LATIN AMERICA AND ITS PEOPLE

LATIN AMERICA AND ITS PEOPLE

VOLUME II: 1800 TO PRESENT

Cheryl E. Martin
University of Texas at El Paso

Mark Wasserman
Rutgers University

PEARSON
Longman

New York San Francisco Boston
London Toronto Sydney Tokyo Singapore Madrid
Mexico City Munich Paris Cape Town Hong Kong Montreal

Acquisitions Editor: Janet Lanphier
Media and Supplements Editor: Kristi Olson
Executive Marketing Manager: Sue Westmoreland
Production Manager: Eric Jorgensen
Project Coordination, Text Design, and Electronic Page Makeup: Electronic Publishing Services Inc., New York City
Cover Design Manager: John Callahan
Cover Illustration/Photo: Pedro Leon. (b1894). Ecudorian. Native festival. © The Art Archive/Archaeological and Ethnological Museum Quito Ecuador/Dagli Orti
Photo Researcher: Photosearch, Inc.
Senior Manufacturing Buyer: Dennis J. Para
Printer and Binder: RR Donnelley & Sons Company
Cover Printer: The Lehigh Press

For permission to use copyrighted material, grateful acknowledgment is made to the copyright holders on page 469, which is hereby made part of this copyright page.

Library of Congress Cataloging-in-Publication Data
Martin, Cheryl English, date-
  Latin America and its people / Cheryl E. Martin, Mark Wasserman.
    p. cm.
  Includes bibliographical references and index.
  ISBN 0-321-06163-2 (single-vol. edition) -- ISBN 0-321-06165-9 (v. 1) -- ISBN 0-321-06167-5 (v. 2)
    1. Latin America--History.   I. Wasserman, Mark, 1946–   II. Title.

  F1410.M294 2004
  980--dc22   2004022815

Copyright © 2005 by Pearson Education, Inc.

All rights reserved. No part of this publication may be reproduced, stored in a retrieval system, or transmitted, in any form or by any means, electronic, mechanical, photocopying, recording, or otherwise, without the prior written permission of the publisher. Printed in the United States.

Visit us at http://www.ablongman.com

0-321-06163-2 (single volume edition)
0-321-06165-9 (volume one)
0-321-06167-5 (volume two)

12345678910–DOC–07060504

*To the students of Rutgers University and
the University of Texas at El Paso,
who have inspired us.*

Contents

List of Features xv

List of Maps and Color Plates xvii

Preface xix

About the Authors xxvii

The New Nations of Latin America 236

Spanish America and the Crisis of 1808 237
    Spain and the Napoleonic Invasion 238
    Representative Government in Spain and America, 1808–1814 240
    The "American Question" 241

Spanish American Grievances and the Crisis of 1808 242
    Mexico 243
    Venezuela 245
    Argentina 245

Spanish American Independence 246
    The Final Campaigns 246
    Regional Conflicts in the Spanish American Struggle for
        Independence 252

The Independence of Brazil 253
    The Portuguese Monarchy in Brazil 253
    Popular Unrest in Brazil 254
    The Culmination of Brazilian Independence 255

The Meaning of Independence 256
How Historians Understand WERE THE WARS OF INDEPENDENCE THE TURNING POINT? 239
Latin American Lives SIMÓN BOLÍVAR AND MANUELA SÁENZ, LEADERS OF SOUTH AMERICAN INDEPENDENCE 250
Slice of Life THE SIXTEENTH OF SEPTEMBER: INDEPENDENCE DAY IN MEXICO 257
Conclusion 260
Learning More About Latin Americans 261

REGIONALISM, WAR, AND RECONSTRUCTION: POLITICS AND ECONOMICS, 1821–1880 262

Dilemmas of Nationhood 263
   Who Governs and What Form of Government? 264
   Federalism/Centralism and Liberalism/Conservatism 265
The Challenge of Regionalism 267
   Argentina, Mexico, Colombia, and Central America 269
   Brazil and Chile 271
A Century of War 272
   Wars of Political Consolidation 274
   Intra-regional Wars 274
   Foreign Wars 275
   Civil Wars 277
   The Impact of War 279
Popular Participation 283
Caudillos 286
The Challenge of Economic Recovery 291
   Obstacles to Development 292
   Export Economies 293
How Historians Understand BENITO JUÁREZ: THE MAKING OF A MYTH 268
Slice of Life THE PARIÁN RIOT: MEXICO CITY, 1828 284
Latin American Lives DR. FRANCIA 289

Conclusion 295
Learning More About Latin Americans 296

10

EVERYDAY LIFE IN AN UNCERTAIN AGE, 1821–1880 298

The People 299
The Large Estates: Haciendas, Estancias, Plantations, Fazendas 301
    Work Life 301
    Domestic Life 304
    Plantations and Slavery 307
Villages and Small Holders 312
    Religion 315
Urban Life and Societal Transformation 315
    The Cities 315
    Transformations 317
Food, Clothes, Shelter, and Entertainment 320
Latin American Lives THE GAUCHO 305
Slice of Life URBAN SLAVES 309
How Historians Understand THE CONSTRUCTION OF RACISM 310
Conclusion 326
Learning More About Latin Americans 326

11

ECONOMIC MODERNIZATION, SOCIETY, AND POLITICS, 1880–1920 328

Economic Modernization 330
    Exports 330
    The Downside of Export-Led Modernization 332

Railroads 334
Modernization and Social Change 335
    Population Increase 335
    New Classes, New Voices 336
    Rural Discontent 340
    Mass Movements of People 341
Politics in the Age of Modernization 342
    A Modernized Military 343
    The Rule of the Ranchers and Planters: Argentina and Brazil 344
    Democracy in Chile 346
    The Aristocratic Republic: Peru 347
    Dictatorship: Mexico 348
Modernization and Resistance 351
    Indigenous Peoples 351
    Resistance in the Countryside 352
    The Mexican Revolution 353

Slice of Life A CHILEAN MINING CAMP 338
Latin American Lives JOSÉ GUADALUPE POSADA (1852–1913), ARTIST OF MEXICO 349
How Historians Understand WHY DO PEOPLE REBEL? 354
Conclusion 355
Learning More About Latin Americans 356

12

BETWEEN REVOLUTIONS: THE NEW POLITICS OF CLASS AND THE ECONOMICS OF IMPORT SUBSTITUTION INDUSTRIALIZATION, 1920–1959 357

Three Crises and the Beginnings of Intensified Government Involvement in the Economy, 1920–1945 359
    The Aftermath of World War I 359

The Great Depression 360
World War II 364
Peacetime Economies 364
Dictators and Populists 365
The 1920s 367
Depression and War 372
Peacetime Politics 378
Failure of the Left and Right 380
Women's Suffrage 382
Slice of Life COLOMBIAN COFFEE FARM 1925 361
How Historians Understand RECONSTRUCTING THE *SEMANA TRÁGICA* (TRAGIC WEEK) IN ARGENTINE HISTORY 368
Latin American Lives ELVIA AND FELIPE CARRILLO PUERTO 373
Conclusion 383
Learning More About Latin Americans 384

13

PEOPLE AND PROGRESS, 1910–1959 385

Socialization in the Factory and the Mine: Proletarianization and Patriarchy 387
A Miner's Day at El Teniente 393
Urbanization and Social Change 395
The Cities 395
Life on the Edge: The Middle Class 398
La Chica Moderna 400
Popular and High Culture 401
Slice of Life VILLAGE LIFE IN PERU 389
How Historians Understand THE VOICE OF THE LOWER CLASSES 396
Latin American Lives FRIDA KAHLO 405
Conclusion 407
Learning More About Latin Americans 407

14

Revolution, Reaction, Democracy, and the New Global Economy, 1959 to the Present 409

The Revolutions: Cuba, Nicaragua, El Salvador, Guatemala, Peru, and Colombia 410
- Cuba 411
- Nicaragua 413
- El Salvador 415
- Guatemala 416
- Peru 416
- Colombia 419

The Tyrannies: Brazil, Argentina, and Chile 419
- Brazil 421
- Argentina 425
- Chile 427

The Exception: Mexico 431
The Struggle for Control of Everyday Life 432
The New Global Economy 433

Slice of Life On the Street in São Paulo 423

Latin American Lives An Argentine Military Officer 428

How Historians Understand Theories of Economic Development and History 434

Conclusion 437
Learning More About Latin Americans 437

15

Everyday Life, 1959 to the Present 439

The Reign of Terror 440
The Quality of Life 442

What Does It Mean To Be Poor? 445

Informal Economy 449

Privatizing Social Security 453

The Cities 456

To Be Poor in the Cities 457

An Urban Migrant's Story 458

The Environment 458

The Globalization of Culture 460

Art 462

Latin American Lives Women Rebels 441

Slice of Life The Barrio/Favela 452

How Historians Understand From the Countryside to the City 454

Conclusion 463

Learning More About Latin Americans 464

Glossary 465

Credits 469

Index 471

LIST OF FEATURES

Latin American Lives

Simón Bolívar and Manuela Sáenz, Leaders of South American Independence 250
Dr. Francia 289
The Gaucho 305
José Guadalupe Posada (1852–1913), Artist of Mexico 349
Elvia and Felipe Carrillo Puerto 373
Frida Kahlo 405
An Argentine Military Officer 428
Women Rebels 441

Slice of Life

The Sixteenth of September: Independence Day in Mexico 257
The Parián Riot: Mexico City, 1828 284
Urban Slaves 309
A Chilean Mining Camp 338
Colombian Coffee Farm 1925 361
Village Life in Peru 389
On the Street in São Paulo 423
The Barrio/Favela 452

How Historians Understand

Were the Wars of Independence the Turning Point? 239
Benito Juárez: The Making of a Myth 268
The Construction of Racism 310
Why Do People Rebel? 354
Reconstructing the *Semana Trágica* (Tragic Week) in Argentine History 368
The Voice of the Lower Classes 396
Theories of Economic Development and History 434
From the Countryside to the City 454

List of Maps and Color Plates

Maps

Latin America in 1830.   265

Gran Colombia: The failed experiment.   272

The War of the Pacific, 1879–1883.   276

The Wars for Northern Mexico, 1836–1853.   277

Latin American boundary disputes in the nineteenth and twentieth centuries.   278

Color Plates

Following page 384

- **Plate 9**   Antonio López de Santa Anna.
- **Plate 10**   C. Penuti and Alejandro Bernheim, *La Batalla de Monte Caseros (The Battle of Monte Caseros)*.
- **Plate 11**   Juan Perón, the populist president of Argentina (1946–55 and 1973–74), and his wife, Eva Duarte "Evita" de Perón.
- **Plate 12**   David Alfaro Siqueiros, *Por una Seguridad Completa para todos los Mexicanas (detalle), 1952–1954 (For the Complete Safety of All Mexicans at Work, detail of Injured Worker)*.
- **Plate 13**   Frida Kahlo, *Las Dos Fridas (The Two Fridas)* (1939).
- **Plate 14**   Favela dwellings in Brazil.
- **Plate 15**   José María Velasco, *Valle de México (Valley of Mexico)*.
- **Plate 16**   Latin American cities with more than one million inhabitants.

Preface

OUR AIM IN WRITING *Latin America and Its People* has been to provide a fresh interpretative survey of Latin American history from pre-Columbian times to the beginning of the twenty-first century. The millions of "ordinary" Latin Americans are the central characters in our story. We look at the many social and political institutions that Latin Americans have built and rebuilt–families, governments from the village level to the nation-state, churches, political parties, labor unions, schools, and armies–but we do so through the lives of the people who forged these institutions and tried to alter them to meet changing circumstances. The texture of everyday life, therefore, is our principal focus.

The Texture of Everyday Life

Life has not been easy for most Latin Americans. Poverty, hard work, disease, natural calamities, the loss of loved ones, and violence have marked many people's lives. Many have lacked educational opportunities and the chance to speak their political opinions openly. In the chapters that follow, we will devote a lot of attention to the daily struggles of men, women, and children as they faced these difficult challenges and adapted to changing times. We are also interested in how people managed to find meaning and enjoyment in their lives. Even in the midst of hardship and tragedy, they came together as families and communities to celebrate, to dance, to eat and drink, to flirt, to marry, and to pray. Our readers will meet the people of Latin American history "up close and personal," in their houses and on the streets, on the shop floors and in the fields, at work and at play, for it is the texture of everyday life that makes the history of Latin America so fascinating and compelling.

The Diversity of Latin America

Latin Americans are a very diverse people. They have spoken Spanish, Portuguese, Nahuatl, Quechua, Maya, Aymara, Guaraní, and scores of other languages. Their ethnic and cultural roots can be traced to the indigenous civilizations of the Americas and to many generations of European, African, and Asian immigrants. A few have been very rich, but many more have been very poor. They have adapted to many different climatic zones, some at altitudes as high as 11,000 feet above sea level. Many Latin Americans have lived in rural areas, but they have also built some of the world's most sophisticated cities, from the Aztec and Inca capitals of Tenochtitlan and Cuzco to such modern industrial giants as São Paulo, Brazil, and Monterrey, Mexico, to cosmopolitan urban centers like Mexico City and Buenos Aires. Following their independence from Spain and Portugal, they have experimented with a variety of political regimes—monarchy, liberal democracy, oligarchy, socialist revolution, and brutal military dictatorships, to name a few.

Despite this diversity, Latin Americans have faced certain challenges in common. European conquest and subsequent shifts in world economic and political configurations have shaped the region's history over the past five centuries. Latin America's rich natural resources have attracted foreign investors who have profited handsomely, while the people who worked in the mines and oilfields have seldom garnered an equitable share of the bounty. The region's ability to produce a stunning variety of agricultural staples has shaped patterns of landholding and labor throughout the region, again to the detriment of the many and the benefit of the few. How to achieve political stability in nations divided by class, ethnic, and regional differences has been an enduring conundrum for Latin Americans, even if they have tried many different means of resolving that dilemma.

Our goal, then, is to explore Latin Americans' common history without losing sight of their diversity, and to compare how the many different peoples of the region have responded to similar situations. We have therefore organized our text thematically rather than proceeding country-by-country. There are too many countries and too much time to cover for us to thoroughly document the history of every Latin American nation. No doubt, some country specialists will feel their area slighted, but textbooks are as much about the choices of what to exclude as they are about what to include. Unlike many other texts on Latin American history, *Latin America and Its People* interweaves the history of Brazil with that of its Spanish-speaking neighbors, rather than segregating it in separate chapters, while also pointing out the special features that distinguish it from other Latin American countries. Volume I includes coverage of those portions of the present-day United States that were once part of the Spanish colonial empire.

Our underlying assumption is that, in order for our students to gain an introductory (and, we hope, lasting) understanding of Latin America, it is best not to clutter the narrative with too many dates and names. We believe that students will remember the major themes, such as the struggle to control local affairs, the impact of war, the transformation of women's roles, and the social changes wrought by economic development. And students will remember, perhaps even more clearly, that many Latin Americans lived and continue to live in overwhelming poverty.

Volume I

Volume I of *Latin America and Its People* looks at the ways in which people have continually reinvented the hemisphere that Europeans called the "new world." This world was first "new" for the nameless ancestors of today's Native Americans, who migrated across the Bering Strait and fanned out across North and South America over the course of many millennia. Generation after generation, they adapted to the many different climatic zones of the hemisphere and gradually accumulated the surpluses necessary to found the great civilizations of the Aztecs, the Inca, the Maya, and so many others. Chapter 1 is devoted entirely to the long trajectory of cultural development in the Americas down to the year 1400 C.E., while Chapter 2 includes an extensive comparative discussion of the Aztec and Inca empires and the simultaneously emerging national monarchies of Spain and Portugal.

Spanish and Portuguese colonists not only found this world very different from what they had known; they also remade it as they discovered its potential for yielding silver, gold, sugar, and other commodities of value to them. The changes introduced by European conquest and colonization profoundly altered the world of the indigenous peoples of the Americas. Over the course of three centuries, the hemisphere witnessed the rise of a new people, the biological and cultural offspring of native peoples, Europeans, and Africans, who yet again made this world something new. Chapters 4, 5, and 6 explore the constantly changing worlds of Latin American peoples under Spanish and Portuguese rule.

The most important theme of Volume I is how ordinary people built these successive new worlds and continually renegotiated the complex and overlapping hierarchies of class, ethnicity, political status, and gender that supposedly governed their lives. Native peoples endured military and political conquest, catastrophic epidemics, highly oppressive labor regimens, and the imposition of a new religion. Yet despite these enormous challenges, they survived and rebuilt their communities, selectively incorporating cultural elements introduced by the Europeans along with traditional practices and beliefs as they formed their new society.

Against what might seem like insurmountable odds, Africans brought to the Americas as slaves managed to retain something of the life they had known before, especially in places where their numbers were sufficiently great that they could form some kind of identifiable community. Some found ways to escape the bonds of slavery and passed that freedom to successive generations of descendants. Like the indigenous peoples, they too borrowed selectively from European cultures.

Throughout three centuries of Spanish and Portuguese colonial rule, Latin Americans of all races and social classes contested, sometimes successfully, sometimes not, the many "rules" that dictated how men and women should behave and how people in subordinate social positions should render deference to those who supposedly ranked above them. Volume I argues that it was not just kings and priests and other authority figures who built the world of colonial Latin America. Men, women, and children of all classes had at least some say in the outcome, even if the colonial state sometimes wielded enough power to silence the most vocal among them.

Volume II

The overarching theme of Volume II is how ordinary people struggled over the course of two centuries to maintain control over their daily lives. This meant that they sought to determine their own community leaders, set their local laws and regulations (especially taxes), establish and keep their own traditions, practice their religion, supervise the education of their children, live by their own values and standards, and earn a living. This endless struggle came to involve more than just the narrow view and experience of their village or urban neighborhood or their friends and neighbors. Rather, it brought ordinary people and their local lives into constant, not always pleasant and beneficial, contact with the wider worlds of regional (states, provinces, territories), national, and international politics, economy, and culture. Although the local struggle forms the backbone of the narrative, we must include summaries and analyses of the contexts in which these struggles occurred, as well. Since all Latin Americans, regardless of country, participated in this struggle, the economic and political narratives proceed thematically and chronologically.

Volume II offers three chapters (10, 13, and 15) that describe the everyday lives of Latin Americans at different points in time. We want students to know what people ate and drank, how they had good times, how they worshipped, where they lived, and what their work was like. The descriptions are individual and anecdotal and collective and quantitative. Thus, it is our hope that students will remember how a Brazilian small farmer raised cassava, or the tortuous efforts of Chilean copper miners. Perhaps, readers will remember the smells of the streets of nineteenth-century cities or the noises of late twentieth-century megalopolises. The struggle for control over everyday life and the descriptions of daily life are related, of course, for the struggle and its context and the reality were joined inseparably. Students should know what the lives were like for which so many bravely and often unsuccessfully fought.

There are other themes interwoven with that of the struggle for control over everyday life. Unlike many other texts in the field, our book gives full and nuanced coverage to the nineteenth century, incorporating the most exciting new scholarship on that period. In the nineteenth century, we assert, chronic war (external and internal) and the accompanying militarization of government and politics profoundly shaped the region's economy and society. We maintain, as well, that race, class, and gender were the crucial underlying elements in Latin American politics. Moreover, warfare, combined with the massive flow of people to the cities, most particularly transformed the place of women.

In the twentieth century, conflict between the upper, middle, and lower classes was the primary moving force behind politics. No ideology from either Left or Right nor any type of government from democracy to authoritarianism has brought other than temporary resolutions. We also follow the continued changes in the role of women in society and politics in the face of vast transformations caused by technology and globalization.

It is also our belief that the history of Latin Americans is primarily the story of Latin America and not of the great powers outside the region. To be sure, Europeans and North Americans invested considerable sums of money and sometimes intervened militarily in Latin America. Their wars and rivalries greatly affected Latin America's possibilities. We do note the importance of such key developments as Mexico's loss of half its national territory to the United States in 1848, the impact of the Cold War on Latin America, and the training that right-wing Latin American military establishments received at the hands of United States military forces in the late twentieth century. But we prefer to keep the spotlight on the people of Latin America themselves.

Special Features

In addition to the main narrative of our book, we have included three separate features in each chapter. Each chapter offers a feature called "Latin American Lives," a biography of an individual whose life illustrates some of the key points of that chapter. Some of these are famous figures such as Simón Bolívar and Frida Kahlo, but others are much less well known. We also give a "Slice of Life" for each chapter—a vignette that takes students to the scene of the action and that illustrates in detail some of the social processes under discussion. We include, for example, living conditions in Chilean copper mining camps in the late nineteenth century, and the circumstances that provoked Mexico City's so-called "Parián Riot" of 1828.

We hope, too, to convey a sense of the methods that historians have used in bringing that texture of everyday life to light and the many debates the intriguing history of Latin America has generated. Each chapter therefore includes a piece entitled "How Historians Understand," designed to give readers better insights into the way that historians go about their work or the ways in which historical knowledge is used and transformed according to the concerns of a particular time and place. In Chapter 9, for example, we show how changing political conditions in Mexico are reflected in the many myths and interpretations that have arisen concerning the life of President Benito Juárez.

Aids to Learning

Since students are at the heart of this enterprise, we have included a number of aids to learning. A glossary explains technical terms and Spanish and Portuguese words used in the text. Discussion questions at the end of the special features Latin American Lives, Slice of Life, and How Historians Understand are intended to stimulate classroom discussion and individual research projects. We have also included suggestions for further reading at the end of each chapter. In keeping with our emphasis on everyday life in Latin American history, we have chosen books that give readers especially clear views of "ordinary" men, women, and children as they went about their daily lives and made Latin America what it is today, at the beginning of the twenty-first century.

We would like to thank the following reviewers for their helpful comments and suggestions:

Rodney R. Alvarez, *University of Central Florida*
Nancy Appelbaum, *State University of New York–Binghamton*
Patrick Barr-Melej, *Iowa State University*
Peter M. Beattie, *Michigan State University*
John F. Chuchiak IV, *Southwest Missouri State University*
Richard Damms, *Mississippi State University*
Francis A. Dutra, *University of California, Santa Barbara*
Joan A. Francis, *Columbia Union College*
Lydia M. Garner, *Southwest Texas State University*
Charlotte M. Gradie, *Sacred Heart University*
Richard Grossman, *Northeastern Illinois University*

Michael R. Hall, *Armstrong Atlantic State University*
Gina Hames, *Pacific Lutheran University*
Mary A. Hedberg, *Saginaw Valley State University*
Andrew S. Hernandez III, *Western New Mexico University*
Andrew J. Kirkendall, *Texas A&M University*
Jose C. Moya, *University of California, Los Angeles*
Daniel S. Murphree, *University of Texas at Tyler*
Lee M. Penyak, *University of Scranton*
Monica Rankin, *University of Arizona*
Arthur Schmidt, *Temple University*
Sister Maria Consuelo Sparks, *Immaculata University*
Karen Sundwick, *Southern Oregon University*
Jason Ward, *Lee University*
Ronald Young, *Georgia Southern University*

CHERYL E. MARTIN

MARK WASSERMAN

About the Authors

Cheryl E. Martin has taught Latin American History at the University of Texas at El Paso since 1978. A native of Buffalo, New York, she received her bachelor's degree from the Georgetown University School of Foreign Service and her M.A. and Ph.D. from Tulane University. She studied at the Universidad de Cuenca, Ecuador, on a Fulbright Fellowship and was a visiting instructor at the Universidad Autónoma de Chihuahua, Mexico. Her publications include *Rural Society in Colonial Morelos* (1985) and *Governance and Society in Colonial Mexico: Chihuahua in the Eighteenth Century* (1996). She also co-edited, with William Beezley and William E. French, *Rituals of Rule, Rituals of Resistance: Public Celebrations and Popular Culture in Mexico* (1994).

Professor Martin has served on the council of the American Historical Association and on the editorial boards of the *Hispanic American Historical Review*, *The Americas*, the *Latin American Research Review*, and *History Compass*, a history website based in Oxford, England. She has received two fellowships from the National Endowment for the Humanities and Awards for Distinguished Achievement in both teaching and research at the University of Texas at El Paso. She currently serves as Graduate Advisor for the History Department. In her spare time, she likes to ice skate.

Mark Wasserman is a professor of history at Rutgers, The State University of New Jersey, where he has taught since 1978. Brought up in Marblehead, Massachusetts, he earned his B.A. at Duke University and his M.A. and PhD. at the University of Chicago. He is the author of three books on Mexico: *Capitalists, Caciques, and Revolution: The Native Elite and Foreign Enterprise in Chihuahua, Mexico, 1854–1911* (1984); *Persistent Oligarchs: Elites and Politics in Chihuahua, Mexico, 1910–1940* (1993); and *Everyday Life and Politics in Nineteenth Century Mexico: Men, Women, and War* (2000). He also coauthored the early editions of the best-selling *History of Latin America* (1980–88) with Benjamin Keen. Professor Wasserman has twice won the Arthur P. Whitaker Prize for his books. Professor Wasserman has received research fellowships from the Tinker Foundation, the American Council of Learned Societies/Social Science Research Council, the American Philosophical Society, and the National Endowment of the Humanities. He has been Vice-Chair for Undergraduate Education of the Rutgers Department of History and Chair of the Department's Teaching Effectiveness Committee. Professor Wasserman was an elected member of the Highland Park, New Jersey, Board of Education for nearly a decade and served as its president for two years. He is an avid fan of Duke basketball and enjoys hiking and travel.

THE NEW NATIONS OF LATIN AMERICA

FOR THREE HUNDRED YEARS, Spain and Portugal ruled their enormous American empires with few serious challenges from people living in the colonies. But within less than two decades between 1808 and 1824, Brazil and most of Spanish America won independence, leaving Spain with just two islands, Cuba and Puerto Rico, and Portugal with nothing. From Mexico to Argentina, the new nations of Spanish America emerged from drawn out, hard-fought wars, costly both in terms of lives lost and damage to the economic infrastructure (roads, buildings, mines). Brazil's independence came somewhat less violently, in 1822, when a son of Portugal's king agreed to become emperor of the new nation, but there too the years since 1808 had witnessed considerable political turmoil.

The movements for independence in Latin America resulted from the convergence of two sets of factors, one international and the other internal to the individual colonies. Although the most important cause of the rebellions for independence was the demand from Latin Americans to obtain more control over

1783	1788	1791	1807–1808	1812	1821	1824
United States wins its independence	Charles IV takes the throne of Spain	Haitian Revolution	Napoleon's armies invade Portugal and Spain	New Spanish Constitution	Mexican independence	Battle of Ayacucho ends wars of independence
	1789 French Revolution		1810 Hidalgo begins Mexican War of Independence		1822 Brazilian independence	

their daily lives, as manifested in local governance and practice of traditions, the timing of the independence movements depended to a considerable extent on events that occurred in the metropolises and in the rest of Europe.

The specific character of the struggles for independence and the kinds of nations that emerged varied greatly across Latin America, reflecting the tremendous geographical and historical diversity of the region. The independence movements were bitterly divided along class and racial lines. On one side stood the wealthy creoles (people who claimed European descent, though born in the Americas), who needed tactical support from the lower classes to win the battles against Spain and Portugal and in the political struggles of nation-building that ensued. At the same time, they despised the masses of poor Indians, blacks, and *castas* (racially mixed people) that surrounded them. One of the principal reasons why the Spanish and Portuguese empires endured so long was that upper-class whites were terrified that any act of rebellion against the mother country might unleash popular unrest that could easily turn against them.

Creole fears were anything but groundless. The colonies were sharply split between the haves and the have-nots, and the gap had widened in many parts of Latin America during the last few decades of the eighteenth century. Popular discontent had mounted accordingly, usually meeting brutal repression by colonial governments and creole upper class. When external events finally began unraveling the ties that bound the colonies to Spain and Portugal, lower classes joined the battles, but with their own agendas in mind. Their specific objectives varied from place to place, but included the abolition of slavery, an end to special taxes levied on Indians, and land reform.

The movements for Latin American independence divided on geographical lines as well. The racially and ethnically diverse people of the countryside thought mostly in terms of local autonomy at the village level and at least initially paid relatively little heed to the ideas of nationhood being hatched by the creole upper classes in the larger cities and towns. The upper classes had their own local and regional loyalties as well. Peruvians and Venezuelans and Argentines all distrusted one another, and people who lived in towns across southern South America resented the domination of Buenos Aires. All of the divisions—racial, social, economic, and geographical—that became so evident during the wars for independence were to shape Latin American politics for much of the nineteenth century.

Spanish America and the Crisis of 1808

The external events that precipitated Latin American independence had their roots in the profound transformations that occurred in Europe and North America during the last half of the eighteenth century and the beginning of the nineteenth century, a period known to historians as the Age of Revolution. The American Revolution, the French Revolution of 1789, and the slave uprising in the French colony of Saint Domingue that gave birth to Haiti, the world's first black republic, affected how Latin Americans viewed their world and the perceptions and actions of metropolitan monarchs and colonial administrators. Napoleon Bonaparte's campaigns to extend French control throughout Western Europe, and the struggle of Great Britain and its allies to thwart him, had profound consequences for Spain, Portugal, and Latin America. Napoleon's invasion of the Iberian Peninsula in 1807 and 1808 provided the catalyst for the Latin American movements for independence.

Spain and the Napoleonic Invasion

In the twenty years leading up to Napoleon's decision to cross the Pyrenees, Spain experienced considerable political turmoil, beginning in 1788 with the death of King Charles III, an energetic monarch who had spearheaded major changes in the administration of his vast empire during his 29-year reign. His successor, Charles IV, proved much less capable, and he had barely assumed the throne when revolutionaries in France overthrew King Louis XVI and inaugurated a "reign of terror" that sent thousands of their countrymen to the guillotine, including the king himself. In 1793, Spain joined its traditional enemy England in a two-year war to stop the new French regime from exporting its radical ideas to the rest of Europe. After 1796, however, the regime in France took a more conservative turn, and Charles IV and his ministers reverted to their traditional policy of supporting France against the British.

Spanish subjects at home and abroad then endured more than a decade of nearly uninterrupted war and the heavy burden of taxation that war demanded. British naval blockades interrupted trade between Spain and the colonies. Popular opposition to Charles IV mounted, while his son Ferdinand openly conspired to depose him. As French troops entered Madrid, Charles gave in to popular pressure and abdicated in favor of Ferdinand. Napoleon then summoned both father and son to France and forced each of them to renounce their claims to the throne, whereupon he proclaimed his brother, Joseph Bonaparte, king of Spain.

Most people in Spain and the colonies did not regard Joseph as their rightful monarch and instead asserted that sovereignty lay in the hands of the people as long as their rightful king remained captive. They experimented with various forms of representative government from 1808 until Napoleon was defeated and Ferdinand VII returned to power in 1814. The six-year interlude of self-rule convinced many colonists that they were fully capable of governing themselves. Creoles, in particular, came to the realization that Spanish governance only siphoned off revenues better used at home and that the cost of colonial administration was so detrimental that it was worth the risk of rebellion.

How Historians Understand | Were the Wars of Independence the Turning Point?

PERIODIZATION—THE DIVIDING OF history into segments and identifying crucial turning points—is a major device historians use to explain and simplify the past. Traditionally, historians have considered the Latin American wars of independence between 1808 and 1826 as the crucial watershed in the region's history, and many Latin American history courses are divided into terms focusing on the colonial and national periods. This interpretation inferred that Latin America abruptly ended its colonial era and entered into modern times with a sharp break from Spain and Portugal. We know, however, that while independence hastened many transformations already underway during the previous century, all vestiges of the colonial order did not disappear in the 1820s. Slavery and discrimination against indigenous peoples endured well past independence, and many laws and government procedures carried over from the colonial regimes to the new nation states. Puerto Rico and Cuba remained colonies of Spain until after 1898. The traditional division of eras obscured critical continuities and made it difficult to assess the effects of change.

During the 1960s, an alternative approach arose, viewing the independence era as part of a broader period stretching from approximately 1720 or 1750 to 1850. This "Middle Period" incorporated the transition from traditional to modern society and from colonial to independent politics. The newly configured century allowed historians to trace the evolution of the trends and forces that caused the independence movements and to evaluate the impact of the end of colonial rule.

Investigating the half-centuries before and after independence has elucidated a number of new themes and hypotheses. First, traditional assumptions that the Spanish Empire was peaceful in the century before 1810 were incorrect. In the Mexican countryside, for example, there was constant unrest. Second, colonial rule was far from omnipotent. Historians had long ago documented corruption and inefficiency, but recent explorations have revealed the considerable extent of local autonomy. We have only scratched the surface of understanding to what degree the innovations introduced by the Spanish Bourbon kings and their counterparts in Portugal not only disrupted accommodations reached earlier, but also began processes of change that independent governments built on after 1830. The Iberian monarchs of the eighteenth century, for example, took steps to reduce the power and political influence of the Catholic Church in Latin America. Many independent governments in the nineteenth and twentieth centuries continued to pursue this objective. Economic development, especially that of frontier regions, was a major concern of late colonial kings and independent governments alike.

(continued on next page)

> **Were the Wars of Independence the Turning Point?** *(continued from previous page)*
>
> While the inclusion of the wars of independence as part of a longer period and as part of longer historical processes has provided much new knowledge and many new insights, the more traditional periodization (adopted by the authors of this text) has considerable advantages. First, the break with Spain and Portugal had an enormous political impact. As we will see in Chapter 9, it set off decades of conflict over who was to rule and how. Independent governments tried for a century to establish their legitimacy and control. Moreover, there is little doubt that the wars of independence were economically cataclysmic. The damage to property and people over the course of nearly two decades of sporadic (and in some places incessant) fighting was enormous. It required nearly the entire century to recover to the level of production and prosperity in 1800. Independent Latin America had broken significantly from the past and begun a new era.
>
> **Questions for Discussion**
>
> What examples of significant historical turning points can you think of that have occurred during your own lifetime? What has changed? What continuities are there? Is periodization a useful tool for understanding history? Why or why not?

Representative Government in Spain and America, 1808–1814

As French troops advanced into Spain in the spring of 1808, Spaniards waged guerrilla warfare against the invading forces. Cities and towns throughout the country formed political bodies known as *juntas* to govern in place of King Ferdinand. They also established a central junta that claimed to speak for the entire Spanish nation and presumably the overseas territories as well. Politically active Spaniards soon began calling for the reestablishment of the Cortes, a parliamentary body that had existed in medieval times but had not met for three centuries. Anxious to win support from Spanish subjects in the colonies, they invited Americans to send representatives to the meetings of the central junta and the Cortes. The latter body first convened in the city of Cádiz in September of 1810, and over the next few years it enacted sweeping political changes for Spain and Spanish America. The most important of these was the writing of a constitution in 1812, a document proclaiming that even if Ferdinand VII were restored to power, he would henceforth rule as a constitutional monarch, in consultation with representatives chosen by the people, thus ending the days of absolutist monarchy.

Americans needed no prodding from Spain to take matters into their own hands in this time of political crisis. Juntas comprised mostly of creoles appeared in cities and towns throughout the empire as soon as news of Ferdinand's captivity reached them. All of these bodies proclaimed their loyalty to Ferdinand.

Many, however, objected to any form of subservience to the ad hoc government in Spain, arguing that they were not colonies but separate kingdoms fully equal to Castile, León, Navarre, Catalonia, and the other peninsular territories that comprised the realm of the Spanish monarch. They were technically correct, for only in the time of Charles III had Spanish bureaucrats begun using the term "colonies" in reference to the overseas possessions.

This sentiment for autonomy gathered strength in early 1810, when a series of French victories forced the Spanish central junta to dissolve itself in favor of a five-member Council of Regency. Americans favoring local autonomy feared that the French armies might overwhelm all Spanish resistance and then Napoleon might impose his regime on the overseas kingdoms. In some places, politically active groups moved quickly to an outright break with Spain. Town councils in Venezuela, for example, convened a national congress that declared independence in July of 1811.

Other Americans preferred to cooperate with the ad hoc government in Spain and welcomed the opportunity to send spokesmen to the sessions of the central junta and the Cortes. Men in cities and towns all over Spanish America participated enthusiastically in elections. The Constitution of 1812 permitted the formation of elected municipal councils (cabildos) in all towns with one thousand or more residents. Hundreds of cities exercised that option. In Mexico, for example, only twenty communities had had cabildos prior to the enactment of the Constitution, while afterwards that number rose to nearly nine hundred. Eighteen new cabildos were formed in Puerto Rico, and dozens more in the highlands of Ecuador. This process empowered men in Latin America as never before. Women, however, were excluded from participating in elections until well into the twentieth century.

The "American Question"

The disruptions to the rule of the monarchy between 1808 and 1814 provided the first practical demonstration of the principles of popular sovereignty and a taste of active political participation for the colonies. Autonomy without independence, however, proved impractical. Moreover, the inherent distrust that both creoles and Spaniards felt toward indigenous and casta peoples permeated the discussions.

The first objections to American autonomy arose in the heated debates over how many American delegates the Cortes would include. Authors of the Constitution of 1812 assumed they would allocate representation according to population. Americans easily outnumbered Spaniards, but they included large numbers of Indians and racially mixed people. Were all of these groups allowed to vote or even counted for purposes of representation? The Constitution of 1812 gave the franchise to Indian and mestizo men but not to castas, whom it defined as people with any trace of African ancestry (Latin Americans themselves used this term to describe many types of racially mixed people). It also excluded felons, debtors, and domestic servants—provisions that might eliminate many Indians and mestizos, and even some people of Spanish extraction, from the political process. Many American upper-class people feared the empowerment of castas and others they considered their social inferiors. Thus, the creoles were torn between their need to assure that their own concerns would receive ample hearing in the emerging political debate and their overwhelming fear of the lower classes. Full representation of all people regardless of ethnicity would have given the Western Hemisphere a three-to-two majority in the Cortes. Not surprisingly, Spaniards opposed this prospect.

The Spaniards prevailed on the question of representation, retaining control of the new parliament and using that advantage whenever their position differed from that of the Americans. One particularly divisive issue was the freedom to trade with all nations, a right that Spain's American colonies had never enjoyed. Spanish merchants preferred to maintain existing rules that allowed Americans to trade legally only with other Spanish subjects. Other American demands included the abolition of crown monopolies and, most crucially, equal access to jobs in the government, the military, and the church.

As they witnessed Spanish intransigence on issues such as representation and freedom of trade, even those Americans who initially favored some degree of cooperation with the new government moved toward a stance of greater self-determination for the overseas territories. Once they began to assert themselves politically, few Spanish Americans were willing to go back to old routines of subservience to the mother country. In the words of Simón Bolívar, a major leader of the independence movement in South America, by 1815 "the habit of obedience...[had] been severed."

Spanish American Grievances and the Crisis of 1808

The uncertainty caused by the French invasion of the mother country exacerbated political and social tensions that had festered in the Spanish colonies for several decades. In many places, eighteenth-century population growth had magnified pressures on relatively scarce land and water resources and heightened tension between Indian villages and wealthy landowners. One historian counted at least one hundred fifty village riots between 1700 and 1820 in central Mexico, two-thirds of them after 1760. A major uprising led by a man who claimed to be descended from the last Inca emperor spread throughout a good part of present-day Peru and Bolivia in the early 1780s.

Administrative changes introduced by Kings Charles III and IV added to the tensions in the colonies. In a sweeping series of innovations known collectively as the Bourbon Reforms, so named because the kings belonged to the same extended Bourbon dynasty that ruled France, they restructured the way they governed the overseas territories. They wished to bind the colonies more closely to the mother country, step up the defense of the empire from foreign enemies, curb the wealth and power of the Catholic Church, and increase the flow of revenue into the royal coffers. New taxes hit everyone regardless of class or ethnicity. Lower-class men feared conscription into new standing armies created for the empire's defense, while creoles chafed under the administration of newly arrived Spanish-born bureaucrats, who cared little for either past practice or American interests. Angry about the new royal monopolies on tobacco, cane alcohol, playing cards, and gunpowder, mobs pillaged government buildings and attacked royal officials in Mexico, the highlands of Ecuador, and New Granada (present-day Colombia). The expulsion of the powerful religious order known as the Jesuits in 1767 spurred additional violence, especially in Mexico. Crackdowns on popular religious expression, political dissent, and labor unrest added to the general climate of discontent.

The disruption of Spanish sovereignty in 1808 brought all of these grievances to the forefront and sparked different kinds of revolts in the colonies. Three of the most important of these upheavals, each with its own special character but all with important implications for the future independence of Latin America, occurred in Mexico, Argentina, and Venezuela.

Mexico

The kinds of political, social, and economic changes that Latin Americans experienced at the beginning of the nineteenth century were especially apparent in the region of Mexico known as the Bajío, located between 100 and 200 miles northwest of Mexico City. As the colony's population grew in the late colonial period, wealthy individuals had invested in the commercial production of wheat, maize, and other crops, taking advantage of the area's rich soil and its proximity to the principal urban markets of New Spain. To expand their estates, these landowners forced many poor sharecroppers and other small farmers off the land.

At the same time, people who had worked in the region's many cloth factories and artisans who had made textiles in their own homes lost their livelihoods when the Spanish crown eased trade restrictions and opened the Mexican market to cheaper merchandise manufactured abroad. Production at the Bajío's silver mines also declined sharply as the new century began, leaving thousands of workers without jobs. Meanwhile, droughts and crop failures added to the misery. In the worst of these agricultural crises, from 1785 to 1786, almost 15 percent of the Bajío's population died of hunger. A new round of crop failures struck the region in 1809. The combined effects of economic change and natural disaster left thousands of people with little left to lose as the nineteenth century began.

Father Miguel Hidalgo y Costilla was a priest in the Bajío, in the town of Dolores, about 20 miles from the old silver mining town of Guanajuato. Born in

1753 to a middle-class creole family, Hidalgo had his own grudges against Spanish authority. He had received his early education at the hands of the Jesuits, and their expulsion from Mexico angered him and many others of his class. As an adult, he read the books of French Enlightenment thinkers who disputed the divine right of kings to exact unquestioning obedience from their subjects. His unorthodox ideas got him dismissed from his position as rector of a college in Valladolid (today, Morelia), one of the principal towns of the Bajío, and he narrowly escaped prosecution by the Inquisition. Policies of the Spanish king also hurt him in the pocketbook. He owned a small hacienda, but in 1804 royal officials seized his property when he could not pay special taxes levied to meet Spain's rising costs of defending itself against Napoleon. Meanwhile, Hidalgo took up his post as parish priest in Dolores. There he tried to promote new industries such as ceramics, tanning, and silk production to help his parishioners to weather the economic hard times they were facing. He also continued to meet with other intellectuals conversant with Enlightenment ideas and disgruntled with the Spanish monarchy.

Hidalgo's concerns and those of many other people in the surrounding region merged with the international crisis provoked by Napoleon's invasion of Spain. Since 1808, the government in Mexico City had been in the hands of conservative forces who favored maintaining ties with Spain at all costs. Father Hidalgo joined one of many conspiracies to overthrow them, and when authorities learned of his plans he decided to take the preemptive strike of declaring open revolt in his famous "Grito de Dolores" on September 16, 1810. Word of his rebellion quickly spread among the desperate and dispossessed classes in the Bajío. Within a few days, Hidalgo enlisted thousands of supporters who held a variety of grievances against the status quo. At its height, his army included sixty thousand people, of whom about 55 percent were Indians and 20 percent were mestizos. In the words of historian Eric Van Young, many rural people joined Hidalgo's insurgency and the many revolts that followed because they were "driven by hunger and unemployment, pulled into the maelstrom of violence by the prospect of daily wages in the rebel forces, the easy pickings of looting, or simply to escape from depressed conditions at home." The Indian rebels also wanted to retain control over their own communities, and for the most part, they did not stray far from their homes to fight. Their concern was less with independence from Spain than with local power and traditional values.

Hidalgo's forces sacked several towns and killed hundreds of Spanish men, women, and children who had taken refuge in the municipal grain warehouse in Guanajuato. Creole elites, some of whom had once flirted with the cause of autonomy, recoiled in horror at the violent turn of events and joined forces with pro-Spanish authorities in Mexico City to crush the insurrection. Within a few months, they captured and executed Hidalgo, but another priest, José María Morelos, continued the fight, controlling virtually all of southern Mexico from

1811 until his defeat in 1815. Followers of Morelos, in particular the casta Vicente Guerrero, then continued guerrilla operations against Spanish authorities for several more years, but continued Spanish control seemed almost certain. It would take another round of events in Spain to propel Mexico toward the final step of independence.

Venezuela

The Bourbon Reforms included an emphasis on the economic development of formerly peripheral parts of the empire. Venezuela was one such region. Cacao production flourished as the popularity of chocolate grew in Europe during the eighteenth century. Its principal city, Caracas, became the seat of a new audiencia, or court of appeals, created in 1786.

Creole upper class in Caracas began efforts to create a self-governing junta in 1808 but succeeded only in the spring of 1810, when they overthrew the audiencia and the Spanish governor. A year later, they officially declared independence, created a three-man executive body, and drafted a constitution that excluded the lower classes from political participation. The new government lasted just a year. After a powerful earthquake hit Caracas in 1812, royalists regained control after convincing the popular classes that God was punishing Venezuela for its disregard for divinely constituted authority.

The young creole aristocrat Simón Bolívar took command of the forces favoring independence and began a campaign to retake Venezuela in the spring of 1813. Like so many others of his social standing, Bolívar detested the lower classes, and his enemies eagerly took advantage of this situation. In 1814, he suffered a humiliating defeat by royalist armies led by a black man named José Tomás Boves and comprised largely of black and mulatto *llaneros* (plainsmen, cowboys by trade) angered at the harsh treatment they had received at the hands of those favoring an independent republic. Boves himself had suffered imprisonment by the insurgents in 1810. Now four years later, his "Legion of Hell" slaughtered wealthy creoles. Boves died on the battlefield, but his troops routed Bolívar and forced him into exile. In Venezuela as in Mexico, the outlook for independence looked grim as Ferdinand VII returned to power in Madrid in 1814.

Argentina

Like Venezuela, southern South America and the port town of Buenos Aires reaped significant benefits from the Bourbon kings' efforts to develop the empire's periphery. Formerly subject to the authority of the Spanish viceroy in Lima, Peru, in 1776 Buenos Aires became the seat of a newly created viceroyalty. The port now became the principal outlet through which silver from Bolivia and hides and tallow from the vast plains of Argentina and Uruguay reached markets abroad. The town's merchants also enjoyed abundant opportunities for contraband with British and Portuguese traders. The population of Buenos Aires quadrupled in the last half of the eighteenth century, reaching almost forty thousand by 1800.

Merchants and civic leaders took pride in the growing prosperity of their community. That sentiment deepened in 1806, when local citizens organized themselves and many of Buenos Aires's blacks and mulattos to drive out a British naval force that had taken control of the city. The following year, this combined militia thwarted yet another British invasion and forced the British to evacuate the city of Montevideo, across the Río de la Plata estuary from Buenos Aires, as well.

Creole militia officers thus positioned themselves to play key roles in the politics of Buenos Aires in the volatile years that followed the Napoleonic invasion of Spain. They figured prominently in a gathering of some two hundred fifty members of the town's upper class in May of 1810. That meeting produced a new governing junta that proclaimed nominal allegiance to Ferdinand VII, but in fact Spanish authority had ended in Buenos Aires, never to reappear. Those who dared to voice opposition to the patriot agenda were soon silenced.

Spanish American Independence

Buenos Aires was the exception, however. Only there, at the southernmost extreme of the empire, did prospects for the political independence of Spanish America seem good when Ferdinand resumed the throne. Everywhere else, the cause of independence appeared doomed. Hidalgo and Morelos were dead in Mexico, and within a few years thousands of those who had fought beneath their banners accepted amnesty from the crown. Bolívar had fled to Jamaica and King Ferdinand sent new armies to crush the Venezuelan rebellion once and for all. Once again, however, the determination of Latin Americans to assert control over their own affairs combined with events in Europe to bring about independence.

The Final Campaigns

Following King Ferdinand's return to power, conservatives quickly persuaded him to dissolve the Cortes and reject the Constitution of 1812. These actions reinforced the determination of those Americans who had decided to break with the mother country and disillusioned those who had hoped he would be a just and fair monarch attentive to the concerns of all his subjects. Despite the many setbacks they had experienced, Americans persisted in their efforts to wear down the strength and morale of Spanish military forces.

Meanwhile in Spain, discontent mounted over Ferdinand's absolutist policies and the increasingly unpopular war in America. In 1820, liberal politicians and army officers forced the king to accept the 1812 Constitution and the convening of a new Cortes. In those parts of Spanish America that still recognized

Portrait of Simón Bolívar.

Iturbide defeating the Royalists.

the tie with Spain, the formation of provincial governments and elections to the parliament proceeded, with the enthusiastic participation of those who had gotten their first experience in representative government between 1808 and 1814. Spain's new leaders hoped the restoration of constitutional government would prove more effective than military repression in ending the movement for independence throughout the colonies. Once again, though, the "American Question" loomed, and most of these leaders remained unwilling to grant the overseas kingdoms an equal voice in government or the liberalization of trade the Americans had long demanded.

The way now lay open for the Americas to make their final break with Spain. In Mexico, the flurry of political activity among the lower classes, once again enfranchised by the resumption of constitutional government, alarmed Mexican conservatives who remembered the excesses of Hidalgo's forces in Guanajuato and elsewhere. At the same time, the upper classes began contemplating a pragmatic partnership with lower-class groups. A decisive moment came in February 1821, when the royalist general Agustín de Iturbide switched sides, forming an alliance with the rebel leader Vicente Guerrero, who had carried on guerrilla operations against royalist forces following the death of Morelos. Iturbide's proclamation of independence, known as the Plan de Iguala, was designed to calm conservatives. He proposed independence for Mexico and the creation of a constitutional monarchy. He also promised protection to the Catholic Church and to all Europeans in Mexico who agreed to support him. Over the next several months, Spanish authority simply collapsed in New Spain, as entire units of the army defected and joined Iturbide. In September of 1821, exactly 300 years after the Spanish conquest of Mexico, Iturbide entered Mexico City in triumph. Meanwhile, the people of Guatemala and the rest of Central America declared their independence from Spain and temporarily became part of Mexico.

In South America, Simón Bolívar returned to Venezuela in 1816 and scored major victories against the Spanish. A key reason for his success was his decision to use black troops, a tactical reversal of his prior refusal to allow them a role in the struggle for independence. Forces that Bolívar recruited with the assistance of Haitian president Alexandre Pétion, in return for a promise that he would abolish slavery in the new nation, helped turn the tide in Venezuela after 1815. Thousands of llaneros also joined with Bolívar at this critical juncture. By 1822, he had assured the independence of the Republic of Gran Colombia, consisting of present-day Colombia as well as Venezuela and Ecuador. He liberated Quito, Ecuador, in 1822.

Meanwhile, the cause of independence won new victories in southern South America, led by José de San Martín, an Argentine-born officer in the Spanish army who had fought against Napoleon in Spain but returned home to join the independence struggle in 1812. San Martín's army set up camp at Cuyo at the base of the Andes in western Argentina, gathering to its side many refugees who had fled Chile after the Spanish had quashed an independence revolt there. After three years of careful preparations, in January of 1817, San Martín led fifty-five hundred troops through treacherous mountain passes, some at altitudes approaching 15,000 feet above sea level, to Chile. Decisive victories over Spanish forces then paved the way for Chile's final independence in 1818.

Chile in turn became the launching pad for San Martín's naval assault on Peru, an expedition that failed to yield immediate results because royalist forces were well entrenched and many Peruvians who supported independence distrusted Argentine and Chilean patriots. In 1821, however, Peruvian creoles declared independence and accepted San Martín as military and civil ruler for the time being, but royalist forces remained firmly in control of much territory in Peru.

San Martín and Bolívar were both strong-willed men and rivals for control of the independence movement in South America. They met in Guayaquil, on the coast of Ecuador, in 1822. At issue was the status of Guayaquil itself, whether this valuable port and naval base would be part of Gran Colombia, under Bolívar's control, or Peru, which San Martín obviously preferred. The Argentine general also hoped that Bolívar would provide troops to assist him in his campaigns

LATIN AMERICAN LIVES

SIMÓN BOLÍVAR AND MANUELA SÁENZ, LEADERS OF SOUTH AMERICAN INDEPENDENCE

BORN IN 1783 to a wealthy family in Caracas, Simón Bolívar has been called the "George Washington of South America" for his efforts in securing the independence of his native Venezuela, as well as Colombia, Ecuador, Peru, and Bolivia. He was well educated and well traveled, having spent his late teens and early twenties visiting Spain, France, the United States, and Italy. While in Paris, he witnessed the coronation of Napoleon as emperor of the French and met the German naturalist Alexander von Humboldt. In 1807, he returned home and became politically active during the period following Napoleon's invasion of Spain.

Bolívar soon took up arms against Spain, fighting in Venezuela and neighboring New Granada (Colombia). Vowing "war to the death" against anyone who opposed the cause of independence, he personally ordered the execution of eight hundred Spanish soldiers being held prisoner in jails and hospitals. When the royalist forces rebounded in 1815, Bolívar retreated to the British island of Jamaica. Late the following year, he invaded Venezuela once again, traveling up the Orinoco River deep into the interior of the continent, where he set up a provisional government. In 1819, he led patriot forces in an assault on New Granada and then headed southward to Quito and on to Peru, where the congress named him supreme dictator. Following General Sucre's victory in Upper Peru, Bolívar joined him and helped organize the new nation of Bolivia, named in his honor.

Bolívar generally distrusted the masses, considering them woefully unprepared for self-government. He did, however, support the abolition of slavery as a tactical move in winning black support for independence. He believed that only strong central governments, headed by authoritarian executives, could ensure the independence of the new nations of Latin America. As author of Bolivia's first constitution of 1826, he included a provision allowing its president to serve for life and choose his own successor. Many of his supporters in Peru wanted to make him their king, but Bolívar resisted the idea that the new countries needed monarchs in order to survive. He repeatedly proclaimed his adherence to the principle of representative government, albeit one restricted to well-educated wealthy, people of his own class. Nonetheless, his ego was enormous, and his jealousy of other heroes, such as José de San Martín, was notorious. Critics accused him of harboring ambitions akin to Napoleon's.

Bolívar hoped that the newly liberated nations of Latin America would form a military and political alliance to protect their hard-won independence. In 1824, he invited each of the Spanish American countries to send delegates to a meeting in Panama. The conference took place in the summer of 1826, with delegates from Mexico, Central America, Gran Colombia, and Peru in attendance. They signed treaties promising to help one another in case of attack by a foreign power and to settle disputes among themselves peacefully. Only Gran Colombia ever ratified the treaties, and Bolívar's dream of a unified Latin America lay far in the future.

In 1828, Bolívar took over dictatorial powers in Gran Colombia, hoping to prevent Venezuelan and Ecuadorian bids for separation from the republic. This effort failed, as regional loyalties proved far stronger than the Liberator's vision of unity, and rivals challenged his leadership and burned his effigy in Bogotá. Bitterly disillusioned, he resigned the presidency in 1830 and died in poverty just months later. Discredited in his own day, Bolívar in time became a national hero in each of the South American republics he helped create. His remains are entombed in a "Pantheon of Heroes" in Venezuela.

Bolívar left behind his long-time mistress, Manuela Sáenz, a native of Quito whom he met when he entered the city in triumph in 1822. Though reared in a convent and married to a British merchant in 1817, she openly lived with Bolívar for the last eight years of his life, accompanying him on his final campaigns in Peru. The Liberator named her to the rank of colonel in his armies. Following Bolívar's disgrace and death, Manuela Sáenz's stature declined. She ended her days running a tobacco shop in Paitá, a tiny fishing village on the coast of Peru, where the American writer Herman Melville met her while on a whaling expedition. When she died of diphtheria in 1856, local authorities burned all her personal effects, including the many love letters she had exchanged with Bolívar, and ordered her buried in a common grave. Sáenz has long been a controversial figure in Latin American history, denounced for immoral behavior by conservatives in her own time and subsequently. In the late twentieth century, new views of Sáenz emerged. A novel by Colombian Nobel laureate Gabriel García Márquez and a film by Venezuelan director Diego Risquez *(Manuela Sáenz)* both portrayed her as a strong, intelligent woman who made significant contributions to the independence of Latin America.

Questions for Discussion
Regional loyalties definitely played a decisive role in the failure of Bolívar's plan for Latin American unity, but did particular personal qualities and actions of Bolívar also play a role? If so, which ones?

against royalist forces in Peru. Bolívar's military position was far stronger, and he won the debate on both counts. In fact, the Guayaquil encounter led to San Martín's withdrawal from the independence struggle. Undisputed leadership of the movement then fell to Bolívar, who occupied Lima in September of 1823. Bolívar's lieutenant Antonio José de Sucre won the final victory for South American independence at Ayacucho, high in the Peruvian Andes, in December of

1824. A few months later, royalist troops stationed in Upper Peru (present-day Bolivia) accepted a general amnesty and agreed to become part of a new republican army of Bolivia.

Regional Conflicts in the Spanish American Struggle for Independence

The surrender of the royalist armies in Upper Peru in 1825 ended Spanish sovereignty in all of the Americas except for Cuba and Puerto Rico. The new republics that replaced the Spanish empire were taking shape, although their final boundaries underwent numerous alterations throughout the nineteenth century and beyond. The nation-states that emerged were the products of age-old local rivalries that drove Spanish Americans apart even as they fought for the common cause of independence. The movement for independence remained rooted in the desire of people from many different social classes to remain in control of their own communities.

Throughout the struggle for independence, the ad hoc governments created in major cities claimed to speak for entire provinces, but smaller towns resisted their domination. Declarations of "independence" proliferated, but the authors of these manifestos often meant independence from Lima or Buenos Aires or Mexico City, and not necessarily from Spain. Under royalist control in 1810, Quito formed a superior junta to preserve the kingdom for Ferdinand VII, to defend the Catholic faith against godless revolutionaries from France, and, as they put it, "to seek all the well-being possible for the nation and the *patria*." For them the word "nation" meant all subjects of the Spanish crown, while the "patria," literally translated as "fatherland," was the Kingdom of Quito, free and independent from the viceregal capitals of Lima and Bogotá. Meanwhile, other towns in the Ecuadorian highlands in turn proclaimed *their* independence from Quito.

In southern South America, many places resisted the hegemony of Buenos Aires, where forces favoring autonomy from the mother country were firmly in control. Paraguay declared itself an "independent republic" in 1813, but again, the issue of concern was independence from Buenos Aires. Montevideo also separated from Buenos Aires, paving the way for an independent nation of Uruguay. People in Upper Peru (present-day Bolivia) faced a double threat to their ability to control their own destinies. This silver-rich region had been ruled from Lima for more than two hundred years, but in 1776 it became part of the new viceroyalty of La Plata, headquartered in Buenos Aires. Now Bolivians took up arms to win freedom from both their present and their former capitals.

The authoritarian actions of governments established in the major cities contributed to these rapidly multiplying struggles for local autonomy. Leaders who were radical when it came to asserting full and outright independence from Spain often served as mouthpieces for the colonial upper class intent on maintaining a firm grip on outlying provinces and on the Indian and casta masses. They restricted the vote to a select few, stifled dissent, and claimed dictatorial powers for themselves. Ironically, it was in the areas controlled by forces loyal to Spain where the very liberal voting provisions of the Constitution of 1812 were most often enforced. In Quito, for example, the same general who had crushed a local movement for autonomy in 1812 supervised elections held throughout Ecuador to choose representatives to the Cortes a year later. He reprimanded a local official who tried to disenfranchise Indians living in remote jungle areas east of the Andes.

Spanish Americans emerged from their wars of independence sharply divided by class and ethnicity and with far more allegiance to their immediate communities than to any larger entity. If anything, the fight for independence may have accentuated those local loyalties by giving people opportunities to articulate why they did not care to be governed by the next town or province any more than they wished to be ruled from Europe.

The Independence of Brazil

Compared to their counterparts in Spanish America, Brazilians attained their independence relatively peacefully, and Brazil remained united rather than split into many small nations. This does not mean, however, that conflict and preoccupation with local concerns were entirely absent from the Brazilian struggle for independence. As in the case of Spanish America, Brazilian independence was triggered by events in Europe.

The Portuguese Monarchy in Brazil

Napoleon's invasion of the Iberian Peninsula unleashed a chain of events that forever altered Portuguese America as well as Spanish America. The French emperor was determined to sever Portugal's long-standing alliance with Great Britain. For decades, policymakers in Lisbon had toyed with the idea of removing themselves from the vicissitudes of European power politics by making Brazil, rather than Portugal, the center of the empire. The rapid approach of French troops in November of 1807 persuaded the government to consider this radical proposal as a temporary expedient in the face of a national emergency. At the time, Queen Maria wore the Portuguese crown, but her son João actually governed as prince regent, and it was he who made the decision to move his entire household and an entourage numbering as many as ten thousand people to Brazil, sailing with a British naval escort. Arriving in Rio de Janeiro in 1808, Prince João declared his intention to remain until the crisis in the mother country had passed. In 1816, Maria died and he became King João VI, while still residing in Brazil.

The presence of the royal court brought dramatic changes to Portuguese America. Intellectual activity flourished with the long-overdue introduction of printing presses at Rio de Janeiro and Salvador, the expansion of education at the primary level, and the establishment of two medical schools and a military academy to train officers for Brazil's new army. Rio de Janeiro thrived as never before, as local merchants found a market providing the court with its many needs. Most important, many Brazilians took pride in their homeland, touting its greatness in new periodicals that circulated in major cities. As one young man from Bahia put it, "Brazil, proud now that it contains within it the Immortal Prince,…is no longer to be a maritime Colony…but rather a powerful Empire, which will come to be the Moderator of Europe, the arbiter of Asia, and the dominator of Africa." In 1815, Portuguese America was proclaimed the Kingdom of Brazil, fully equal with the mother country.

Other changes proved less welcome, however. Brazilians had to shoulder new tax burdens to pay for the expanded bureaucracy and the costs of waging war against the French in Portugal. Willingly at first but with increasing reluctance as time passed, prominent citizens of Rio de Janeiro vacated their homes to accommodate the courtiers and bureaucrats who accompanied the king to Brazil. People in Bahia in the northeastern part of the country chafed under Rio de Janeiro's growing dominance over them. Although the government in exile officially encouraged trade with all nations, it also bound Brazil more closely than ever before to an economic dependence on Great Britain that stifled the growth of local manufacturing.

Popular Unrest in Brazil

Some Brazilians dared to express their opposition to the adverse effects of the Portuguese occupation, and King João was no more sympathetic to their concerns than King Ferdinand was to the grievances of his American subjects. In March of 1817, a revolt began in Pernambuco in the northeast after royal authorities arrested a number of army officers and others suspected of harboring treasonous sentiments. The rebels destroyed images of the king and his coat of arms, proclaimed a republic, and trumpeted ideals voiced by their contemporaries in Spanish America, among them personal liberty, equality before the law, support for the Catholic religion, and devotion to their homeland, or patria. They also expressed their hatred toward the many Portuguese-born Europeans who had settled in Brazil in the years since 1808, but vigorously denied rumors that they advocated an immediate end to African slavery, a mainstay of the Brazilian economy. The revolt spread throughout the northeastern part of Brazil, the area that most resented the heavy hand of the royal government based in Rio de Janeiro.

King João was aghast at what he called "a horrible attempt upon My Royal Sovereignty and Supreme Authority." His forces suppressed the rebellion within

Coronation of Emperor Pedro I, Rio de Janeiro, 1822.

just two months and about twenty of its leaders were executed, but the king could no longer take his Brazilian subjects for granted. He brought new armies over from Portugal and stationed them in Rio de Janeiro, Salvador, and Recife. The king was determined to snuff out any signs of unrest on either side of the Atlantic.

The Culmination of Brazilian Independence

Indeed, King João had cause for concern that the people of Portugal might attempt to throw off his authority as well. Discontent within the military sparked a revolt in August of 1820 that strongly resembled the Spanish coup of that same year. The participants called for the convoking of a Cortes and the writing of a constitution modeled after the Spanish document of 1812. They also demanded that King João return to Lisbon, and he prudently acquiesced. Before embarking from Rio de Janeiro in April of 1821, he placed his 22-year-old son Pedro in charge as prince regent of the Kingdom of Brazil.

This was a period of important political change in Brazil. With the blessing of the Portuguese Cortes, many towns and cities formed juntas, asserting their local autonomy rather than accepting the continued domination of the government in Rio de Janeiro, much as Spanish Americans of their time tried to free themselves from the control of capital cities. The Cortes also ordered the dismantling of superior tribunals created during King João's residency, and the local governing juntas refused to send tax revenues to Rio de Janeiro. The cumulative effect of these changes was to reduce Prince Pedro's authority, so that, in effect, he functioned as little more than the governor of the capital city and its immediate surrounding area. Affluent residents of Rio missed the good times their city had enjoyed between 1808 and 1821, and those imbued with a sense of Brazilian national pride fretted over the splintering of the great Kingdom of Brazil into a series of petty autonomous provinces, each under the jurisdiction of a separate local junta.

Meanwhile, delegates in the Cortes worried with considerable justification that those opposed to these constitutional changes might rally around Prince Pedro. The Cortes therefore commanded the prince regent to return to Portugal, as his father had done several months previously. In January of 1822, Pedro announced his decision to stay in Brazil, evidently convinced that the Cortes's order constituted a supreme disregard for royal authority. Over the next several months, he moved ever closer to those favoring a complete break with the mother country. The final break came on September 7, 1822, and Pedro I became the "constitutional emperor and perpetual defender" of Brazil, a position he held until 1831, when he abdicated in favor of his son, Pedro II, who in turn ruled until Brazil finally became a republic in 1889.

The Meaning of Independence

As they went about setting up governments, leaders of the new nations of Latin America borrowed very selectively from the egalitarian rhetoric of the North American and French Revolutions. They eagerly invoked ideas of representation and freedom of expression when it came to claiming a voice for themselves in governing their homelands. Taking their cues from France and the United States, Latin America's leaders forged a new concept of citizenship, calling on all who lived within their borders to place loyalty to the nation above any ties to their church, family, or local community.

The kind of equality proclaimed by the more radical factions of the French Revolution terrified them, however. At the same time, fighters both for and against independence sought to enlist the lower classes on their side. Various insurgent leaders in Spanish America promised to abolish the tribute, a special tax on Indians and blacks levied by on the colonial state. In Peru, the insurgents also ordered an end to the mita, a highly oppressive system of forced labor that had sent thousands of Indians to work in silver mines and other enterprises. The tribute and the mita both symbolized the power of the colonial state that the insurgents were anxious to destroy. Indians often had few reasons to trust privileged creole patriots, and sided with the Spanish. In Peru and Bolivia, for example, Indians comprised the bulk of the royalist armies. After independence, many leaders declared that the people formerly known as "Indians" were now citizens of the new national states. In practice, however, many forms of discrimination lingered long beyond the end of colonial rule.

Slice of Life   The Sixteenth of September: Independence Day in Mexico

THE LEADERS of Latin America's new nations not only had to set up governments and rebuild economies disrupted by the independence wars; they also had to convince their people to pay allegiance to the nation. Historians sometimes speak of nation-states as "imagined communities" in which people who do not have face-to-face contact with one another, and who may not have much in common, all see themselves as citizens of the nation. In practical terms, forging these new communities in Latin America meant getting people as diverse as, for example, pampered creole aristocrats in Mexico City, Zapotec-speaking Indians in Oaxaca far to the south, and farmers who eked out a living on the far northern frontier of New Mexico, to set aside their racial, economic, linguistic, and cultural differences and swear loyalty to the new republic of Mexico.

Most Latin Americans of the early nineteenth century, whatever their backgrounds, did in fact see themselves as part of a universal community, that of the Catholic Church. Those who took command of the new national governments strove to persuade their citizens to transfer their loyalties from the church to the nation, and they borrowed some of the tools the church had used for centuries to instill a sense of community among the faithful. National holidays now competed with religious ones, and the heroes of the independence wars were invoked as examples of patriotism, much as saints had served as examples of Christian piety.

Leaders of Mexico lost little time in setting up a new ritual calendar intended to enkindle a sense of nationalism from Oaxaca to New Mexico. Foremost among the days they chose to commemorate was September 16, the anniversary of Father Hidalgo's "Grito de Dolores" of 1810, the proclamation that had ignited the first phase of Mexico's wars for independence. The initial celebration of September 16 took place in Mexico City in 1823. The festivities included the ringing of church bells, a splendid parade with music supplied by a military band, and speeches extolling the virtues of the new nation. The remains of national hero José María Morelos were brought to Mexico City for burial. Just as saints' days had offered a variety of secular entertainments in addition to the religious observances, the independence celebrations of September 1823 featured music and theatrical presentations in the Alameda, the city's centrally located park. Fireworks shows at the zócalo, the main plaza facing the cathedral, lasted far into the night.

From 1825, a private, voluntary organization supervised the celebration in Mexico City. For 30 years with only one exception, when U.S. troops occupied the city in 1847, the *Junta Patriótica* (patriotic committee) oversaw the events. Beginning on the night of September 15 and continuing throughout the next day, there were patriotic speeches, artillery salutes, music, theater,

(continued on next page)

The Sixteenth of September *(continued from previous page)*

and fireworks. The junta, the President of the Republic, and other dignitaries marched through the city's streets on the morning of the sixteenth. Schoolchildren sang patriotic hymns specially commissioned for the occasion. The people of Mexico City turned out in droves dressed in their best. The junta also marked the day with charitable works such as cash payments to disabled or impoverished veterans and to widows and orphans of rebels who died in the wars. In the 1820s, poor children received new clothes. Every prisoner in the Mexico City jails received a good meal, a packet of cigarettes, a bar of soap, and one *real* (a coin, worth one-eighth of a peso) on September 16. In the provinces, the holiday was marked with equal fervor, if not with equal splendor. In San Luis Potosí, for example, local dignitaries marched and tossed coins to the assembled crowds, who also enjoyed music and fireworks.

From the 1820s to the present, the timing, scale, and specific content of Mexico's independence festivities varied according to the political climate of the time. Sometimes, members of the nineteenth-century upper class muted the celebrations because they feared a rekindling of the same kind of popular unrest that Hidalgo's proclamation had unleashed. On some occasions, they suspended all observances except for a few speeches in Congress. In times when national governments felt more securely in control, they praised the revolutionary aspirations of Hidalgo and Morelos, hoping to win the allegiance of the lower classes. The first celebrations of Mexican independence had commemorated Agustín de Iturbide's triumphal entry into Mexico City in September of 1821 along with Hidalgo's Grito de Dolores, but later leaders chose to focus exclusively on the first phase of the movement, when Hidalgo and Morelos had so forcefully articulated the grievances of the masses, even though it had been Iturbide's actions that had secured Mexico's final independence from Spain. Iturbide's victory represented the consummation of upper-class negotiations with insurgents—a backroom deal. Subsequent leaders of Mexico had more to gain politically if they claimed to be the heirs of Hidalgo and Morelos, even if their outlook and their means of governance far more closely resembled those of the conservative Iturbide. Ironically, the symbol of the people's movement, Father Hidalgo, triumphed just as governments grew strong enough to encroach upon the very local autonomy for which the people had fought.

Questions for Discussion

Are patriotic holidays effective in promoting a sense of national loyalty? Why or why not? What are some other means that governments use to win people's allegiance? Are there means that are available to governments today that were not available to the leaders of the new Latin American governments in the early nineteenth century?

Royalist commanders throughout the hemisphere promised freedom to slaves who helped them fight the rebel forces. Similar offers went out from insurgent camps as well, but sometimes blacks were advised that they would have to wait patiently for these promises to be fulfilled. In 1812, for example, the revolutionary junta at Buenos Aires told the city's slaves, "Your longed-for liberty cannot be decreed right away, as humanity and reason would wish, because unfortunately it stands in opposition to the sacred right of individual liberty." By "individual liberty," the Argentine patriots meant the property rights of slaveowners. Even when the offers of freedom were genuine, creole leaders of the independence movement often showed extreme prejudice toward blacks even as they tried to recruit them, and many people of color cast their lot with the royalists. After independence, victorious creoles devised means to deny blacks access to the political process in their new nations. Only in places where slavery was no longer economically viable did they carry through with their wartime promises to abolish slavery.

Both sides in the independence struggle also sought the support of women. Women often accompanied soldiers into battle, preparing meals, nursing the wounded, and sometimes taking up arms themselves. In South America, Bolívar's

Miguel Hidalgo, leader of Mexican independence.

companion Manuela Sáenz played a prominent role in the final battles for independence. Throughout the Americas, women served as spies for royalist and patriot armies alike. María Josefa Ortiz de Domínguez, wife of a royal official in the Bajío and nicknamed "La Corregidora," alerted Father Hidalgo and his co-conspirators that the authorities had learned of their plot. Women smuggled weapons, and—in one instance in Mexico—a printing press, to insurgents and persuaded soldiers in the royalist armies to desert. In Mexico City, however, a women's organization called the *Patriotas Marianas* drummed up support for the royalist cause. Despite the active involvement of many women in the independence movement, the new leaders of Latin America, like those who commanded the United States and all the nation-states of nineteenth-century Europe, included only males in their definition of who was entitled to play an active role in civic affairs.

Conclusion

In most of Latin America, the wars of independence were long, drawn out, brutal contests. The Spaniards had defeated the insurgencies in the first phase by 1815. Popular and creole movements (in New Spain and northern South America, respectively) failed because of the deep-seated mutual distrust between the upper classes on one hand and Indians and castas on the other. Upper-class fear of the indigenous and mixed population cut short Hidalgo's campaign, and the unwillingness of creoles to make concessions to the lower classes in New Granada insured Bolívar's initial defeats. Undercurrents of class and race war added a vicious, murderous aspect to the fighting.

Beginning about 1817, the tide turned in favor of independence, in part because the creoles learned from past mistakes and reached temporary arrangements with the lower classes, such as the llaneros of Venezuela and Vicente Guerrero's guerrilla forces of southern Mexico. Politics in Europe also played a role in pushing the colonies toward the final break with the mother countries. Following his restoration to the Spanish throne, King Ferdinand VII had paid little attention to colonial concerns, and the representative assemblies that reemerged in Spain and Portugal in 1820 proved intransigent on issues of vital concern to Latin Americans. Colonial upper classes finally felt confident they could declare independence and contain popular discontent without help from overseas. From 1817 to 1824, Spanish and Portuguese authority yielded to independent governments from Mexico to southern South America.

Soon after taking power, leaders of the new Latin American governments began declaring national holidays that honored the heroes of independence and their victories on the battlefield, but more than a decade of war left most Latin Americans with little to celebrate. Parts of the region were in ruins, and hundreds of thousands had died. Many survivors, armed and mobile, had nothing to which they could return. Facing an uncertain future, those who did have resources hesitated to invest in new enterprises. It would take much of Latin America a century to recover economically from the wars of independence. Poverty in turn undermined the political stability of the new republics.

And while it was easy enough to create new symbols of nationhood such as flags, monuments, and coinage, much more difficult was the task of forging new national identities, "imagined communities" in which racially and culturally disunited peoples who thought mostly in terms of their own towns and villages could live together and come to see themselves as Mexicans or Peruvians or Brazilians. As we will see in the following chapters, the resulting tensions would undermine the stability of Latin American politics for a half century.

Learning More About Latin Americans

Chambers, Sarah C. *From Subjects to Citizens: Honor, Gender and Politics in Arequipa, Peru, 1780–1854* (University Park, PA: Pennsylvania State University Press, 1999). A look at how ordinary people in one Peruvian community experienced the transition from colonialism to independence.

Kinsbruner, Jay. *Independence in Spanish America: Civil Wars, Revolutions, and Underdevelopment* (Albuquerque, NM: University of New Mexico Press, 2000). Good overview of the process of independence.

Kraay, Hendrik. *Race, State, and Armed Forces in Independence-Era Brazil: Bahia, 1790s–1840s* (Stanford, CA: Stanford University Press, 2001). An examination of independence and early state-building in one of Brazil's historic sugar-producing regions.

Schultz, Kirsten. *Tropical Versailles: Empire, Monarchy, and the Portuguese Royal Court in Rio de Janeiro, 1808–1821* (New York: Routledge, 2001). How the temporary presence of the Portuguese monarchy transformed life in the capital of Brazil.

Walker, Charles F. *Smoldering Ashes: Cuzco and the Creation of Republican Peru, 1780–1840* (Durham, NC: Duke University Press, 1999). Gives key insights into the roles played by the indigenous people of Cuzco in forging independence and a new national state.

9

REGIONALISM, WAR, AND RECONSTRUCTION
POLITICS AND ECONOMICS, 1821–1880

THE NEWLY INDEPENDENT countries of Latin America confronted two enormous challenges. The first was the need to persuade people who lived within their boundaries to render allegiance to the nation-state. Second, they had to rebuild their economies following the widespread destruction of the prolonged wars of independence. But before they could undertake these efforts, they had to resolve endless, seemingly intractable, disputes over who was to rule and what type of government was most appropriate. Most important, the new nations had to overcome the fact that the majority of people thought about politics in terms of their village, town, or province. Their concerns centered on how best to earn their livelihoods and maintain their local traditions, and for centuries, they had stubbornly resisted outsiders' attempts to meddle in their affairs. As we saw in Chapter 8, this regionalism shaped the independence struggle in many parts of Latin America, and it would continue to frustrate the efforts of nineteenth-century politicians bent on forging national communities.

Class and ethnic divisions further stymied nation-building, as people of different social classes fought for control of the new national governments. Under-

1814–1840	1829–1852	1836–1838	1857–1860	1879–1883	1865–1870
Dr. Francia rules Paraguay	Juan Manuel de Rosas dominates the Río de la Plata	Peru–Bolivia Confederation	War of the Reform in Mexico	War of the Pacific (Chile v. Peru and Bolivia)	Paraguayan War or War of the Triple Alliance

1822–1831	1829		1846–1848	1862	
Pedro I rules in Brazil	Gran Colombia breaks up		Mexican War with the United States	Argentine unification	

lying all politics was the deep fear the white upper classes had for the lower classes—comprised of African Latin Americans, native peoples, and mixed bloods—in part the result of a series of Indian and slave rebellions during the half century before the end of colonial rule.

Nor was there any kind of consensus about the form that governments should take. Some called for monarchy as the only way to guarantee stability, while others favored representative government. Among the advocates of democracy, some wanted a broad franchise, while others preferred to limit political participation to a select few. Often, charismatic strongmen, called *caudillos,* who were able to impose order by either mediating or coercing the various competing groups, took the reins for long periods. Finally, for many Latin Americans the struggle for independence was just the beginning of a cycle of intermittent and devastating warfare that would last for much of the nineteenth century. Civil conflicts, wars with neighboring Latin American nations, and invasions launched by nations outside the region all took an enormous toll in human lives, wreaked economic havoc, and undermined all efforts at achieving some kind of national political cohesion.

Building strong economies proved equally daunting. The damage caused by the wars of independence was extensive. The lack of continuity caused by changes in the form of government and turnover in personnel made economic development difficult.

Dilemmas of Nationhood

The new leaders of Latin America embarked upon nationhood with many ideas about political life, but no clear blueprint of the forms their national governments should take. They all had recent experience with kings, much of it unfavorable. The principal model of self-government at the national level was that of the young United States, but some political leaders found it unsuitable for Latin America. Like their neighbors to the north, the larger nations grappled with the question of whether to create a strong central government headquartered in the national capital or to leave substantial power in the hands of state, provincial, or local governments. Given the profound attachment that many Latin Americans had to their own regions and towns, this dilemma of centralism versus a loose confederation proved especially vexing. Then, too, Latin America's leaders disagreed about how much change their societies needed. What institutions and practices left over from the colonial period should be retained, and what colonial legacies should be discarded? In particular, they quarreled over the proper role of the Catholic Church in their societies and how best to make their economies more productive. But before they could address any of these questions, they had to settle the argument over who was to control the new national governments.

Who Governs and What Form of Government?

From independence through the 1870s, four broad groups vied in the political arena. At the top were the large landowners, prosperous merchants, mine owners, and church officials. All over Latin America, these wealthy, influential whites expected full well to rule the newly independent nations for their own benefit. Their plans for domination did not always go smoothly. Divided themselves over important political issues and facing their own economic difficulties, they also met resistance from the lower classes in the countryside and the cities. Military forces—national armies, provincial militias, and locally based armed units—comprised the second major contender for power in the newly independent Latin American countries. Most of the time, they served the interests of the upper classes, but often military officers themselves coveted high political offices. The many wars of the nineteenth century reinforced the position of military leaders in national affairs. Third, a small middle group known variously as *gente decente* (decent people) or *hombres de bien* (men of worth) consisted of professionals, bureaucrats, lower-level clergy, and merchants associated closely with the upper classes and who, in many cases, handled the day-to-day operations of governments.

Lastly, the lower classes demanded a place in the national debates. In rural areas, they included sharecroppers, tenant farmers, small merchants, muleteers, and landless workers, while in the cities, artisans, small merchants, unskilled and skilled workers, domestics, and street vendors could all be found in their ranks. Although the upper classes commanded considerable resources and usually dominated political struggles, the lower class wielded influence at the local levels. The upper classes feared them but also needed their support, especially in times of civil war or foreign conflict. Lower-class people could thus negotiate with the upper classes for a share of political power and other concessions. In some parts of Latin America, especially Mexico and Peru, the first fifty years after independence provided considerable opportunity for lower classes, particularly in the countryside, to compete in politics and to influence national events.

The second dilemma the new nations confronted was how they were to govern themselves. The largest nations, Brazil and Mexico, initially tried monarchies. Their upper classes were most comfortable with what they had grown used to under Spanish and Portuguese rule. In Mexico, Emperor Agustín I lasted little more than a year (1821–1822). The Brazilian monarchy, however, endured for 67 years (1822–1889) and two emperors, Pedro I and Pedro II. For the most part, Latin Americans chose republican forms of government with chief executives, legislatures, and judiciaries. The new republics generally limited political participation to literate male property owners. Although there were often elections in the republics, they were usually unrepresentative or fraudulent. Turbulent politics frequently resulted in the rule of dictators, who

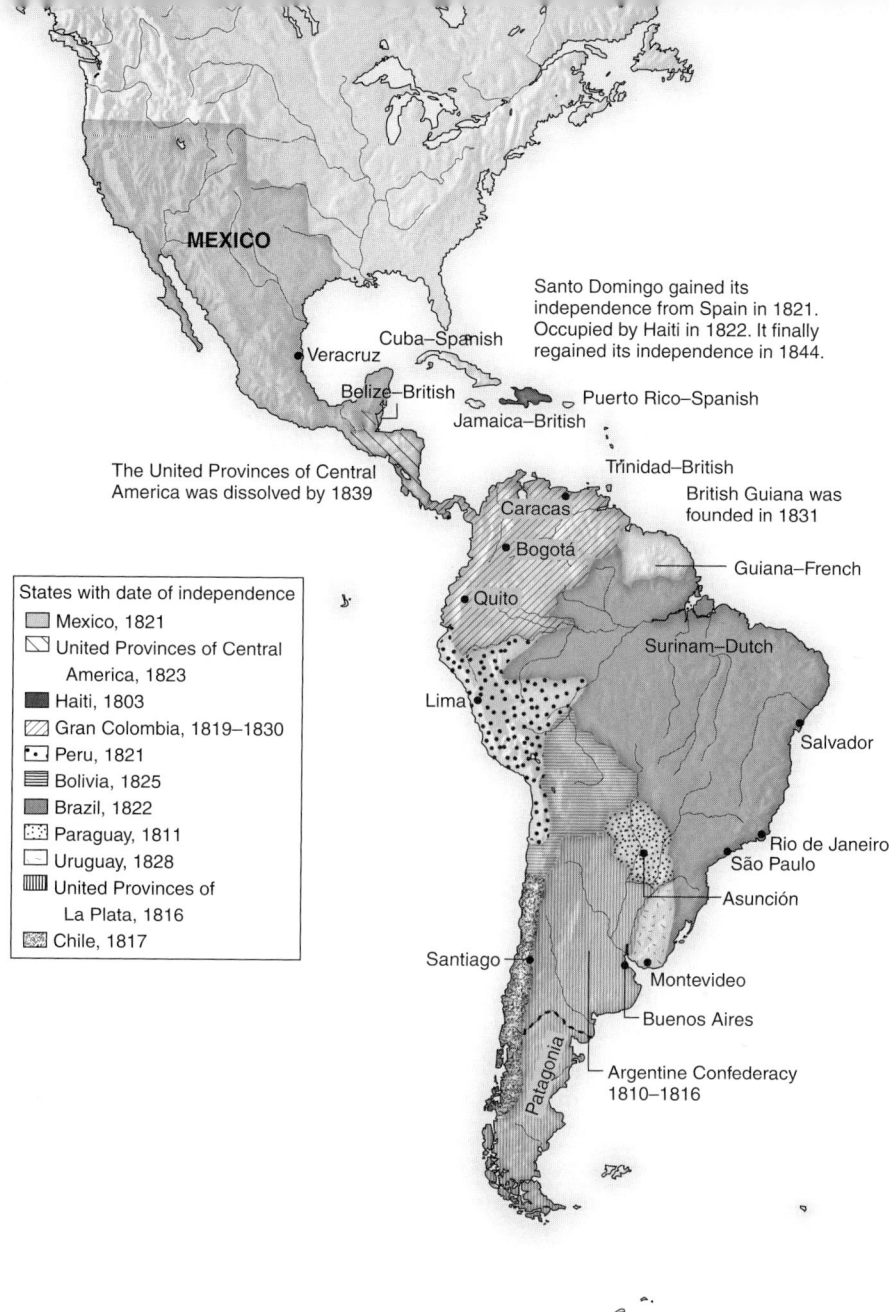

Latin America in 1830.

usually did the bidding of the upper classes. Some of the dictatorships did away with elections and representative bodies, while others maintained only the façade of democracy.

Federalism/Centralism and Liberalism/Conservatism

Even as regionalism and mutual distrust were the essence of their political struggles, Latin Americans framed their discourse initially in terms of federalism versus centralism and, by mid-century, in terms of Liberalism versus Conservatism.

At the national level, these political ideologies focused on the conflict between regional and national loyalties and visions. Federalists wanted a weak national government and strong provincial (state) governments. They were usually provincial upper class whose fortunes rested on large landholdings. They sought to maintain their long-held prerogatives derived from centuries of autonomy under colonial rule. Centralists, on the other hand, demanded a strong national government. They tended to be military officers, upper-class residents in the large capital cities (often merchants), top echelon government bureaucrats, and high-ranking clergy. Their economic interests often depended on the national government. Neither faction of the upper classes trusted the lower classes, but, nonetheless, relied on their lower-class neighbors, especially in the countryside, for armed support.

During the middle decades of the century, the wars over the form of government extended to issues such as the place of the church in economy and politics, the role of collective landholding in economic development, and the merits of free trade as opposed to protectionism. The debate between federalism and centralism was then subsumed within the conflict between Liberalism and Conservatism. Liberals supported federalism (except in the Rió de la Plata), opposed the Roman Catholic Church as an economic and political force, and advocated free trade. Liberals rejected the colonial past and promote capitalist economic development. Accordingly, they sought to end communal landholding (residents of a village owned their lands as a collective, not individually), which had, dating from before the arrival of Europeans, formed the basis of indigenous communities. Liberals believed that these collective landholdings, as well as the vast lands held by the Catholic Church, could become more productive if private individuals were allowed to develop them. Not surprisingly, large landowners, especially in the provinces (away from the large capital cities) often counted themselves among the most outspoken Liberals. The landowners as federalists sought to maintain their political autonomy from the national government. They and powerful merchants favoring an end to trade barriers formed the Liberal base among the upper classes. Provincial landowners also sought to maintain their political autonomy from the national government and therefore backed the federalist position. But the crucial goal for the Liberals was modern economic development. When they discovered in the last quarter of the nineteenth century that federalism was incompatible with modernization, they became centralists.

Conservatives argued that the church served as the guarantor of social stability and accused the Liberals of godlessness for attacking the church's prerogatives. For much of the nineteenth century, Conservatives were centralists and vice versa. Among their ranks could be found military officers, upper clergy, top echelon government bureaucrats, some large landowners, and upper-class residents in the large capital cities who were merchants and landowners. The military, for the most part, divided along the lines of the national army and local militias. The national army sided with the centralists/Conservatives and the militia with the federalists/Liberals. The middle classes, who resided in the cities, were centralists because they found employment as bureaucrats in the national government.

Whether Liberals or Conservatives, the privileged groups distrusted and often despised the lower classes while at the same time enlisting their support. For most poor people in cities and countryside alike, the everyday struggle to provide for their families remained paramount. In rural areas, such issues as access to good land and freedom from oppressive taxation stood at the center of the lower classes' political agenda. Maintaining local religious and community traditions free from outside interference also assumed great importance in small towns and rural villages throughout Latin America. Many country people joined the independence movements in great part to reassert the local autonomy they had lost under colonial administrative reforms during the eighteenth century. To them, ideology mattered less than regaining control over local affairs. They often changed alliances, establishing ties with whatever regional and national forces seemed least likely to intrude on local prerogatives. Lower-class concern for local issues helped make regionalism a driving and seriously disruptive force in nineteenth-century Latin American politics.

The Challenge of Regionalism

The histories of almost every nation in Latin America recount decades of struggle to forge regions into larger entities and build national identities. The centuries-old desire for local autonomy on the part of many lower-class people lay at the heart of Latin American regionalism, but many other factors also worked against any quick achievement of national unity. Geography played a decisive role. Mountains, deserts, and jungles often impeded easy overland transportation and communication and made it difficult to determine clear national and provincial boundaries. In Mexico, the lack of navigable rivers further hindered contact among people across its vast territory that extended from present-day California to Central America. Linguistic differences and racial antagonisms divided many countries as well. Although a small group of upper-class whites in each country by the 1810s had imagined nationhood, the vast majority of the people owed loyalty to their home villages or cities. Mexico, Central America, northern South America, and Argentina all required a series of civil wars to create nations from regional conglomerations. Bolivia, Paraguay, and Uruguay owed their status as separate nations to their efforts to escape from the control of Argentina. Brazil escaped the ravages of civil war but still experienced serious conflicts among its many regions. Only Chile did not struggle to unify. It maintained orderly politics for sixty years, and Chilean presidents succeeded one another at ten-year (two five-year terms) intervals until 1890.

How Historians Understand | Benito Juárez: The Making of a Myth

BENITO JUÁREZ WAS PRESIDENT of Mexico from 1858 to 1872. Mexico's first Indian head of state led the nation through its bloodiest civil war, the War of the Reform (1858–1860), and its longest foreign war, the French Intervention (1861–1867). During his distinguished career, Juárez served at every level of government in both elected offices and the courts: from city councilor, to state legislator, national congressman, state governor, cabinet minister, and president; from district judge to chief justice of the Supreme Court of the Nation. Almost single-handedly, by force of his own determination, Juárez assured the triumph of Liberalism as the dominant political ideology and began the process of creating Mexico as a nation from the conglomeration of regions which had emerged from independence. Despite his obvious importance in nineteenth-century Mexican history, the myth of Benito Juárez has changed over time to reflect its creators' needs at the time. In the words of historian Charles Weeks: "…what Mexicans say about Juárez represents what they want to believe about themselves, as individuals and as a nation."

Because his career bridged and overlapped the careers of the two most vilified figures of nineteenth-century Mexican history, Antonio López de Santa Anna, who dominated politics from 1828 to 1855, and Porfirio Díaz, the dictator from 1876 to 1911, Juárez should have attained the status of the nation's greatest hero. But mythical status came hard. In the fragmented politics of the era, his leadership was never uncontested. Two rivals vied for the presidency against him in 1861. He faced opposition to his continuation as president, during a time when the nation was at war, after his term ended in 1865. Two opponents confronted him in the elections of 1868 and 1872. (In the latter year he died shortly after his reelection.) Despite having defeated the French and their figurehead, the emperor Maximilian, Juárez found himself demonized by his enemies as a dictator.

For the first fifteen years after his death, Juárez was almost forgotten. His successor, Porfirio Diaz, had tried twice to overthrow him by force and the two men had ended as enemies. Díaz initially sought to get out from under Juárez's shadow. A radical change in attitude toward Juárez took place in 1887, when Díaz sought reelection for the first time. Díaz had served as president from 1877–1880, sat out for a term, run for election again in 1884 and again in 1888. Díaz needed to place himself as the heir to Juárez of the mantle of Liberal leadership and it legitimized him for Juárez also to have run for reelection in a time of national crisis. The opposition to Porfirio Díaz supported the myth of Juárez, as well. They saw him as the champion of anti-clericalism (anti-Roman Catholic Church), a strong legislative branch of government, and individualism. The celebration of Juárez the hero peaked in 1906 with the centennial of his birth.

Juárez then became a symbol of the radical opponents of Díaz, who sought to revive his program—democracy, and anticlericalism— that Díaz had betrayed. The major opposition to Díaz, which arose in 1910 led by Francisco I. Madero, named its political clubs after Juárez. Ironically, they called themselves anti-reelectionists. Madero deeply admired Benito Juárez as the epitome of legality. Madero's followers called him the modern day Juárez. During the Revolution (1910–1920), Juárez emerged in yet another reincarnation as the model of a strong president. Amid the chaos and episodic tyranny of civil strife, Juárez stood for strength and law. The revolutionary leaders eventually constructed a centralized state led by a president with vast powers. They raised Juárez to hero status in order to legitimize strong presidential rule.

Questions for Discussion
Was Juárez a popular figure among common folk or just an icon created by the ruling class to suit its own purposes at various times? In the contest for control over their everyday lives, where did Juárez and his politics fit in? How do you think it is possible for historians to separate themselves from their times and to evaluate historical figures evenhandedly?

Argentina, Mexico, Colombia, and Central America

The rivalries between federalists and centralists and Liberals and Conservatives were often bitter and brutal. Four areas, Argentina, Mexico, Colombia, and Central America, required a series of civil wars to amalgamate nations from their disparate regions. Independent Argentina (originally the Viceroyalty of Río de la Plata) consisted of four regions: the city and environs of Buenos Aires, the area along the coast north of Buenos Aires, the territory across the river (nowadays Uruguay), and the interior (west of Buenos Aires to the Andes mountains). From the outset of independence, the people of the Río de la Plata struggled among themselves based on regional loyalties. Centralists, primarily export-oriented landowners and merchants in Buenos Aires, favored a unified, secular nation with an economy based on free trade. They earned their fortunes by exporting animal products, such as salted meat, to Europe. They also sought to limit the influence of the church and advocated religious freedom. Against them stood the regional bosses, usually landowners with armed cowboy (*gaucho*) followers, who objected to a strong central government and supported the church and fiercely fought to maintain their provincial autonomy.

The old Viceroyalty of Río de la Plata, the colonial administrative unit, disintegrated as a political entity immediately after independence. It would take more than four decades to unite what is today Argentina. The northeast (Corrientes,

Entre Ríos, and Santa Fe provinces) sought to throw off the domination of Buenos Aires as early as 1810. Upper Peru (now Bolivia) broke away in 1810, then Paraguay in 1811. Montevideo (across the river in present-day Uruguay) simultaneously rejected the rule of Buenos Aires. In 1819, several coastal and interior provinces declared themselves independent republics, each ruled by a local warlord.

The city of Buenos Aires, which was the strongest political and military entity in the Río de la Plata, led the struggle for centralization. Bernardino Rivadavia (1821–1827) and Juan Manuel de Rosas (1829–1852) established Buenos Aires's dominance until the provinces reasserted their autonomy, overthrowing Rosas in 1852. After nearly a decade of warfare, Buenos Aires finally defeated provincial forces in 1861 and imposed unification. Delegates from the provinces elected Bartolomé Mitre (1862–1868), the victorious general, Argentina's first president in 1862. He then used war with Paraguay (1865–1870) to further strengthen the power of the national government at the expense of provincial autonomy. By the mid-1870s, the government had eliminated the last of the regional bosses. The achievement of a centralized nation-state had been costly, however, requiring two civil wars and an external war.

Regionalism was also at the core of nineteenth-century Mexican politics. In Mexico, centralists and federalists alternated in power through the 1850s. The experiment with monarchy immediately after independence was short-lived. Emperor Agustín I, who as Agustín de Iturbide had forged the negotiations between the upper classes and rebel guerrilla leaders that obtained independence from Spain in 1821, failed to unite the country and fell to a federalist insurgency. Mexico's first elected president, Guadalupe Victoria (1824–1829), a hero of the guerrilla wars of independence, managed to balance the two factions. From 1829 until 1855, as the battle between federalism and centralism teetered back and forth, Antonio López de Santa Anna dominated the political landscape, holding the presidency on 11 separate occasions. Santa Anna began as a federalist, but quickly changed views when confronted with the fragmentation of his country. The centralists ruled for a decade from 1836 to 1846, lost out to the federalists from 1846 to 1853, and reasserted themselves in 1853. The loss of Texas in 1836 and defeat in the war with the United States (1846–1848) badly discredited the centralists led by Santa Anna. The federalist-centralist struggle was then subsumed in the new conflict between Liberals (who were federalists) and Conservatives (who were centralists). A terrible civil war erupted, which ended only in 1867 with the defeat of the centralists-Conservatives. Mexico began to come together under the presidency of Benito Juárez (1858–1872), a Liberal, who unified the nation through his heroic struggle against the French Intervention from 1862 to 1867. The Conservatives allied with the French and, as a result, suffered devastating defeat. Like Argentina, the emergence of Mexican nationhood had required a series of brutal civil wars and an external war in which there were hundreds of thousands of casualties.

Regionalism destroyed independence hero Simón Bolívar's grand dream of a unified northern South America. From 1821 to 1830, Bolívar, as president, built Gran Colombia out of Ecuador, New Granada (presently Colombia), and Venezuela. But by 1830, despite his enormous efforts, the three nations had separated and were individually beset by centrifugal forces. Ecuador divided into sharply distinct regions tied economically to the outside rather than to each other. The height of its regional divisions occurred in 1859, when no fewer than four governments with capitals in four different cities claimed to rule. Colombia was more divided than Ecuador. There were six major regions, five with an important city at its center: Cauca (Popayán), Antioqueña (Medellín), the coast (Cartagena), the Central Highlands (Bogotá), the northeast (Vélez), and the llanos (coastal plains). Francisco de Paula Santander, one of Bolívar's important lieutenants who was president from 1832 to 1837, maintained an unsteady peace. But after he left office, federalists and centralists fought a series of bitter civil wars from 1839 until 1885. Venezuela, through the skills of José Antonio Páez, another important lieutenant of Bolívar, resisted regional fragmentation into the 1850s. However, the nation erupted into the Federal Wars from 1859 to 1863, which resulted in a federalist victory. The triumph was short-lived, however, because in 1870 Antonio Guzmán Blanco (1870–77, 1879–84, and 1886–88) reestablished centralized rule. In neither Colombia nor Venezuela did civil wars settle the conflicts between federalism and centralism.

Central Americans struggled against each other for much of the nineteenth century. In 1821, they put their fates in the hands of Mexico, joining the newly independent empire of Agustín de Iturbide. With the fall of Iturbide, a Central American congress met to declare the independence of the United Provinces of Central America in 1823, but the government of the United Provinces never gained control as the region plunged into civil war. Although the central government continued, the individual states increasingly expanded their influence. By 1865, Guatemala, under the rule of José Rafael Carrera (chief of state, 1844–1848, 1851–1865), defeated unification once and for all. In Central America, as in Argentina and Mexico, it took civil war to establish nation-states. Nothing, however, could unite the region.

Brazil and Chile

Although Brazil experienced no widespread civil wars, it, too, suffered deep regional divisions. Regional leaders never ceased their opposition to the nation's first ruler, Pedro I, and finally forced him to abdicate in 1831. Regional rebellions erupted during the 1830s, when a regent ruled during the minority of the heir to the throne. (Pedro I abdicated when his son was only four years old.) With Brazil seemingly on the verge of dissolution in 1840, Pedro II became emperor at age fourteen. War with Paraguay (1864–1870) to some extent served to push some Brazilians to think in national terms. Pedro II kept Brazil together until he abdicated, when regional tensions again overwhelmed the monarchy in 1889.

Thus, to a large extent, regionalism determined Brazil's political fate, though the nation did not have to pay as great a price in bloodshed as had Mexico and Colombia. Only Chile did not struggle to unify. Chile maintained orderly politics for sixty years. Chilean presidents succeeded one another at ten-year (two five-year terms) intervals until 1890.

A Century of War

War was the second major factor in the political instability in Latin America, as well as the primary reason for the lack of economic development. Hardly a year went by when there was not a war or some kind of military action somewhere in Latin America (see Tables 9.1 and 9.2). Warfare inflicted enormous physical and economic damage; disrupted commerce, communications, and transportation; and drained governments of scarce financial resources. Political scientist Brian Loveman has

Gran Colombia: The failed experiment.

Table 9.1

International Wars and Foreign Invasions in Latin America during the 19th Century

1823	Mexico v. Central America
1825–1828	Cisplatine War: Brazil v. Buenos Aires
1828–1830	Gran Colombia v. Peru
1829	Spain v. Mexico
1833	Great Britain takes Falkland Islands
1833	United States force in Buenos Aires
1836–1839	Chile v. Peru-Bolivia Confederation
1836	Mexico v. Texas
1838	Pastry War: Mexico v. France
1838–1840	France blockades Río de la Plata
1838–1851	La Guerra Grande: United Provinces v. Uruguay
1838–1865	Central American Wars
1840–1841	Panama v. New Granada
1840–1845	France and Great Britain blockade Río de la Plata
1840	Peru v. Bolivia
1843–1850	Great Britain occupies parts of Central America
1846–1848	Mexico v. United States
1851	Brazil, Río de la Plata, and Uruguay v. Buenos Aires
1852–1853	United States lands force in Argentina
1853	United States lands force in Nicaragua
1854	United States lands force in Nicaragua
1853–1854	William Walker filibuster in Baja, California, and Sonora, Mexico
1855	United States lands force in Uruguay
1855–1856	William Walker conquers Nicaragua
1856	United States lands force in Panama
1857	United States lands force in Nicaragua
1858	United States lands force in Uruguay
1859	United States displays force in Paraguay
1859	United States force in Panama
1860	William Walker filibuster in Honduras
1861	Tripartite (Great Britain, France, Spain) Intervention in Mexico
1861–1865	Reoccupation of Santo Domingo by Spain
1862	Great Britain in Central America
1862–1867	French Intervention in Mexico
1863	Guatemala v. El Salvador
1864–1866	Peru, Chile, Bolivia, and Ecuador v. Spain
1864–1870	War of the Triple Alliance: Paraguayan War
1865	United States force in Panama
1864–1871	Guatemala and Honduras v. El Salvador
1868	United States lands force in Uruguay
1868	United States lands force in Colombia

(continued on next page)

Table 9.1

International Wars and Foreign Invasions in Latin America during the 19th Century *(continued)*

1876–1885	Central America
1879–84	War of the Pacific: Chile v. Peru and Bolivia
1885	United States force in Panama
1888	United States force in Haiti
1890	United States force lands in Argentina
1891	United States force in Haiti
1891	United States force in Chile
1894	United States force in Brazil
1895	United States force in Colombia
1896	United States force lands in Nicaragua
1898	United States force in Nicaragua
1894–1895	Great Britain in Central America
1898–1899	United States v. Spain (Cuba)

Sources: C. Neale Ronning, ed. *Intervention in Latin America* (NY: Knopf, 1970); David Bushnell and Neill Macaulay, *Latin America in the Nineteenth Century*, 2d. ed. (NY: Oxford, 1994): 305–309; and Brian Loveman, *For La Patria: Politics and the Armed Forces in Latin America* (Newark: SR Books, 1999): 45–47.

identified four categories of wars in Latin America: transnational wars of political consolidation; international wars between Latin American nations; wars against foreign military intervention; and civil wars.

Wars of Political Consolidation

The best examples of wars of political consolidation were actually unsuccessful in unifying the contesting countries, leading instead to the dissolution of large confederations. The Argentine Confederation fought against Brazil from 1825 to 1828 in order to maintain its control over the territory that became Uruguay, which was once a part of the Viceroyalty of Río de la Plata. Uruguay emerged as a separate nation in a compromise to bring about peace. One of the longer wars of political consolidation took place in Central America, where the struggle for unification dragged on from 1824 to 1838, ending in failure. Peru and Bolivia, once together as part of the Viceroyalty of Peru, also failed to unify, engaging in a fruitless war from 1836 to 1841.

Intra-regional Wars

The most important wars between Latin American nations were the War of the Triple Alliance (1864–1870) and the War of the Pacific (1879–1883). The War of the Triple Alliance, or Paraguayan War, in which Paraguay fought against the alliance of Argentina, Brazil, and Uruguay, was the most prolonged and destructive of the inter-Latin American conflicts. The war began when Brazil invaded Uruguay (which Brazil claimed was part of its territory) and

Table 9.2

Major Civil Wars in Latin America during the 19th Century

Year	Name	Nation
1826–1829, 1837–1840	Unnamed	Central America
1828–1830	Unnamed	Chile
1839–1842	War of the Supremes	Colombia
1854–1867	Plan de Ayutla; War of the Reform, French Intervention	Mexico
1851–1861	Unnamed	Argentine Confederation
1859–1863	Federal Wars	Venezuela
1890–1891	Civil War	Chile
1893–1894	Civil War	Brazil
1899–1902	War of the Thousand Days	Colombia

Paraguay in response crossed a sliver of Argentine territory to attack the Brazilian province of Rio Grande do Sul. Argentina, Brazil, and Uruguay (with a government that was a puppet of Brazil) then allied and turned on Paraguay in May 1865. The war devastated Paraguay. It lost between 8 and 18 percent of its population and 38 percent of its pre-war territory. Its industries were ruined. After the peace, alliance troops occupied parts of Paraguay for eight years. All of the progress of the previous half-century toward a self-sufficient, relatively economically egalitarian society ended. Political instability followed for the next six decades.

Another extremely destructive conflict between Latin American nations was the War of the Pacific. Chile fought Peru and Bolivia over access to nitrate fields. Chile and Bolivia had a long-standing disagreement over the territory–located in a disputed area in northern Chile, southern Peru, and western Bolivia–while Peru and Chile disputed control over the taxes on nitrate deposits. Chile won a drawn-out struggle and occupied Peru from 1881 to 1883. Peace brought a substantial victory for Chile, for it acquired the nitrate fields and thus a monopoly on the world's supply of this fertilizer. Bolivia lost its access to the Pacific Ocean, which was a serious detriment to its future economic development.

Foreign Wars

The most devastating war with a nation outside the region was the Mexican War with the United States (1846–1848). Mexico had lost its northern province of Texas in 1836 to North American settlers, who had revolted against Santa Anna's imposition of centralist rule. Mexico never recognized the independence of the Republic of Texas and warned the United States that any attempt to annex Texas would be considered an act of war. In late 1845, the United States, ignoring Mexico's

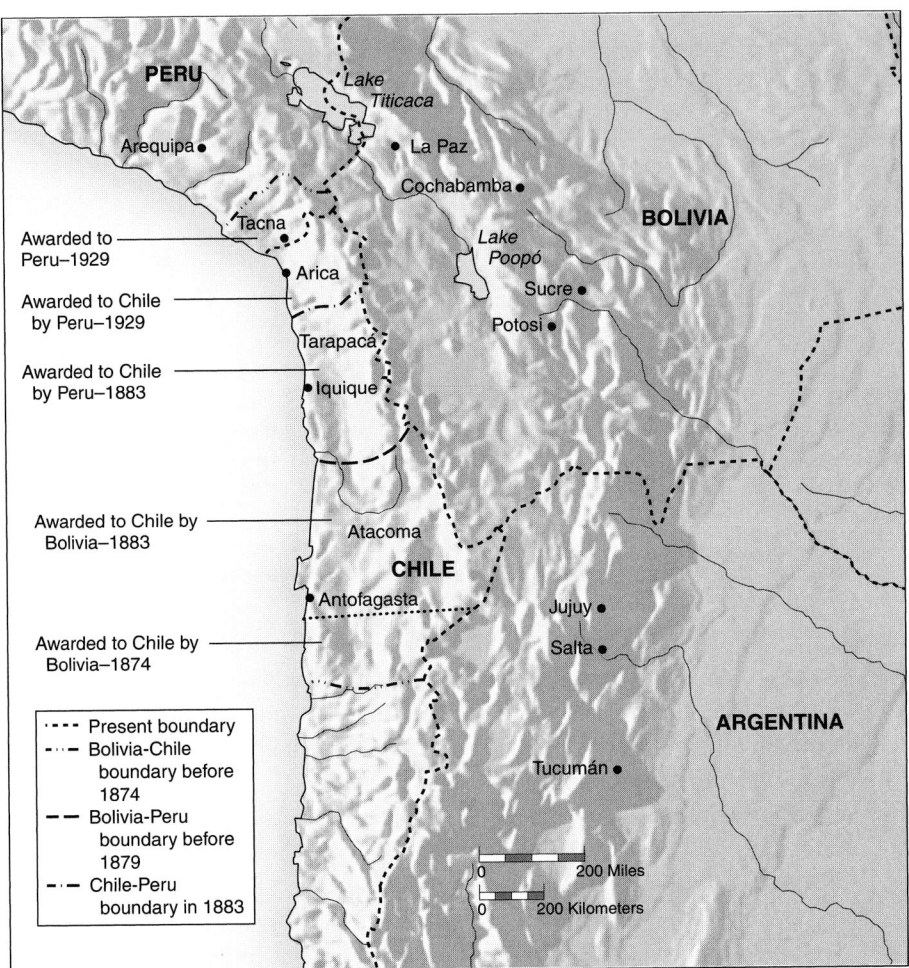

The War of the Pacific, 1879–1883.

protests, annexed Texas. A few months later, a clash between Mexican and U.S. forces in south Texas led to war. In a relatively short but costly conflict, the United States eventually captured the major cities of Monterrey, Veracruz, and ultimately Mexico City. Mexico lost half its national territory, including present-day Texas, Arizona, New Mexico, and California.

In addition to the actual wars themselves, the potential for war with neighbors over boundaries and other issues was continuously present. Argentina and Chile disputed each other's rights to Tierra del Fuego. Peru and Ecuador were at odds over their Amazonian territories. The threat of foreign intervention was constant. For a decade after independence, Mexico feared Spain would attempt to reconquer it. It also anticipated invasion by the United States for almost a century after the two ended their war in 1848. Central America and the Caribbean lived in the shadow of U.S. intervention from the 1850s.

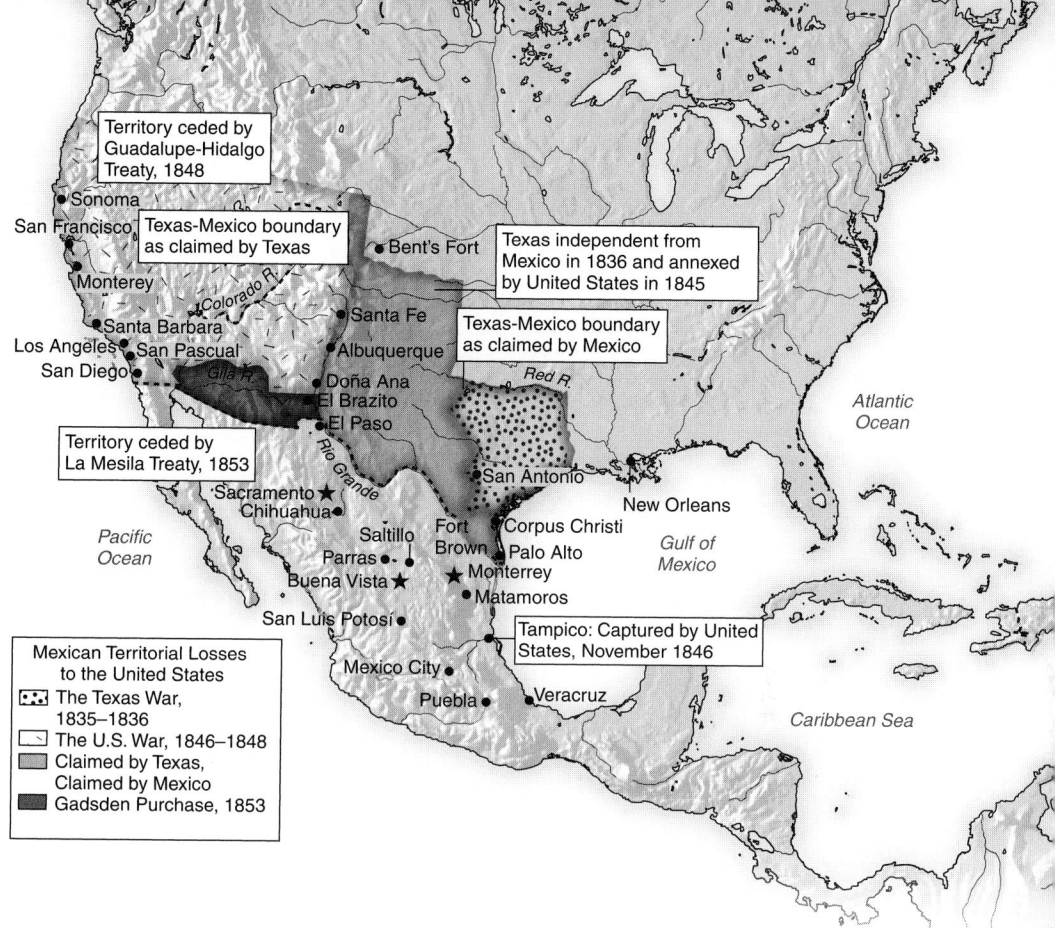

The Wars for Northern Mexico, 1836–1853.

Civil Wars

The small civil wars that plagued Latin America in the nineteenth century were innumerable (see Table 9.2). There were 11 "national level rebellions" in nineteenth-century Colombia alone. From 1831 to 1837, Brazil endured continuous rebellions in Maranhão, Bahia, Minas Gerais, Mato Grosso, and Rio Grande do Sul. Thirteen military uprisings occurred in Peru in the months between June and October 1840. From 1852 to 1862, there were 117 uprisings of one type or another in the Río de la Plata.

The struggles between Liberals and Conservatives in some countries, Mexico and Colombia for instance, erupted in brutal warfare during the middle decades of the century, as the conflicts over the place of the church in society, politics, the economy, and over collective landholding intensified. These were emotional issues, for at stake were the very essence of day-to-day life–control over one's religion and livelihood. By the mid-1840s in Mexico, Liberals and Conservatives were unwilling to compromise. Liberals propounded egalitarianism and individualism. These required the destruction of what they saw to have

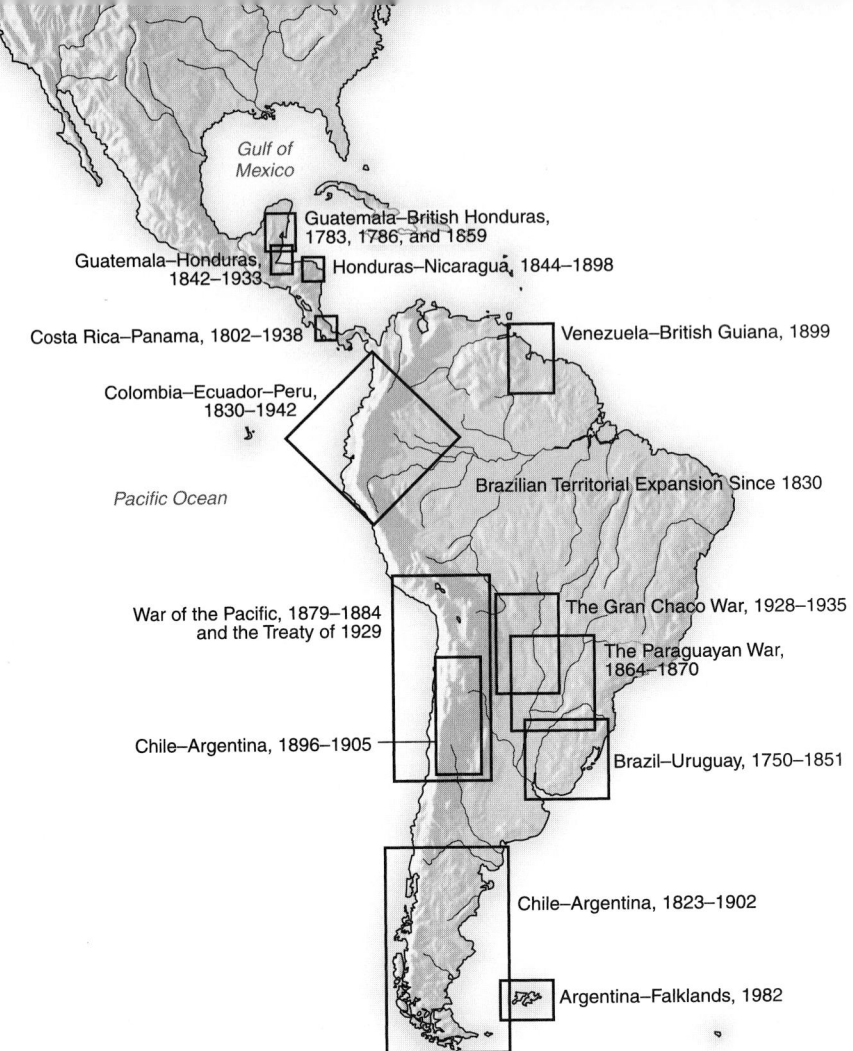

Latin American boundary disputes in the nineteenth and twentieth centuries.

been the crucial elements of the colonial state: the church, the military, and the collective landholdings of communal (for the most part, Indian) villages. They believed that the church, as a large landowner and holder of enormous funds acquired through bequests and tithing (a 10 percent tax on income), was an obstacle to economic development. The church and the military, with special privileges (such as their own courts), violated the principles of equality, an idea dear to the hearts of many Liberals. The Liberals regarded the church and communal villages as impediments to both an individualistic society and economic development. Liberals sought to take away the church's enormous economic holdings. Liberals also sought to break up village communal landholding, thereby creating a class of small farmers, which would form the base of civil society. By breaking up village communal landholding, the Liberals sought to transform villagers into a class of small farmers who would adhere to the tenets of the free market and private property and who would form the base of civil society. Conservatives believed in a civil bureaucracy based on the Spanish colonial model, a powerful military, and the Roman Catholic Church. They sought to preserve the colonial economic and social order with themselves, of course, at the top of the hierarchy. Conservatives favored strong central governments.

People in the countryside, the vast majority of Mexicans, resisted the assault on their landholdings and their local autonomy, regarding the Liberal program as a threat to their whole way of life. Their daily existence revolved around access to land, local customs, and religion. Neither upper-class faction proposed an acceptable program. The Liberals sought to abolish collective land ownership (villages owned the land, but resident families worked specific assigned plots and helped out neighbors at planting and harvest), install an ethic of capitalist individualism, and weaken the Catholic Church. But it was more than just elections, land, and taxes, for as the century wore on, common people resisted the incursions of modernity, such as the efforts to diminish the role of the church in marriage and education and the drive to expand government oversight into aspects of private life. Liberals sought to transform urban and rural lower classes into docile workers who would toil without protest, refrain from gambling and drinking, and procreate new employees. The Conservatives did not seek to undermine village traditions, but threatened the whole structure of local self-rule through centralization.

From 1854 to 1867, Liberals and Conservatives fought a vicious civil war over the issues of communal landholding and the place of the church, including the Plan of Ayutla Revolt (1854–1855), which ousted Santa Anna for the last time, the bloody War of the Reform (1858–1860), and the French Intervention (1862–1867). The Liberals ultimately won the struggle because they won over the people of the countryside. Communal villages sided with the Liberals despite the fact the Liberals advocated destruction of communal landholding because the Liberals, as federalists, also advocated local autonomy in governance. Villagers calculated that it did not matter what laws the Liberals enacted nationally; as long as the villagers controlled their own local governments, they could evade them. The crucial factor was local autonomy.

The Impact of War

The effects of warfare were profound both politically and economically. Wars militarized society, gave political prominence to military leaders, undermined democracy, widened ethnic divisions, diminished daily life, killed tens of thousands of people, destroyed property, transportation, and communications, and squandered scarce resources. They made economic development nearly impossible and thus prevented any substantial improvement in living conditions for most Latin Americans. (See Chapter 10.)

Constant warfare militarized society as formal national and informal regional armed forces proliferated. The regular army functioned at the national level to defend the nation against external threats, but often its units attempted

A soldier in the Río de la Plata in the nineteenth century.

and succeeded in overthrowing the national government. In addition, there were local militias that formed the power bases of regional bosses who challenged national unity and authority. It seemed at times that everyone was armed.

Warfare spawned countless military leaders who dominated high government office in many countries. Six civilians and sixteen generals served as president of Mexico between 1821 and 1851. Three of the civilian presidents lasted just a few days. Two generals, Antonio López de Santa Anna and Anastasio Bustamante (1830–1832, 1837–1841), dominated Mexican politics for the first half of the nineteenth century. The men who overshadowed all others in the politics of the Río de la Plata were in the military. Juan Manuel de Rosas was a noted military commander. Bartolomé Mitre (1862–1868) won fame for winning the decisive battle for Argentine unification in 1861. Despite its reputation as perhaps the most stable of the continent's republics, Chile was ruled by military officers through its initial three decades. Ramón Freire (1823, 1826–1827) was a hero of the war of independence, as was Joaquín Prieto (1831–1841). Manuel Bulnes (1851–1861) was the hero of the war against the Peru–Bolivia Confederation (1837–1839).

Military leaders who became presidents did not necessarily bring chaos or dictatorship, but constant warfare, nonetheless, did much to undermine the precarious democracies of nineteenth-century Latin America. The presence of so many military figures gave politics an authoritarian air. Moreover, in times of war, governments often suspended civil liberties, such as freedom of the press and freedom of speech. National legislatures, when confronted with war emergencies, regularly chose to temporarily suspend the rule of law in order to bestow extraordinary powers on the president.

Wars rubbed raw old ethnic and class divisions. The civil wars at mid-century in Mexico exacerbated local rivalries in the countryside to the extent that vengeance became an integral part of everyday life in the villages. There had been too many atrocities to be forgotten. One civil conflagration in Mexico in the 1840s, the Caste War of Yucatán, nearly resulted in the overthrow of white rule on that peninsula. In Peru, the War of the Pacific ripped open ethnic scars as Chinese coolies and rural blacks in the south sought vengeance for mistreatment. These conflicts only accentuated the fears of the upper classes.

Economically, wars were devastating. Lack of reliable sources makes it impossible to accurately assess the damage of a century of wars, but there is sufficient anecdotal evidence to suggest it was debilitating in some areas. The mining sector was initially hardest hit. It took decades for production in the mines of Bolivia, Peru, and Mexico to regain their colonial levels. The destruction of mine shafts by flooding, scavenging of equipment, and deteriorating roads impeded redevelopment. No better example exists than Bolivia. It emerged from the wars of independence with its mining industry in ruins. In 1800, there were several hundred mines and forty refineries in Potosí, the leading mining center in all of South America. By 1825, there were only fifty mines and fifteen refineries in operation, and the value of silver production fell by more than half. It would take thirty years for the industry to regain 50 percent of its highest colonial production.

The human cost of war in terms of casualties was sometimes catastrophic, as in the case of Paraguay in the War of the Triple Alliance. In Yucatán, in Mexico's southeast, more than one hundred thousand lost their lives in the vicious rebellion during the late 1840s. Perhaps three hundred thousand people lost their lives in Mexico's War of the Reform a decade later. The tremendous losses among young males profoundly altered family structures and gender relations (see Chapter 10).

Wars and military preparedness bankrupted national governments. Armies drained scarce, precious financial resources that would have been better spent on roads and schools. The cost of the military was nowhere more evident than in Mexico. In the mid-1830s, there were 13 divisional generals and 18 brigadiers with combined salaries of 159,000 pesos per year on the payroll. This was in an army that could muster only eight thousand soldiers to fight the Spanish invasion in 1829. One subsequent regime spent 10 million pesos in three years on new equipment in an effort to win the army's loyalty. In 1836, the Mexican military expended 600,000 pesos a month, while government revenues totaled only 430,000 pesos. These figures did not include the cost of the Texas War (1836), which added another 200,000 pesos a month! Needless to say, this left no money for other functions of government. Dictator Rosas of Buenos Aires maintained a standing army of twenty thousand and a militia of fifteen thousand. His military rarely absorbed less than half the budget, and in 1841 military expenses took three-quarters. In both these examples, the threat of foreign invasion was constant. Mexico feared Spain and the United States, while Buenos Aires worried about the Brazilians, the British, and the French.

Because armies regularly expanded and shrank in size, there were always a substantial number of out-of-work soldiers who were unwilling to return to their former homes to toil as tenants or peons on a hacienda or the communal holdings of their villages. Many became bandits. Lawlessness followed. From the 1820s to the 1860s, it was virtually impossible to travel between Veracruz, Mexico's major port, located on the Gulf of Mexico, and Mexico City without being held up. Some stagecoaches were robbed several times over the course of a single trip. It was not uncommon for passengers to arrive at their destination wrapped in newspapers, having been relieved of all their worldly possessions en route. This disorder greatly discouraged commerce and thus impeded economic development.

Not all of the effects of war were adverse, however. The military provided unparalleled upward social mobility. Indians, mulattos, and mestizos obtained unprecedented opportunities for economic and social advancement through war. Many of the national leaders who emerged from the wars of independence and subsequent conflicts came from lower-class origins. Notable among them was Porfirio Díaz, who was dictator of Mexico in the last quarter of the century. Mobilization in Brazil during the Paraguayan War had conscripted mostly black and mulatto troops. The war probably assured the end of slavery as an institution, for slaves earned their freedom for military service. Returning soldiers were not the docile work force they had been when they went to war. Some veterans received money bonuses and land grants. Others who had received nothing for their service refused to return to the status quo before the war.

Constant warfare undoubtedly eroded the fabric of everyday life and politics. Ironically, however, a few international wars may have actually contributed to the creation of nationalist sentiment and helped forge a sense of nationhood. Its two wars against Peru and Bolivia unquestionably helped consolidate sparsely populated Chile. These clear victories boosted popular association with the nation. The War of the Triple Alliance, which came only three years after unification, promoted a sense of Argentine naional identity. The valiant fight of Benito Juárez against the French Intervention in Mexico also produced the first extensive sense of nation and Mexicanness.

Popular Participation

Regional fragmentation, divisions among the upper classes, and war provided unusual opportunities for lower-class participation in political affairs during the first five decades after independence. Although Latin American civil conflicts rarely involved more than a few thousand troops, local and regional bosses required regular retainers recruited from their areas. Manpower requirements necessitated concessions and inducements. While personal loyalties were sometimes sufficient to secure followers, lower-class supporters demanded not only personal gain, such as wages, war booty, and promotions, but more importantly, maintenance of local autonomy for villages and protection from laws against collective land ownership and taxes.

Popular participation in the politics of nation-building resulted from the need of the lower classes at the very least to exert some influence over their everyday lives. As we have discussed, the policies of neither upper-class faction were acceptable. Country people increasingly opposed both Liberal and Conservative policies to develop the economy. The struggle to maintain control over their daily existence in the countryside manifested itself in the vast conflict over local autonomy, which translated into the national conflict between federalism and centralism. This in turn led the lower classes into broader political participation. In search of supporters, national leaders courted the concerns of everyday people, who comprised the armies of various competing factions.

In the cities, local issues revolved around food prices and employment. Riots were important expressions of political involvement in urban settings. Protests erupted in Latin American cities as a result of the high cost of corn and beans. For example, in 1831, the populace of Recife, Brazil, attacked Portuguese merchants believed to have been price gouging.

There were also a number of instances where the urban lower classes played crucial roles in national politics. Mexico City's lower classes formed the backbone of Iturbide's support during his last days. However, he was unwilling to use their support to maintain power, so strong was his sense of solidarity with the upper class and his fear of the lower classes. Mexico City dwellers erupted again in 1828 in the Parián Riot (see Slice of Life: The Parián Riot) in support of Vicente Guerrero, the hero of the war of independence, in his campaign for president. Mobs in the streets of Rio de Janeiro helped to force Pedro I to abdicate in 1831.

The lower classes also influenced national politics in some instances when they were willing to fight foreign invaders long after the upper classes, who, while looking after their own self-interests, surrendered to or collaborated with the enemy. After the United States army had defeated Santa Anna's army in a series of battles on the outskirts of Mexico City in 1847, the general withdrew from the

Slice of Life   The Parián Riot: Mexico City, 1828

IN NINETEENTH-century Latin America common folk struggled constantly both to sustain themselves—furnishing sufficient food, adequate shelter, and safety for their families—and to maintain some measure of control over their everyday lives. During the first five or six decades after independence, the lower classes exercised a degree of political influence because the upper classes were divided, and in some places, periodically at war among themselves. Urban and rural working-class folk participated in the politics of the time in several ways: as voters in local elections; as soldiers in civil wars and revolts; as allies of upper-class factions; and as perpetrators of specific, directed incidents of urban violence. Upper-class Latin Americans needed the lower classes to fight their battles and as allies. Nonetheless, the wealthy and powerful were wary, often fearful, of the lower classes, knowing full well that to arm the masses risked unleashing the dangerous forces of centuries of pent-up resentment. The Parián Riot, which occurred in Mexico City in 1828, was an instance in which the lower classes took part in political events, leading to a tumultuous episode that shook the Mexican upper classes to their very core.

As in most history, the upper classes wrote the narrative of the riot and, consequently, the actual events of the day were slanted in a way unfavorable to the masses. On the early afternoon of Thursday, December 4, 1828, simultaneous to and probably in association with a popular revolt that broke out against President Guadalupe Victoria (1824–1829), a crowd of five thousand assaulted and looted the luxurious shops located in the Parián Building in Mexico City's Zócalo. It ended sometime the same evening. Upper-class chroniclers of the era depicted the riot in graphic terms, such as a "savage invasion," "murders in cold blood," and a "stain on the pages of our history." We know that the rioters were people of the lower classes and some soldiers, probably part of the troop sent to bring the tumult under control.

There were two murders, neither committed by the lower classes (but by upper class), and there was considerable damage to stores and houses around the Zócalo. Most of the heavy destruction actually resulted from three days of street fighting that preceded the riot. Considerable disorder followed, with the wealthy of the city notably absent from the streets.

The revolt against President Victoria began on November 30. The lower classes rushed to support the upheaval led by Vicente Guerrero, a hero of the long guerrilla war that had led to independence. One observer estimated 30,000 to 40,000 people, 20 to 25 percent of the population of the capital, fought on the side of the rebels. Most soldiers abandoned the government and joined the rebellion.

Upper-class Mexicans disdained Guerrero, an uneducated, dark-skinned casta. Guerrero advocated two policies that were especially popular among the capital's poor. He propounded protective tariffs for the native textile industry, where many lower-class and artisan city dwellers earned their living. He also proposed to expel the remaining Spaniards, many of whom were quite wealthy and, given the dire straits of the Mexican economy, were bitterly resented. It may have been that some rioters shouted "Death to the Spaniards" as they stormed into the Parián. Many of the merchants in the building were Spaniards.

The Parián riot was indicative of the politics of lower-class mobilization in the first decades after independence. Mexican upper classes both in the cities and in the countryside needed popular support. But this came at a price—sometimes mobilization got out of control. In the countryside lower classes demanded local autonomy for their villages and delay in the implementation of many of the modernizing policies so dear to upper-class hearts. By mid-century it was clear to the Mexican upper class that the price of lower-class cooperation was too high. The Parián riot remained an indelible memory for Mexico's rich and powerful. Their fear of the masses, to their mind, was justified.

Questions for Discussion

Both during the colonial and early independence eras, Mexico had a long history of urban riots as a means for the common people to express their dissatisfaction with their governments. What were the alternative strategies for the lower classes in negotiating with the upper classes?

capital. The population of the city continued to fight, however, sniping and throwing debris from the rooftops at the North American troops. During the War of the Pacific (1879–1883), after the total defeat of the Peruvian army, the civilian country people of the central sierras and the south of Peru continued to fight under the leadership of General Andrés Cáceres against the invading Chileans. Upper-class Peruvians collaborated with the invaders. In both Mexico and Peru, the upper classes signed disadvantageous peace treaties at least in part because they feared the expansion of popular upheavals.

Throughout the nineteenth century, the upper classes faced a decided dilemma. They needed support from the lower classes, but they were not always pleased with their allies, for the masses were not easy to control once an uprising began. They lost control of the 1831 revolt in Recife, Brazil, when slaves joined in hoping to obtain their freedom. In 1835, outraged blacks and Indians in Belém, Brazil, joined and then overwhelmed an upper-class-led revolt seeking independence for their province, engaging in widespread destruction of property and attacking wealthy whites. It took the government five years to finally quash the rebels. The death toll for this bloody uprising reached thirty thousand, approximately one-fifth of the provincial population.

The new rulers of Latin America were more successful at re-imposing traditional gender roles in politics. Females were crucial participants in the wars of independence on both sides. This, of course, upset long-held views that women's place was in the home in the private sphere. The male casualties endured during the decades of war in some areas, however, created demographic imbalances that threatened male domination (see Chapter 10). In Argentina, females were in the majority until mid-century. The upper classes realized full well that in times of war and disruption, families rather than governments would hold society together. They therefore insisted on the model of a male-dominated family. In order to maintain stability, the upper classes sought to maintain long-established gender roles.

Caudillos

Strong leaders, known as caudillos, often emerged to bridge the gap between the upper and lower classes and temporarily bring order to disrupted politics. The term caudillo refers to a leader whose notoriety and authority arose from the local level, where he had attained a reputation for bravery. The caudillos of the nineteenth century who first emerged from the wars of independence were often landowners who obtained their economic and manpower bases from their position. The caudillo's army frequently was comprised of the workers on his hacienda. He was tougher and meaner than any of his followers. A web of patron–client relations (informal and personal exchanges of resources between parties of unequal status) served as the cement of his support. Usually, these relations formed a pyramid with ever more powerful participants above. Typically, a landlord expected labor, deference, loyalty, and obedience, while the employee in turn received a basic level of protection and subsistence. Many caudillos solicited support among the lower classes and consequently earned their fierce loyalty.

Juan Manuel de Rosas, who dominated Buenos Aires and allied provinces from 1829 to 1852, was perhaps the most famous nineteenth-century caudillo (see the list of caudillos in Table 9.3). He embodied the qualities of the nineteenth-century Latin American leader. He was rough, brave, ruthless, tyrannical, and a sharp political strategist. Rosas was a military leader with a common touch. As a child growing up on a large cattle estate (*estancia*) he learned the ways and language of the people who inhabited the vast plains of the Pampas, including the Indians, who at times fiercely resisted the onslaught of settlers, and the gauchos. He shared their austere lives, learning to do everything the plainsmen could do, but better. Although he came to own vast tracts of land and many enterprises, Rosas presented himself as one of the people. He adhered to their "code" of honesty and discipline. It is said that he once

Table 9.3

Caudillos

Country	Name	Years
Chile	Bernardo O'Higgins	1822
	Diego Portales	1831–1841
Ecuador	Juan José Flores	1830–1835, 1839–1845
	Tomás Cipriano de Mosquera	1845–1849, 1863–1864, 1867–1868
Mexico	Antonio López de Santa Anna	1828–1854
	Benito Juárez	1858–1872
	Porfirio Díaz	1877–1911
Paraguay	José Gaspar de Francia	1815–1841
	Carlos Antonio López	1844–1862
	Francisco Solano López	1862–1870
Venezuela	Simón Bolívar	1821–1830
	José Antonio Páez	1831–1835, 1839–1843, 1861–1863
Costa Rica	Juan Mora Fernández;	1824–1833
	Tomás Guardia Gutiérrez	1870–1882

ordered his servant to give him 20 lashes for being a bad gaucho and when, unsurprisingly, the servant balked, Rosas threatened him with 500 lashes if he did not comply with the order. Virtually unchallenged through the 1840s, Rosas succumbed to his provincial opponents in 1852.

Like many other caudillos, Juan Manuel de Rosas had a crucial base of support among the lower classes of both the city and the countryside. His multi-class coalition relied on Indians and blacks to fight on his side. He organized a personal retinue of blacks and mulattos from the poor of Buenos Aires and had a wide following among the gauchos of the Pampas. The lower classes regarded Rosas as the protector of their way of life. They proudly resisted economic progress and attacks on Catholicism. Unlike other landowners, Rosas did not always fight the Indians, but rather mostly negotiated and bargained. He provided Indian leaders (caciques) specified tribute of cattle, sheep, horses, yerba mate, tobacco, and salt. As a result, Indians respected Rosas.

Rosas turned Afro-Argentines into a pillar of his regime, relying on them for his war machine. Through his wife Encarnación, he worked with African mutual aid societies. Rosas lifted the previous bans on African street dances that reached the pinnacle of their popularity during his rule. His daughter Manuela attended dances and danced with black men. Once when the provincial government was strapped for money, 42 black nations (mutual societies) made special contributions. Rosas named his urban home after the black saint Benito de Palermo. His

Juan Manuel de Rosas was the most famous Latin American caudillo of the first half of the nineteenth century.

propaganda was written in African Argentine dialects. Through his wife and daughter, Rosas lavished gifts and attention on poor Afro-Argentines. By 1836, Buenos Aires ended the forced draft for freed slaves and in 1839 ended the slave trade. Rosas promoted blacks to high military rank and took others as personal retainers. His maintaining a large military force had considerable benefits for the chronically underemployed lower classes, for he disbursed 900,000 pesos in salaries. He distributed land to the poor who were willing to live on the frontier and rewarded loyal soldiers with land.

Heroism and charisma were no guarantees for a long or successful political career. Several of the foremost figures of the wars of independence suffered tragic fates. Like Simón Bolívar, Bernardo O'Higgins suffered early defeats at the hands of the Spaniards, but ultimately was triumphant in winning independence for Chile. As ruler, he lasted only until 1822. Antonio José de Sucre, one of Bolívar's best generals, was the first president of Bolivia (1825–1828). He failed at his extraordinary attempts to end the oppression of the Indian population. His successors, Andrés Santa Cruz (1829–1839), attempted unsuccessfully to unite Bolivia and Peru. (See also Latin American Lives: Dr. Francia.)

LATIN AMERICAN LIVES

Dr. Francia

Dr. José Gaspar Rodríguez de Francia, along with Juan Manuel de Rosas and Simón Bolívar, epitomized the strong leaders who, after the wars of independence, attempted to impose their broad vision for nation-building. All of these figures have inspired endless controversy, but no one has remained as unknown, and perhaps as misunderstood, as Dr. Francia, who ruled Paraguay from the early 1810s until his death in 1840. Vilified by the outside world as a madman, Dr. Francia enjoyed considerable popularity among the common folk of Paraguay and built an efficient, honest government and a comparatively egalitarian society.

Dr. Francia was born on January 6, 1766. After receiving his early education at home, he attended the University of Córdoba, in Argentina, graduating in 1785. He taught Latin at a seminary in Paraguay for a number of years until forced to resign because of his radical ideas on religion and politics. He then became a highly successful lawyer. He spoke Guaraní, the language of the local indigenous peoples, whom he represented in legal matters for little or no fee. Dr. Francia also acquired a substantial amount of land, which gained him access to Paraguayan politics and society.

On May 14 and 15, 1811, Creole officers, alarmed at the possibility that Spanish royalists would sell out to the Portuguese, staged a coup, overthrowing the colonial regime, though they did not immediately seek independence. Dr. Francia quickly emerged as the leader of the Paraguayan government. He was instrumental in keeping Paraguay from the clutches of both Portugal (Brazil) and Buenos Aires in the years from 1811 to 1813, eventually leading the region to independence in 1813. The next year he wrote the new constitution at a genuinely popular assembly comprised of predominantly lower-class delegates.

Unlike other leaders of independence such as Bolívar, who led the movement for liberation in northern South America from his home country, Venezuela, Dr. Francia succeeded in acquiring impressive popular support, dominating his nation's politics for a long period. He sought to destroy the bases of the old Spanish upper class, removing all Spaniards from public office. He selected judges and military officers from the general population rather than relying only on upper-class whites. Unlike many of the other leaders of his time, Dr. Francia refused to allow any monuments in his honor, and had no streets or buildings named for him. His integrity and honesty were legendary. He acquired no fortune and, in fact, his government salary were almost always in arrears. He accepted no gifts. Living as a semi-secluded bachelor, he left no heirs and, consequently, when he died the state confiscated his belongings in accordance with the laws he himself had promulgated.

(continued on next page)

DR. FRANCIA *(continued from previous page)*

Without doubt, Dr. Francia was a dictator who ruled Paraguay with an iron hand. He professed to implement the will of his people as was made known in the popular assemblies of 1814 and 1816. Thereafter, however, he limited public gatherings. After an unsuccessful conspiracy to oust him in 1820, Dr. Francia imprisoned 500 opponents for the next twenty years, but he carried out few political executions. Dr. Francia was particularly tough on the Catholic Church and large landowners. He expropriated the property of monasteries and took over financial control of the Catholic Church, ruthlessly cutting its expenses. Dr. Francia crippled the upper classes through land expropriations and forced contributions, which eroded their economic base. His system of fines and confiscation prevented upper classes from exercising indirect influence through their financial resources. His policies sharply curtailed export trade with Argentina, another important source of upper-class wealth. He did not allow members of the upper class to hold any office.

The dictator operated a highly efficient government. Although facing a chronic shortage of trained, competent personnel, Francia maintained fiscal stability, built a strong defense industry, manufacturing firearms and uniforms and building ships, reduced taxes to a minimum, balanced the budget, and adopted land reform. There was also a public works program and the nation's first public education system. Unfortunately, like other Latin American nations, Paraguay spent an inordinate amount of its funds on the military, because of the constant threat from Argentina and Brazil, which resulted in the Cisplatine War from 1825 to 1828. He pared down the government to the point at which it consisted of only a chief of police, minister of the treasury, governmental secretary (who acted as attorney general and minister of the interior), the defender of the poor, and a small staff. He divided the nation into twenty regions, each with only three officials: a commander, a tax collector, and a judge. Residents elected local officials. Early on he engaged in a fierce, successful anti-corruption campaign. The dictator personally audited the books of government tax collectors. He even fired his own brother for incompetence.

His reform program was aimed at improving the plight of the lower classes. It reduced the most onerous taxes on population left over from colonial times, cutting by more than half the alcabala or sales tax and the 10 percent tithe on agricultural production. Property confiscated from the church and the wealthy made up for revenue losses from tax reductions. Later in his rule the sale of products manufactured by the state were its largest revenue producers. The state also operated its own estancias. He presided over remarkable successes in education with widespread advances in literacy. The land the government expropriated from large landowners it leased to the landless at moderate rents. Perhaps 6,000 such homesteads with 49,000 people, 13 percent of the population, received land. The government supplied homesteaders with clothes and tools as well as cattle. Paraguay enjoyed a measure of economic success. It went from an importer of beef to an exporter. Eventually, the government had to limit the amount of cattle so as to assure other agricultural production and to limit ecological damage to the land from the livestock. Dr. Francia had tremendous success at economic diversification. Paraguay did not develop as a mono-cultural (one-crop) economy. One proof of Paraguay's economic and political success was the growth of the population from 100,000 in 1798 to 375,000 in the 1830s. Most of the increase came from migrants seeking a peaceful place to live.

His enemies wrote the history of Paraguay, portraying him as a cruel tyrant, crazy for power, who ruled in a reign of terror, isolating Paraguay in order to assure his dictatorship. But recent scholarship has depicted him as a benevolent dictator, who brought peace, prosperity, and egalitarianism to his nation. In doing so he had alienated the upper classes, which ultimately triumphed over him by writing Paraguay's history.

Dr. Francia was the only Latin American independence leader to succeed in implementing his vision of a unified nation. Paraguay remained stable and relatively prosperous until the 1860s, when war destroyed all of the accomplishments of a half century.

Questions for Discussion

Compare the career of José Gaspar Rodríguez de Francia with that of Juan Manuel de Rosas of the Río de la Plata. Do you think they ruled with popular support or through coercion? How did lower- and middle-class support for these leaders contribute to the struggle for control over their daily lives?

The Challenge of Economic Recovery

Regionalism and war affected Latin American economic development for a half century after independence. Regionalism created an uncertain political environment, which frightened investors, while war unproductively consumed vast human, material, and financial resources. In Mexico and elsewhere, the loss of territory deprived the nation of valuable resources. During the years from 1810 to 1870, Latin American economies, with a few exceptions, stagnated due to the inability or unwillingness of the upper classes to establish governments that could create stable environments for commerce and industry. Institutional obstacles left from the colonial period, the widespread damages and disruptions caused by the wars of independence and subsequent upheavals, and the lack of capital further stifled economic growth. After 1850, the situation slowly began to change, as booming markets for Latin American agricultural staples and minerals, along with European capital investment in mining and transportation brought renewed economic growth. From 1850 until World War I (1914), most nations in the region attached their economic fortunes to the burgeoning export markets in

Western Europe and the United States. Still, those committed to the economic development of Latin America faced substantial obstacles.

Obstacles to Development

In many regions, geography was a major obstacle to development. Most of Latin America lacked inexpensive transportation and easy communications. The cost of moving products to market was prohibitive. The Spanish colonial government had never invested much in roads and the wars of independence left existing roads in disrepair. With the exception of the Río de la Plata, few major waterways ran through population centers. Coastal trade was not important in the nineteenth century. The lack of transportation greatly limited the establishment of national and regional markets.

Laws, attitudes, and institutions inherited from the colonial period further hindered growth after independence. These included local and regional autonomy; over-regulation and under-enforcement of rules; indifference to long-term planning and preference for short-term benefits; concentration on the export of precious minerals; state monopolies of commodities such as liquor and tobacco; strict limitations on international trade (including with neighboring nations); widespread corruption; a tradition of smuggling; and failure to invest in roads and ports. Three hundred-year-old colonial habits and tendencies were not easy to break.

There were considerable institutional constraints to economic enterprise. Laws were often arbitrary and capricious, changing from regime to regime, and easily subverted through corruption. Laws often differed from region to region within the same nation. Each region also imposed its own taxes. Perhaps most important was the lack of modern systems of banking. The lack of credit handicapped both industry and agriculture. The shortage of capital prevented the repair and maintenance of mines, and haciendas were not repaired or maintained. The church, which had acted as a major source of credit during the colonial era, lost its primary base of income when the new governments abolished the tithe (an annual tax of 10 percent on all income collected by the colonial government from individuals for the church). The church's funds were still considerable, but they were tied up in land and virtually unredeemable loans to landowners. Europeans, with the exception of a few brief (mad) years in the 1820s, were unable or unwilling to invest in Latin America. Governments also experienced chronic revenue shortages because the newly independent states did away with many royal taxes and, because of their incompetence, were unable to collect those taxes that remained. The flight of Spaniards with their capital in the aftermath of the independence wars drained Latin America of crucial investment funds.

The new nations sought to make up for the lack of capital during the 1820s by borrowing funds abroad in the form of government loans. Several of the founders, like Bolívar, obtained loans from British investors, which they used to buy arms. From 1822 to 1825, seven Latin American nations (Brazil, Buenos Aires, Central America, Chile, Colombia, Mexico, and Peru) contracted for more than 20 million (British) pounds debt (see Table 9.4). Not surprisingly, economic difficulties prevented repayment. All the Latin American nations except Brazil remained in default of these debts for a quarter century. This foreclosed the possibility of attracting external capital to the region. After 1850, Europeans were attracted once again with the upturn of Latin American agricultural and mineral exports.

Export Economies

Although the general trend for the region as a whole was bleak for much of the first half century, as continuous war and periodic political disruptions impeded economic growth, several nations prospered because of increasing demand for agricultural commodities. Buenos Aires became one of the remarkable economic success stories of nineteenth-century Latin America. Even when fighting raged, its foreign trade expanded. Markets for hides and cattle by-products flourished. A new industry arose to process hides and salt meat. The Río de la Plata provided the slaves of Brazil and the working class of Europe with their food. In 1825, forty processing plants (*saladeros*) slaughtered seventy thousand head of cattle. By 1850, they slaughtered three hundred thousand head of cattle and

Table 9.4

Foreign Loans to Latin American Governments, 1850–1875

| | (£ thousands) | | Purpose % | | |
	Total no. of loans	Nominal value	Military	Public works	Refinance
Argentina	7	13,488	20	68	11
Bolivia	1	1,700		100	
Brazil	8	23,467	30	13	57
Chile	7	8,502	37	51	12
Colombia	2	2,200		9	91
Costa Rica	3	3,400		100	
Ecuador	1	1,824			100
Guatemala	2	650		77	23
Honduras	4	5,590		98	2
Mexico	2	16,960	70		30
Paraguay	2	3,000		80	20
Peru	7	51,840	10	45	45
Santo Domingo	1	757		100	
Uruguay	1	3,500			100
Venezuela	2	2,500		30	70

Source: *Encyclopedia of Latin American History and Culture*, ed. Barbara A. Tenenbaum (New York: Charles Scribner's Sons, 1996), 2:590.

horses. Entrepreneurial landowners began to raise sheep to provide cheap wool for the carpet factories of New England and Great Britain. Buenos Aires evolved into a complex of stockyards, slaughterhouses, and warehouses. The vast plains around Buenos Aires, the Pampas, became an enormous, efficient producer of agricultural products. In a more modest example, Venezuela experienced a coffee boom that brought two decades of prosperity from the 1830s through the 1840s.

After mid-century, European markets expanded rapidly. The increasing affluence of a growing population in Europe, a crucial aspect of which was the transfer of people from agriculture to industry, created a demand for Latin American products. Because most European nations were self-sufficient in basic agricultural staples, at first demand centered on luxury and semi-luxury commodities such as sugar, tobacco, cacao, coffee, and (later) bananas. Salted and dried beef also became a preferred part of the European diet. As industrialization in Europe accelerated, so too did the demand for raw materials. Cotton production grew rapidly during this period to meet the demand for inexpensive clothing. As the population continued to grow in Europe, there was less land available for raising livestock, and Europeans looked abroad for their tallow, hides, and meat. As Europe required more and more efficient agricultural production, the demand for fertilizers rose. Latin America had the natural resources to fill these demands.

The Haitian revolution of 1791, which destroyed the island of Hispaniola as the major sugar-producing region, sharply altered the trends of sugar production. Cuba and Brazil were the main beneficiaries. Brazil, which once had been the world's largest producer of sugar but whose ability to compete on the world market had atrophied by the end of the colonial era, was presented with new potential markets. Brazil grew 15 percent of the world's sugar in 1815. This boom resuscitated the old sugar regions of the northeast, especially Bahia and Pernambuco. Production doubled in the 1820s and nearly doubled again the following decade. Brazil's output was 20,000 tons a year in 1800, rising to 40,000, then 70,000, and finally surpassing 100,000 tons in the 1850s and 200,000 by 1880.

Perhaps the most spectacular case of the rise and fall of an export economy occurred in Peru. The demand for fertilizers in Europe created an enormous demand for the natural fertilizer guano (bird excrement) found on Peru's offshore islands. Beginning in 1841, shipments of guano for export rose sharply, reaching 350,000 tons a year within a decade. The Peruvian government used the prospects of future revenues from guano to compile an enormous debt. It also used guano funds to build the country's major railroad lines. By the early 1880s, however, guano deposits were nearly exhausted, and nitrate came on to the market as an alternative fertilizer. Consequently, the guano boom ended. Peru was left with huge debt to foreign companies and no possibility of repaying it because the revenues from guano had ceased.

A pattern of boom and bust cycles emerged. Latin America's national economies reacted to market forces using their competitive advantages in the production of agricultural and mineral commodities. Before 1850, when the market demanded mostly agricultural products, domestic entrepreneurs responded. Later in the century, however, when the demand was for minerals, foreign investors played an ever-increasing role. Latin American nations became increasingly dependent on foreign capital and vulnerable to fluctuations in world markets as the nineteenth century closed. Economic recovery from a century of war and political upheaval rested on an extremely precarious base.

Conclusion

The nineteenth century was a difficult time for governments and ordinary people in Latin America, but some progress occurred nonetheless. Once established, nations displayed remarkable continuity and cohesion in the face of strong regional forces. Despite the high turnover among high officeholders and the occurrence of civil wars, there were elements of stability in Latin American politics. Not infrequently, one or two figures dominated for a decade or more, though not continuously occupying the presidency. For example, Mexico had 49 national administrations between 1824 and 1857, and only one president, Guadalupe Victoria (1824–1829) finished his term. However, five chief executives held office on three or more separate occasions. Two, Anastasio Bustamante and Antonio López de Santa Anna, headed the nation for approximately half this period.

The high turnover was deceptive elsewhere as well. Though at times upheavals beset its politics, four men dominated Venezuela, José Antonio Páez (1831–1835, 1839–1843, 1861–1863), the Monagas brothers (José Tadeo and José Gregorio, 1847–1858), and José Guzmán Blanco (1870–1877, 1879–1884, 1886–1888). Peaceful successions occurred in 1835, 1843, 1847, 1851, and 1855. Although there were periods of violence in Bolivia after independence, three presidents held sway for its first quarter century, Andrés Santa Cruz (1829–1839), José Ballivián (1841–1847), and Manuel Isidoro Belzú (1847–1855). Other nations, most notably Brazil and Chile, were relatively stable. Pedro I (1822–1831) and Pedro II (1831–1889) ruled for more than six decades. Chilean presidents followed successively by election from 1831 to 1891. Rosas ruled the Río de la Plata from 1829 to 1852. Argentina's presidents followed one another by election from 1862 to 1930. Three dictators ruled Paraguay from 1815 to 1870.

Peru was perhaps the worst case of unstable politics. From its independence in 1821 to 1845, there were twenty-four major regime changes and more than thirty presidents. From 1821 to 1824, Peru was the major battleground between the northern armies of Simón Bolívar and the last bastions of Spanish rule.

Bolívar's armies remained in Peru for three years after defeating the Spaniards. Protesting Peruvians finally pushed them out in 1827. During the next decade or so, innumerable outbreaks shattered the peace until strongman Agustín Gamarra (president 1829–1833 and 1839–1841) emerged to dominate the political fracas, interrupted only by Bolivian caudillo Andrés Santa Cruz, who conquered Peru and established the Peru–Bolivia Confederation from 1836 to 1838. During the early 1840s, Peru came apart. Finally, General Ramón Castilla established a measure of order from 1845 to 1862 (as president 1845–1851 and 1855–1862), despite fighting a vicious civil war in 1854 and 1855.

Stability was more evident at the regional and local levels of politics. In Mexico, state (regional) politics were mostly in the hands of locally prominent merchant and landowning families who ruled for generations through control of municipalities and courts. In the Río de la Plata, provincial leaders like Estanislao López in Santa Fe ruled for decades. In Brazil, local bosses, known as colonels, and their families ran roughshod for generations.

Moreover, this era was in some ways the most democratic era in Latin America until nations introduced unlimited universal suffrage and mass voting after World War II. The lower classes not only participated in government, particularly on the local level, but also took part indirectly in national politics and helped shape the political debates. It was also the period of the most extensive economic equity in Latin American history. In some areas, large landholdings suffered from disruptions and uncertainties. War and the expansion of the armed forces provided opportunities for upward mobility for the lower classes, including people of color.

Post-independence Latin America, as we will see in the succeeding chapter, was by no means the Garden of Eden, but common people had control over their everyday lives, a role in national politics, and often a chance to get ahead. The next fifty years were not to be as kind.

Learning More About Latin Americans

Barman, Roderick J. *Citizen Emperor: Pedro II and the Making of Brazil, 1825–91* (Stanford, CA: Stanford University Press, 1999). This is the best biography of the man who had the longest rule in Latin American history.

Graham, Richard. *Patronage and Politics in Nineteenth-Century Brazil* (Stanford, CA: Stanford University Press, 1990). Graham delves into the intricacies of politics in Brazil.

Halperin-Donghi, Tulio. *The Aftermath of Revolution in Latin America.* Trans. Josephine de Bunsen (New York: Harper Torchbooks, 1973). Halperin has written a brilliant exposition of the impact of the wars of revolution.

Jacobsen, Nils. *Mirages of Transition: The Peruvian Altiplano, 1780–1930* (Berkeley, CA: University of California Press, 1993). Traces change in the Peruvian altiplano.

Mallon, Florencia E. *Peasant and Nation: The Making of Postcolonial Mexico and Peru* (Berkeley, CA: University of California Press, 1995). Studies the ins and outs of rural local politics in communities in Mexico in Peru.

Thurner, Mark. *From Two Republics to One Divided: Contradictions of Post-Colonial Nationmaking in Andean Peru* (Durham, NC: Duke University Press, 1997). A study of the relationship between country people and the state in the early post- independence era.

Wasserman, Mark, *Everyday Life and Politics in Nineteenth Century Mexico: Men, Women, and War* (Albuquerque, NM: University of New Mexico Press, 2000). A lively exposition of what it was like to live in the nineteenth century.

10

EVERYDAY LIFE IN AN UNCERTAIN AGE, 1821–1880

THE UNCERTAIN POLITICAL environment and frequent warfare adversely affected the material well-being of a large number of people of all social classes in Latin America during the sixty years after independence. The absence of consistent rules and regulations, the widespread lawlessness, and the physical damage to property and loss of life resulting from armed conflict often made day-to-day living quite difficult and substantially transformed important aspects of society, most importantly gender relations. Despite these ofttimes troubled conditions, ordinary folk continued to earn their living and conduct their private lives much like their ancestors had for decades, even centuries. Much changed profoundly over the course of the nineteenth century, but as much—good and bad—stayed the same. Ordinary people and to some extent their wealthier neighbors as well, particularly in the countryside, resisted the transformations sought by centralizers and modernizers.

The vast majority of Latin Americans during the nineteenth century lived in rural areas either as residents of large estates or villages with collective or small individual landholdings. Only a minority of country dwellers owned their own lands, though many were tenants or sharecroppers. In Brazil, most people in the countryside were slaves, forcibly brought in large numbers from Africa until 1850, when the trade in slaves from Africa ended as the result of enormous pressure put on the Brazilian government by Great Britain. A significant minority of Latin Americans lived in large cities, such as Mexico City, Buenos Aires, Lima, Rio de Janeiro, and São Paulo. Wherever they resided, most common folk lived in poverty, often barely surviving. Work, whether one was employed on a large estate or on one's own plot of land or in the mines or as a domestic in another wealthier family's home in the city, was never easy. Latin Americans toiled long and hard for their sustenance. However difficult their labor, Latin Americans took pride in their jobs and did them well (no matter how much their bosses may have complained about them). Latin Americans, no matter how poor they were, mostly enjoyed their lives. There were *fiestas* (festivals) and other entertainments, the comfort of one's family, and the pageantry and solace of the Catholic Church.

The contrasts between rich and poor were enormous. Wealthy landowners often lived in palatial splendor in the cities, while only blocks away workers struggled in filth and squalor. Moreover, the well-to-do often had little empathy for those less fortunate than they.

Let us turn now to the lives and work of Latin Americans, rich and poor.

The People

First, who were the people who populated the newly independent nations? Latin America emerged from the colonial era with an ethnically diverse population, which had, during the eighteenth century, recovered from the horrific losses suffered in the sixteenth century, when the number of people had fallen by as much as 90 percent, mostly as a result of epidemic diseases brought by the Europeans. The vast majority of Latin Americans were Indians, Africans, or castas. Typical of Mexico at the turn of the nineteenth century, the population of the state of Puebla was 75 percent Indian, 10 percent white, and 15 percent castas. Less than one-third of Brazil's population was white, the rest black or mulatto. More than 30 percent were slaves. In the early 1820s, out of a total of 1.5 million Peruvians the white population counted only about one hundred fifty thousand. Mestizos numbered between two hundred ninety thousand and three hundred thirty-three thousand. The African slave population was an estimated fifty thousand. The remaining million people were Indians. Approximately 65 percent of the people of Central America were Indian, 31 percent ladino (mestizo and mulatto), and 4 percent white.

The disruptions that followed independence slowed demographic growth (see Table 10.1), and, as a consequence, in general the region's economies stagnated. Mexico's population grew only at an average annual rate of 1 percent. Its population increased from 6 million in 1820 to 7.6 million inhabitants in 1850. Brazil's population rose more quickly, from between 4 and 5 million inhabitants at independence (1822) to 7.5 million by the early 1850s. But the increase resulted primarily from the rise in slave imports; the number of Brazilian slaves increased from 1.1 million in 1820 to between 1.7 and 2.25 million in the 1850s.

Table 10.1

The Population of Latin America in the 19th Century

Nation	1820	1850	1880
Argentina	500,000+	1,800,000 (1869)	
Bolivia		1,378,896 (1846)	
Brazil	4–5,000,000	7,500,000	
Chile	1,000,000 (1835)		2,100,000 (1875)
Colombia			
Ecuador	496,846 (1825)		1,271,761 (1889)
Mexico	6,000,000	7,600,000	
Paraguay			
Peru	2,488,000	2,001,203	2,651,840
Uruguay			
Venezuela	760,000	1,660,000 (1860)	2,080,000
Costa Rica	63,000	101,000	137,000 (1870)
El Salvador	248,000	366,000	493,000 (1870)
Guatemala	595,000	847,000	1,080,000 (1870)
Honduras	135,000	203,000	265,000 (1870)
Nicaragua	186,000	274,000	337,000 (1870)

Unlike the other new nations, Argentina experienced rapid population growth, as its half million people in the 1820s increased to 1.8 million by 1869. Latin America experienced growth after 1850, as Mexico's population rose to 15 million and Brazil's to 22 million by 1910. But to give an idea of what this stagnation meant in the first half of the century, the population of the United States rose from less than that of Mexico's in 1800–just over 5 million–to 92 million in 1910. The United Kingdom went from 11 million to 45 million during the same period. Population growth accounted for a large portion of the difference in economic progress between Latin America and these industrial leaders. While Latin America failed to grow economically, the United States and the United Kingdom expanded exponentially. Latin America has never been able to make up for the fifty or so years of economic and demographic stagnation.

The colonial heritage of large, dominant cities continued in post-independence Latin America. Mexico City's population fluctuated between one hundred fifty thousand and two hundred thousand. Rio de Janeiro experienced growth from one hundred thousand inhabitants in the 1820 to two hundred seventy-five thousand in the 1850s. Buenos Aires blossomed from fifty thousand inhabitants in 1810 to ninety thousand in 1850 to one hundred eighty-nine thousand by 1869. As we will see later in this chapter, the expansion of the cities outpaced governments' ability to provide a healthy and prosperous environment for their residents.

The Large Estates: Haciendas, Estancias, Plantations, Fazendas

Most Latin Americans earned their living on the land, for the most part planting, maintaining, and harvesting crops and tending to the livestock of their wealthier neighbors. Other Latin Americans toiled on lands owned either collectively by the residents of their home villages or individually by themselves and their families. Some worked as both employees and owners. Whichever the circumstances, the land represented more than just a living. Farming or ranching was a way of life. As we will see, life in the countryside in the nineteenth century was difficult. Sometimes, as in the case of slaves, conditions were oppressive. But even those worst off, including slaves, made lives for themselves with humor, love, grace, and at times even anger.

A large number of Latin Americans resided on large estates (known as *haciendas, estancias,* or *fazendas* in Mexico, Argentina, and Brazil, respectively), where they worked for the landowner or leased land as tenants or sharecroppers. In rural areas, the owners of these large properties (known as *hacendados, estancieros,* and *fazendeiros*) controlled much of the land. Conditions on Latin American large estates varied widely according to era, region, property size, and crops under cultivation.

At the top of hacienda society in Mexico was the owner, the hacendado, and his family. Beneath him were the supervisors and administrators, headed by the chief administrator or *mayordomo*. Usually males headed haciendas, but occasionally a widow operated a large property. Mayordomos in the Río de la Plata managed the larger estancias, directing employees, keeping records, and communicating with the owner. The mayordomo controlled his workers through subordinate foremen (*capataces*). On smaller ranches the foreman took the role of the mayordomo. The living conditions of the capataces were hardly better than those of the workers. The mayordomo, however, was well paid.

Work Life

Country people worked long, hard hours on the estates. On the Mexican large estates, there were two types of employees: permanent and temporary laborers. Permanent labor included resident peons (unskilled laborers), tenants, and sharecroppers. A hacienda's temporary labor came from neighboring villages, whose residents supplemented their incomes from communally held land or family plots by working seasonally at planting and harvest. Commonly, the hacienda's sharecroppers and tenants earned extra money by working for their landlord.

While some hacendados farmed their own land with their own employees, the most common arrangement was a mixture of owner and sharecropper or tenant-cultivated lands. Tenants paid their rent to the hacendado in the form of cash or a portion of the harvest. Though most tenants leased small plots, there were a few who leased entire haciendas. Sharecroppers paid the landowners with a preset part of the harvest, usually 50 percent. What may have been a typical arrangement in the central region of Mexico between the hacendado and his employees and tenants was as follows. Resident peons earned wages and rations of corn to feed their families and received the use of small plots of land for cultivation. Tenants received a hut, firewood, seeds, and some pasturage, along with their plots, in return for half their crop. Occasionally, tenants worked for the hacendado and earned additional cash. For peons, the crucial part of the arrangement was the corn ration. Custom obligated hacendados in some areas to provide peons with the ration, regardless of the market price of corn. Because corn comprised 75 percent of a peon family's diet, this arrangement assured the peon's basic staple, even in periods of drought and crop failure, and partially insulated him and his family from the effects of inflation, which resulted from shortages of staples arising from crop failures. Tenants and sharecroppers had no such security and their well-being depended on the vagaries of the weather. A good-size plot with oxen and plenty of rain might turn a profit, but there were no guarantees. We do not know very much about the situations of day laborers other than that agricultural wages varied according to the available supply of labor.

Conditions on the haciendas varied according to region, depending on the availability of labor. A relatively dense population, concentrated in mestizo or Indian villages, as in the central area of Mexico, meant a large pool of potential workers and, therefore, low wages and less favorable terms for tenants and sharecroppers. Labor shortages, as in the far north and the far south, produced one of two outcomes: heavy competition for workers, which raised wages and added benefits, such as advances on wages; or intensified coercion to retain employees.

Debt peonage was the most notorious aspect of hacienda labor relations. In this system, peons went into debt to the hacienda in order to pay church taxes, church fees, expenses for rites of passage such as marriage, baptism, and burial, or for ordinary purchases at the hacienda store. Peons then would be obligated to work until they repaid the debt. But the peon, of course, often could not repay it. In some regions, multiple generations were tied to the hacienda, since children were expected to repay their parents' debts. Debt peonage in a few areas was nearly indistinguishable from slavery. On one of the great estates of northern Mexico, the owner dispatched armed retainers to hunt peons, who tried to escape their obligations. Some historians have observed, however, that debt was not always to the disadvantage of the debtor, for in some areas debt served as a kind of cash advance or bonus, attracting peons to work on a particular hacienda. In these instances, it was understood by both debtor and creditor that the debt was not to be repaid. Debt, therefore, became a device to attract and keep workers.

The Hacienda del Maguey, a grain and livestock estate in central Mexico, provides us with an example of relatively benign living and working conditions. The normal workday on this hacienda lasted from 6 A.M. to 6 P.M. There were breaks for breakfast and a traditional midday dinner followed by a resting period, or *siesta,* which lasted for two to three hours. The complete workday was eight to nine hours long, which, compared to the contemporary industrial workforce in the United States and Western Europe, was not arduous. The workload was heaviest at planting, weeding, and harvest times.

Peons on the Hacienda del Maguey, according to the calculations of historian Harry Cross, were relatively well treated. The average peon laboring in the fields probably needed 2150 calories a day. His family, two adults and two children, required 9000 calories. The ration of corn provided by his employer contained 75 percent of this caloric need. The rest of the diet consisted of *frijoles* (beans), chile peppers, lard, salt, and meat. The peon added to these staples wheat flour, rice, and sugar, which he bought at the hacienda store. (Usually, there were no other stores in the area. Sometimes the employer allowed employees to purchase goods only at the hacienda store.) The typical family would also gather herbs, spices, and cacti from the countryside at no cost. Alcoholic beverages, particularly *pulque*–the fermented juice of the maguey plant–were consumed in large quantities, providing vitamins. The combination of beans and corn produced most of the diet's protein.

But not all haciendas treated their peons quite so well. A passerby noted the conditions for resident peons on the Sánchez Navarro estate in northern Mexico in 1846: "The poor peon lives in a miserable mud hovel or reed hut (sometimes built of cornstalks, thatched with grass). He is allowed a peck of corn a week for his subsistence, and a small monthly pay for his clothes...." Peons generally earned 2 or 3 pesos a month and 1 or 2 pecks (a peck equals a quarter bushel or 8 quarts) of corn a week. The Sánchez Navarro family paid their highly valued shepherds and cowboys (*vaqueros*) a bit more, 5 pesos a month and 2 pecks of corn a week salary, but these modest wages hardly covered an average family's necessities.

The Hacienda de Bocas, located 35 miles north of San Luis Potosí, also in central Mexico, for which we have extensive records for the 1850s, provides another example of hacienda life. Bocas had between three hundred and fifty and four hundred permanent workers. The better-off minority of these had free title to land they used for a house, corral, and farming. The best-treated permanent workers also received a corn ration. A resident earned 6 pesos a month, slightly less than $1.50 a week, with a corn ration of 15 liters a week. Since this was not enough to feed his family–1 liter a day per adult was necessary for sustenance–he purchased another 7 or 8 liters a week on account for 0.125 pesos each, leaving him with roughly fifty centavos a week to cover all the family's other expenses. The worker received a plot of 3000 square meters for which he paid no rent. He bought seed for planting from the hacienda. Other purchases during the year included food, sandals (*huaraches*), leather pants, and a burial. His expenditures totaled just over 72 pesos for the year, approximately the same amount as his annual salary. Temporary workers on the Hacienda de Bocas, however, did not have nearly such favorable circumstances, earning 10 pesos a month (if they labored 30 days) and having no guarantee of subsistence rations provided the permanent workforce. Few of the 794 tenants and 200 sharecroppers at Bocas in 1852 made ends meet without supplementing their incomes with temporary work for the hacienda.

Work was equally hard in the Río de la Plata, where most of the employees on the estancias were wage labor called in for cattle branding and horse breaking. There were a few permanent workers who tended cattle or sheep and rode the perimeter looking for strays. Each maintained a hut and a corral in his area. Routine work consisted of tending to the herds and rounding them up every morning. Shepherds' chores were to wash and shear, brand, and slaughter, as well as to tend the herd. Cowboys earned wages, while shepherds shared in the profits. Some owners gave their shepherds one-third to one-half the increase in their flocks per year. Other sheepherders earned up to one-half of the sale of wool, grease, and sheepskins. Cowhands, in addition to their flat wage, got rations of salt, tobacco, *yerba mate* (very strong tea), and beef, and perhaps a small garden plot. The estancias employed Europeans, mixed bloods, and both free and enslaved blacks. Part-time workers came from the interior of Argentina and Paraguay. Native-born mestizos and mulattos, migrants from the interior, tended cattle, while immigrants raised sheep, farmed, and traded. Labor for the cattle roundup and sheep shearing came from nearby rural communities. When labor was scarce, temporary workers earned more. Estancieros had to pay high wages to skilled workers, such as sheep shearers, who could demand as much as 40 to 50 pesos a day plus food. A native-born laborer, with his own string of horses, could hire himself out at 20 to 25 pesos a day in cattle-branding season. Some estancieros offered advances and credit at the ranch store to attract laborers. Workers, however, were often paid irregularly or in scrip to be used at assigned stores. Real wages for agricultural labor rose from 7.5 gold pesos per month in 1804 to 12 pesos in 1864. Wages remained relatively high until the late 1880s, when immigration and improved stock-raising methods ended the labor shortage.

Domestic Life

The differences between the affluent and the poor were particularly evident in the conduct of their everyday lives. Daily routine for both men and women among the upper classes focused on work and meals. Wealthy women on the hacienda spent much of the morning, beginning around nine, doing needlework together in the drawing room in what was called "virtuous silence." After the midday meal each female family member carried out chores before retiring for a nap (siesta). During the mid-afternoon, the women gathered again to continue their needlework. Male and female joined at eight in the evening to say prayers and eat the evening meal. Another hour of needlework followed while one of the men read aloud to the family.

LATIN AMERICAN LIVES

The Gaucho

THE HISTORY OF the gauchos (cowboys) of the Argentine plains, known as the Pampas, reflects the evolution of the region's politics and economy in the post-independence era. They were the symbol of regionalism, fierce local independence, the crucial role of the lower classes in politics, and the importance of the export economy. The gauchos were originally a product of the vast growth of wild herds of horses and cattle on the Pampas during colonial times. They roamed far and wide, taking the livestock that they needed to survive. To Viceroy Arredondo in 1790, they were "vagabonds," who "live by stealing cattle from the estancias and selling the hides…to the shopkeepers…." During the wars of independence, gauchos were among the rebels' best troops. After the wars, they comprised the local private armies of the numerous regional chiefs who ruled in the Río de la Plata. As the Argentine economy grew, finding export markets for hides, tallow, and dried salted beef, gauchos worked on the expanding estancias. During the first half of the nineteenth century their services were in such demand both as soldiers and as ranch hands that they escaped worker discipline. Time was against them, however. Eventually, modern technology in the form of barbed wire and a glut of immigrant agricultural labor ended their independence.

To many upper-class Argentines, the mixed-blood gauchos were a symbol of backwardness. Domingo F. Sarmiento, in his famous polemic (*Life in the Argentine Republic in the Days of the Tyrants*) against Juan Manuel de Rosas, the notorious gaucho leader who ruled Buenos Aires from 1829 to 1852, treated the gauchos as representatives of "barbarism." He saw them as impediments to Argentine development.

Dressed in little more other than a poncho, mounted on horseback, armed with rope and knife, the gaucho was a formidable sight. He subsisted on

Gauchos comprised the lower-class support for local political bosses of nineteenth-century Argentina.

(continued on next page)

THE GAUCHO *(continued from previous page)*

meat, a bit of tobacco, and strong yerba mate (a type of tea). He lived simply in huts, roofed with straw. "The walls were sticks driven vertically into the ground, and the chinks were filled with clay...." There were neither doors nor windows. Furniture consisted of perhaps "a barrel for carrying water, a horn out of which to drink it, a wooden spit for the roast, and a pot in which to heat the water for mate." To cook and keep warm, the gaucho burned dung, bones, and fat. There were no chairs or tables or beds. The gaucho needed only a knife, for he ate only meat. Gauchos were skilled horsemen. They were enthusiastic brawlers, and loved to sing, gamble, and drink. Clothes, shelter, and food, of course, made the gaucho no different from the other Latin Americans who struggled to make their living in the nineteenth century.

Like other members of Latin America's working classes, cowboys in the Río de la Plata and Venezuela were important participants in the wars of independence and the uncertain politics and warfare of the early nineteenth century. Their glory days did not last long, however, for the export economy demanded their subordination. The undisciplined gaucho was not an acceptable employee in the modern economy. The history of the Argentine gaucho paralleled that of many other lower-class Latin Americans, who defended their local prerogatives, customs, and traditions in an ever more difficult struggle against government centralization and economic modernization.

Sharecropping arrangements on the livestock estancias were relatively favorable through the 1860s because of labor shortages. Sharecroppers provided their labor and perhaps some small investment and shared in the expenses, while the landowner furnished the sheep, tools, equipment, and modest lodging. The sharecropper earned a set percentage of the product—wool, tallow, sheepskins, and new lambs.

As the century wore on and agricultural exports grew, estancieros sought to transform the native-born worker into a dependent, hardworking, stable peon, but met great resistance to their efforts. Workers in the countryside had a long tradition of escaping labor discipline, commonly taking a day off whenever they felt like it. Gauchos had gained rights to leisure time on the numerous fiesta days. Employers also frequently had to endure a lack of respect from their peons, who could and did regularly insult their foremen and owners. Most native-born workers refused to perform any work on foot—such as plowing, ditch digging, gardening, or repair work. Estancieros had to supervise workers closely to prevent theft. As a result, even when the estanciero lived in the city he had to spend much time on the ranch. Gauchos retained their freedom because the growing economy increased demand for their services. Restrictive laws and military recruitment never succeeded in limiting the mobility of workers. Cowboys would work for a few months, ask for their pay, and move on. Raising wages only delayed the inevitable. Sometimes peons left work without notice. There was always another job. This all began to change in the second half of the century, as immigrants became the most important source of wage labor in Buenos Aires province.

Questions for Discussion
How did the life of an Argentine gaucho compare with that of a Mexican worker on a hacienda? Why were gauchos able to exert their independence, and thus control over their daily lives, so successfully during the first half of the nineteenth century?

Women administered the domestic sphere and, at times, may have taken over as heads of family when husbands were away. Girls stayed at home while the boys went to school. The young women learned needlework and enough reading to carry out religious observances. One of the more curious relationships existed between wealthy families and their household servants, who simultaneously were part of and separate from the family. A hacienda's rich and poor children grew up together, even shared confidences, but friendship was never a possibility, because the social barriers between classes were too great.

Plantations and Slavery

Brazilian slaves lived perhaps the hardest lives of all the Latin American poor. About two-thirds of Brazilian slaves worked in agriculture. And of these, the largest group, one-third, worked on coffee plantations in the environs of Rio de Janeiro or São Paulo. Another large number toiled on sugar plantations in the Northeast. On plantations, particularly in the south, masters practiced swift, brutal discipline. They regarded slaves as "by nature the enemy of all regular work." Planters lived in constant fear that their slaves would rebel.

At the beginning of the nineteenth century, Brazil had 1 million slaves and during the next fifty years imported another million. Slave life expectancy was not that different from the rest of the population, 23 to 27 years. The crucial problem was for the child born in Brazil to survive infancy. One-third of all male slave babies died before the age of 1 and just a little less than one-half died before the age of 5. If a slave male reached the age of 1, he was likely to live until he was 33.5. If the slave child survived until age 5, then he could expect to live to over 43 years. Twenty-seven percent of female children died before reaching the age of 1 and 43 percent died before age 5. If the female lasted until age 1, she could expect to live until 25.5, and if she endured to age 5, she would likely reach 39 years.

Slaves born in Africa had difficulty in adapting to the new climatic and biological environments and, as a result, their mortality rate was high. In the northeast, the climate was very humid and hot, with sudden drops in temperature quite common; chills resulted in pulmonary diseases. Diseases such as tuberculosis, scurvy, malaria, dysentery, and typhus were endemic. Slaves lived in unhygienic conditions and medical care was crude or unavailable. Slave deaths in Brazil always exceeded births, and only the constant importation of newly enslaved people from Africa permitted the slave population to increase.

The flow of slaves ended in 1850, when under pressure from the British, the Brazilians ended the trade. This brought about a massive transfer of slaves from the cities and towns to the countryside and from regions where markets for export crops were in decline to those areas where exports flourished. Between 1851 and the early 1880s, approximately two hundred thousand slaves were sent from northeastern and far southern Brazil to the southeast coffee country.

Underlying slave relations with fazendeiros were coercion and violence. The slave owner required slaves to be loyal, obedient, and humble. In return, a slave might expect to be made part of the patron's family with all the accompanying protections. However benign this bargain in the short term—slaves became skilled artisans and attained positions as overseers—ultimately there was confrontation and resistance on the part of the slaves. They refused to surrender either their cultural heritage or their dignity. Slaves resisted passively, slowing down the pace of work or working shoddily. Sometimes they refused to do work not in their job descriptions. Cooks would not do housework, for example. Occasionally, they struck back violently. Running away was not uncommon. Those who fled found haven in isolated communities, known as *quilombos*. Slaves created their social and family life, which was both separate from and intimately attached to the world of their masters. Whatever the approach—harsh or paternalistic—taken by the planters, few were entirely successful in controlling their slaves.

Most slaves worked in the fields in regimented gangs closely supervised by overseers. Corporal punishment—whipping or placement in stocks, for example—was common. The workday lasted sixteen to seventeen hours, night work was rare, except when milling sugar and drying coffee. Though it may seem surprising, slaves did get breaks during the day. And while everyday work was always hard, it was probably only truly unbearable for short periods during harvest.

Many slaves had occupations other than field hands. Men were given all the skilled positions repairing equipment, constructing buildings, and sewing clothing. Planters even rented the services of slave artisans to other landowners. As a result, fewer male slaves and more women planted, weeded, and harvested. Slaves were also domestic servants. Slaves who worked in the masters' houses or as artisans experienced better living conditions than those in the fields.

In the nineteenth century most slaves worked in the São Paulo coffee region. The typical plantation had seventy to one hundred slaves, though the largest coffee fazendas contained as many as four hundred. The average adult slave took care of well over three thousand trees. Each slave produced approximately 1000 kilograms of coffee.

The slaves' daily routine began with breakfast, which consisted of coffee, molasses, and boiled corn. Slaves then said their prayers and divided into work teams, led by supervisors who were themselves slaves. At 10 A.M. slaves ate a meal of corn porridge, black beans, and pieces of lard covered with a thick layer of manioc flour. Sometimes they also ate highly seasoned sweet potatoes, cabbage, and

Slice of Life Urban Slaves

NOT ALL slaves worked in the fields of the plantations. A few toiled in the plantation home of the master. Others had skilled occupations in processing sugar and coffee. A surprising number of slaves worked in the cities, primarily as domestic servants, but also as artisans and in other jobs.

In 1872 in Brazil, slaves comprised 11 percent of the industrial work force. Approximately thirteen thousand worked in textile factories. Slaves also made up 15 percent of construction workers, and slave women represented 8 percent of all seamstresses. Many of these slaves lived in the cities, numbering some one hundred eighteen thousand in total, or roughly 15 percent of the population.

Urban slaves usually found themselves in one of three possible situations (or some combination thereof). They could have the traditional relationship with their masters; they could have a traditional relationship but be rented out to a third party; or they could be self-employed. The latter arranged housing for themselves. Self-employed slaves were a lucrative enterprise for their masters, for they generated considerable income. Slaves were bakers, barbers, carpenters, masons, porters, and prostitutes. It is likely that slaves in the cities had more control over their everyday lives than their counterparts on the plantations. Nonetheless, they were no less subject to abuse or the other hazards of survival. Thomas Ewbank, a traveler from the United States, observed at mid-century: "Slaves are the beasts of draught as well as of burden. The loads they drag...are enough to kill both mules and horses."

In Rio de Janeiro, the constant demand for domestic servants arose from the need for services later supplied by urban utilities and public works. As late as 1860, homes in the city had neither piped water nor a sewerage system. Residents also had no refrigeration to store food, which spoiled easily in the tropical climate. Servants carried water, washed laundry, and shopped. Most indoor chores were centered around the kitchen, where slave servants were skilled cooks. There was, too, considerable cleaning in the dusty, dirty city in houses chock full of furniture and other objects. Other servants saw to the chamber pots. Wet nurses fed the babies. Trusted servants in the home were highly valued by wealthy families. Parents might pass them down to their children so as to assure a reliable staff when the younger generation established households of their own.

While an important minority of slaves worked independently in the cities or held relatively privileged positions in their owners' households, they, nonetheless, remained in bondage. The master still controlled their fate.

Questions for Discussion

How did the lives of urban slaves compare with those on the plantations? How and to what extent were slaves able to shape their own living and working conditions (and thus exert some control over their daily lives)?

> **How Historians Understand** | The Construction of Racism

THE FEAR THE UPPER classes had of the lower classes that so impeded political developments in Latin America during the nineteenth century had its foundation in racism. Africans and Indians were people of color and, as such, were widely disdained, if not hated, by white Europeans. Historians, many of whom were prominent public intellectuals and politicians, were the pillars of nineteenth-century racism. It is worth asking how and why historians legitimated these destructive beliefs.

By mid-century an "insidious pseudo-scientific racism" had overwhelmed Argentina. In their desire to modernize, Argentines firmly believed that European immigration was the only method to "civilize" their nation. Juan Alberdi, one of Argentina's leading intellectuals and author of the Constitution of 1853, disdained non-whites, writing that to populate the Pampas with Chinese, Asian Indians, and Africans was "to brutalize." Domingo Sarmiento, another notable Argentine intellectual and later president of the nation from 1868 to 1874, was another proponent of European immigration because he believed mixed bloods and Africans to be inferior. These men and others believed that Argentina in the 1850s was a mestizo country and that it would not progress unless it was Europeanized. Part of the whitening campaign was for Argentine historians and government bureaucrats to have Afro-Argentines disappear from its history and excluded from the census. Chileans, like Argentines, saw to it that Africans disappeared from their history. They, too, firmly believed that development would come only with Europeanization.

In Peru, intellectuals retained their hostility to Afro-Peruvians even after the abolition of slavery in 1861. One insisted that "the Negro [is] a robber from the moment he is born…." Another thinker decried that "in South America, civilization depends on the…triumph of the white man over the mulatto, the Negro, and the Indian."

Abolition of Slavery

Country	Year
Argentina	1861
Bolivia	1831
Brazil	1888
Chile	1823
Colombia	1850
Costa Rica	1825
Cuba	1886
Ecuador	1852
El Salvador	1825
Honduras	1825

Mexico	1829
Nicaragua	1825
Paraguay	1870
Peru	1854
Uruguay	1846
Venezuela	1854

The failure of Latin American governments to abolish African slavery at independence was not only an indication of the powerful political influence of planters, but also of the underlying fear and contempt the white upper classes felt for Africans.

Free and enslaved Africans were not the only victims of racism. In Argentina, Mexico, and Chile, governments conducted campaigns of extermination against nomadic peoples, who they believed stood in the way of progress. These indigenous peoples fought back fiercely. In the north of Mexico, for example, the Apaches, Yaquis, Comanches, Mayos, and Tarahumara resisted incursions until the end of the century. In Yucatán the Maya Indians came close to eliminating whites from their peninsula in a bloody rebellion that began in 1847. It was only in the late twentieth century, however, when historians finally told the stories of this resistance. Until then, Indians had been labeled as barbarians, obstacles to the betterment of society. The Mexican historians of the era, such as Lucas Alamán and Carlos María Bustamante, had low regard for the nation's Indian peoples, even though by virtue of Mexico's first Constitution (1824) all Mexicans were equal before the law. Alamán once said that "it would be dangerous to enable the Indians to read the papers."

Historians are products of their times. Nineteenth-century historians like Alamán, mostly from upper-class origins, shared the same prejudices and fears of the others of their status.

Questions for Discussion
Why do you think that historians in nineteenth-century Latin America, like Domingo Sarmiento and Lucas Alamán, were so biased against people of color? Why do you agree or disagree with the assertion that race underlay all of the region's politics during the century after independence?

turnips. At 1 P.M. there was another break for coffee and a corn muffin. Dinner was eaten at 4 P.M. Work then went on, often until well after dark, as late as 10 or 11 P.M. Finally, before retiring, slaves received a ration of corn, a piece of dried meat, and some manioc meal. They usually lived in a single unpleasant building. Some were given the use of a plot of land to raise coffee or vegetables and were even allowed to sell these crops and keep the proceeds. Coffee planters did not give slaves a day off on Sunday because they feared that religious or social gatherings of the entire slave population would lead to trouble. Instead, to prevent the possibility of any kind of unified revolt, different groups of slaves were given different afternoons off during the week.

Within the larger plantations, African slaves established their own communities, resembling small villages. There they forged a new culture adapting African ways with those of the Americas. In these communities, they established families. Almost all native-born slaves married. And though they were not usually married by the Church, the fazendas commonly recognized the marriages. Maintaining the family was difficult, however, for there was always the possibility of separation resulting from the sale of one or more family members. And the reality of high mortality rates among slaves was a perpetual threat to family stability. On the plantations, enslaved women were subordinate in marriage to their husbands (like their free counterparts). Religion also played an important part in plantation slave communities. Slaves practiced godparenthood *(compadrazgo)*, in which close friends of the parents of a child would act as godparents who were obligated to care for the child in case its parents died. Slaves also synthesized their African religions with Catholicism, producing a folk Catholicism and religious cults, such as *candomblé, voudoun,* and *santería.* African deities, for example, took on the guise of Catholic saints.

Villages and Small Holders

The majority of the rural population in Mexico and Peru consisted of Indians, who continued to live as in colonial times in relatively autonomous villages. The small, individual plot of land used for family subsistence farming was the basis of rural life. Villages existed in both symbiotic and conflicting relationships with haciendas. Villagers relied on the estates for work to supplement earnings garnered from working their own lands. Haciendas, in turn, depended on village residents for temporary labor and tenants. Nonetheless, haciendas and pueblos not infrequently clashed over land and water rights. The relationship was, perhaps, most equal in the years from 1821 to the mid-1880s, a period when war and uncertain political conditions badly weakened the haciendas economically. Villages traded their political support for increased local autonomy and protection of their lands.

We should be careful not to idealize rural life, particularly in the villages. In Mexico, the *pueblos* (villages) had their own forms of social stratification with local bosses (caciques), municipal officeholders, and lay leaders of religious organizations comprising the upper level. Small traders, muleteers, and some of the larger tenants (in terms of the amount of land they rented) at times joined the top group. At the bottom were poorer residents who worked permanently or temporarily as hacienda peons and tenants.

Generally, village leadership came from male elders, who nominated people for local offices, made decisions in times of crisis, and oversaw all dealings by local officeholders with the wider society. Elders attained their elevated status through hard work on the community's behalf or, perhaps, through economic achievement. As the century wore on, the ability of the elders to act justly and to reach community consensus lessened, because of the intrusions of state and national governments on their autonomy.

Politically, residents of all villages concerned themselves primarily with the protection of their individual and collective landholdings and minimizing taxes (both of which required local autonomy), as well as the right to govern their everyday affairs without interference from state or national governments. Taxes oppressed country people and throughout the nineteenth century were a never-ending source of friction between them and the various levels of government. Country people also bitterly opposed coerced military service. It was not uncommon for the armies of various factions to raid villages in order to drag off their young men, the loss of whom badly disrupted the local economy and society.

Not uncommonly, there was a considerable measure of competition, petty bickering, and serious disputes among villagers. In many places, like Oaxaca in southeastern Mexico, inter-village conflict was endemic, as rival pueblos fought perpetually over land and water.

For most rural dwellers in Mexico and elsewhere, life revolved around their individual plots of land and their families. Country people lived in two worlds: The first was the subsistence economy, retaining ancient practices; and the second was the money and wage economy, the boundaries of which country people carefully limited. Indian people, such as the Maya of the Yucatán peninsula of Mexico, fiercely resisted the discipline and values of the plantation or the industrial workplace. North American John Lloyd Stephens, who traveled extensively in the peninsula in the 1840s, reported that "The Indians worked as if they had a lifetime for the job." Working slowly, though, was only one strategy for resisting the demands of overbearing employers. Any attempts to alter existing custom or wages were met with resistance in the form of strikes or mass migrations.

All rural Mexicans utilized the family as an economic unit both on their own plots and on the haciendas. Families, men and women, worked together in the fields, especially during planting and harvest. The men worked their eight- to nine-hour days at the hacienda or, perhaps, even longer on their own land or in helping neighbors at planting and harvest times. Women's responsibilities went far beyond. They had to rise early, well before dawn, to prepare the family's food. The backbreaking work of making tortillas took hours. Since the men required both breakfast and lunch to take along to the fields, the women had to prepare enough for both meals early in the day. They drew the water, brought the wood for the fire, cared for the children, prepared three meals, did the wash, and spun and wove. They also made pottery and then hauled it to the Sunday market. When men were hired on to a hacienda, it was quite common for the women in their families to function either as field hands or as domestics in the hacienda house—work for which they received no pay. But market day each week in the village, when Indians from surrounding towns sold their produce and bought what they needed, provided a welcome respite from the dull and routine. All was not drudgery, for at the market women vendors had the opportunity to gossip and laugh with friends. Employment opportunities for women in rural areas were very limited and, consequently, a large number of young women migrated to the cities, where, for the most part, they entered domestic service.

Families planted land watered only by erratic rainfall. If the rains did not come, people either starved or went deeper into debt in order to purchase their food. Often, the plots were cultivated by slash and burn, whereby a field was cleared from forest or scrub, the debris burned for ash fertilizer, and the land tilled with a wooden digging stick. Crops quickly exhausted this land after only two or three years, whereupon the farmer abandoned it. Usually, it took seven years for the land to restore itself for cultivation.

Life was equally difficult in Argentina for small landowners. The family farm was the most common productive unit on the vast plains of the Río de la Plata. Most farmers lived in comparative modesty on land they worked with family members and a few hired hands. In one sector of Buenos Aires province, almost 70 percent of the landholdings were smaller than 5000 hectares in 1890. The typical rural residential unit was a farm or small ranch with six to eight persons: a man, his wife, their children, a peon, an orphan, and perhaps a slave or *liberto* (a slave born after 1813 who was to remain a slave until 21 years of age). The constant turnover of land tenure attested to the fact that farming was a hard life.

In the Brazilian Northeast, small farmers eked out a living raising the region's staple crop, cassava. To plant the cassava, farmers cleared the land with an iron axe and set fire to the brush. Their slaves then used hoes to heap the earth into small mounds. These prevented the cassava roots from becoming waterlogged and rotting during the winter rainy season. Two or three pieces of stalk cut from growing plants went into each little mound. Corn or beans were planted in the rows between the mounds. In about two weeks, the cuttings took root and poked through the soil. For several months, slaves would weed. There were also natural enemies, such as ants, caterpillars, and livestock, to keep from the fields. After nine to eighteen months the central stalks sprouted small branches. Below ground each plant put down five to ten bulbous roots, which the farmer harvested.

The slaves then prepared the cassava for processing into coarse flour *(farinha)*. Most important was to eliminate poisonous prussic acid from the roots, which involved scraping, washing, grating, pressing, sifting, and toasting. Workers first scraped the roots with blunt knives and washed them. Then they grated or shredded the roots with a grating wheel. The pulp fell through the wheel and dried overnight to remove the prussic acid. The fine white sediment that collected at the bottom of the trough, when dried, washed, and sifted, became tapioca. The grated pulp of the cassava root was sifted into a coarse grain with the texture of moist sand. Slaves placed the sifted cassava on a large griddle made of glazed clay or copper and then lightly toasted it over an open hearth, stirring often to prevent burning. Toasting made it taste better and removed the last of the prussic acid. Cassava was a crop that could be planted or harvested at any time. Harvesting, moreover, could be delayed for a year before the roots would spoil.

Religion

The influence of Catholicism was everywhere. Almost every small town had at least one chapel. Many had several churches. Much of a village's social life revolved around religious celebrations and rites of passage. Local priests often lived only in the larger villages or towns, periodically traveling through the villages in their districts to perform masses (Catholic religious services) and sacraments (baptism, marriage, burial). Though clergy were counted among the most important figures, most country people rarely encountered a priest. As a result, the folk Catholicism practiced in the countryside retained many indigenous customs from pre-Christian times. Christian saints not uncommonly had characteristics indistinguishable from those of gods long ago worshipped by pre-Columbian peoples. Perhaps the most important religious institutions in the countryside were the cofradías, the village organizations that maintained the church and funded religious celebrations.

Religion occupied a central place in rural life and permeated popular culture. For the wealthy, for example, reading was mostly devotional literature. While devotional artwork decorated the houses of the rich, altars with candles, flowers, and likenesses of saints often occupied a corner of a poor family's hut.

Urban Life and Societal Transformation

In size, Latin American cities rivaled any in the world. Often situated in physically beautiful settings with impressive colonial architecture, they were at once splendiferous and horrifying. They were unsanitary and dangerous, filled to overflowing with poverty-stricken people. The cities, too, were crucibles of change, for it was in the urban areas that modernization most directly confronted tradition. It was in the cities that the transformation of the role of women most starkly occurred.

The Cities

With 137,000 people in 1800 and 168,846 in 1811, Mexico City was the largest city in the Western Hemisphere and the fifth largest city in the western world. Half its population was of Spanish descent, with the rest comprised of Indians, mixed bloods, and African Mexicans. During the next three decades through the 1850s, because of periodic epidemics, the population of the city fluctuated between 160,000 and 205,000 and migration from the countryside, rather than natural increase, accounted for the net population growth. At the beginning of the nineteenth century, Rio de Janeiro had between 50,000 and 60,000 people. But its population rose to 100,000 in 1838; 228,743 in 1872; and 423,000 in 1890. The city's residents included immigrants from Portugal, Spain, and Italy, free blacks and mulattos, and white Brazilians from the hinterlands. Buenos Aires in the second half of the century was the fastest-growing large city in Latin America, rising to become the largest city in the region by 1890. By 1914, in all the Americas, only New York exceeded it in number of inhabitants. Half the city's population was foreign born. The city also expanded geographically, extending over 125 square kilometers, up from 14 square miles in 1850. In the 1890s, Argentines responded to this explosive growth by building a deep-water port.

The physical spaces of the cities were impressive. But their beautiful buildings and picturesque settings hid dismaying conditions for its inhabitants. Mexico City was laid out in a grid with an enormous central plaza, the Zócalo. The great cathedral stood at the north end, with the palace of government on the east, and the offices of the municipality on the south. Five causeways furnished access to the city over the lake beds. As a legacy from Aztec times, the city was divided into distinct sections, known as barrios. The outer margins of the city were left to the poor, while the affluent lived in the central area. Rio de Janeiro was located in a setting of overwhelming physical beauty, but was just as shabby and disease-ridden as Mexico City. With narrow, stinking streets and crowded tenements, it was jam packed with poor people. In contrast, Buenos Aires at midcentury was little more than a large village. One Scottish traveler remarked that there was a "filthy, dilapidated look" to the houses. It had none of the physical beauty of Rio de Janeiro or the impressive buildings of Mexico City. One could find pastureland with grazing livestock twenty blocks from the central plaza.

The cities were unsanitary and unhealthy. The Spaniards had built Mexico City on the ruins of the great Aztec capital Tenochtitlan and surrounding dry lake beds, which flooded during rainy season, when it was common for the central plaza to be knee-deep in water and outlying districts to be transformed into lakes. At times, canoes were needed for urban transport. During the rainy season, the floods dumped a "foul concoction of mud, garbage, and human feces" into the houses. Like Mexico City, Buenos Aires had poor drainage, so when rains were heavy even paved streets were difficult to pass. Much of Rio de Janeiro was built on filled-in swampland, resulting in similar problems with drainage.

Mexico City never had enough water or sufficient waste disposal (nor does it today). The air smelled horribly from the sewage and the garbage and piles of trash. Walking the thoroughfares of the city was dangerous to one's health. The city dumped trash into Lake Texcoco, which unfortunately was one of the most important sources of municipal drinking water. Unsanitary conditions had an

Mexico City in the nineteenth century was noisy and unsanitary.

enormous cost. Diseases such as smallpox, scarlet fever, measles, typhoid, and cholera were endemic. In 1840, smallpox killed more than two thousand children, while cholera killed almost six thousand in 1833 and nine thousand in 1850. Cholera killed fifteen thousand in Buenos Aires in 1870. These diseases and others, such as diarrhea and dysentery, undoubtedly were closely associated with the wretched living conditions. Like Mexico City, Rio de Janeiro was also chronically short of water. Originally, a system of fountains had supplied water, but it proved inadequate. In the 1860s, the city built a new system of reservoirs to hold water from mountain streams.

Governments, whose minimal resources were used up to finance their armies, were simply unable to provide the public works necessary to make the cities healthy and safe. As the migration from the countryside to the city intensified during the last half of the nineteenth century, conditions grew worse.

Transformations

Life in the cities in nineteenth-century Latin America was quite different than in the countryside. To be sure, the social structure was just as stratified and rigid, work was equally hard and as badly paid, and the gap between rich and poor was equally wide. But the move to the cities removed much of the support of the villages, especially that of extended kinship. Migration most transformed the situation of women, who came to urban areas often without father or husband and had to function in public spaces (like factories and markets), make their own living, and as often as not act as head of their own household.

Society in Mexico City was divided into very small upper and middle classes separated by vast differences in wealth and status from the great majority of poor people. High civil government and ecclesiastical officials, merchants, and wealthy mine owners and landowners comprised the upper classes. Next in the strata came professionals, such as doctors, lawyers, prosperous merchants, civil servants, industrialists, and other business people, who formed an upper middle class closely associated in outlook with the uppermost classes. The middle sectors consisted of small shopkeepers, tradesmen, artisans, and the better-off skilled workers. At the bottom were unskilled workers, peddlers, artisans of low-prestige trades, and others who lived at the margins of society, such as prostitutes and beggars (*léperos*). For 80 percent of urban dwellers, wages were barely sufficient for subsistence and there was never enough steady employment. Only 30 percent of those employed had full-time jobs.

The most common occupations were domestic service, manual labor, and artisan. Of the skilled workers, shoemakers, carpenters, and tailors were the most common. Among the unskilled, the most numerous were bricklayers, domestics, and street peddlers. The average daily salary was .5 to 1.0 peso per day for skilled workers and .25 to .50 for unskilled, while the minimum cost of subsistence was .75 to 1.0 peso per day. (Until late in the century, the peso was equal to the U.S. dollar.) Because of the stagnant economy and a labor surplus, wages did not rise much, if at all, through the 1830s. A large number of tiny businesses supplied consumer goods; many conducted their commerce on dirty blankets in the filthy main market. Only 1.4 percent of city residents owned any property.

Women made up between 57 and 59 percent of the inhabitants of Mexico City and the majority of the migrants from the countryside throughout the first half of the nineteenth century. As with the men, almost all were castas or Indians who came from the densely populated regions around the capital. These brave, determined women, many single and aged 15 to 29, left their rural birthplaces in search of a better life.

A quarter of all women worked, accounting for one-third of the total work force in the capital. Over a third of caste woman and almost half of Indian women worked. Sixty percent of women worked as domestic servants. Twenty percent sold food from their homes, on the street, or in the markets. Other occupations ran the gamut from midwives to peddlers and waitresses. Women fared no better than males in the conditions and remuneration of employment. Work was hard to come by and wages were paltry. Even those who found employment were underemployed. Worse still, women were limited to the worst-paying occupations. The most likely jobs, in domestic service, they regarded as humiliating. Although some servants were well treated, they owed "submission, obedience, and respect." They were on call 24 hours a day and were often paid no more than their room and board. Because there were so many young women available for domestic service, the labor market precluded any improvement in conditions. The factories paid no better, although work there was considered more honorable than domestic service. Conditions in the textile and tobacco industries, large employers of women, deteriorated considerably over the course of the 1820s and 1830s. Women were not allowed into the clergy, the military, or government bureaucracy, which were, of course, the main paths to upward mobility.

In 1870, 63 percent of free women and 88 percent of slave women in Rio de Janeiro were gainfully employed. Only a very few had professional employment as midwives, nuns, teachers, or artisans. Women were prohibited from holding jobs in the government bureaucracy and in law and medicine. Women found work in commerce only as street vendors or market sellers because employers preferred males as clerks and cashiers. More often women found jobs in the textile and shoe industries. By far and away the most common occupation for women was, as in Mexico City, domestic service. Over 60 percent of free working women and almost 90 percent of urban slave women were servants.

The exodus of women to cities began the profound transformation of women's status. Urban women, often separated from their families, did not conform to the traditions of male-dominated society. When women arrived in the city, they remained surprisingly independent, though desperately poor. In Mexico City, slightly less than half were married. Eighty percent of females married at some point, either in formal or informal unions, but most spent only a small portion of their lives married. If they migrated from the countryside, they delayed marrying. Because of the higher mortality rate among men, it was likely that they would be widowed. One-third of adult women were single or widowed at the time of the censuses (1811 and 1848). Seventy percent of married women between 45 and 54 had outlived their husbands. Rich or poor, women spent much of their lives on their own.

An average woman in the Mexican capital bore five children. With infant mortality (death before age 3) estimated at 27 percent, it was likely that she would outlive at least one of them. Although two-thirds of adult women bore children, less than half of these women had children at home.

What all this means is that, for much of their lives, a substantial proportion of Mexico City's women headed their own households as widows. Widowhood afforded wealthy women a degree of independence. This, of course, should not be exaggerated, for in many cases among the wealthy, an adult son or son-in-law controlled the finances and negotiated the outside world for the woman. Half of white women headed their own households in 1811, while only a third of caste or Indian women did so. Wealthy widows benefited from inheritance laws, which forced the division of an estate among spouse and children. The wife would always have at least some control over the estate. Because affluent males commonly married late, the number of offspring was often limited, thus keeping the widow's share of the estate larger. These kinds of calculations, of course, were of no consequence to the poor. Poor women could barely subsist. They had few alternatives other than to turn to men for support. Even then survival was uncertain. Children were the only old-age insurance. Surely, they would care for and support their parents in their old age.

Poor women worked out of necessity. Men's incomes alone could not generally support an average family. Families simply could not subsist without the woman's earnings. Marriage and motherhood did not put an end to a woman working outside the home. It may, however, have changed her occupation. Domestic service was not a possibility because it required living in separate residences. Self-employment, on the other hand, allowed women to care for their children while generating income. They could prepare food for sale, sew, operate small retail establishments, or peddle. The result was that women dominated the markets.

Marriage was an unequal institution. A wife was expected to accept submission to her husband and to "obey him in everything reasonable." Domestic violence was common. The double standard was widely practiced; that is, it was perfectly acceptable for men to engage in extramarital relations, while it was totally unacceptable for women to do so.

Food, Clothes, Shelter, and Entertainment

For most Latin Americans the fabric of everyday life—the food they ate, the housing that sheltered them, and the clothes that covered them—remained much the same throughout these tumultuous decades of the nineteenth century. Nowhere were disparities between social classes as clear as in these three basic aspects of daily existence.

The three basics of the Brazilian diet were black beans, dried meat, and manioc flour, with occasional game, fruit, molasses, and fish. The average Mexican's diet consisted of maize, beans, squash, and *chiles,* with small amounts of eggs, pork, meat, and cheese. The corn tortilla was an essential staple. Women shucked the corn and soaked the kernels in water with small bits of limestone, which loosened the sheath of the corn, imbued it with calcium, and increased the content of amino acids. The latter created proteins from the mix of corn and beans, crucial in a diet that lacked meat. Next the women beat the corn in the grinding bowl for hours. Finally, small pieces of the resulting dough were worked between the hands—tossed, patted, and flattened out—until no thicker than a knife blade, after which they were thrown on the steaming hot griddle *(comal)*. The combination of maize tortillas and beans (tucked inside the folded tortilla) was not only delicious, but also provided almost all of the required daily protein. (The more prosperous could afford to get more of their protein by eating greater amounts of meat, mostly pork.) Squash, which is made up of 90 percent water, supplied badly needed liquid in an arid land and filler to make meals more satisfying. Chiles added to the beans were the source of crucial vitamins A, B, and C and also killed bacteria that caused intestinal disorders. Water or pulque was drunk with the meal, and lump sugar provided something sweet. The urban poor took few meals at home for there was no place in their crowded rooms for cooking appliances.

The diet of the middle class, while modest, was more varied and nutritious. In a respectable house in Rio de Janeiro, residents woke to a cup of strong coffee. Later on in the morning they ate bread and fruit. The afternoon meal consisted of hot soup, then a main course of fish, black beans sprinkled with manioc flour, rice, and perhaps vegetables and, on occasion, well-cooked meat or stewed or roasted chicken. Two favorite dishes that took hours and hours of preparation were *feijoada*, which required black beans to be soaked overnight and cooked for hours with fatty pork, and cod soaked for twenty hours and then baked. Desserts were sweets, such as fruit glazed with a paste made from guavas and sugar, or candy made from egg yolks, egg whites, and sugar, and was accompanied by highly sweetened strong coffee.

In Mexico City breakfast started with a hot drink—chocolate for the adults or corn gruel (*atole*) for the children—and then toast, biscuits, or pastries with coffee and milk. At eleven o'clock chocolate or atole was drunk with anisette. The large meal, served in mid-afternoon, consisted of bread, soup, a roast, eggs in chile, vegetables, and beans flavored with pickled onion, cheese, and sauce. Dessert was honey with grated orange on a toasted tortilla. A light dinner in the evening was comprised of a spicy sauce (*mole*), stewed meat, and a lettuce salad. A small staff served the meals.

For wealthy Mexicans, food was plentiful, varied, and rich, and meals were leisurely. In the morning, at eight o'clock, they partook of a small cup of chocolate with sweets. Two hours later, they ate a hearty breakfast of roasted or stewed meat, eggs, and beans (boiled soft and then fried with fat and onions). Dinner was at three in the afternoon. It began with a cup of clear broth, followed by highly seasoned rice or some other starch, a meat course consisting of beef, mutton, pork, fowl, or sausages, various vegetables and fruits, and dessert. After such repast a siesta was in order. At six, there was a warm drink of chocolate or, in summer, a cold, sweet beverage. Cigars and conversation or a walk followed. Wealthy families ate supper at ten. Roasted meat, salad, beans, and sweets comprised this "light" meal. Domestics served all meals on elegant china and silverware with tablecloths and napkins.

Differences in dress between the affluent and poor were equally as striking as the differences in their diets. Rich urban women conformed to the latest fashions from France, often adding traditional Spanish garb, such as the *mantilla* (a shawl, usually made of lace, worn over the head). Diplomat Brantz Mayer described one woman in church in Mexico in the 1840s: "She wore a purple velvet robe embroidered with white silk, white satin shoes, and silk stockings; a mantilla of the richest white blond lace fell over her head and shoulders, and her ears, neck, and fingers were blazing with diamonds." The dandies who frequented the fashionable spots in Mexico City might wear a "French cutaway suit, American patent leather shoes and an English stovepipe hat." The more sedate wore broadcloth suits and silk hats.

Few Mexicans, of course, could afford rich silk and woolen apparel. Frederick Ober described mestizo dress in the early 1880s: "In the warmer regions he wears (on Sundays) a carefully plaited white shirt, wide trousers of white or colored drilling, fastened round the hips by a gay girdle, brown leather gaiters, and broad felt hat, with silver cord or fur band about it." Ranchers wore "open trousers of leather ornamented with silver, with white drawers showing through, a colored silk handkerchief about the neck, and a *serape*–the blanket shawl with a slit in the centre...." The women "seldom wear stockings, though...feet are often encased in satin slippers; they have loose, embroidered chemises, a woolen or calico skirt, while the *rebozo*–a narrow but long shawl–is drawn over the head, and covers the otherwise exposed arms and breast."

Poor Mexicans dressed in simple, practical clothes. They wore sandals or went barefoot. Their footwear was made simply and easily from rawhide or plaited fibers. Despite the laws that demanded they wear pants and hats in public, Indian men usually wore a breechcloth. Other rural Mexicans wore cotton shirts without collars and buttons and pants with long legs that covered their feet. Belts were strips of rawhide or cloth. The serape, a brightly covered woolen blanket, was an all-purpose garment, which protected its wearer from the elements. The one common luxury was a straw hat. Rural women wore no fancier apparel than the men. Indian women often wore only a few yards of cloth wrapped around their bodies. Rebozos were used similarly to serapes, protecting women from the elements and, in addition, providing modesty. The rebozo when folded just the right way could be used to carry small children. Other women wore a scarf bound at the hips with a girdle extended to the feet. A broad mantle with openings at the head and arms covered the upper part of the body. This wool garment was often ornamented with colorful embroidery. Wealthier Indian women wore a white petticoat with embroidery and ribbons. Some girls wore simple white cotton dresses with the head, neck, shoulders, and legs below the knees left bare. Women also wore heavy earrings and necklaces of cut glass. On their feet were the same sandals worn by men or no shoes at all. Mostly, they went without head covering, and often, men and women carried rosary beads.

As in the case of diet and clothing, housing, too, sharply differentiated the classes. The wealthy lived in opulence. In larger cities, houses of the affluent often had two stories. The ground floor in these buildings was for shops or other businesses, while the second floor was for the family. The house of Vicente Riva

Palacio, well-known soldier-statesman, had fifty rooms. One entered through an impressive stairway leading to the living quarters. The stairs and the floors of the corridors were made of the finest Italian marble. Tropical plants decorated the halls, and an aviary was filled with singing birds. Of the numerous rooms, there were three parlors, a grand salon, and two smaller salons. There was also an impressive private chapel adorned with luxurious drapes and beautiful religious ornaments. Mirrors and massive sideboards took up the walls of the dining room, measuring 100 by 50 feet. On these shelves were thousands of pieces of china, crystal, and silver. Thirty bedrooms each had a bedspread of velvet, silk, lace, and crochet, each one more elegant than the last, hand-stitched linens, and brass bedsteads and canopies. The large living room had furniture with golden trim, fabulous mirrors and chandeliers, and rich carpets. The ceilings were 30 feet high. The family had its own 200-seat theater. Maintaining this remarkable establishment required 35 servants.

Guillermo Prieto, the noted social critic, described the typical middle-class home in Mexico City, which was considerably more modest: "A steep stairway led to a corridor paved with red varnished millstones. (The middle class usually lived on the second floor...because of the flooding that periodically afflicted the city, and the servants occupied rooms on the first floor.) The corridor was embellished with cages filled with stuffed birds, squirrels, wind chimes, and earthen crocks packed with stored foods and vegetables. Landscapes...adorned the walls. Comfortable chairs and couches...furnished the principal chamber.... In the bedroom were a large bed of fine wood, easy chairs, and wardrobes. The small children of the family slept in the halls. Those of a small family slept with their parents in curtained compartments of the main bedroom. The dining room contained a washstand holding towels, soap, straw, and a scouring stone for scrubbing. Colored vegetables, pots and pans, and jars lined the kitchen walls...with strips of garlic and pepper for a festive air."

In contrast to the comfort of the urban well-to-do, housing for farmers in the countryside was little more than a hut. Because wood for construction or fuel was very expensive in these deforested or arid areas, neither lumber nor bricks were practical. (Wood was too costly for use in ovens that baked bricks.) Consequently, in temperate climates, country people constructed their huts with adobe made from sun-baked straw and mud blocks. In the highlands, houses consisted of brick (or stones plastered with mud) with a flat roof constructed of beams laid close together with a covering of finely washed clay, carefully stamped. Stone walls were built without mortar. In the tropics farmers built their huts with saplings and leaves held together with mud. Occupants drove hewn logs into the ground to support the beams and roof and used bamboo sticks for the walls. The normal hut measured 20 by 15 feet and contained one room with no windows and no flooring other than packed earth mixed with ashes. Doorways (without doors) provided ventilation and light. Most commonly, roofs were made either with thatch or by laying rows of poles across the tops of walls that were then covered with one or two feet of dirt and a layer of pine boards. Where it was colder, roofs were covered with shingles. Native vegetation, such as palm leaves or straw, served in the tropics.

The kitchen area, where a fire burned continuously, was outside or in a separate, smaller building. The metate for tortillas was beside the fire. Huts had no furniture. Mats known as *petates* served as sleeping pallets. Better-off rural dwellers might have a fancier bed consisting of four mounds of clay crossed with rough boards. No one could afford bedding or mattresses. Men and women slept in their clothes, wrapped in *serapes* and rebozos in cold weather. Since most people had only the clothes they wore, there was no need for chests or closets. Pottery and baskets stored food and whatever possessions they owned. The only decoration in the hut was a picture of the Virgin of Guadalupe or a saint. Most regions required no heating, and no one could afford it anyway. The more prosperous rancheros lived in slightly less simple abodes. They might have a bench and table and board beds with mats and skins for pillows. There might also be low stools around the table for use during mealtimes.

Poor people in Mexico City lived in rooms rented in crowded tenements *(vecindades)*. Because the city endured periodic flooding, ground-floor rooms were constantly damp. Badly ventilated, filthy, and crowded, the vecindades were breeding grounds for disease. Apartments lacked cooking facilities, which meant most of the poor took all their meals from street vendors. Not everyone was fortunate to have a roof over his or her head. Joel Poinsett, the United States Minister in 1824, estimated twenty thousand people slept on the streets. In Buenos Aires, most of the poor lived in small, ugly houses on the outskirts of the city. About a quarter of the resident in 1887 lived in tenements *(conventillos)*, where they and their many children inhabited tiny rooms piled high with garbage and filth. In Rio de Janeiro, many of the new immigrants and internal migrants lived in crowded slums known as *corticos*. As in Mexico City the fashionable suburbs sprang up on the periphery, while the core of the city became the ever more crowded home of the poor.

As miserable as statistics and anecdotal evidence depict everyday life, people found ways to enjoy themselves. The church, family, drinking, and gambling provided the most common entertainment for people of all classes. The solemn church masses were great spectacles. The rites and rituals, resplendent priests, and majestic music surely were the best entertainment of the time. While no parish in the capital or anywhere else duplicated the magnificence of the great cathedral in Mexico City, there were many inspiring churches elsewhere to stir the people. Even in villages with modest chapels, a visiting clergyman might put on a good show without the trappings of opulence.

Religious fiestas took up a large number of days; in Aguascalientes, Mexico, for example, in the 1860s there were forty per year. They were occasions of both solemn consideration and joyous fun. The cities, towns, and villages prepared carefully for these celebrations. Streets were repaired and cleaned. Processions marked the special days. On Palm Sunday, the march represented Jesus' entrance into Jerusalem. On Good Friday, the crucifixion procession took place. Repentant sinners paraded half-naked with crowns of thorns. Mexico City celebrated Corpus Christi in unusual splendor. The archbishop conducted mass in the great cathedral in the Zócalo after which he led a grand parade from the church through adjacent streets, walking under a canopy of white linen, decorated with a red border. Everyone who was anyone—presidents, generals, cabinet ministers—appeared in full regalia. The procession was a time to show off. The wealthy displayed their fine clothes, perhaps imported from Paris. The surrounding homes were decked out with carpets, flowers, flags, and streamers. And a vast crowd of costumed people of different races and colors watched as the spectacle passed before them.

One of the most important holidays was the Day of the Dead, celebrated in late October and early November. The celebrants burned massive numbers of candles and consumed large quantities of food. Poor Indians expended years of earnings in remembrance of departed loved ones. The night of the last day of October, families decorated their homes with flowers and candles and set out a colorful mat on which they lay a feast to lure the dead children back. The next day, the family repeated the ritual, adding other dishes too hot for children, such as turkey mole and tamales. On this day, they offered liquor. The Day of the Dead celebrations indicated that Mexicans knew death well and did not fear it.

Drinking was an important aspect of religious celebrations and, perhaps, for many, a crucial outlet for alleviating the pain of daily life. It became a serious problem among the poor as the alienation of urban life and industrialized working conditions became widespread at century's end. Pulque was the alcoholic beverage of choice. The maguey (agave) cactus has leaves of up to 10 feet in length, a foot wide, and eight inches thick. After some years, it sends up a giant flower stalk, 20 to 30 feet high, on which grow greenish yellow flowers. The plant dies after it blooms. Just before it is about to emit its stalk, the Indians cut into the plant to extract the central portion of the stem. The incision leaves only the thick outside rind, forming a natural basin two feet deep and a foot and a half in diameter. The sap that would feed the stem, called *aguamiel* (honey-water), oozes into the core and is extracted. A small amount is taken to ferment for 10 to 15 days. This becomes the *madre pulque,* which acts as a leaven inducing fermentation in the aguamiel. Within 24 hours it is pulque. As one draws off the pulque, one adds aguamiel to the mix. A good maguey yields 8 to 16 liters of aguamiel a day for as long as three months. Although the pulque has a lumpy consistency, tastes something like stale buttermilk, and smells like rotted meat, it is quite nutritious and many believe it helps digestion.

Another popular diversion was gambling, which many observers of the time believed was a Mexican obsession. Cockfighting was a passion. It necessitated considerable preparations. Handlers bred and selected the cocks carefully, fed them strictly, and trained them assiduously. The event required an arena 6 feet in diameter fenced in by 3-foot boards with benches around it. From the gallery, spectators urged on and bet on their favorites. The spectacle of the birds was bloody and brutal. The brave cocks exhausted themselves, but would not quit until one of the two contestants lay dead. Money then changed hands.

Of the different types of entertainment available in Mexico during this period, bullfighting was the most famous. Thousands frequented the Sunday afternoon spectacles in Mexico City. Although it was a sport shared by all classes, status was clear by virtue of seating. The wealthy sat in the shade, while the masses suffered the sun. The spectacle proceeded in traditional stages. The bull entered to have *picadors* and *matadors* goad and tease him with lances and red cloaks. They had to be agile to avoid death on his horns. Then, amid trumpet sounds, his tormentors stuck small lances into his neck. The bull, snorting, thundering to no avail, attacked anyone and anything. Finally, the chief matador emerged, with more trumpets, to do battle armed with his red cloak and long blade. After some flourishing, the matador plunged his weapon between the bull's shoulder blades and into its heart.

Conclusion

Life in the first seven decades of the nineteenth century was, for all but the wealthiest classes, difficult indeed. Latin Americans struggled in their poverty. Most people resided and worked in the countryside either on large estates, in communal villages, or on small farms. A small percentage found employment in mining camps. Growing numbers saw better futures in the great cities. Inept and corrupt governments, war and banditry, and stagnant economies tormented nearly everyone. In the half-century to come, new forms of work would emerge. Modernization would make life worse rather than better.

However difficult their lives, Latin Americans sought to preserve their customs and traditions. The best means at their disposal was to defend local governance. As we have seen in Chapter 9, political and economic instability had allowed the lower classes to maintain their autonomy, at least in the countryside, for decades after independence. Political centralization and economic development would in the succeeding half century undermine local prerogatives and erode the practice of everyday life as they had known it for centuries.

Learning More About Latin Americans

Barickman, B.J. *A Bahian Counterpoint: Sugar, Tobacco, Cassava, and Slavery in the Recôncavo, 1780–1860* (Stanford, CA: Stanford University Press, 1998). Explores economics and society in the Brazilian northeast.

Beezley, William H. *Judas at the Jockey Club and Other Episodes of Porfirian Mexico* (Lincoln, NE: University of Nebraska Press, 1987). Explores popular culture at the end of the century.

Burns, E. Bradford. *The Poverty of Progress: Latin America in the Nineteenth Century* (Berkeley, CA: University of California Press, 1980). Classic argument against the European notion of progress.

Calderón de la Barca, Frances. *Life in Mexico* (Berkeley, CA: University of California Press, 1982). Sometimes biting observations by foreign diplomat's wife.

Fowler-Salamini, Heather, and Mary Kay Vaughn, eds. *Women of the Mexican Countryside, 1850–1990* (Tucson, AZ: University of Arizona Press, 1994). Essays on the social history of women in everyday life.

Graham, Sandra Lauderdale. *Caetana Says No: Women's Stories from a Brazilian Slave Society* (New York: Cambridge University Press, 2002). The lives of a woman slave owner and a woman slave.

Graham, Sandra Lauderdale. *House and Street: The Domestic World of Servants and Masters in Nineteenth-Century Rio de Janeiro* (Austin, TX: University of Texas Press, 1992). A study of lower-class women who worked as domestics.

Johns, Michael. *The City of Mexico in the Age of Diaz* (Austin, TX: University of Texas Press, 1997). Mexico City, warts and all.

Mattoso, Katia M. de Queirós. *To Be a Slave in Brazil, 1550–1888* (New Brunswick, NJ: Rutgers University Press, 1986). The most thorough analysis of what it was like to be a slave in Brazil.

Stein, Stanley J. *Vassouras: A Brazilian Coffee County, 1850–1900* (Princeton, NJ: Princeton University Press, 1985). Classic study of a coffee plantation.

Wasserman, Mark. *Everyday Life and Politics in Nineteenth Century Mexico: Men, Women, and War* (Albuquerque, NM: University of New Mexico Press, 2000). A lively rendition of what life was like in nineteenth-century Mexico.

11

Economic Modernization, Society, and Politics, 1880–1920

THE PERIOD FROM 1880 to 1920 was a time of momentous changes in the world economy. Railroads, steamships, telegraphs, and telephones made it possible for people, goods, ideas, and money to move rapidly across oceans and international boundaries. In Western Europe and the United States, most people now lived in cities and earned their livelihoods in industry rather than agriculture. The population of these areas grew in both numbers and affluence, creating demand for a wide range of agricultural products, such as beef and grains for consumption and cotton and wool for wear. New industries required minerals, like copper for electric wire, and other commodities, like petroleum for internal combustion engines. Large corporations emerged to provide the capital, technology, and administrative know-how in a global process of economic modernization.

1876	1888	1910	1912	1916	1919
Porfirio Díaz takes power in Mexico	Abolition of slavery in Brazil	Mexican Revolution begins	Sáenz Peña Law in Argentina extends male suffrage	Election of Hipólito Yrigoyen as president of Argentina	Semana Trágica in Buenos Aires
	1889 Empire overthrown by military in Brazil		1912 Foreign investment in Latin America reaches $US 8.5 billion	1917 Mexican Constitution	
	1891 Chilean civil war ousts president José Manuel Balmaceda; parliamentary rule begins				

These transformations had especially profound economic, political, and social consequences in Latin America. Beginning in the 1870s and continuing to the 1920s, Latin America experienced an extraordinary trade boom, especially in exports. The construction of thousands of miles of railroads and the refurbishing of seaports eased the flow of products from Latin American mines and fields to waiting North Atlantic markets. Europe and the United States not only provided expanding markets, but they provided new technologies and capital to facilitate the extraction of agricultural and mineral resources. Economic growth brought a measure of prosperity, but it was unequally distributed. Workers in the region's mines and nascent industries experienced harsh working conditions and often received scant compensation for their contributions to the growing economies. Poor farmers, usually indigenous peoples who still held their land communally, often lost their holdings to large estates that sought to increase their acreage in order to produce more agricultural commodities for export. Aided and abetted by national governments, who looked unfavorably on collective landholding as an impediment to progress, land expropriations created a large class of landless rural people, whose customs and mores had for centuries revolved around collective and individual landownership. Meanwhile, as the region became more closely tied to the world economy, it became exceptionally vulnerable to fluctuations in overseas markets. The resulting boom and bust cycles wreaked havoc in many countries. Major depressions in the world economy in the 1890s and again in 1907 sparked political conflict in various Latin American countries.

Export-led modernization brought enormous political and social changes to Latin America. Emerging from the violent decades that followed independence, many nations experienced long periods of political stability, dominated by land-based upper classes ruling through rigged elections or dictatorships. This political stability was vital to the modernization process, but economic development generated forces that ultimately threatened that stability. The export boom created two new, crucial social classes—an urban middle class and an urban industrial working class—whose demands for equality and equity eventually brought an end to the rule of the large landowners. The export economy expanded the size and role of governments, which needed a growing number of white-collar workers who obtained middle-class status. These workers formed one component of the new middle class. Economic opportunities in boom times created an entrepreneurial group of small-scale businesspeople, who also joined the ranks of the middle class. This middle sector commonly formed the foundation of rising political parties.

Meanwhile, railroads, mining, food processing, and other new industries stimulated by the export economy required growing numbers of workers. In some countries, massive immigration—made possible by rapid development of railroads and steamship lines—helped fill the demand. The new export economies needed large numbers of unskilled workers, but the new technology also required many workers with specialized skills. Workers of all ranks, but particularly those who were highly skilled, organized labor unions and joined political parties in search of improved living and employment conditions.

Workers' grievances joined with those of dispossessed farmers to form an increasingly volatile political climate. The crisis, known in some countries as the "Social Question," intensified after 1900. Those who ruled struggled to maintain their position. Some upper classes grudgingly made concessions to the middle and lower classes, while others stubbornly refused. During the first two decades of the twentieth century, many cities and mining regions witnessed violent protests against upper-class oppression, but only in Mexico did these protests lead to revolution. Almost everywhere, however, the rule of large landowners drew to a close.

Export-led development brought with it not only profound economic and political dislocations, but wrenching social changes as well. The old ruling classes faced the erosion of the patriarchal norms that underlay their positions of power. The urbanization, industrialization, and migration that accompanied export-led development undermined traditional gender roles and family structures that cast fathers and husbands as the heads of families and men as the sole actors in the political sphere. Women's positions in the family, the workplace, and the public arena changed. Feminism rose to demand that women be recognized as important contributors to the construction of modern nations. Women sought equality under the law, both inside and outside the family. Not only was the public rule of the upper classes under attack, but the private basis of their position as well.

Economic change notwithstanding, the core of the political struggle remained control over everyday life. Urbanization and industrialization merely shifted the locations, altered some of the methods employed, and broadened some of the goals. In the countryside, struggle continued much the same as it had before against the intrusions of central authority. To country people, modernization and centralization meant a widespread assault against their culture and traditions.

Economic Modernization

After nearly a half century of stagnation with interludes of export boom, much of Latin America entered into a period of economic growth from the 1880s through the First World War, resulting from the influx of new technologies and capital, mostly from abroad, and the advent of domestic peace. Massive new railroad networks were both the products of modernization and the engines of further economic development. They also facilitated national consolidation in ways unimaginable before 1880.

Exports

The development of export agriculture and industry was at the core of the economic, social, and political transformations of the era. The export boom displayed several notable characteristics. First, most nations concentrated on one or two export commodities. Second, the booms were not sustainable, for the most part, for more than a decade or two at a time. International markets for primary products were cyclical, and busts inevitably followed booms. Third, the question of who actually benefited from the expansion of exports is subject to unending debate. Finally, linkages between the export economy and domestic sectors of the Latin American economies were not consistent. As a result, the growth of exports did not necessarily stimulate overall economic development.

The industrialized nations of the North Atlantic (Great Britain, France, Germany, and the United States) greatly increased their population and general prosperity after 1850. Annual income per capita doubled. The market demand for agricultural staples, such as grain, meat, and wool, exceeded locally available supplies, while increased affluence stimulated demand for more "exotic" products, such as coffee, cacao, sugar, and bananas. Simultaneously, technological advancements in agriculture and industry created additional demands for primary materials. New farming techniques required fertilizers, for example. Intensifying industrialization created a need for mineral ores such as lead, silver, gold, tin, zinc, and copper. The invention and widespread use of the internal combustion engine expanded demand for petroleum. Technological improvements in metallurgy and mining made it possible to extract minerals from previously unusable sources and cut down on the bulk and cost of ore shipments. New railroads and communications and the introduction of steamships facilitated the transportation of raw materials. The new ships reduced the Buenos Aires to Europe route to weeks. Refrigerated shipping made it possible to send even fresh meat and other delicate commodities across the ocean.

Latin American nations possessed the natural resources to help satisfy the North Atlantic market for food and minerals. The industrialized nations supplied capital, technological expertise, and administrative organization to extract and transport these commodities. A vast inflow of foreign investment stimulated the expansion of exports. By 1913, foreign investment in Latin America reached $8.5 billion, of which railroads accounted for $2.9 billion. The largest other sectors of investment were in government obligations (bonds), mining, and public utilities.

Great Britain accounted for the largest share of foreign investment in Latin America, nearly $5 billion. Between 1900 and 1914, the British doubled their holdings in the region. The British were a notable presence in Chilean nitrate mining and Mexican petroleum. United States capital was second in importance to the British and concentrated in Mexican railroads and mining, Cuban sugar production, and Central American plantations and railways. Between 1900 and 1914, U.S. investment in Latin America quintupled. Mexico received the most capital, more than $1 billion. U.S. investors mostly sought export industries. Before 1914, the third largest source of foreign investment was Germany. Germans invested heavily in Argentina, Brazil, and Mexico (over $100 million in each). The First World War, however, broke most of Latin America's commercial and financial ties with Germany.

Growing demand in the North Atlantic economies, transportation improvements, and massive foreign investment all combined to increase Latin American exports enormously. Some of this growth began as early as the mid-nineteenth century, but the pace accelerated greatly after 1880. Between 1853 and 1873, Argentine exports grew sevenfold. By 1893, they had doubled again. Brazilian coffee exports more than doubled in the years between 1844 and 1874 and quadrupled between 1874 and 1905. Colombian, Costa Rican, and Venezuelan coffee exports also increased spectacularly. Total Mexican exports rose nearly 700 percent from 1878 to 1911. Bolivian tin exports jumped by 1200 percent from 1897 to 1913.

The burgeoning export economy had important positive effects. In 1916, Argentina's per capita national wealth ranked approximately 10 percent less than that of the United States, but 62 percent higher than that of France. By 1914, Argentina's per capita income exceeded that of Spain, Italy, Switzerland, and Sweden and compared with Germany, Belgium, and the Netherlands.

The Downside of Export-Led Modernization

Despite overall growth, export-led modernization proved a mixed blessing for Latin Americans. While statistically impressive, the rise in per capita income masked the fact that this wealth was not equitably distributed. Wealthy landowners became fabulously rich, while the situation of the rest of the population remained the same or deteriorated.

Moreover, few Latin American nations were able to sustain steady high growth. Only Argentina and Chile expanded their exports at a rate averaging over 4 percent from 1850 to 1914. Argentina averaged over 6 percent, a truly impressive accomplishment. The other nations had spurts of growth followed by long periods of stagnation. By World War I, however, exports seemed to reach a ceiling, either because the products of these nations dominated the world market to such an extent that little room for growth remained or severe competition had arisen and market share inevitably fell.

Latin America's vulnerability to world market fluctuations was exacerbated by the fact that most nations continued to rely on a limited number of export commodities. To be sure, in the first decade of the twentieth century, there were a number of efforts to diversify from the model of one or two raw material exports, but concentration of exports persisted. In five Latin American nations (Bolivia, Chile, Cuba, El Salvador, and Guatemala) in 1913, one commodity comprised more than 70 percent of exports. In five more nations (Brazil, Ecuador, Haiti, Nicaragua, and Panama), one product accounted for over 60 percent of exports. And in three others (Costa Rica, Honduras, and Venezuela), one commodity accounted for over 50 percent. The most diversified export nations were Argentina, Colombia, and Peru. Argentina was the most successful with grains (wheat, linseed, rye, barley, and maize) and livestock (chilled and frozen beef, lamb, wool, and hides).

Most Latin American export economies became dependent on a handful of consuming nations and therefore found themselves vulnerable to economic fluctuations in those countries. Four markets, the United States, Great Britain, Germany, and France, together accounted for 90 percent of the exports in ten countries and more than 70 percent in eighteen. Only Argentina avoided this heavy dependence on the four markets. Although Great Britain purchased 25 percent of Argentine exports, seven other nations took more than 3 percent each. Latin America relied just as heavily on the same nations for imports. Only Uruguay obtained less than 70 percent of its imported goods from the United States, Great Britain, France, and Germany. In 1913, the United States and Great Britain each accounted for approximately 25 percent of Latin American imports.

The foundation of Latin American trade was the shipment of primary commodities in return for manufactured goods. Historians have long debated the equity of this system. Some have maintained the terms of trade were unfair because manufactured goods constantly rose in price while commodity prices declined. The statistics for trade and prices are not very reliable and those that are available do not show firm trends. The advantage, however, was not always with the industrialized nations. Primary prices fluctuated from 1850 to 1913. The prices of manufactured products also varied. Brazil, for example, actually improved its terms of trade (the relationship between exports and imports) between 1850 and 1913, but there were wide fluctuations within the period. Mexico's terms improved markedly, but Chile's deteriorated rather badly.

The impact of export-oriented development strategies is also heatedly argued. Advocates claim that these strategies stimulated the other sectors of the economy, particularly industrialization. Some export commodities require processing, such as butchering and chilling meat, tanning hides, and milling flour. Sugar production, as we have seen, is as much an industrial as an agricultural enterprise. Exports drove the construction of railroads and other transportation. At the same time, however, export commodities often drained the nation of resources, leaving little or nothing for other economic activities. In nations where capital was chronically scarce, the export machine allowed precious few resources to trickle from that sector. Some export economies, notably petroleum drilling, operated in enclaves without enhancing the overall economy.

The rapid rise of the various export economies of the region did not necessarily lead to development of the non-export economy. Industrialization, the usual measure of economic modernization, did not automatically derive from increased primary exports. In general, the nations with the most varied export product base were the most likely to develop. Those economies that relied on one product were the least likely to develop.

Finally, export booms inevitably ended. Agricultural commodities wore out the soil, causing production gradually to decline. This was particularly the case for coffee in Central America, Venezuela, and Haiti around 1900. Bananas were vulnerable to disease and natural disasters. More important, world market demand was fickle. For example, demand for Brazilian rubber skyrocketed at the turn of the century, creating fabulous fortunes, only to fall precipitously when competitors from Southeast Asia flooded the market and, later, chemists invented a substitute.

Railroads

Railroads were, perhaps, the greatest technological agents of change and they provide a good illustration of the benefits and drawbacks of modernization. They were the "backbone" of the export economy, bringing unparalleled prosperity to some regions and unmitigated misery elsewhere. The expansion of the railways was spectacular (see Table 11.1). The railroad system of Argentina increased from 1600 miles in 1880 to 10,400 miles in 1890 and 21,200 miles in 1914. Mexico had less than 400 miles of railroads in 1880, but by 1910 it had constructed nearly 15,000 miles of track.

Railroads provided inexpensive transportation for agricultural commodities, minerals, and people. The rail networks opened up new lands for cultivation. In Argentina, they made it possible to cultivate grains on the rich soil of the Pampas and to push livestock raising farther and farther south into the semi-arid region of Patagonia. Brazilian planters spread coffee cultivation to the vast interior of São Paulo. Railroad transportation facilitated the recovery of the Mexican mining industry.

The new transportation systems brought together nations torn by regionalism. They enabled governments to exert their authority in previously autonomous areas. What were once months-long journeys for armies took only days and day trips took only hours. Railroads enabled people to travel farther and at less cost than ever before. Walking to the mines of northern Mexico from the center of the nation was an impossible dream, but the railroad carried pas-

Table 11.1

Railways in Latin America, 1880–1920 (Number of Miles)

	1880	1900	1920
Argentina	1,600	10,400	21,200
Brazil	2,100	9,500	17,700
Chile	700	8,300	13,000
Peru	1,100	2,700	5,100
Latin America	7,200	34,500	62,900

Source: Frederick Stirton Weaver, *Latin America in the World Economy*, p. 69.

sengers to potentially better lives for minimal expenditure. It also created truly national markets for the first time.

Despite their obvious benefits, railroads were also a symbol of unwanted modernization. People frequently resisted them. In Mexico during the last quarter of the nineteenth century, there was violence in almost every region where tracks were laid for the first time. It was not unusual for people anywhere in Latin America to throw rocks at the train cars as they passed, so hated were the engines of progress. The railroads disrupted old patterns of landholding. Their presence raised the value of land. In areas where indigenous people owned lands collectively and individually and grew subsistence staple crops, government officials and large landowners forced them off their properties. The greedy landowners then converted production to commercial crops, which they sent to urban and international markets by means of the railroads. This process created a large, landless class of poor rural people, and thus a pool of inexpensive labor, and cut the total production of staple crops, which in turn caused the prices of basic foodstuffs to rise. The subsequent inflation undermined the living standards of both the middle and working classes.

Modernization and Social Change

The economic and technological transformation described in the preceding section triggered great changes in Latin American society. First, improved diets and medical care, coupled in many countries with a steady stream of immigrants, brought a substantial increase in population, most particularly in urban areas. Second, new social classes arose, complicating the social hierarchy and political agendas for the region. Third, discontent mounted in the countryside. Finally, people were on the move–from rural areas to cities and mining camps, from overseas to Latin America, from one country to another. All these changes had a profound impact on the daily lives of men, women, and children throughout Latin America.

Population Increase

As we saw in Chapter 9, the decades following national independence were pervaded by warfare throughout Latin America. These conflicts cost many lives, and the population growth that many areas had experienced in the late colonial period came to a halt. By the 1880s, however, the populations of Latin American nations began to grow once more. The population of Argentina doubled between 1895 and 1914, from 3.9 to 7.8 million. Brazil's went from 10.1 million in 1872 to 30.6 million in 1920. Cities exploded. (See the growth of Brazilian cities in Table 11.2.) The population of Buenos Aires went from one hundred seventy-eight thousand in 1869 to nearly 1.6 million in 1914. Other than Hamburg, Germany, it was

Table 11.2

The Growth of Brazilian Cities, 1872–1920

		Population		
City	1872	1890	1900	1920
Rio de Janeiro	274,972	522,651	811,443	1,157,093
São Paulo	31,385	64,934	239,820	579,093
Salvador	129,109	174,412	205,813	283,422
Recife	116,671	Not available	113,106	238,843
Belém	61,997	Not available	96,560	236,402
Porto Alegre	43,998	52,421	73,674	179,263

Source: June E. Hahner, *Poverty and Politics: The Urban Poor in Brazil, 1870–1920*, p. 7.

the fastest-growing city in the Western world. Lima, which because of the War of the Pacific and subsequent civil wars, did not begin to grow until the 1890s, jumped from one hundred four thousand in 1891 to two hundred twenty-four thousand in 1920. Guayaquil, Ecuador, grew from twelve thousand to ninety thousand between 1870 and 1920.

New Classes, New Voices

Latin America's new middle classes derived in part from the gente decente (decent folk) of the colonial era, who were mostly light-skinned people who did not work with their hands. Color, race, and status were all elements in delineating this group. There were few Africans, mulattos, Indians, or mestizos among the gente decente. In many places, such as Peru and Brazil, an affluent, educated mestizo or mulatto might find acceptance into the middle or upper classes.

White-collar workers fit between the gente decente and the lower classes, a decidedly ambiguous situation, where they sought respectability, but had incomes scarcely above poverty. According to the 1908 census for Lima, there were 6610 white-collar workers, of which a little over 50 percent were white, 25 percent were mestizo, less than 10 percent were Indian, 15 percent were Asian, and a tiny number were black. They felt little affinity toward the lower classes from which they had recently risen. Their main fear was that they might fall back into the lower class. No matter what the white-collars believed, upper-class acceptance was at best uncertain. These white-collar workers were, according to D.S. Parker, "marginal figures at best. With no family name and no connections, they were only capable of moving into the lowest rung of the commercial ladder. Poorly paid for long hours, ruthlessly exploited, and lacking any job security, their highest realistic expectation was to receive a steady pay check and to wear a clean shirt." Nearly all white-collar workers were men. In 1908, only 1 percent of the women in Lima worked in white-collar occupations. This began to change only after World War I.

Other groups also belonged to the heterogeneous middle class. In Buenos Aires, the middle class, mostly of immigrant origin, operated the small businesses mentioned earlier. The city was filled with bakers, brewers, carpenters, printers, blacksmiths, and keepers of small shops. The number of manufacturing establishments in Argentina increased from fewer than three thousand in 1853 to twenty-three thousand in 1895 and forty-eight thousand in 1914.

For most of the middle class in Latin America—especially white-collar employees, owners of small businesses, and practitioners of the crafts—their status was precarious at best. Administrative and clerical positions often depended on the good will and good fortune of their bosses. Proprietors of small enterprises rarely had assets other than their own skills. Few middle-class people owned their own homes.

The rapidly emerging industrial working class was also quite diverse. In mining, its members ranged from unskilled peons, who carried 200-pound sacks of ore up rickety ladders from deep tunnels to the surface, to experts in explosives. On the railroads, common pick-and-shovel men toiled with locomotive engineers. In meat-packing there were unskilled meat carriers and skilled butchers. The number of industrial workers in Argentina grew from one hundred eighty thousand in 1895 to four hundred ten thousand in 1914. While the meat-packing plants were large enterprises, most of the firms were small. Thousands of workshops manufactured an enormous variety of products. European immigrants owned between two-thirds and four-fifths of all industrial concerns and comprised from one-half to two-thirds of the workers. In Mexico, the expanding mining and textile industries swelled the ranks of the working class. The number of workers in Lima, Peru, rose from ninety-five hundred in 1876 to more than forty-four thousand in 1920, and in Callao, Lima's port, their number doubled between 1908 and 1920. Women and children comprised one-fifth of the working class employed.

Expanding literacy rates among the middle classes and some sectors of the working classes gave these groups greater access to information about national affairs and emboldened them to demand a voice in political debates. In Brazil, to cite one example, only 19.1 percent of all Brazilian men and 10.4 percent of all women were literate in 1890. By 1920, literacy had improved to 28.9 percent for men and 19.9 percent for women. Literacy was much higher in the cities. By 1920, 65.8 percent of the men and 54.5 percent of the women in São Paulo and Rio de Janeiro had learned how to read and write.

The emergence of these new middle-class and working-class groups added new voices to the political debates in Latin America by the early twentieth century. A growing number of these voices were female. Although women comprised a tiny percentage of white-collar employees, they entered the urban work force and gained access to at least a rudimentary education in unprecedented numbers. As factory workers, operators of small businesses, and heads of households, they

Slice of Life — A Chilean Mining Camp

LIFE IN the mining camps of Brazil, Chile, Mexico, and Peru was difficult, dangerous, and expensive. Spanish and Portuguese colonial enterprises had little success in attracting voluntary labor to the camps without substantial monetary inducements or coercion. The indigenous peoples steered clear of the mines as much as possible. The advent of a freer labor market and the introduction of modern technology during the nineteenth century did not change for the better the living and working conditions. "Labor in the copper mines of the nineteenth century was harshly disciplined, intense, and brutal."

Chilean copper mines were small and totally lacking in modern technology. Chilean mine owners had no capital, suffered poor transportation, and lacked a dependable labor supply. Who would want to work in a copper camp? The mines were usually isolated, accessible to the outside world only by several days of hard travel through rugged terrain. Most were located in the mountains with inhospitable weather.

Treatment of the miners was abominable. Armed guards patrolled the camps. If caught stealing ore, miners were subject to corporal punishment. The physical labor was arduous. Miners worked with hammers and chisels and carried 200-pound sacks of ore up rickety ladders. Charles Darwin observed that the miners were "truly beasts of burden." Miners had little time for meals, working from dawn until dusk.

Mining Camp. The work was back-breaking and dangerous.

Conditions changed somewhat during and after World War I, when copper prices rose because of increased demand. Large international corporations invested in the copper industry after the war. They brought in new technology, such as the widespread use of dynamite. The big companies paid relatively high wages and had better living conditions than the small Chilean operations. This was not saying much, however.

The cost of living in the camps skyrocketed, and working conditions were still unendurable. Tunnels were hell-like, with heat from underground gases and cold and wet. Copper dust swirled in the air, making it nearly impossible to breathe. Respiratory diseases were rampant. Accidents took place as the result of cave-ins, falls down chutes (down which ore also flowed), asphyxiation, and dynamite explosions. At the enormous El Teniente mine in 1920, there were seven severe mining accidents a month. Housing for single workers was makeshift, usually just tents in the smaller camps. Often, twenty men were packed into one room. Families resided without ventilation, electricity, or light in hovels made of wood and aluminum boards. Two families often shared two-room apartments in the barracks. The floors were dirt. There was no heat and the cold was unbearable.

The mines recruited workers from the southern agricultural regions, especially the Central Valley, where the concentration of landholding pushed landless people to seek work in the mines and cities. *Enganchadores* (less-than-honest recruiters) haunted the bars and plazas, buying drinks and getting men drunk. After the workers signed contracts, they woke up the following morning hung over and on a train bound for the north. The enganchadores advanced money that had to be worked off. Since the companies needed workers who were at full strength for the arduous work, they often rejected the men brought by the recruiters. Agricultural labor went back and forth from the farming regions to the northern mines. Many rural workers spent a year in the mines for the high wages and then returned home to pay their debts or settle on a plot of land. Others migrated north in the off season to accumulate enough money to buy their own land. There were high levels of turnover among the labor force. Many worked just long enough to amass some cash and then off they went. In 1917, El Teniente employees averaged only 18 to 20 days' work. Workers often left without notice. They asked for their pay, but more often than not the company withheld it. The harsh conditions were frequently too much for the country people who came to work. Miners, who were too sore to work, missed days. The extreme changes in temperature caused illness and damaged morale. To make matters worse, foreign supervisors in the large companies often were racially prejudiced.

Women moved in and out of the camps, working as domestic servants, preparing and selling food and alcohol, and offering paid solace to the men. Women came to the camps mostly independent of men, looking to earn and save money, perhaps to start again elsewhere. They ran their own households,

(continued on next page)

A Chilean Mining Camp *(continued from previous page)*

raised children, and struggled mightily to make ends meet. Formal marriage was unlikely, for life was too transient.

Both men and women resisted the efforts of large, foreign companies to institute labor discipline. Mobility and independence were highly valued by the workers and widely opposed by the companies. It took decades to instill the industrial work ethic.

In the mining camps, the workers and bosses directly confronted each other over the control over everyday life. The struggle was a microcosm of the general relationship between the upper classes and lower classes throughout Latin America during the nineteenth century.

Questions for Discussion
Compare the lives of Chilean miners to those of Argentine gauchos. What were the social and economic processes that gradually limited their independence? How did the miners assert their control over their own lives?

---

acted independently of traditional family ties and increasingly sought equal treatment in both private and public spheres. Feminists among them asserted their equality with men, while insisting on their differences as well. They used the regard society had for them as females to establish their role in the public sphere and their position as working women to campaign for societal reforms. Feminism called for a redefinition of the traditional notions of the home as women's space and the street as forbidden. At stake were the long-held values of honor and the double standard. They challenged the basic structure of the family, seeking to end the legal subordination of women and the illegality of divorce. Ultimately, women sought to obtain suffrage. Initially, however, they focused on securing equality under the law and better health care for women and children. Their active voices changed the nature of political discourse in the modernizing nations of Latin America.

Rural Discontent

Although the emergence of middle and industrial working classes had limited effect in rural areas, there were other disruptive trends. Generally, conditions for rural working people deteriorated rather badly. In central Mexico, for example, wages had stagnated while purchasing power declined. In Mexico, land expropriations by politicians and large landowners left many landless rural dwellers, who toiled either for small remuneration on the great estates or abandoned their villages to labor in the mines and cities, or across the U.S. border. The ownership of land was concentrated among the upper classes. At the same time in some areas, such as northern Mexico and the Argentine Pampas, the number of owners of small farms increased. In the Mexican north, small holders were a vocal and prosperous group that deeply resented unfairly high taxes and government centralization.

In Argentina, rural conditions for farm tenants, cattle peons or shepherds, and seasonal laborers varied. Landowners no longer recognized any traditional, patriarchal obligations to look after the welfare of their employees, in return for which they had received both labor and loyalty. As in Mexico, there was a sector of small farmers, mostly tenants, who increased their numbers and prospered. Tenants, for example, operated 69 percent of the cereal farms in 1916. When boom times in the cattle industry raised land prices, farmers found it cheaper to rent large parcels rather than to buy relatively smaller properties. The larger the farm, the higher the output and income. By the 1910s, however, many tenants, chronically in debt to suppliers, lived in desperate conditions.

In both rural Argentina and Mexico, the onslaught of centralization grew more intrusive because landowners and governments sought not only to extend their control to local governance, but also to modernize owner-labor relations. This meant that the ruling classes attempted to transform age-old customs and traditions that lay at the core of rural society. Regional autonomy remained strong in Argentina, but rural society changed to suit the needs of the estancieros. However, in Mexico, where the traditional village structure remained strong despite unending assaults by the national government, rural protests led to revolution in 1910.

Mass Movements of People

Latin American leaders, even before independence, had dreamed of populating their vast nations with immigrants from Europe as part of their effort to modernize their economies. Many governments made attracting foreign settlers a matter of public policy. Argentine Juan Bautista Alberdi proclaimed that "to govern is to populate." For the upper class and intellectuals, disdainful of their indigenous and mestizo brethren, an influx of Europeans was the way to "get rid of the primitive element of our popular masses." Domingo Sarmiento, the liberal ideologue who was president of Argentina (1868–1874), claimed that only mass immigration could "drown in waves of industry the Creole rabble, inept, uncivil, and coarse that stops our attempt to civilize the nation." Despite the fervent wishes of upper classes almost everywhere, few Latin American countries attracted many immigrants. Five nations, Argentina, Brazil, Uruguay, Cuba, and Mexico, drew the preponderance of the new arrivals.

From 1860 to 1920, 45 million people left Europe to go to the Western Hemisphere (see Table 11.3). Massive immigration occurred in Argentina, Brazil, and Cuba. From 1904 to 1914, on average, one hundred thousand immigrants a year found their way from Italy and Spain to Argentina. Much of the new middle and working classes derived from the immigrant and migrant population.

Table 11.3

Destination of European Emigrants to Latin America, ca. 1820–1932

Country	Number of immigrants
Argentina	6,501,000
Brazil	4,361,000
Uruguay	713,000
Cuba	1,394,000
Mexico	270,000
Chile	90,000
Venezuela	70,000
Peru	30,000
Paraguay	21,000

Source: José C. Moya, *Cousins and Strangers: Spanish Immigrants in Buenos Aires, 1850–1930,* p. 46.

The export economies demanded labor and, consequently, Peruvian cotton and sugar industries brought in Chinese coolies, the construction of the Panama Canal drew British West Indians, and the Dominican Republic exploited Haitian workers for plantations. By the beginning of the twentieth century, then, an increasingly diverse population demanded a say in the affairs of Latin American nations.

Politics in the Age of Modernization

The spectacular growth in Latin America's national economies in the late nineteenth and early twentieth centuries was accompanied by an equally impressive degree of political stability that stood in marked contrast to the recurring political upheavals that had occurred during the first few decades after independence. Political stability fostered economic growth by guaranteeing a safe climate for domestic and foreign investment. Economic growth in turn gave the ruling classes the tools they needed to maintain order—professionalized and better equipped armies to repress dissidents and sometimes act as arbiters of political disputes, railroads to carry troops quickly to the scene of any potential disorder, and contracts to keep the middle classes happy. The philosophy of positivism was the ideological underpinning of the ruling classes during this era. Developed by Frenchman Auguste Comte (1798–1857) and infused with social Darwinism by Herbert Spencer (1820–1902), positivism emphasized reason, science, order, and progress, which fit nicely into the efforts of the Latin American upper classes to modernize their nations.

The political stability of the age of modernization assumed a variety of forms. In Argentina and Brazil, ranchers and planters played a dominant role in national politics, but large landowners figured heavily in the power structures of all Latin American countries during this era. Chile demonstrated a fair degree of democracy, while in Peru an "Aristocratic Republic" held sway. The long dictatorships of Porfirio Díaz (1876–1911) in Mexico and Antonio Guzmán Blanco (1870–1888) in Venezuela brought a measure of peace and prosperity at least for those who enjoyed the favor of the regime in power.

The rise of the new middle and urban working classes and the widespread encroachments on traditional rural politics and society undermined this stability. In 1910, Mexico burst into revolution that tore it apart for nearly a decade. In other countries, political parties representing the new classes and labor unions formed to contest upper-class rule. By the first decade of the twentieth century, the challenges to the ruling classes were profound.

A Modernized Military

Latin American military establishments reflected the transformations of the times. In Argentina, Brazil, Chile, and Peru, upper classes sought to modernize and professionalize the armed services. As early as the 1860s (El Salvador) and 1870s (Guatemala), Latin American governments began to import European consultants to update their militaries and make them into more professional organizations. These foreign missions inculcated a sense of separateness, nationalism, and impatience, which reconstructed the military in a way that ultimately made it the major threat to democracy in the region. The military was a crucial ally of the upper classes, for the two groups envisioned similar futures of order and economic development. As the social pressures from below increased, the professional, apolitical, incorruptible military convinced itself ever more of its own virtue. Officers came to despise civilian politicians. Concurrently, middle-class people entered the armed services as a route toward upward mobility. As a result, Latin American militaries were integral participants to the struggles over the "Social Question."

The revamped militaries recreated their officer corps through education at special military academies and a career system based on merit. The old-timers, veterans of the wars and civil wars of the nineteenth century, had often made their way "up from the bootstraps" or received patronage appointments. The new career routes kept the young officers—at least in theory—away from politics. Technology changed the military, as it did society as a whole. Railroads, cannons, rifles, machine guns, and telegraphs altered warfare. Ironically, professionalization took place when the region was at peace. After the War of the Pacific, there were no more external wars until the Chaco War between Paraguay and Bolivia in the 1930s. Nonetheless, militaries expanded their role in society and politics.

Isolated and confident (though untested in most cases), Latin American militaries set themselves up as arbitrators of their nations and saw themselves as saviors of their fatherlands. One Argentine army officer wrote in 1911: "The army is the nation. It is the external armor that guarantees the cohesive operation of its parts and preserves it from shocks and falls." No constitutional guarantees, moreover, could dissuade the military from its duty to insure that governments responded to the needs of the nation. It proved impossible to keep the military separate from politics.

As composition of the officer corps changed substantially over time—especially in Brazil and the southern cone—and officers came to represent the middle class (often sons of immigrants), they more and more adopted middle-class values. Officers were conservative and ambitious. But the military was far from unified. As in the upper classes, there were divisions between those who those who wanted to crush all dissidents and those who were willing to compromise with the new urban classes. In Chapter 12, we will see how these disagreements evolved as the militaries asserted more power and influence.

The Rule of the Ranchers and Planters: Argentina and Brazil

A pattern emerged all over Latin America in which export-dominated economies experienced successive booms and busts, with the downturns leading to political unrest and sometimes rebellion. This pattern was evident in Argentina and Brazil during the depression of the 1890s, though none of the resulting rebellions overthrew the existing order. The large landowners of Buenos Aires and the Pampas and the coffee planters of Brazil who dominated politics in their respective nations from the mid-nineteenth century until the 1920s were willing to concede very little, if anything, to the new groups. In Argentina, the large landowners accommodated only the middle classes, while they harshly repressed the urban working class. The Brazilian upper class stubbornly refused any compromise. Eventually, it would split over tactics toward the new classes.

General Julio A. Roca dominated Argentine politics at the end of the century, first through puppets from 1892 to 1898 and then as president from 1898 to 1904. He advocated economic growth financed through foreign investment in the export sector. He kept the provinces in line with patronage and force. But Roca presided over a house of cards. The landowners split into factions, one that supported him and his hard line toward the lower classes and the other that sought progressive reform. Both groups feared the changes taking place in Argentine society, but they differed over what to do about them. Fortunately for the upper classes, the new classes also divided. The middle class took refuge in the Radical Party (Unión Cívica Radical). The working class divided its allegiance among various leftist parties centered in Buenos Aires.

The first setback for the rule of the large landowners in Argentina occurred during the early 1890s. The Radical Party staged two unsuccessful revolts, which served as warnings to the upper classes that they would have to consider some sort of concessions to the emergent working and middle classes. Eventually, the upper classes consented to expand voting rights to all males through the Sáenz Peña Law of 1912. The Radicals, who changed their violent tactics in order to participate in elections, triumphed in the presidential vote of 1916 with their candidate Hipólito Yrigoyen (1916–1922, 1928–1930).

The Radicals evolved into a coalition of dissident landowners, like Yrigoyen, and the new middle class based in Buenos Aires. They were committed to popular democracy and honest government, but when confronted later in the 1910s with the necessity of siding with the working class or the wealthy, they chose the latter. The landowners and middle class who comprised the Radical Party primarily were concerned with protection of the beef industry and access to political patronage (government employment). The leftist political parties sought better wages and working conditions.

The Buenos Aires working class divided into anarchists and socialists. The anarchists sought to obtain better conditions for workers through confrontation with the government by means of the general strike. In response, the government took drastic measures, such as deporting strike leaders and using civilian vigilantes to attack the anarchists. In 1910, a government crackdown against threatened demonstrations at the nation's centennial broke the movement. Argentine socialists were moderates, who supported democracy and sought primarily to redress the inequalities of income distribution. They sought to raise living standards by both raising wages and lowering prices. They also advocated women's suffrage. Founded in 1894 by Juan B. Justo, the Socialist Party (Partido Socialista) was an alliance of professionals, skilled workers, and small-scale manufacturers. The fact that most members of the working class were immigrants and not citizens of Argentina badly hampered the electoral efforts of the Socialists because non-citizens could not vote. Neither anarchists nor socialists made more than a passing mark on Argentine electoral politics. Nonetheless, they frightened enough of those in power into making some concessions to the lower classes.

The onset of depression in 1913, lasting until 1917, further undermined upper-class rule and created widespread discontent among the middle and working classes. World War I drastically curtailed trade and shortages drove up the cost of living. As a result, the Radical Yrigoyen won the presidential election of 1916. Yrigoyen proved a masterful politician, promising change, but never specifying his program. The Radicals built a formidable political machine founded on patronage. The Radicals, never in control of both houses of Congress, were neither able nor inclined to implement extensive reforms. Yrigoyen confronted his greatest crisis in 1919, when strikes in Buenos Aires led to widespread violence. The Radicals sided with the upper classes and crushed the unions in what became known as the Tragic Week (Semana Trágica).

Brazil followed a similar pattern, but the emergent classes were weaker and the upper classes stronger than in Argentina. Regionalism remained a major force, with state governments more influential than the national government.

In the 1880s, Brazil experienced two enormous political and economic shocks. First, the monarchy proclaimed the abolition of slavery on May 13, 1888. Then, on November 15, 1889, the army overthrew the Empire, thus beginning the First Republic (1889–1930). Thereafter, a fragile alliance of state upper classes ruled Brazil until this arrangement broke down in 1930 at the outset of the Great Depression.

At first, the military ruled. The Republic's first two presidents, Deodoro da Fonseca (1889–1891) and Floriano Peixoto (1891–1894), were military officers. Eventually, large landowners took the reins of power. They had to share control with state-level alliances of local political bosses, known as colonels, who presided over the rural hinterlands through a strict system of patron–client relations. The colonels' clients obligated themselves to vote as ordered in return for patronage and protection.

An alliance of São Paulo coffee planters and Minas Gerais cattle barons controlled the national government. By agreement, the major states, Minas Gerais and São Paulo, alternated their representatives in the presidency. (This agreement was the so-called *café com leite* alliance.) Of eleven presidents during the First Republic, six came from São Paulo and three from Minas Gerais. A third state, Rio Grande do Sul, muscled its way into the mix after the turn of the century. Brazilian states exercised considerable autonomy. They had control over their own finances and militaries. The State of São Paulo had a well-equipped state militia with as many as fourteen thousand men. State governments could even contract foreign loans. The coffee planters openly used government for their own economic gain, relying on the national and state governments to buy their surplus crops. Brazil's slower industrialization delayed the development of pressure from below for a decade or two after other Latin American nations confronted the social question.

Democracy in Chile

Chile's landed upper class ruled until 1920. But it, too, was vulnerable to the downturns of the export economy. As in Argentina and Brazil, the depression of the 1890s brought unrest. Until 1890, the Chilean system had a strong president and weak legislature. As the size of the government grew, the amount of patronage jobs at the president's command increased also, thereby enhancing the power of the office even more. President José Manuel Balmaceda (1886–1891) encountered unparalleled rancor and divisions because to many Chileans he symbolized the corrupt, coercive system that had held power for so long. Balmaceda's opposition, which sought to hold free elections and modify the balance of power, stalemated Congress in 1890, virtually paralyzing the national government. When the president closed Congress (which was legal), it established a rival government and defeated Balmaceda in an eight-month-long civil war.

During Chile's so-called "Parliamentary Republic" from 1891 to 1920, Chilean politics reached an impasse. The government's inability to meet the demands of the emerging classes led to recurring crises during the 1920s. The working class increased in numbers as people moved into the mines and cities from the countryside. Inevitably, they sought ways to protest their brutal labor and living conditions through unions. In the 1890s, there were riots in the nitrate fields, where conditions were unimaginable. Conflict worsened in the first decades of the new century. Disturbances in Santiago in 1905 cost the lives of sixty people. A devastating earthquake in 1906 virtually destroyed Valparaíso, Chile's major port. There was a depression from 1907 to 1908. Nitrate demand fell during World War I and then recovered, only to give way to depression after the war. The worsening economic crisis led to terrible strikes in 1919; one in Santiago involved fifty thousand workers. Arturo Alessandri emerged in 1920, promising to accommodate the demands of the new classes, and won election to the presidency. The upper class again was unwilling to compromise, creating a political stalemate. Reformist military officers, impatient for change, overthrew Alessandri in 1924. Only then was the impasse broken, but only temporarily.

The Aristocratic Republic: Peru

Thirty or forty families dominated Peruvian politics at the turn of the century. They were large landowners and businesspeople tied closely to the export sector. Often, they knew Paris, France, better than they did the Peruvian countryside. The racist upper class viewed Indians and castas as backward barbarians. From the mid-1890s until 1919, Peru experienced an era of peace and stability, known as the "Aristocratic Republic." Like everywhere else, however, the inevitable downturns brought discontent and unrest.

The War of the Pacific (1879–1883) left the nation's economy and politics in ruins. Exports fell sharply. Andrés Avelino Cáceres picked up the pieces of Peruvian politics from 1885 to 1895, first as president and then through puppet rulers. Cáceres had led an army of central highland country people in guerrilla warfare against the Chileans. These same followers backed him for the presidency in 1885. He settled Peru's foreign debt, allowing a resurgence of foreign investment. Nicolás de Piérola (1879–1881, 1895–1899), a former president, ousted him in 1895 because an economic depression eroded his popular support. Piérola presided over a considerable measure of development, led by expanding exports of agricultural commodities and minerals and accompanied by a surge in urban manufacturing. He also set out to pare and recast the military. Unfortunately, not everyone participated in the good times. Increased agricultural exports caused landowners to seek to expand at the expense of individual small and communal landholdings. A boom in wool exports, from alpaca and sheep, resulted in large landowners pushing small proprietors off their land, which in turn created widespread unrest.

During the First World War, Peru experienced rebellions in the countryside, uprisings of Chinese immigrant laborers, and protests by university students. Social unrest exploded in 1919 with huge strikes in Lima and Callao. The presidential election in 1919 returned to power former president Augusto B. Leguía (1908–1912, 1919–1930), who ruled for the next 11 years. His solution to the nation's economic problems was an extensive program of public works construction that was devised to provide employment.

Dictatorship: Mexico

In Mexico, dictator General Porfirio Díaz, in conjunction with the landed upper class, the military, and a cadre of professional bureaucrats, ruled Mexico for 35 years (1876–1911), presiding over an era of unprecedented economic development. Some observers regarded him as the most powerful leader in the Western Hemisphere. He built his regime on a shrewd combination of consensus and coercion. A raw pragmatist, Díaz wove an intricate web of alliances among once fragmented regional upper classes. He held them together using the revenues generated by his export-based economic strategy. Don Porfirio, as he was called, was a masterful politician who was simultaneously both feared and admired. He was a war hero, recognized as one of the commanders at Puebla, where Mexican troops won a great military victory against French invaders on May 5, 1862. (The *Cinco de Mayo,* or Fifth of May, is a national holiday in Mexico.) Díaz was often magnanimous in victory, when it was to his political advantage. However, he could be equally ruthless. When early in his regime a subordinate asked him what to do with captured rebels, Díaz told him to "kill them in cold blood." His rural police, the *Rurales,* kept order in the countryside with the *Ley fuga,* according to which prisoners were often "shot while trying to escape."

During Díaz's rule, Mexico's economy grew spectacularly. Domestic peace and the end of foreign invasions combined with burgeoning markets for Mexican agricultural commodities and minerals and the inflow of international capital in search of profitable investments to cause unprecedented economic expansion. The Díaz government sponsored the construction of more than 10,000 miles of railroad. It oversaw the investment of $1 billion in U.S. capital and a nine-fold increase in trade from 1877 to 1911.

Despite peace and prosperity, however, there was a dark underside to both Mexico's economy and politics. As in other export economies, Mexico endured periodic booms and busts. There were downturns during the mid-1880s, the early 1890s, and from 1907 to 1909. The booms brought prosperity, but the busts caused widespread suffering among the urban and rural working class. Economic depressions caused political disruptions by undermining the conditions of the emerging working and middle classes and by disrupting the delicate system of political arrangements between Díaz and regional upper classes. Díaz's web of political

LATIN AMERICAN LIVES

José Guadalupe Posada (1852–1913), Artist of Mexico

During the late nineteenth century, there arose in Mexico a thriving business in broadsheets, which celebrated events such as murders, gory bullfights, natural disasters, and banditry. Country people living in the cities purchased them to get an alternative view to the official accounts of the dictatorship of Porfirio Díaz. We can look at surviving copies and piece together a cogent history of life in Mexico City at the turn of the century. The best known printer of these broadsheets was Antonio Vanegas Arroyo. The most popular artist of the era, José Guadalupe Posada, did most of the illustrations for the Vanegas Arroyo broadsheets. Posada's art was often satirical, poking fun at those in political power. He is, perhaps, most well known for his *calaveras,* skeletal figures used in the celebrations of the Day of the Dead.

Posada left no writings and only bare traces of his personal life. He was born into modest circumstances in Aguascalientes. He showed talent from an early age, apprenticing to a lithographer at 16. As a young man, he got into trouble when he drew cartoons that satirized local authorities. Posada then fled to León, Guanajuato, where for the next 16 years he was a commercial artist. In 1888, he moved to Mexico City. There he worked for Vanegas Arroyo and also illustrated for a number of magazines openly opposed

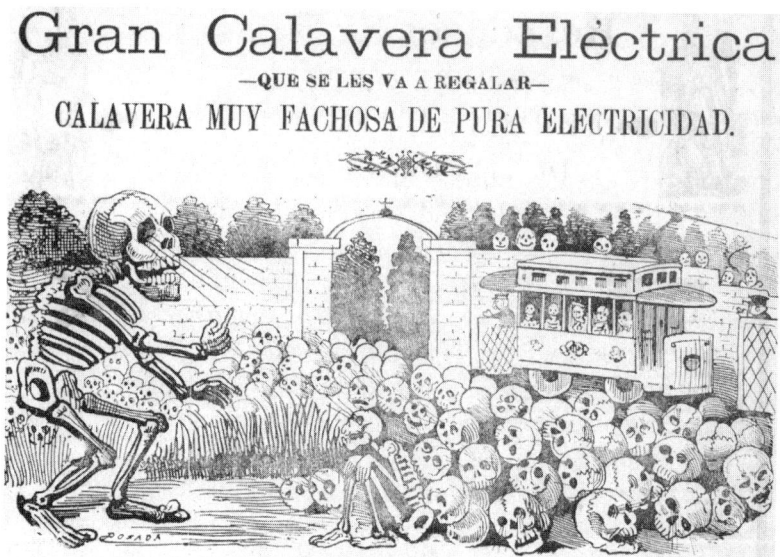

José Guadalupe Posada was famous for his satirical drawings of calaveras (skeletons).

(continued on next page)

> **JOSÉ GUADALUPE POSADA** *(continued from previous page)*
>
> to Díaz. He was, by his financial and social standing, an urban artisan, rather than an intellectual.
>
> Posada was nearly unknown in his own era. The major art critics of the day ignored him. Posada was resurrected from obscurity during the 1920s as an artist of the people by the great muralists Diego Rivera and José Clemente Orozco and French artist Jean Charlot. The circle of revolutionary artists saw Posada as a precursor of the upheaval of 1910. Orozco copied the calavera style of Posada. One of his famous works, *Gods of the Modern World* (1932), displays the style.
>
> Posada stated in his artwork the basis of the middle-class opposition to the Díaz regime. He satirized the dictatorship's unfairness and venality. He was also among those early twentieth-century artists who gave a voice to the struggles of the common folk for fairness and justice. Like so many Latin American artists in the twentieth century, Posada tried to make sense of an unjust world through his talent and humor.
>
> **Questions for Discussion**
>
> In places and times where there are no honest and fair elections for public office, how do subordinated people protest? How do artists and musicians contribute to the political discourse?

alliances depended on his ability to reward cooperation with jobs, tax exemptions, subsidies for businesses, and other benefits. The economic downturn in 1907 allowed him insufficient resources to pay for cooperation. Ungrateful upper-class allies looked for opportunities to free themselves from the dictator.

At the same time as the economic crisis undermined his support among the upper classes, the countryside had reached the point of rebellion. Improved transportation and widened markets for agricultural commodities both in Mexico and abroad had sharply increased land values. Political officials and large landowners, particularly in the mid-1880s and in the decade after 1900, undertook to expropriate the lands of small owners and the communally held lands of Indian villages in order to expand both their landholdings and the pool of cheap, landless labor. As a result, there was an undercurrent of agrarian discontent throughout the dictatorship. Crises evolved because the economic downturn in 1907 had limited the alternative employment possibilities of landless people in rural areas. They previously had found jobs in the mines, the cities, and the United States. The depression deprived them of these opportunities. Country people also protested the loss of local autonomy. Through a system of appointed district leaders *(jefes políticos)* the Díaz dictatorship had eliminated elections to local offices. These district bosses in some areas proved extraordinarily intrusive, meddling even in private matters.

Coinciding crises helped bring down the dictatorship after 1900. The most immediate was the furor over succession. Díaz was 74 when reelected president in 1904. His vice president, Ramón Corral, occupied the post because he was one of the most unpopular officials in Mexico and was, therefore, no threat to Díaz. None of the obvious successors dared to show ambition. If Díaz was to run for reelection again in 1910 at 80, few expected he would live out his term. The second crisis was the depression of 1907, which erased many of the gains of the Díaz economic miracle. The oil that greased the wheels of the political arrangements of the dictatorship evaporated. The emerging middle class saw its businesses ruined. All the unfairness of the regime, under which the middle class suffered discrimination in taxation, the courts, and the banking system, was laid bare in the downturn. Third, the upper classes squabbled and divided. Old-time enemies of the dictator, who had bided their time, content to be bought off, saw an opportunity to even old scores. The depression left the urban and rural working classes with little to lose. It was time to fight.

Modernization and Resistance

The export boom presided over by the upper classes hid inherently unfair societies. The benefits from prosperity accrued to only a small minority. The new middle classes were extremely vulnerable to economic downturns. They saw their modest gains erode in the economic depression during the first decade of the twentieth century and during the inflation of World War I. The mines and new factories paid pitiful wages and offered miserable working conditions for new migrants from the countryside and immigrants from abroad. Workers agitated for better compensation and working conditions, but also against the regimentation that domestic and foreign employers tried to impose upon their daily lives. Meanwhile, rural people lost their lands and their livelihoods to the forces of the export economy. Some migrated in search of better opportunities elsewhere, but others stayed where they were and revolted to regain or retain their landholdings and control over their daily lives. National leaders in a number of countries grappled with the question of how best to draw indigenous peoples into the new capitalist nation-state. Resistance then was inevitable in the face of the intrusion of the world market and national authorities.

Indigenous Peoples

Many Latin Americans of the upper class and urbanized middle classes regarded the indigenous population as a serious impediment to national progress. Positivists in Mexico shared this view, and the Díaz regime alternated between ignoring and trying to exterminate indigenous peoples. Apaches in the north of Mexico were at times subject to bounties on their scalps. Conversely, some of the victorious factions in the revolution that overthrew Díaz adopted a conscious policy of glorifying the nation's indigenous heritage. Archaeologists and historians rediscovered the great cultures that had existed before the arrival of the Europeans. The brilliant muralists of the 1920s and 1930s further illuminated the Indian past.

The place of indigenous peoples also provoked much discussion in Peru, where the humiliating defeat in the War of the Pacific caused a reevaluation of the nation's priorities and policies. Peruvian intellectuals concluded that Indians required reform. Fired by the 1889 novel *Aves sin nido* by Clorinda Matto de Turner, which exposed the harsh exploitation endured by Indians in a small Andean town, a new movement resolved to rediscover Indian Peru. U.S. archaeologists rediscovered Machu Picchu, the long-lost Inca city, further fueling interest in Indian Peru. After World War I, the movement shifted from a willingness to study Indians to more revolutionary goals. A few envisioned a new nationalism that glorified the Indian past. A second strain of indigenismo arose from José Carlos Mariátegui, the noted Marxist intellectual, who tied indigenismo to socialism. He advocated radical land reform to end the centuries-old oppression of Indians by the hacienda system.

Resistance in the Countryside

The first, and perhaps most crucial, source of opposition to modernization was in the countryside. During the first half of the nineteenth century, political disruptions and inadequate transportation kept land values down. As we observed in Chapter 9, after mid-century, Liberals attempted to create a class of small farmers that they believed, following the model of England and the United States, would form the basis for both capitalism and democracy. Their efforts to break up the landholdings of the Catholic Church and communal indigenous villages backfired, however, because politicians and large landowners inevitably ended up with much of this property. A number of nations, notably Argentina and Mexico, gave away vast tracts of public lands to the politically well connected, which concentrated landholding even further.

As we have seen in the instances of those Latin Americans who threw stones at passing railroad cars, not everyone accepted the notion that modernization and economic development were good. In addition to the deep-seated distrust of central authority intruding on local prerogatives, there were also a number of other sources of resistance to modernity.

On a number of occasions, country people offered violent resistance to modernization. Two such movements erupted in Brazil. The first occurred in Canudos, an estate in the northern part of the state of Bahia, where Antônio Conselheiro and his followers set up a community in 1893. Deep in the backlands, it grew into a considerable city of twenty to thirty thousand people. The local upper class—and eventually the national government—viewed Canudos as a threat to their rule. Several military expeditions were sent and the people of Canudos defeated them. Finally, in October of 1897, the federal army destroyed the city and slaughtered its last five thousand residents. The events were made famous by the book *Rebellion in the Backlands* by Euclídes da Cunha. Another movement, the *Contesdado,* took place in the border area between the states of

Paraná and Santa Catarina in southern Brazil. The rebellion started in 1911, led by José María, whom his followers regarded as a saint. The processes of modernization in both the countryside and the city had alienated many of the people who joined the movement. There were among them unemployed former small farmers thrown off their lands as railroads spread out across the land. Others were railroad workers abandoned after their contracts expired. Despite the death of their leaders, rebels continued to fight until late 1915. Meanwhile, widespread banditry swept Brazil during the same years as the Canudos and Contesdado rebellions. People who had lost their lands or ended up on the wrong side of local political disputes filled bandit ranks. Their soldier-bandits were poor dark-skinned people who made up the majority of the rural population.

The Mexican Revolution

Nowhere was the impact of the rapidly developing export economy dominated by foreign investors clearer than in Mexico, where a diverse coalition of discontented people waged a revolution of unprecedented duration and cost. In 1910, a multi-class alliance of dissidents from the upper class, middle-class people who had suffered financial ruin in the depression of 1907, country people whose lands the upper class had expropriated, and unemployed workers rallied around Francisco I. Madero, a disaffected, wealthy landowner, toppled Porfirio Díaz from power. The depression of 1907, the uncertainty of succession, and the deteriorating state of the army and police had badly weakened the Díaz regime. In the spring of 1911, the coalition ousted Díaz, who prudently embarked on a comfortable retirement in Paris, never to return to Mexico. But the consensus among Madero's followers soon crumbled as landowners and landless country people clashed over land reform and the middle and lower classes disagreed over the importance of property rights. Dormant regionalism, suppressed temporarily by Díaz, reawakened as well.

In 1913, supporters of Díaz took advantage of the disintegration of the revolutionary coalition and the resurgence of regionalism to briefly reestablish the old regime without Díaz. General Victoriano Huerta took over the reins of the counterrevolutionary movement, betraying Madero and ordering his execution. Others then formed a loose partnership of revolutionary movements to defeat Huerta in 1914. Their leaders included Venustiano Carranza, another alienated northern landowner, Pancho Villa, a bandit-businessman from Chihuahua (also in the north), and Emiliano Zapata, a village leader from the state of Morelos (just south of Mexico City). This alliance did not last even as long as Madero's. Carranza, representing the dissident landowners, clashed with the *Zapatistas* (followers of Zapata) who advocated wide-ranging land reform. Villa and Carranza disliked each other intensely. Villa and Zapata allied since they both stood for the lower classes. The three factions set upon each other in a brutal civil war that lasted until 1917. In those three years, there was virtually no functioning government in Mexico.

How Historians Understand | Why Do People Rebel?

THE ERA FROM 1880 to 1920 was tumultuous. New emergent classes pushed for their place in politics, economy, and society. Upper classes struggled to maintain their positions. Country people sought to return to what they had under the protection of the Catholic monarchs of the Iberian empires. Technological innovations disrupted society at all levels. The international movement of ideas, people, and money reinvented the ways that men and women worked, lived, and interacted. Yet, despite all these upheavals and rapid changes, only in one country, Mexico, did the people rise up in revolution. It is an enduring and important question in Latin America as to why only in Mexico the lower and middle classes allied and destroyed the old regime.

Most people in Latin America had lived with a (sometimes considerable) degree of day-to-day oppression. The daily struggle to subsist consumed their days; they had little time or energy to plan, let alone carry out, a rebellion. At some points in history, however, individuals have ignored survival in order to rise up against their oppressors (though such occurrences are rare). Historians have almost universally failed to discern what caused these rebels to risk everything.

Within the Mexican case itself, there are questions as well. Why did some groups or individuals rebel and others not? Why did some country people, permanent residents on the haciendas, for example, remain at peace, while northern small landowners led the overthrow of Porfirio Díaz? Why did some large landowning families join the Revolution, while others fought it to the death?

The most difficult questions arise about why individuals participated in uprisings. It is very unusual to find sources that give insight into motivations. In the Mexican case, historians have compiled a large number of oral interviews and discovered criminal court records, which reveal personal stories. But these sources are not available for all regions or eras.

Of all the groups that rose in rebellion against Porfirio Díaz in 1910, the most elusive have been country people. Everyone concedes that rural people were central to the Mexican Revolution, but there is some disagreement as to why exactly they revolted. Did country people fight to restore their lost lands? Did they resist the encroachments of centralized government on their local prerogatives? Do people risk their lives for land or religion or local autonomy? It is nearly impossible for an historian in the twenty-first century to get inside a country person's head. Modern-day historians simply have not been able to penetrate the worldview of the late nineteenth-century rural dweller.

Historians and social scientists have formulated various theories, based on such notions as rising expectations, class conflict, moral economy, and mob behavior, to try to understand why people rebel. Because of the paucity of evidence, they have validated none of these. Analysts have tried to circumvent the lack of direct evidence (such as the actual words of the participants) by examining the possible grievances, the economic circumstances, and the political crises that might have led to discontent and eventually revolution. Thus, historians build circumstantial cases without proof of causality.

Perhaps the most convincing and plausible attempts at figuring out the mental state of various individuals and members of groups have appeared in the fiction of the Mexican Revolution. The works of such authors as Mariano Azuela *(The Underdogs),* Martín Luis Guzmán *(The Eagle and the Serpent),* and Carlos Fuentes *(The Death of Artemio Cruz)* give insights into the reality of the rebels through the imaginary conversations and thoughts of their characters. The novelists often portray the revolutionaries as petty, greedy, and murderous. There are few heroes. And some, like Azuela's Demetrio Macías, were less than admirable.

How then do we obtain a truer picture of the revolutionaries and their motivations? It is unlikely that historians can ever really know. There will always be pieces of the puzzle missing.

Questions for Discussion

Without benefit of an extensive written record to which to refer, how do you think historians can understand how working-class and country people thought? How can the historian of the twenty-first century "get into the heads" of people who lived decades, even centuries, in the past?

By 1917, however, Carranza emerged triumphant with the brilliant assistance of his best general, Álvaro Obregón, another northerner. Carranza owed much of his victory to his ability to win over the working class and some rural people with promises (later unfulfilled) of reforms. Carranza also appealed to members of the middle class because he defended private property rights and offered political patronage. The revolutionaries promulgated the Constitution of 1917, which provided for extensive land reform, workers' rights, and other wide-reaching reforms. Carranza then split with Obregón over the extent to which the government would implement the provisions of the constitution. Obregón, who favored reforms, overthrew Carranza in 1920 and made himself president. Meanwhile, Zapata and Villa continued guerrilla warfare until 1919 and 1920, respectively. Mexico's bloody struggle had lasted a decade and cost the lives of between one and two million people. The Revolution also devastated the nation's economy. It would be well into the 1930s before most economic indicators recovered to 1910 levels.

Conclusion

In 1920, middle-aged and elderly Latin Americans could look back on the enormous changes that had occurred in their lifetimes. Those who lived in the cities could see signs of "progress" all around them—streetcars, automobiles, modern office buildings, banks, and factories. In the more fashionable parts of town, they could marvel at the lavish homes and other symbols of the conspicuous consumption of the upper classes. More people could read and write than ever before. Outside the cities, other evidence of change could be found. Railroads crisscrossed the countryside, although they were concentrated along routes that served the new export economies. Large estates and modern farm machinery produced crops for sale in nearby cities and markets overseas, while small farmers found it increasingly hard to produce the subsistence crops they needed to support themselves and their families.

With the notable exception of Mexicans, this generation of Latin Americans had seen fewer wars than their parents or grandparents, but only the most naïve among them would have predicted that social peace would last indefinitely. Some of them had witnessed massive strikes by urban workers in the turbulent aftermath of World War I. Rural discontent was in evidence everywhere as well. Intellectuals and some political figures began to carve out a more active role for indigenous peoples, and women began to demand changes in the home, the legal system, and in society as a whole. In Chapter 12 we shall see how Latin Americans met these and other serious challenges in the coming decades.

Learning More About Latin Americans

Dore, Elizabeth, and Maxine Molyneux, eds. *Hidden Histories of Gender and the State in Latin America* (Durham, NC: Duke University Press, 2000). Essays on women, the state, and society.

Gwynne, Robert N., and Cristobal Kay, eds. *Latin America Transformed: Globalization and Modernity* (New York: Arnold, 1999). The impact of vast change in the twentieth century.

Haber, Stephen, ed. *How Latin America Fell Behind: Essays on the Economic Histories of Brazil and Mexico, 1800–1914* (Stanford, CA: Stanford University Press, 1997). Essays that attempt to account for the lack of Latin American economic development.

Lavrín, Asuncíon. *Women, Feminism, and Social Change: Argentina, Chile, and Uruguay, 1890–1940* (Lincoln, NE: University of Nebraska Press, 1995). Traces the feminist movement in the Southern Cone.

Wasserman, Mark. *Everyday Life and Politics in Nineteenth Century Mexico: Men, Women, and War* (Albuquerque, NM: University of New Mexico Press, 2000).

Weaver, Frederick Stirton. *Latin America in the World Economy* (Boulder, CO: Westview Press, 2000). An overview of the role of external economic factors in Latin American economic development.

12

BETWEEN REVOLUTIONS
THE NEW POLITICS OF CLASS AND THE ECONOMIES OF IMPORT SUBSTITUTION INDUSTRIALIZATION, 1920–1959

THE ERA FRAMED by the end of the Mexican Revolution (1910–1920) and the beginning of the Cuban Revolution (1959) continued, augmented, and refocused the conflicts and dilemmas of Latin America's politics and economy, which emerged from the transformations experienced in the preceding four decades. Battered by recurring crises—two world wars and a debilitating depression—and the exigencies of the superpower confrontation we know as the Cold War, Latin America struggled to answer the questions raised at independence and discussed in Chapter 9: Who was to govern (and for whom) and how were they to govern? Latin American upper classes fiercely resisted the strident demands of the middle and urban working classes, whose rise we studied in Chapter 11. Refurbished and reformed militaries established themselves as crucial participants in politics, mostly as conservatives, but on occasion as moderate and even radical advocates of social justice. For the most part, however, the upper classes allied

1914–1918	1919–1930	1933	1937	1939–1945	1952
World War I	Augusto B. Leguía dictator of Peru	Cuban Revolution ousts dictator Gerardo Machado	Getúlio Vargas overturns his own government and establishes the Estado Novo	World War II	Fulgencio Batista returns to Cuba as dictator
	1924 Young military officers overthrow president Arturo Alessandri in Chile	1929–1941 Great Depression	1938 Lázaro Cárdenas expropriates foreign oil companies in Mexico		1946 Juan Perón elected president of Argentina

with the military against labor organizations and popularly based political parties, the primary advocates of the lower classes. Armed forces anointed themselves as the ultimate arbiters of civil society, intervening periodically when differing versions of democracy faltered.

The profound changes brought about by urbanization and incipient industrialization altered not only relationships between classes but between men and women. Women entered the public political and economic arenas, forcing readjustments to traditional patriarchy. Old notions of women's role, sexuality, and honor underwent important transformations. During this period, women fought for and eventually won suffrage.

Constant battles between moderates and hardliners in the upper classes and militaries were reflected in the rise and fall of democracy and dictatorship. Many members of the upper classes and allied military officers realized the necessity of altering the economic and political system, at least so as to minimally satisfy the demands of the lower and middle classes for better living and working conditions and for electoral and economic fairness. Compromise was difficult because the ruling classes of most nations were no longer homogeneous, making consensus virtually unattainable, and intransigent elements of the upper class–military alliance were unwilling to make concessions. The most notable divisions arose because export economies had created a brash new class of industrialists and entrepreneurs whose interests were not always in harmony with the landowning class. The militaries were divided as well, usually between old-line upper-class senior officers and up-and-coming middle-class junior officers.

The lower classes strove for their voice in politics and the economy by joining labor unions, though these mostly served skilled workers. With expanded male suffrage, workers were valuable allies for rival middle- and upper-class political parties. Left political groups, such as the Socialists and Communists, experienced only modest success. With the exception of the brief Socialist Republic proclaimed in Chile in 1932 and Chile's and Cuba's popular front (alliances of Left and center political parties) governments of the late 1930s and early 1940s, none of the leftist parties ever shared national power. The working class more commonly attached itself to a rising political leader, like Colonel Juan Perón (1946–1955, 1974–1976) in Argentina, who traded concessions, such as wage increases, for support. A number of other democratic leaders and dictators also relied on the support of the middle and lower classes. Thus, populism, comprised of cross-class alliances brought together by a charismatic leader advocating social reform, dominated the politics of the era.

The struggle for control over their everyday lives continued to be at the center of lower-class demands. Although the increasing migration of people to the cities muted somewhat the demands for local autonomy in the countryside, they remained at the core of Mexican politics into the 1940s (and perhaps longer). The strength of regionalism forced even dictators like Juan Perón in Argentina and Getúlio Vargas in Brazil to ally with provincial and state political bosses, who obtained the support of the people of the countryside by defending local customs and traditions.

At the same time, Latin American governments grew more powerful. Important sectors of the national ruling classes came to realize that they could not obtain their goals of modernization, most critically industrialization, without national governments becoming more active in the economy. Concerned with the industrial base of national security, the new industrialists and organized labor joined elements of the military to institute extensive tariff protection for domestic manufacturing. Furthermore, beginning in the 1930s, with the onset of the prolonged economic crisis, governments took crucial roles in the economy. The resulting resurgent drive for modernization became known as import substitution industrialization.

Nonetheless, exports fueled the economies of Latin American nations throughout all the crises. The plight of the region depended on the booms and busts of the international markets for agricultural commodities and minerals. Political instability or stability and the choice between dictatorship or democracy often (though not always) derived from the status of the economies of the individual nations.

Three Crises and the Beginnings of Intensified Government Involvement in the Economy, 1920–1945

As we observed in Chapter 11, the export boom from the 1870s to the 1910s stimulated industrialization, mainly in the form of processing agricultural commodities. The spectacular growth of exports ended after 1920, however. Three great crises—the two world wars and the Great Depression—disrupted international trade and capital markets for prolonged periods (1914–1919, 1929–1941, and 1939–1945). Latin American upper classes reassessed their nations' reliance on the exportation of commodities and the importation of consumer goods.

The Aftermath of World War I

World War I revealed the extreme uncertainties and costs of the booms and busts associated with reliance on exports. In theory, the war should have stimulated exports and benefited the region, as European countries placed their economies on a wartime footing. Instead, the war pointed out the vulnerability of Latin America to temporary stoppages in the flow of goods and capital back and forth across the Atlantic Ocean. During the early part of the war, the demand for Latin American commodities plummeted. Government revenues dropped sharply, which led to government deficits. When the demand for strategic materials finally rose, other factors, such as the rising cost of imports, mitigated the benefits. Latin American exports obtained high prices, but only for a short period.

The brief boom proved detrimental to Latin American agriculture in the long term, for many farmers borrowed to increase their lands under cultivation to fill demand, only to face ruin when Europe recovered its agricultural capacity and the rest of the world once again gained access to European markets. The most startling case was the Cuban "Dance of the Millions." In two years, sugar prices soared from 4 cents to over 20 cents a pound, only to plunge even lower than they had begun. In anticipation of booming prices, Cuban sugar growers greatly expanded landholdings and production, only to confront disaster when prices dropped.

With competition from abroad cut off by the war, domestic manufacturing seemingly had unprecedented opportunities. Unfortunately, machinery and capital were not available. The United States furnished an alternative market, but during the war it could not supply Latin America with all the needed industrial equipment, materials, and capital.

Despite the lessons of the world war and the nasty, though brief, depression in 1920 and 1921, Latin American economies remained export-oriented throughout the decade. Unfortunately, overall international trade grew far more slowly than it had in the previous decades. From 1913 to 1929, the volume of trade rose an average of only 1 percent per year. To make matters worse, Latin American nations confronted harsh competition for this stagnant global market. It was nearly impossible to increase market shares of primary commodities because there were other, often cheaper, producers elsewhere. Latin American nations were already operating at high efficiency, so they could not significantly decrease costs.

Circumstances were right for the development of modern manufacturing. Urbanization had brought together a relatively more affluent population that demanded consumer goods. The expanding middle and laboring classes furnished a growing market. Improved transportation and communications expanded the market to the countryside. Domestic manufacturing, however, could not compete successfully against its external rivals unless protected by government. Internal markets were simply too small to obtain economies of scale. Typically, manufacturing plants operated at a fraction of capacity. World War I briefly cut off outside competition. As a result, some nations, such as Brazil, Chile, and Peru, experienced modest growth in manufacturing. Argentina and Uruguay made little or no headway. Mexico, of course, suffered through a decade of civil wars during the world conflagration.

The Great Depression

As the 1930s began, Latin American economies remained highly concentrated on a few export commodities sent to a handful of markets. One product accounted for at least 50 percent of the exports in ten countries (Bolivia, Brazil, Colombia, Cuba, the Dominican Republic, El Salvador, Honduras, Guatemala,

Slice of Life: Colombian Coffee Farm in 1925

THERE ARE two quite distinct forms of coffee production: the plantation (fazenda in Brazil, *finca* or hacienda elsewhere) and the small, family-operated farm. Two nations, Costa Rica and Colombia, are particularly known for the latter. Between 1920 and 1950, small producers came to dominate Colombian coffee production. Small holdings required, as one historian observed, a "lifetime struggle in which ingenuity, hard work, and a good measure of luck…" were crucial elements.

The small operators did not always own their own property. On the huge plantations in the older coffee regions, permanent workers (*arrendatarios*) obtained the right to farm a small parcel on which they grew corn, yucca, plantains, and sugar cane and raised fowl or livestock. In return for the use of the land, the worker undertook an obligation to labor ranging from a few days to nearly a whole month on the plantation, depending on the size and quality of his plot. The coffee estates also employed temporary workers, small farmers from other areas, contracted for harvest and paid according to the amount of coffee beans they picked. Temporary labor weeded the groves as well. A third type of worker, the *colono,* contracted to open up new lands for coffee production, clearing the land, planting new trees, and caring for them for four years. The colono then sold the trees to the plantation owner and renounced all rights to the land. The colono also cultivated food crops between the trees for family subsistence.

In the newer coffee regions, small- and medium-sized family farms predominated, the latter operated by sharecroppers or renters. The sharecroppers received half the harvest in return for caring for the trees and processing the beans. They got one-third if they did not dry and de-pulp the beans. Although there were some medium-sized farms with sharecroppers, for the most part these operations relied on family labor.

The small farmers had to adapt to the environment and the family's limited resources. The topography made it impossible to use mechanized machinery, so farmers used axes and fire to clear the land and hoes to weed it. Colombian farmers planted their crops in vertical rows on the severely steep slopes so they could weed standing upright. (Weeding bent over was excruciating work.) The farmers planted using a *barretón,* a heavy wedge-shaped implement with an iron tip and a long straight wood handle that the farmer poked into the soil. The farmer then placed corn or a coffee seedling into the resulting hole in the ground. Clearing was done with a *peinilla* or *machete.* They planted food crops between the rows of coffee trees not only to provide sustenance for themselves, but also to help prevent erosion. Shade trees, such as plantains, were also planted to inhibit erosion (through root systems), but they also provided the additional benefit of leaves that could

(continued on next page)

Colombian Coffee Farm in 1925 *(continued from previous page)*

be used as fertilizer for the coffee trees. Shade also slowed the growth and ripening of the coffee beans, so that they matured at the proper pace. Pigs and fowl wandered in the fields, eliminating insects and supplying fertilizer. Family farms grew many crops. The smallest concentrated on subsistence. Plantains, bananas, manioc, corn, and beans were among the staples. Corn was grown on the least fertile land.

The work was hard and long. The males usually did the heavy work of clearing, planting, and weeding. Women and children helped with the harvest. Once the de-pulping, washing, fermenting, drying and selecting took place, they put the coffee beans into burlap sacks and transported them by mule or horse on difficult trails to coffee towns where they were sold to merchants and traders.

Farm families lived simply. Corn, eaten in soups and bread, was the staple of their diet. It also was fed to the fowl and pigs, which in turn were eaten by the family on special occasions. The usual meal was soup and starch with small bits of salted beef or pork purchased in town. The farmers also bought most vegetables. Many farmers grew citrus and mango trees. In the warmer zones, they also grew sugar cane. From this sugar cane, they produced brown sugar cakes called *panelas* and the molasses that was later fermented and distilled to yield aguardiente or rum. These provided sweets and alcoholic beverages.

Family members usually produced most of what they needed, except for some male clothing (pants, shoes, and boots). Poor children wore little or no clothing. The women made baskets, mattresses, and candles. To survive, the families had to be frugal and self-sufficient.

Housing was made of bamboo and thatch with dirt floors. Washing was done in local rivers and streams. Human wastes were dropped in the fields, which was terribly unsanitary for water supplies and resulted in the transmission of intestinal diseases. The tropical zones were generally unhealthy. Intestinal parasites were common.

In Colombia, small producers engaged in constant, often violent competition with their neighbors. The prevalent clientelist politics forced them to participate in partisan wars, such as *La Violencia*. It had been the hope of Latin American liberal politicians during the nineteenth and twentieth century that small farmers, as they had in some parts of Europe and the United States, would form the bedrock of democracy. In Colombia, however, they were at the heart of conflict.

Questions for Discussion

Compare the lives of Colombian coffee farmers with other small farmers, such as cassava growers in Brazil. Why was violence so integral a part of conditions in the countryside? Was violence a result of the local loss of autonomy?

Nicaragua, and Venezuela). Four nations, the United States, Great Britain, Germany, and France, provided 70 percent of the trade. This concentration put the region in serious jeopardy when the great economic crisis came.

The world-wide Depression wrecked havoc with Latin American economies. Between 1928 and 1932, export prices tumbled by more than half in ten countries. Oil and bananas were the only commodities that fell only moderately. Mineral producers were hit the worst. Bolivia, Chile, and Mexico suffered the decline of both unit volume and prices. Customers for minerals worked off stockpiles rather than make new purchases. Argentina's exports fell from about $1.5 billion in 1929 to $561 million in 1932. Cuban sugar was all but ruined. Between 1928 and 1932, Cuba's national per capita income fell by one-third and Chile's gross national product (GNP) dropped 35.7 percent. Export prices continued to fall until 1934, rising sharply in 1936 and 1937, and falling again for the next two years.

Recovery from the Depression began between 1931 and 1932. The fastest recoveries, where the gross domestic product (GDP) rose 50 percent or more from 1931 to 1939, took place in Brazil, Mexico, Chile, Cuba, Peru, Venezuela, Costa Rica, and Guatemala. Argentina, Colombia, and El Salvador came back more slowly, with their gross domestic products increasing 20 percent in these years. The worst off were Honduras, Nicaragua, Uruguay, Paraguay, and Panama. Real GDP in Colombia exceeded its pre-Depression level in 1932. The same was true for Brazil in 1933, Mexico in 1934, and Argentina, El Salvador, and Guatemala in 1935, while Chile and Cuba, where the Depression was most severe, recovered later in the decade. Honduras, dependent solely on bananas, did not reach its pre-crisis GDP until 1945. The recovery of external trade in the 1930s was at least partly the result of a shift away from markets in Great Britain and the United States to those in Germany, Italy, and Japan. By 1938, Europe bought over half (55 percent) of Latin America's exports and supplied nearly half (45 percent) of its imports.

The Depression acted much like World War I in that it impeded the flow of imports to Latin America. But again, manufacturing did not necessarily flourish. Obviously, domestic markets shrunk during the early 1930s, but opportunity existed once recovery was underway. However, low productivity, the result of shortages of cheap power, lack of skilled labor, lack of credit, obsolete machinery, and overprotection (tariffs that were too high), hindered development. The Depression also shut off the flow of capital into the region from Europe and the United States. The only way to modernize was through some form of government intervention. National governments established agencies such as CORFO (Chilean National Development Corporation) in Chile to foster industrialization that the private sector was unable or unwilling to undertake. Mexico nationalized its petroleum industry and railways in the late 1930s. In Uruguay, the government owned the meatpacking and cement industries.

World War II

World War II hit Latin America harder than the Depression and previous world war. The British market shrunk when it went on war footing, and the British blockade of Europe cut off recently expanding continental European markets. U.S. programs such as lend-lease and the Export-Import Bank never replaced the shortfall in either finance or commerce. Some of the lost market was made up with inter-Latin American trade, which went from 6 percent to 16 percent of the total exports and 25 percent of imports.

The drop in imports after 1939 should have provided impetus for further Latin American industrialization, but wartime inflation again kept the level of consumer consumption static. Rising prices eroded real wages and purchasing power. Nonetheless, industrialization expanded in several nations. The United States fostered industry by supplying technical assistance through various agencies. Governments established non-consumer industries, such as the Volta Redonda steel works in Brazil. Wartime cooperative programs with the United States added to the responsibilities of governments. Confiscating and operating Axis-owned businesses thrust the government directly into the economy.

Latin American nations accumulated tremendous reserves from the sale of exports during the war, which led to inflation. This in turn created an ever-widening gap in the distribution of income. Very few workers' wages and middle-class salaries could maintain their real earnings in the face of rising prices. Those who had assets, on the other hand, saw them appreciate. This increase in the cost of living had created social unrest by the end of the war.

Peacetime Economies

Peacetime solved few of the region's crucial problems. First, markets in the United States shrunk. As in the aftermath of the First World War, Latin America suffered from the decline of U. S. purchases of primary products and the elimination of the cooperative mechanisms for funneling technical assistance and capital into Latin America. All wartime commodity agreements ended. Second, to make matters worse, the markets Latin Americans gained during the war in Latin America were lost. Cheaper European and U.S. products pushed out Latin American goods. Latin American nations were further disadvantaged because their governments did not devalue their currencies, making their exports more expensive abroad. Third, the United States, confronted by the threat of Soviet communism, turned its attention to rebuilding Europe. U.S. government resources were no longer available. Latin America was forced to rely on its insufficient private sector. Fourth, slow European recovery (until the advent of the Marshall Plan for European recovery in 1948) limited potential markets. The outbreak of the Korean War (1950–1954) sent prices up again, but only briefly.

Fifth, Latin American nations faced a dilemma as to how to spend their large foreign exchange reserves built up during the war before they were eroded by inflation. One option was to repay defaulted external debt. Argentina paid off its external debt by 1949. Argentina also nationalized foreign-owned properties, such as the railroad network, using foreign exchange reserves to pay for them. Mostly, however, Latin Americans disposed of the reserves by spending them. The spending spree set off a wave of inflation.

With limited resources available from abroad and dismal market opportunities, Latin America turned inward in the late 1940s. Most governments instituted tight restrictions on imports, both to end the spending spree and to protect domestic manufacturing. The export model looked unpromising because postwar depression in Europe erased traditional markets with no prospects for quick recovery. Moreover, European nations set up high tariffs to protect their domestic agriculture. Latin America shared minimally in the vast post-war expansion of international trade. In 1946, Latin America had 13.5 percent of the world's exports. By 1960, the region's share of exports had fallen to 7 percent.

The growing consensus among government officials and intellectuals was that Latin America could no longer rely on the export model. Some nations sought to diversify their exports, others adopted the policies of Import Substitution Industrialization, and another smaller group attempted both. These goals proved illusive. In the most advanced countries (Argentina, Brazil, Chile, Colombia, Mexico, and Uruguay), the easiest steps toward industrialization were already taken. The next stage was to be far more demanding in terms of capital and technology. Domestic enterprise was unable or unwilling to risk capital. This left the field open to either multinational corporations (which were eager to enter protected markets) or state-owned companies.Unfortunately, the ISI strategy for development had crucial flaws. Domestic manufacturers were hard pressed to compete. They were so highly protected by tariffs that they were extremely inefficient. To make matters worse, the small size of domestic markets meant there were no economies of scale. Often, domestic manufacturers operated at less than full capacity. They could not compete outside their home countries. Moreover, industrialization was itself import-intensive; it needed capital goods available only from abroad. Foreign exchange paid for technology, royalties, licenses, and profits, creating a further drain of scarce capital. With the exceptions of Brazil and Mexico, the 1950s were a time of economic stagnation in the region. Meanwhile, the developed nations were on the path to unprecedented prosperity, leaving Latin America behind.

Dictators and Populists

The Social Question remained preeminent in Latin American politics throughout the years of world wars and economic crises. The constant conflict and negotiation between the upper, middle, and lower classes (at least the organized elements) and between genders framed political parameters. The region alternated limited democracy and dictatorship, for the most part, but not always, in correlation with booms and busts of the world market. Good times allowed democracy to function. Bad times brought increased conflict between classes and the imposition of coercive governments by the upper class allied with the military. Of course, each Latin American nation had its own political culture. Not every society reacted the same way in every instance to good and bad times.

The 1920s brought a wave of popularly elected leaders prepared to make concessions to the new aspiring classes and the changing circumstances of women. Hipólito Yrigoyen, the head of the Radical Party in Argentina, and Arturo Alessandri in Chile both eventually fell victim to military coups. Augusto B. Leguía in Peru and Gerardo Machado in Cuba transformed themselves from populist leaders into dictators, when economic depression eroded their support.

The 1920s and 1930s were troubling times for the traditional social order. The upper and, to some extent, the middle classes feared their societies were coming apart. The challenges from below grew. Perhaps the greatest uncertainties evolved from the transformation of women's roles. Women worked in visible urban settings in factories and offices. They organized and staged strikes. The new "free" woman—sexually active, cigarette smoking—was not always the pliant, passive mother of old. As in the case of working- and middle-class aspirants, however, feminists found it difficult to obtain their goals in the face of resistance from the male hierarchy. Their major goal, equality in law, was not forthcoming until the 1930s, and suffrage took even longer.

Women's organizations received assistance from liberal and populist political parties. A handful of liberals viewed changing laws to reflect women's new roles to be part of the modernization process crucial to development. Women were active participants in the multifaceted campaigns for social reform all over the region. They sought not only their vote, but also better working, sanitary, and health conditions for everyone. As Latin American governments haltingly involved themselves in public welfare, women made these activities their own as social workers and teachers.

In both Argentina and Peru, the upper classes, through populist leaders Yrigoyen and Leguía, shared power with the middle class. As long as the export economy stayed strong and the national government did not attempt far-reaching reforms, the tension-filled alliance held. The Depression of the 1930s, however, put the upper and middle classes into competition for scarce, shrinking resources. Ultimately, the upper classes used coercion to maintain their status. In Chile, politicians could not reach consensus. As a result, the younger elements of the military twice intervened to force concessions to the middle and lower classes.

Modern women in Brazil.

The 1920s

In Argentina, the Radical Party alliance between the middle class and elements of the landowning upper class dominated politics during the 1920s. Heavily reliant on government patronage to bolster their support, the Radicals required prosperity to generate the revenues to pay for their strategy. Marcelo T. Alvear (1922–1928), one of the country's richest landowners, succeeded Yrigoyen as president in 1922. The Radicals in 1926 enacted the law of women's civil rights, which provided that women had all the rights of men, thereby removing gender limits to the exercise of all civil functions (but not the vote). Despite the Radicals' split into pro- and anti-Yrigoyen factions, Yrigoyen reestablished his base among the middle class and recaptured the presidency in 1928. The economic downturn that began in 1928, however, sharply curtailed the ability of the Radicals to provide patronage employment for their followers. The military, which had long opposed Yrigoyen, impatiently overthrew him in September of 1930.

Yrigoyen's case clearly illustrates two aspects of Latin American politics of the era. First, populist politics succeeded only when government revenues were sufficient to fund patronage. Second, the precarious alliance between the upper

> **How Historians Understand** | Reconstructing the *Semana Trágica* (Tragic Week) in Argentine History

CLASS CONFLICT, AS WE have seen in Chapters 11 and 12, was always just beneath the surface in Latin America. And as we will see in Chapter 14, the political outcomes of these confrontations depended to a considerable extent on the middle class. When the demands of the lower classes threatened the middle class (nearly always), its members sided with the upper class–military alliance against workers and country people. One of the first instances of the middle class behaving thusly was during the red scares after World War I. The Semana Trágica was tragic because the middle class panicked believing the government had lost control over the lower classes. But class conflict was not the only factor in the tragedy, for it brought together the festering prejudices Argentines felt for the vast wave of new European immigrants that had poured into their country over the preceding half century. In particular, it displayed Argentine anti-Semitism, for much of the violence Argentines committed was against the Jewish community. Perhaps easily dismissed at first by historians as an abhorrent event, the intensifying activities of the Argentine Right and its accompanying anti-Semitism over the course of the twentieth century has led to some reevaluation of this initial assessment.

The week began as a strike in a metallurgical factory in Buenos Aires, which evolved into a general strike in December of 1918 and January of 1919. The strike led to violent reprisals from the upper classes. The national government sent police and the army against the strikers. In mid-January, the government brokered an agreement that ended the conflict. The disturbance clearly frightened the urban middle and upper classes, who believed the government had "lost control" of the situation and allowed a communist conspiracy to run amok. Many blamed Jews for the troubles because they identified Jews with the Left. Most Jewish immigrants in Buenos Aires had come from Russia, where a revolution had recently (1917) taken place.

Amid the tensions of those days, rumors flew about plots from abroad. Some vigilantes formed militias to protect their neighborhoods from the workers. Other groups took to the streets from January 10 through 14. Allied with the police, they attacked Jewish neighborhoods, arresting people and destroying property. The Argentine Navy played a crucial role in encouraging, arming, and leading the vigilante groups.

In light of the universality of the anti-Left riots of the post-World War I era (the Palmer Raids in the United States, for example), historians paid little attention to the anti-Semitic aspect of the event. Later, Argentina, like most of the world, closed its doors to Jews fleeing Nazi Germany during the 1930s. Again, because the situation was commonplace, no historian remarked. Many commented on the military rightist regime's affinity for

Germany during World War II; Argentina had steadfastly refused to declare war against the Axis powers until the last day of the conflict.

Anti-Semitism reappeared publicly during the dire crisis of the 1960s and 1970s. The military governments (1966–1973 and 1976–1983) fired Jews from positions of prominence. In the early 1970s, rightist paramilitary groups killed Jews suspected of Left sympathies. When the army instigated the "Dirty War," Jews bore the brunt disproportionately. The harrowing story of newspaper publisher Jacobo Timerman's imprisonment and torture was, perhaps, the least daunting, for many Jewish young people filled the rolls of the disappeared ones.

Questions for Discussion

Given the propensity of Argentines, particularly of the Right, toward anti-Semitism in times of domestic strife, should historians look for patterns within society? Are these acts, some decades apart, indicative of wider aspects of Argentina's history that historians should explore? Why did the Argentine middle class turn on the lower classes in the period after World War I? Why do people in crisis look for scapegoats? Why were Jews convenient scapegoats in 1919 Argentina?

and middle classes disintegrated rapidly when the two groups had to compete for scarce resources or when their interests clashed. Their ties, forged from their mutual fear of the lower classes, proved unstable. When there was conflict, the side with the strongest links to the armed services, most often the upper classes, won out.

As had the Radicals in Argentina, Peruvian politicians sought to find answers to the Social Question by appealing to the middle class and by adopting a vast program of public patronage. In Peru, former president Augusto B. Leguía (1908–1912, 1919–1930) returned from exile in 1919 to topple the old order (the "Aristocratic Republic"). With strong backing from middle- and lower-class voters, he proclaimed *La Patria Nueva* (the new fatherland). He proposed a stronger interventionist state, which would modernize and grow the economy, financed by foreign investment and increased exports. Leguía undertook a far-reaching reform of all aspects of government operations. The center of his administration was a massive program of public works. He rebuilt Lima into a beautiful modern city and constructed nearly 10,000 miles of roads. Leguía's plan, with the help of a large inflow of U.S. investments and expansion of the U.S. market for Peruvian products, was successful until 1930, when the Depression sharply limited the funds available.

Leguía focused on the middle class and country people as his bases of support. To appeal to the former, he vastly expanded the government bureaucracy and the educational system, quadrupling the number of public employees and doubling the number of students. Leguía took advantage of growing unrest in the Indian countryside, where indigenous peoples and landlords were at bitter odds. The president regarded the landlords as impediments to his drive to centralize power. As we will see in the case of the Mexican revolutionary government in the 1920s and 1930s, Leguía tried to insinuate the government as intermediary between landlord and landless. But this effort to woo country people foundered when Leguía realized the extent to which the farmers had organized independently and the degree to which they were militant in their demands. The end of his efforts to forge an alliance with country people came when the army and local authorities killed two thousand small farmers and landless residents in two uprisings in 1923.

Like Yrigoyen and so many after him, Leguía learned that populism was only as successful as its economic program. Because of the Depression, after 1928 the flow of funds from the United States halted. He had to slash government expenditures in 1929 and 1930. Leguía could not survive the crisis of the Depression. On August 25, 1930, Colonel Luis M. Sánchez Cerro led a military coup. A cheering crowd of one hundred thousand greeted him in Lima. With the support of the poorest classes, Sánchez Cerro won the presidential election in 1931.

The Chilean upper classes steadfastly refused concessions to the middle and lower classes. As a result, Chile's Parliamentary Republic (1891–1920) simply did not work. Social unrest escalated as the government was unable to ameliorate the economic crisis and hardship brought on by the First World War. Strikes tore apart the northern nitrate region. Out of the turmoil of the late 1910s rose veteran politician Arturo Alessandri Palma. Drawing support from the working class, promising sweeping reforms, and professing an interest in women's issues, Alessandri won the presidential election of 1920 by a razor-thin margin. For four years, however, Alessandri was unable to overcome congressional opposition to his program. Impatient junior officers, led by Major Carlos Ibáñez del Campo and Major Marmaduke Grove Vallejo, seized the government. Their administration decreed a law in 1925 that extended the property rights of married women. A new constitution in 1925 restored strong presidential rule (lost in the 1890 civil war). Alessandri returned to complete his term, only to resign months later. Ibáñez took office as president in 1927 and quickly moved to curtail civil rights. Until 1930, his foreign loan-financed spending spree brought a measure of prosperity. The world Depression, however, was especially harsh in Chile, which was heavily dependent on mining exports. Massive street demonstrations forced Ibáñez to resign in mid-1931.

In Cuba as well, populism evolved into dictatorship in response to the Depression. The terrible collapse of sugar prices in 1920 after the spectacular post-war boom devastated the Cuban rural middle class (known as *colonos*). New president Alfredo Zayas (1920–1924) carried on the two-decade-old tradition of ineffective, corrupt government. The middle class and workers organized to protest the rampant corruption and the insidious influence of the United States, which by virtue of the Platt Amendment to the Cuban Constitution of 1902, acted as the island's protector. Appealing to these sentiments, veteran politician Gerardo Machado won the 1925 presidential election. Despite his increasingly brutal methods, a relatively prosperous sugar economy and an enormous public works program financed by extensive foreign loans, which employed thousands, enabled him to maintain his regime. Cuban women were especially active during the 1920s in support of democracy and equality. In 1928, Cuban women's organizations hosted a hemispheric conference that proposed an equal rights treaty to the region's leaders. In 1929, sugar and tobacco prices crashed and the ensuing crisis wore away at Machado's popularity. He lasted until August 1933, when a coalition of students and military officers forced him out.

In Argentina, Peru, Chile, and Cuba, leaders with reform programs had emerged, supported by the urban middle and working classes. Yrigoyen, Leguía, Ibáñez, and Machado encountered difficulties when economic depression limited their ability to provide employment in government and build public works projects. All turned to coercion. Each of these leaders lost the confidence of the middle and working classes and was toppled by the military.

Mexico differed from the other cases because the middle class, allied with workers and country people, had won the Revolution and controlled the national government. The new ruling group, comprised of middle-class northerners (from the state of Sonora in particular) did not share power with the upper classes because civil war had ruined much of the pre-Revolution upper class. The main problems facing the revolutionary regime were rebuilding the economy, satisfying the demands of the victorious revolutionaries, and unifying an army fragmented by regional and personal loyalties. From 1920 until the mid-1930s, Mexicans struggled to reach a balance between reconstructing their nation's economy after a decade of destructive civil war and satisfying the various revolutionary factions. Middle-class demands for equal and fair access to education, employment, and economic opportunities were, perhaps, the easiest to meet. They sought, in particular, the expansion of government to provide them jobs. The needs of rural dwellers and urban workers, however, encountered more resistance because they threatened private property rights, of which their middle-class allies were the firmest advocates. Landless villagers had fought in the Revolution to regain the lands stolen from them and their ancestors by hacendados. The Constitution of 1917 guaranteed the return of these lands. Nonetheless, the revolutionary government redistributed land only when necessary politically because the leaders of the revolutionary government feared land reform might undermine private property rights and would decrease agricultural production and thereby impede economic recovery from the civil war. Moreover, during the 1920s a new landowning class, many of them ex-revolutionary military officers, emerged to oppose the implementation of land reforms. The revolutionary regime was willing to allow industrial labor to organize as long as the unions affiliated with the Regional Confederation of Mexican Workers (CROM), whose leader, Luis Morones, was a close ally. Presidents Álvaro Obregón (1920–1924) and Plutarco Elías Calles (1924–1928) balanced reconstruction and reform and survived a series of major rebellions that shook the Revolution to its core. Obregón won reelection in 1928, but an assassin's bullet killed him before he took office. Calles ruled from behind the scenes, as three puppet presidents filled out the six-year term until 1934. He solved the problem of the fragmented army, when he founded (1929) and built a new political party, the National Party of the Revolution (PNR), which brought together the disparate factions and wayward generals.

Brazil had the weakest middle and lower classes in Latin America in terms of political strength in 1920. Nonetheless, the old order fell apart when it experienced the Depression of the 1930s. The First World War had spawned only mild, brief strikes. However, the power-sharing arrangement between the upper classes of the largest states gradually broke down during the course of the succeeding decade. When the upper classes of São Paulo (the other participants were the states of Rio de Janeiro and Minas Gerais) refused to alternate out of the presidency in 1930, it set off a rebellion. Plummeting coffee prices added to the crisis. An unequal coalition of dissident regional upper class, disgruntled mid-rank army officers, and disparate urban middle class revolted to overthrow the Old Republic. Out of the uprising, Getúlio Vargas, governor of Rio Grande do Sul and the defeated presidential candidate of 1930, emerged to rule Brazil for the next 15 years.

Depression and War

To meet the crisis of the Depression of the 1930s, most of Latin America turned away from democracy to military dictatorship or civilian dictatorship with strong military support. The major exception was Mexico, which instead constructed a one-party regime. A number of important experiments took place, such as the *Concordancia* in Argentina, the Socialist Republic in Chile, the *Estado Novo* in Brazil, and the revolutionary administration of Lázaro Cárdenas in Mexico. Almost all were short-lived. Although each aimed to end conflict between classes, only Cárdenas's reforms brought social peace.

Leftist ideologies, such as socialism and communism, often flourished as intellectual exercises, particularly among university students, but they were no match for upper-class and military opposition. More eclectic, though at times offering relatively radical programs, leftist political parties, like the American Popular Revolutionary Alliance (APRA) in Peru and the National Revolutionary Movement (MNR) in Bolivia, proved more enduring and influential. In the short term, local variations of rightist ideologies, most importantly corporatism and fascism, had greater impact, but quickly receded.

LATIN AMERICAN LIVES

Elvia and Felipe Carrillo Puerto

ELVIA (1876–1967) and her brother Felipe Carrillo Puerto (1874–1924) were respectively among the foremost feminist and radical leaders of the post-revolutionary era in Mexico. Elvia once said that "I want...women to enjoy the same liberties as men...to detach themselves from all the material, sensual, and animal, to lift up their spirituality and thinking to the ideal...to have a more dignified and happier life in an environment of sexual liberty and fraternity." As governor, Felipe carried out in Yucatán the most extensive redistribution of land outside of Morelos. Together in their brief time in power, they created the most progressive state government in post-revolutionary Mexico in terms of women's rights.

Elvia and Felipe Carrillo Puerto were two of fourteen children born in the heart of the *henequen* region. (Henequen was used to make twine.) Their father was a small merchant. Both lived and worked during their formative years among the poor Maya of the region, learning their language, customs, and traditions.

Elvia Carrillo Puerto was a feminist, activist, politician, administrator, and teacher in Yucatán and Mexico City for much of the twentieth century. She was a controversial figure in Yucatán as the sister of Felipe, and her activities defined Yucatecan feminism during the 1920s. Married at 13 and widowed at 21, she scandalized Yucatán's traditional society by living with men to whom she was not married as well as marrying three times. When her brother was killed during a rebellion in 1924, she had to flee the state and returned only once in the next forty years.

Elvia worked as a rural schoolteacher to support herself and her son after her first husband died. She saw at close hand the horrors of poverty and malnutrition in the countryside. She was well read (Marx, Lenin, and others), especially for a woman of her status and time. She joined the movement against the dictator Porfirio Díaz in 1909 and kept up her work as a teacher and organizer through 1915. In 1912, she organized the state's first feminist league. In the late 1910s, she moved to Mexico City, for a short time sharing a house (1921–1922) with her brother, who was then a deputy in the federal congress. She married again, divorcing in the early 1920s and remarrying in 1923. In 1921, Elvia was the first woman elected to a seat in the state congress of Yucatán. After her exile from Yucatán, Elvia held a series of administrative posts in the capital. She continued to organize feminists, founding a succession of important feminist groups.

Felipe, as the radical governor of the state of Yucatán (1922–1923), led one of the failed "Laboratories of the Revolution" during the 1920s. He was killed in a brief rebellion that failed nationally but succeeded in Yucatán in

(continued on next page)

> **ELVIA AND FELIPE CARRILLO PUERTO** *(continued from previous page)*
>
> 1924. As a youth, Felipe was a small landholder, mule driver, trader, and railroad conductor. During the 1910s, he spent time with the agrarian movement of Emiliano Zapata in Morelos before attaching himself to General Salvador Alvarado, the socialist governor of Yucatán. Felipe took over the Socialist Party of the Southwest, the governing political party of Yucatán, when Alvarado left the state in 1918. Felipe tried to get the people involved in politics. He was also a proponent of Mayan culture and history. Carrillo Puerto, however, was too radical for the so-called "Sonoran Dynasty" made up of presidents Álvaro Obregón and Plutarco Elías Calles. They readily abandoned him during the revolt by army officers, led by Adolfo de la Huerta, in 1923.
>
> The siblings Carrillo Puerto symbolized the unfulfilled promise of the Mexican Revolution at its turning point during the 1920s. A series of local and state radical initiatives all fell victim to the harsh practicalities of rebuilding a war-ravaged nation and the hard-eyed greed of the victorious generals. Elvia, who lived four decades longer, however, never seemed to have given up her dreams of women's equality.
>
> **Questions for Discussion**
> In some ways, the careers of the Carrillo Puerto family were microcosms of the failures of both the Mexican Revolution and Mexican feminism. Why did both fail? Or do you think that one or the other did not fail? Do you think that the Carrillo Puertos had the same goals as their constituents in the latter's battle for control over their everyday lives?

Argentina began the decade of depression with the hard-liners among the upper class in control, but they eventually gave way to compromise. General José F. Uriburu, who led the rightist, nationalist, minority faction of the coup against the Radicals, became president of Argentina in 1930. His group repudiated compromise with the lower classes and favored an all-powerful state. General Agustín P. Justo led the dominant faction, which sought only to rid the nation of the corrupt Yrigoyen regime. Justo became president in 1932, putting together a coalition (known as the Concordancia) comprised of old-line conservatives, Independent Socialists (primarily from Buenos Aires), and, most importantly, anti-Yrigoyen Radicals. The new conservative alliance confronted the Depression by balancing the budget, paying the foreign debt, encouraging exports, and discouraging imports. The Justo administration introduced Argentina's first income tax, which substantially cut the government's reliance on trade taxes for revenues, and established a central bank, which gave the government unprecedented influence on the management of the economy. The Depression did not hit Argentina as hard other Latin American nations and, as a result, the upper-class regime was relatively benign. The moderate Concordancia continued to govern when Roberto M. Ortiz took over as president in 1938.

In Chile during the 1930s, the upper classes made concessions to urban workers and women, but were unwilling to accommodate demands for land reform in the countryside. For a year and a half after the fall of Carlos Ibáñez, Chileans stumbled from one government to another. One of these was the Socialist Republic, led by Marmaduke Grove, which lasted for 100 days in 1932. Former president Arturo Alessandri won a new term in the election of 1932. By 1935, Chile had recovered from the economic crisis and this allowed him to make overtures to the lower classes. He permitted extensive labor union organization and instituted a very effective process of mediating employer–employee disputes. A law in 1934 expanded women's freedoms and property rights, though men still maintained legal authority in the family. Alessandri was less generous in the countryside. His police massacred one hundred country people in 1934, when they protested their treatment at the hands of landowners. The candidate of a coalition of center and Left parties, known as the Popular Front (an alliance of parties of the center and Left), Pedro Aguirre Cerda, captured the presidency in 1938. His administration initiated government involvement in economic development with establishment of the National Development Corporation (CORFO). Aguirre Cerda also cracked down hard on rural mobilization, sacrificing the oppressed rural population, in order to obtain support from landowners for his economic program.

Social ferment and economic crisis led Brazil to dictatorship. Like the post-Revolution Mexican government during the same period, Getúlio Vargas (1930–1945) obtained the support of selected sectors of the middle and lower classes. White-collar and industrial workers formed the base of his support. However, he was never able to create a wide political consensus, instead ruling by decree. Vargas's appeal to the masses was more show than substance. He incorporated unions into his system, but benefits, such as higher wages and other improvements, came at the expense of labor union autonomy. Three years after winning election as president by vote of a constituent assembly (1934), Vargas, in order to prevent new elections, engineered a coup against his own government, establishing the *Estado Novo* (New State) in 1937. Vargas no longer made even a pretense of popular support. Brazil had proceeded from a coup that overthrew an elected government to an elected government and finally to a dictatorship, all under Vargas's rule.

In Peru, various forms of populism failed because the military remained steadfastly opposed. Sánchez Cerro represented the same middle class that had formed the core of Leguía's following. He, like Leguía, extended his mass support by abolishing conscription, instituting secular marriage and divorce, and distributing food to hungry people. Despite his populist notions, he relied on the upper classes for his administration. His "Conservative Populism" promised to restore the old social and economic structure, but at the same time offered the lower classes land reform, social security, and equal rights for Indians. After a bitter election campaign in 1931 against APRA's Victor Raúl Haya de la Torre, Sánchez Cerro lasted through 16 terrible months of civil war and economic crisis until assassins murdered him. General Oscar Benavides (1933–1939), who had been provisional president earlier (1914–1915), took over. Despite issuing a general amnesty, he engaged in a continuing struggle with Haya's followers in APRA. Peru recovered more quickly than other nations in the region from the downturn, as exports surged beginning in 1933. Benavides cancelled the 1936 elections when he was apparently losing and ruled as dictator for the next three years. Modest conservatives with inclinations toward expanding slightly the role of government served as presidents from 1939 to 1948. Like Brazil, Peru experienced short periods of stability, but the Social Question remained unanswered.

Mexico experienced the most far-reaching reforms and consequently the longest era without upheaval. The Mexican Revolution in 1934 had seemingly reneged on its promises (set forth in detail in the Constitution of 1917). Seventeen years after its victory, however, the new president, Lázaro Cárdenas, implemented long-awaited reforms. His major accomplishment was to redistribute 49 million acres of land to 15 million Mexicans, one-third the population. As we discussed in Chapter 11, rural Mexicans had fought the Revolution for land. Cárdenas fulfilled the promises first uttered by revolutionary leader Emiliano Zapata to return these lands to the lower class. As a result, the president bestowed an aura of legitimacy on the post-Revolution regime that lasted another half-century. During the Cárdenas administration, the average wages of urban workers more than doubled. The president undertook major efforts in public health and education. In 1938, Cárdenas expropriated the foreign-owned petroleum companies operating in the country, when they refused to obey a Supreme Court order to increase the wages of their employees. He also reorganized the official party in 1938, transforming it from a loose alliance between revolutionary generals, regional bosses, and labor leaders into an organization responsive to four major sectors: labor unions, rural organizations, the military, and government bureaucrats (middle class). Cárdenas did not, however, fulfill his promise to amend the Constitution to insure equal rights for women. Reform reached its acme in 1937. The government avoided bankruptcy only because the United States bailed it out with huge purchases of silver and gold. Land redistribution had disrupted food production, worsening conditions for the lower classes. Cárdenas had gone as far as he could, for there was enormous opposition among the post-Revolution upper class to any further radical policies and the nation did not have sufficient resources to carry out further reform.

Manuel Ávila Camacho (1940–1946), a member of a family that controlled the state of Puebla, and Miguel Alemán Valdés (1946–1952) succeeded Cárdenas as president. They led a sharp turn to the center and a shift to policies to produce economic growth. The rhetoric of revolution, nonetheless, continued. Alemán and Adolfo Ruiz Cortines (1952–1958) presided over the second great Mexican economic miracle (the first occurred under Porfirio Díaz). Mexico flourished as the official party consolidated its support among the middle class by providing large numbers of jobs in the government bureaucracy and government-operated businesses and free education at the fast-expanding National University (UNAM).

Only in Mexico was the ruling group substantively responsive to the demands of the middle and working classes. Country people and the urban middle class obtained the land and opportunities for which they had fought so long and hard. As a result, Mexico prospered until the 1960s and maintained unparallel political stability.

Cubans rose up in popular rebellion against Gerardo Machado in 1933. The victorious revolutionaries, comprised of a coalition of university students, noncommissioned military officers (sergeants, corporals), and political opponents of Machado, encountered strong disapproval from the United States government. Sergeant-stenographer Fulgencio Batista emerged from the plotting and violence as the power behind the scenes. Batista used similar methods as other populist leaders of the era, appealing to the working class from which he had come. He won election as president in 1940 and led the island through the Second World War. He retired peacefully and went to Florida in 1944. Cuba, like Mexico, had achieved a measure of stability through concessions by a government run by the middle class (with a few leaders from the lower classes as well) to the needs of the middle and working classes.

Argentina became the setting for the most notorious populist regime in Latin America during the twentieth century. Political crisis accompanied the cutoff of European markets for Argentine grain during World War II, when severe illness forced president Roberto Ortiz (1938–1942) to turn over his office to his archconservative vice president Ramón S. Castillo (1942–1943), who alienated the moderates in the Concordancia and was eventually overthrown by the military in June of 1943. As it had in 1930, the officer corps divided into moderates and hard-liners. The latter, known as the United Officers' Group (GOU) consisted of nationalists who opposed entering the war on the side of the Allies. A succession of three generals failed to establish stable government, but eventually, the charismatic Colonel Juan Domingo Perón emerged.

Perón and his wife, Eva (Evita) Duarte de Perón, towered over post-war Argentina. Perón, though the military ousted him in 1955, was a major influence until he died in 1974. Peronism was the most important example of the alliance between a dictator and the lower classes. He built a base of support among organized labor, known as the shirtless ones (*descamisados*) in 1943 and 1944. The unions received his backing as long as they remained loyal to him. Perón became vice president of Argentina in 1944. Military hard-liners pushed him out of the government in 1945, but a massive demonstration by workers in October of 1945 rescued him. Perón won the presidential election in 1946. Unlike Yrigoyen and Leguía, both of whom drew support from the middle sectors, Perón's politics was based on the urban working class with strategic allies among conservative bosses in the provinces.

Perón repaid the working class for its support, greatly improving working conditions and benefits. Real wages rose by 20 percent between 1945 and 1948. The president led the way toward massive government involvement in business enterprise with the establishment of a state agency for marketing all of the nation's agricultural exports and another that administered industries confiscated from German citizens during the war. His government also operated shipbuilding and steel firms. He nationalized the railroads and telephone service. After 1950, however, post-war prosperity ended. Stagnation and inflation tormented the economy. Real wages fell 20 percent between 1948 and 1952. Like the other populists, Peron found that he was unable to pay for his program in times of downturn and lost support. He shifted his strategy away from popular appeal to repression. The middle and upper classes grew bitter in their opposition. Nonetheless, he maintained his hold on the masses, winning an overwhelming reelection in 1951. The economy stagnated, inflation rose, his regime grew increasingly harsh, leading to the military overthrowing him in 1955.

One unique aspect of Perón's rule was the crucial role played by his wife Eva Duarte de Perón, a former actress. Evita, as she was known, exerted enormous influence through her Eva Perón Foundation, which funded medical services and provided food and clothes for the needy. She was Perón's connection to the lower classes. She was one of them. Unfortunately for Juan Perón, Evita died in 1952.

Peacetime Politics

The first major revolutionary movements to arise from the ashes of World War II took place in Guatemala in 1945, when a group of young, reformist military officers overthrew the long-running dictatorship of Jorge Ubico (1930–1945), and in 1951 in Bolivia, when a coalition of country people, miners, and the middle class, under the banner of the National Revolutionary Movement (MNR), toppled the conservative government backed by landowners, industrialists, and the military. The Bolivian Revolution implemented widespread land reform, destroying the traditional landowning class, nationalized the tin mines, the producers of the nation's major export, enfranchised all males and females, and virtually eliminated the military.

More common was a profound shift to the Right, as the upper class–military alliance, in the midst of the international Cold War between the communist Soviet Union and the capitalist United States, struck hard against the threat of communism in Latin America. Anti-Left dictators arose in Chile, Colombia, Cuba, and Venezuela in the early 1950s.

After a number of years under the rule of Left and Left-center coalitions, in 1948 Chile turned to the Right with the enactment of the Law for the Permanent Defense of Democracy, which forbade the Communist Party from political participation. Chileans seemed fed up with the politics that had led to inflation and foreign domination of the nation's major industries. Former dictator Carlos Ibáñez took advantage of widespread discontent to bring together an odd coalition of Socialists, feminists, the middle class, and deserters from the parties to win the election of 1952. Unable to build consensus, he repeated his earlier policies of repression, especially against labor unions. His major innovation was to vastly intensify and broaden government involvement in the economy, establishing a central bank and also state enterprises in major industries such as sugar, steel, and petroleum. Colombians looked to Conservative General Gustavo Rojas Pinilla, as dictator of Colombia, who tried to bring peace to a nation wracked by civil war. He lowered the level of violence for perhaps two years, but he could not survive through an economic downturn. Fulgencio Batista returned to rule Cuba in 1952, overthrowing a corrupt, democratically elected regime, and presided over a measure of prosperity on the island until the late 1950s. Batista, like Ibáñez and Rojas Pinilla, used harsh repression to govern instead of his earlier appeal to the masses. A young lawyer, Fidel Castro, led a rebel band in the mountains of southeastern Cuba, which gradually attracted support and allies among the middle class and workers in the cities to defeat Batista's army in late 1958. Reformers alternated with dictators in Venezuela. A group of officers, calling themselves the Patriotic Military Union, overthrew the president of Venezuela in 1945, but the Democratic Action Party (AD), led by Rómulo Betancourt, outmaneuvered the officers and installed a civilian government. Three years later, Marcos Pérez Jiménez took the reins as dictator until 1958, when the military overthrew him and returned Venezuela to democracy. In Brazil, Getúlio Vargas joined Batista and Ibáñez as former presidents, once discredited, who returned to power. He won election as president in 1950 mainly because of the support given him by the working class of the big cities. Economic stagnation and inflation, however, badly eroded real wages and drastically undermined his base among workers. Amid a scandal over his role in the attempted assassination of a political rival, Vargas killed himself on August 23, 1954. Ironically, his death at his own hands prevented a military coup and paved the way for the continuation of civilian rule under Juscelino Kubitschek (1955–1960).

In each of these cases, neither populism nor coercion succeeded in establishing social peace. Reform was possible only in times of economic boom. Populism disintegrated during economic downturns. Efforts to win the support of the middle and lower classes through public patronage and concessions to labor unions required booming economies to pay for them. Coercion was unsustainable without some concessions to the middle and lower classes. The upper classes and military were willing to make only superficial accommodations. The basic unfairness and unjustness of Latin American society remained.

Failure of the Left and Right

The major populist experiments all failed in the long term. Their success, as we have seen in the cases of Yrigoyen's Radical Party and Perón's movement (known as *peronismo* or *justicialismo*) were tied closely to the fortunes of their nation's export economy and the unbending opposition of the hard-line elements of the military and upper classes.

Perhaps the most auspicious failure of populism in Latin America was APRA in Peru. Victor Raúl Haya de la Torre founded APRA in 1924 in Mexico as an international organization of students. When he returned to Peru in the late 1920s to run for president, Haya de la Torre gained support among labor unions and the middle class. APRA's program consisted of opposition to U.S. imperialism, unification of Latin America, internationalization of the Panama Canal, nationalization of land and industry, and solidarity for oppressed peoples. Although its leadership was middle class, the party extolled the Indian past and sought to adapt the majority of Peruvians who were Indians into modern life. Haya refused to join the international communist movement and in 1928 split with the Peruvian communist party and its leader, José Carlos Mariátegui. Haya believed that with its tiny industrial working class, socialism was not possible in Peru. He saw instead the middle class leading a cross-class alliance. With the upper classes and military adamantly opposed to Haya, he was never to gain the presidency, though APRA was often an influential force in Peruvian politics. After losing in the election in 1931, Haya led a revolt, during which the APRA executed a number of military officers. In retaliation, the victorious upper class–military alliance outlawed the party in 1932. Nonetheless, APRA played a major role in the regime of Manuel Prado (1939–1945). Haya moved APRA to the center during the 1940s, ending its plotting and eliminating its anti-imperialist rhetoric to the point of exhibiting a favorable attitude toward the United States. In 1945, Haya and APRA returned to their old strategy and planned a revolt. At the last minute, however, Haya struck a deal with Prado to withdraw his support from the revolt in return for legalizing the party. The dictatorship of Manuel Odría (1948–1956) again outlawed the APRA and forced Haya to flee to the Colombian embassy in Lima, where he resided until 1954. APRA would make a comeback in the 1960s, but for its first four decades it made little headway against the entrenched upper classes.

The most successful and extensive reforms took place in Bolivia. Bolivia's MNR sought to create a strong centralized state with middle-class leadership of

Symbol of the First Congress of the Pro-Emancipation Movement of Chilean Women.

a cross-class alliance. Formed in 1940, it was heavily influenced by the nationalistic elements of European fascism. In 1943, the MNR helped Major Gualberto Villaroel overthrow a conservative military government. Villarroel in turn fell in 1946 without accomplishing much reform. Conservative governments followed until 1951, when the MNR, which adopted a much more radical program, won the presidential election with Victor Paz Estenssoro. After the military intervened to prevent Paz's victory, the MNR rose in rebellion in 1952 allied with organized labor. The MNR carried out extensive land reform, nationalized the tin mines, which produced the nation's most important export, and enacted universal suffrage without literacy requirements. For the first time in centuries, the Indian population had access to land and politics. After the initial radical transformations, the MNR shifted to the center, partly because in the throes of the Cold War the United States exerted enormous influence. The party balanced the rival interests of small landowners, who had become conservative when they received land, and tin miners, who sought a more radical program. The MNR maintained its power until overthrown by the military in 1964.

The APRA failed in Peru and the MNR succeeded in Bolivia because the APRA alienated the military, which remained inalterably opposed, while the MNR defeated the Bolivian military. As importantly, the MNR, unlike the APRA, enjoyed a cross-class alliance between the middle and urban and rural lower classes.

Women's Suffrage

Industrialization and urbanization transformed the place of women in society. As we have seen, women always worked and were often single heads of households in the nineteenth century. At times, they were crucial participants in politics, as in the military aspect of the Mexican Revolution from 1910 to 1920. The upper-class men who controlled government had to find a satisfactory way to recognize the realities of these transformations. This also required a reassessment of such concepts as public and private space, honor, and gender (see Chapter 13).

Latin American feminists of this era (the first wave of feminism) were comfortable in defining themselves as mothers and wives, emphasizing their childbearing and nurturing. They did not seek to gain equality with men but rather to eliminate laws and conditions that impeded their roles as women. They also used their status as mothers and teachers to further their argument for their participation in the public sphere. Feminists' early successes were in revising civil codes to eliminate the legal inequality of married women and in bringing to light important social welfare issues. Because in many Latin American nations elections were meaningless, suffrage was not a crucial issue until the 1920s. Furthermore, not all feminists agreed on the value of women participating in the corrupt male world of politics. In fact, some doubters believed that the female vote would be overwhelmingly conservative and thus impede their program. Women obtained suffrage in only four Latin American nations prior to World War II (see Table 12.1).

Table 12.1

Women's Enfranchisement

Nation	Year	Nation	Year
Ecuador	1929	Argentina	1947
Brazil	1932	Chile	1949
Uruguay	1932	Bolivia	1952
Cuba	1934	Mexico	1952
El Salvador	1939	Honduras	1955
Dominican Republic	1942	Nicaragua	1955
Panama	1945	Peru	1955
Guatemala	1945	Colombia	1957
Costa Rica	1945	Paraguay	1961
Venezuela	1947		

Conclusion

Import substitution economics and populist politics dominated the era from 1920 to 1959. Latin American ruling classes sought to industrialize and modernize their nations, while maintaining the political status quo. The urban middle and working classes simultaneously looked to better their living and working conditions and to have a meaningful say in government. In the countryside, small property owners and landless workers wanted either to maintain what they had or acquire lands previously stolen from their ancestors by the greedy upper class and to defend their control over their local traditions and values.

Import substitution, which protected Latin American manufacturing from foreign competition, did not succeed, despite two world wars and the Depression. Most Latin Americans were too poor to constitute extensive enough markets that would enable domestic industries to obtain economies of scale. The capital required for industrialization had only three possible sources: domestic private credit, domestic public funds, or foreign investment. Given the high risk involved with such enterprises, domestic private capital was unwilling to invest. Although Latin American banking had emerged by 1900, it had only a scattered impact on import substitution industrialization.

Foreign investment was unavailable through much of the period because of the world wars and economic crises. As a consequence, Latin American upper classes had to expand the role of government in economic enterprise. Both public and private capital, however, relied almost entirely on the export sector to generate revenues for investment. And as we have seen, the export sectors were subject to booms and busts and therefore unreliable.

Populism with its cross-class alliances had its moments when it seemed to be the answer to the Social Question. Charismatic leaders like Yrigoyen and

Perón who were willing to distribute patronage and other economic benefits to their loyal followers enabled years of social peace. The price was high: sham elections and loss of institutional independence for popular organizations. More importantly, populism, like ISI economic policies, was built on sand. It relied on booming exports to pay for the public works, expanded bureaucracy, and higher wages and benefits. When export booms ended, populism often deteriorated into oppressive dictatorship.

The struggles of ordinary Latin Americans remained much the same as they had since independence. The upper classes sought as always to maintain what they had—wealth and power. They were reluctant to share either. Those at the bottom of the economic scale fought to preserve their control over their everyday lives: to feed, clothe, and shelter their families, and to preserve that which was worth keeping of their local values and traditions.

The inability of Latin American economic policies and politics to lead to development and to answer the Social Question intensified societal tensions. When combined with the threatening specter of the Cold War struggle between communism and capitalism, these tensions would produce the conditions that in turn created two decades of tyranny and civil wars.

Learning More About Latin Americans

Bergquist, Charles. *Labor in Latin American History: Comparative Essays on Chile, Argentina, Venezuela, and Colombia* (Stanford, CA: Stanford University Press, 1986). Places workers at the center of Latin American politics.

Besse, Susan K. *Restructuring Patriarchy: The Modernization of Gender Inequality in Brazil, 1914–1940* (Chapel Hill, NC: University of North Carolina Press, 1996). Traces the changes in gender relations in the first half of the twentieth century.

Caulfield, Sueann. *In Defense of Honor: Sexual Morality, Modernity, and Nation in Early Twentieth Century Brazil* (Durham, NC: Duke University Press, 2000). Explores the role of public honor in gender relations.

Chant, Silvia, with Nikki Craske. *Gender in Latin America* (New Brunswick, NJ: Rutgers University Press, 2003). Excellent overview.

Craske, Nikki. *Women and Politics in Latin America* (New Brunswick, NJ: Rutgers University Press, 1999). Another insightful overview.

Dore, Elizabeth, ed. *Gender and Politics in Latin America: Debates in Theory and Practice* (New York: Monthly Review Press, 1997). Provocative essays.

Dore, Elizabeth, and Maxine Molyneux, eds. *Hidden Histories of Gender and the State in Latin America* (Durham, NC: Duke University Press, 2000). A collection of essays on the nineteenth and twentieth centuries.

Gwynne, Robert N., and Cristobal Kay, eds. *Latin America Transformed: Globalization and Modernity* (New York: Arnold, 1999). Examines changes from all angles.

Plate 9 Antonio López de Santa Anna dominated Mexican politics and military during the first half of the nineteenth century.

Plate 10   C. Penuti and Alejandro Bernhein. *La Batalla de Monte Caseros*. The Battle of Monte Caseros in 1852 marked the defeat of long-time dictator Juan Manuel de Rosas.

Plate 11 Juan Perón, the populist president of Argentina (1946–55 and 1973–74), and his wife, Eva Duarte "Evita" de Perón.

Plate 12 David Alfaro Siqueiros, *Por una Seguridad Completa para todos los Mexicanos (detalle), 1952–1954 (For the Complete Safety of all Mexicans at Work, detail of Injured Worker)*. Siqueiros was one of the three great Mexican muralists who focused their art on working people.

Plate 13 Frida Kahlo, *Las Dos Fridas* (*The Two Fridas*) (1939). Kahlo was one of the greatest Latin American painters of the twentieth century.

Plate 14 Favela dwellings were built board by board and brick by brick by resourceful Brazilians.

Plate 15 José María Velasco, *Valle de México (Valley of Mexico)*. Lakes and agricultural land still predominated in the Valley of Mexico during the nineteenth century.

Plate 16   Latin American cities with more than one million inhabitants.

13

People and Progress, 1910–1959

IN THE ERA FROM the 1910 to 1960 Latin America underwent a vast transition from rural, agriculturally based traditions to urban middle and working class "modern" life. This transformation was manifested not only in the politics of popular organizations and upheavals, but also in all aspects of everyday life, such as employment, housing, food, popular entertainment, and art. The prolonged processes of altering gender roles, begun in the nineteenth century, continued. The struggle for control over everyday life, particularly in the countryside, became as much cultural as political, though no less intense as a result.

Change was not uncontested. In the countryside, especially, people resisted transformations of their long-held values and practices. Interestingly, it was not only rural dwellers that struggled against modernity, but also its promoters, the Latin American upper classes. They looked on mass popular culture as vulgar—the products of the slums—and regarded with suspicion the repercussions of migrations and industrialization. The wealthy and powerful were torn between their goals to transform their nations and the lower classes and their worries about whether they could control these needed changes.

The transition from countryside to city and from rural agricultural to urban industrial worker or middle class did not transform the attitude of the upper classes toward the lower. The rich and powerful continued to fear the poor. The wealthy, as we have seen in previous chapters, grappled with the social question in politics and economy and allied with most elements of the armed services and the middle class to control the masses. This was reflected in a saying in Brazil: "The social question is a question for the police." It was not enough, however, merely to maintain their control over the lower classes through government coercion. The upper classes tried mightily to force all aspects of social life and culture to conform to their need to rein in the urban lower classes. They sought to transform immigrants and migrants into a quiescent proletariat loyal to the nation (sometimes known as the patria or fatherland). Moreover, they attempted to exert similar influence over the transformation of gender roles, particularly the place of women, in the rapidly changing urban society. Through the state, Latin American upper classes sought to shape the families, relationships, homes, leisure time, and tastes of workers to maintain their (male) hegemony (patriarchy). This meant potentially massive intrusions into local and personal prerogatives.

The rural-to-urban continuum was and continues to be the most crucial process in Latin America. In 1950, 61 percent of the population was still rural. But from 1950 to 1960 alone nearly 25 percent of rural Argentines abandoned the countryside for the cities; 29 percent of Chilean country people and 19 percent of Brazilian rural folk did the same. They left their homes because there was neither land nor jobs available to them. Increasing concentration of land ownership severely limited their opportunities to obtain their own plots. Land reform projects distributed marginally productive properties without possibilities to get credit to purchase equipment and other improvements. Burgeoning populations added to the pressures on the accessible land. To make matters worse, large landowners required fewer year-round laborers because of technological innovations and changes in crops. Many export commodities needed only seasonal workers (at planting and harvest). In contrast to the deterioration of conditions in rural areas, the cities offered more employment, better opportunities for education—and therefore upward mobility—and improved health care. However miserable the living conditions in the slums of the cities, they were infinitely better than in the countryside, and however limited the possibilities in the metropolises, they were glaring rays of hope compared to the large estates and villages.

Everyday life, of course, remained, as it had in the nineteenth century, a constant struggle. Most Latin Americans remained poor and uneducated. Literacy of those over 15 years of age was 50 percent. Only 7 percent of the people possessed a secondary education. If anything, work became harder. Large companies rather than small, family-operated workshops employed most industrial workers. Impersonal bureaucracies replaced personal relations. The streets of the cities, noisy and smelly, polluted and unsanitary in the previous century, deteriorated. The vast influx of people who came from the countryside and from abroad increased the pressures on existing facilities and public works beyond the breaking point. Like the Europeans and North Americans before them, modernizing Latin Americans cared little that their relentless drive to develop economically decimated their forests and pastures and polluted their water and air.

The contrasts and ironies were striking. Latin American upper classes during the first half of the twentieth century rebuilt the cores of the largest cities to emulate London or Paris. Governments built the Teatro Nacional (now the Palacio Nacional de Bellas Artes) in Mexico City and the Teatro Colón in Buenos Aires and constructed the elegant avenues of Rio de Janeiro and the Avenida de Mayo in Buenos Aires. At the same time, more and more people crammed into the decaying tenements and the deplorable conditions in the vast tracts of the city untouched by renovations.

Socialization in the Factory and the Mine: Proletarianization and Patriarchy

The migration of Latin Americans from the countryside to the cities resulted primarily from inability to earn a decent living in agriculture. For the lower classes, conditions in rural areas had deteriorated steadily since independence. Work on the farms and ranches, if available, remained as hard and as badly paid as ever. Employment was erratic or seasonal. It was impossible to do more than scratch out the barest living. More than likely, rural workers faced lifelong indebtedness to their bosses or landlords. At a ranch in northwestern São Paulo state in Brazil in 1929, for example, fifty laborers rose at 4 A.M. to eat a breakfast of bread and coffee after which they cleared fields to plant pasture for cattle. The men ate lunch at 8 A.M. and consumed their third meal, consisting of beans, rice, and pasta, at 2 P.M. There was much more to do, so their toils did not end until dusk. Although the food was plentiful, there was no more provided after the early dinner. Famished, the workers purchased additional food—perhaps cheese and bread or candy—from the ranch store, buying on credit, to be charged to their salaries. The conditions for tenants were as precarious as in the preceding century. Chilean estates, for example, provided a house and a small parcel of land in return for their labor. The landlord could change the arrangements at a moment's notice and evict or move the tenants. Usually, the alternative was disadvantageous to the tenant. Protest was futile, for the police and military were at the service of the landowner. In short, conditions for rural workers had not changed at all since the nineteenth century.

Living in any one of thousands of small villages in Peru or Mexico offered little better. The villages were often isolated, reachable only over muddy or dusty potholed roads hours from any city. There was no electricity. Many of the inhabitants of the Indian and mestizo villages, especially women, spoke only their Indian language, such as Quechua and Aymara in the Andean nations or Nahuatl in Mexico.

Despite their modest meals—in the Andes people ate simple stews, filled with potatoes and vegetables, shreds of chicken, beef, or pork in good times, with wheat or barley bread—it was nearly impossible to feed a family from the production of a small, individually owned plot of a few acres. As a result, country people sought work elsewhere on neighboring estates and farms, mines, and cities. The movement of people was constant from the mid-nineteenth century. Country people in Chile often left their farms for short periods to work in the mines, drawn by high wages and the possibility of saving enough to buy their own land. When the farmer-miner accumulated enough money after a few months, he went back to the estate where his family members were tenants or to his own parcel. Manuel Abaitúa Acevedo, who first traveled to El Teniente copper mine in Chile in 1924 from home in an agricultural town, was typical of the early migrations. He initially worked nine months and returned home. The next year he worked for four months and in the following two years one month each. In 1928 he worked for five months. The dream for Manuel and others in his situation, of course, was to someday save enough money to buy one's own land.

Not every aspect of rural life was dismal. Two machines seem to have had significant impact on the countryside. In Mexico, the *molino de nixtamal,* which ground soaked maize kernels into the damp flour that comprised tortillas, wrought a revolution in the everyday lives of women, allowing them to escape hours and hours of hand grinding that for centuries had begun before dawn. The sewing machine, many of which operated through foot power rather than electricity, formed the basis of the clothing industry. It facilitated home piecework production, permitting women to both work and tend to their families. Sewing machines also eased the transition to more western style modern clothing. Electricity and radio would have enormous effect, but they were not universally accessible until the 1950s. Only 40 percent of the residents of Huaylas, a village in Peru, for example, had electricity in 1963.

The history of María Elisa Alvarez, a Medellín textile worker, illustrates how women, like men, bravely left their villages and estates in order to improve their situation, acquired skills, and moved on when necessary. María Elisa arrived in Medellín, Colombia, at age sixteen after toiling on a coffee plantation for five years. She had also sold cured tobacco, sweets, and produce on the streets of her hometown. María Elisa was in domestic service for one year in the city, but then went to the textile mills. She worked for a few months and then labored at a small dyeing shop and a local hospital. Having learned enough as a nurse's assistant to care for a patient, she gained employment caring for the invalid son of a wealthy family. She later quit because the son was unpleasant. From there, she obtained employment in the factory she had worked in years before and then found a position in another mill, where she stayed until retirement. By all counts, this does not seem an unusual pattern of work, but María Elisa and her sisters worked in a culture that disapproved of their employment outside the home. Nonetheless, they persevered.

Once the migrants from the countryside arrived in the cities or the mining camps, the long process of socialization and accommodation began. Not only were the sights, sounds, and smells different, but they were engaged immediately in the struggle over their customs, traditions, and demeanor. They entered

Slice of Life — Village Life in Peru

HISTORIAN FLORENCIA Mallon conducted extensive research in the villages of the neighboring Yanamarca and Mantaro Valleys in the central highlands of Peru that provides us with an illuminating picture of the lives of rural people. The land is fertile and well watered by the Yanamarca and Mantaro Rivers. The area lies on the major transportation routes to both important mining regions and the tropics. The mines furnished a market for its livestock and produce.

At the beginning of the twentieth century, small to medium-size farms whose proprietors enlisted the help of family labor to grow alfalfa, wheat, and vegetables, predominated. In the higher altitudes around the valley, people raised livestock and grew potatoes and quinoa. The holdings were much larger in this area. They drew labor from local villages.

There were some proprietors who owned plots in three zones: the humid lowlands located in the center of the valley, the valley slopes, and the flat lands on the other side of the mountains. This practice, of course, replicated the ancient Incas' approach to farming and commerce. To illustrate how the country people diversified, Mallon tells us the story of Jacoba Arias, an Indian who spoke only Quechua, from Acolla in the Yanamarca Valley. She owned 14 hectares (2.47 acres = 1 hectare) divided into small parcels scattered in different growing regions. She also owned 40 sheep, 3 teams of oxen, 6 bulls, 1 cow, and 3 mules. They provided the family with milk and cheese, meat and lard. The sheep supplied wool for her family's clothes. The mules allowed her to engage in small-scale commerce.

Farming the slopes down to the valleys was no easy task. The environment often changed radically even in a single plot, with variations in soil and climate. The farmers had to intimately understand the land. They had to adapt their methods and crops meticulously to the land, according to the soil, the temperature, and the amount of sunlight and rain. Families also adjusted to the needs of the farm and the capabilities of their members. Young children and the elderly tended the livestock because these duties required less arduous work. No time was wasted. The shepherds, for instance, spun wool thread while they watched the flock.

Family farmers diversified their economic activities to make ends meet. Agricultural work was seasonal. Everyone participated in planting and harvest. Spinning thread, weaving, and household chores were major year-round tasks. Some men, usually young and single, worked in the mines or as muleteers, transporting goods. Others made handicrafts, like shawls, hats, ponchos, blankets, or woodcarvings. In a good year, there was an agricultural surplus to be used for purchasing extras, perhaps coca and alcohol. In bad years, the balance shifted to handicrafts or the family might sell some livestock.

(continued on next page)

Village Life in Peru *(continued from previous page)*

Agriculture was a risky enterprise under the best of circumstances. An early frost, hail, or too little or too much rain might bring disaster. Because family size was not planned, inheritance eventually divided up the land to the point that no one family could subsist. Some families augmented their property by working the farms of other owners in return for splitting the harvest between them. Some families tended other livestock owners' animals in return for half the newborn sheep or cattle. There was also an arrangement by which one farming household and one livestock-raising household cooperated. The latter's sheep fertilized the fields of the former, and the two families tended to and shared the crops.

Godparenthood enhanced cooperation between local families. On the occasions of a baby's first haircut, baptism, marriage, and roofing of a new house, children obtained six godparents, who, tied with the bonds of affection and respect, looked out for them in difficult times. Usually, one of the families was better off, but the arrangement worked to the benefit of both families because the wealthier had access to labor (and perhaps political support), while the less affluent could expect assistance in case of poor harvests or conflicts.

Governance in each village in the region consisted of two or more administrative units with their own officials. These entities oversaw community projects such as cleaning the irrigation ditches or planting community fields. There were also cofradías, religious lay brotherhoods, that sponsored the local saint's celebrations. Each of these organizations had a mayordomo to administer the celebration. He had to pay for the expenses not covered by the income from cofradía lands. The people of the community came together in these shared tasks. There was, of course, always conflict, ranging from petty arguments to more serious disputes over landownership.

Questions for Discussion
Compare village life in Peru with that of village life in Mexico. Why do you think the upper classes so mistrusted villagers even though the former need the latter's support in the politics of the nineteenth and twentieth centuries? Of the villages in Peru and Mexico which were more successful in retaining their autonomy over time?

---

into the struggle between workers and industrial companies over work habits. The conflict between worker and company is evident in the histories of two important industries, textile manufacturing in Medellín, Colombia, and copper mining in Chile. In both cases, companies sought to transform feisty country bumpkins into passive, stable, productive workers. In the face of critical changes in gender relations, large companies attempted to control workers' lives to an extraordinary extent. Workers resisted mightily. The process of negotiation between employees and employers shifted over time to reflect new market conditions and technological innovations.

Textile workers, mostly recent migrants from rural areas, were a rambunctious group. In the early days, they fought among themselves and with supervisors, played tricks, and needled each other and the bosses. They often did not show up for work or abruptly walked off the job. A series of strikes during the mid-1930s led owners to adopt different strategies in order to introduce stronger discipline to their unruly workers. The strikes combined with two other transformations to cause the industrialists to revise their strategies. Because firms had grown larger and more bureaucratic and owner families no longer supervised their operations from the factory floor, they no longer fostered personal relations with their employees. In addition, the introduction of large looms, which the bosses believed were best operated by men, drastically reduced the number of women employees. Through the 1930s, Medellín's textile and clothing factories, like most in Latin America, heavily employed women, but, as a result of these changes, by the end of the 1950s men far outnumbered female workers.

In their struggle to reacquire control over the work place in the 1940s, employers followed a two-tier strategy: on one hand providing desirable benefits for their employees, and on the other hand seeking to influence all aspects of their employees' lives. Colombian industrialists wanted a "sober, industrious, married" work force. Male heads of household were judged more stable employees. The companies targeted the role of women as crucial in their strategy of control. The bosses viewed female textile workers as a threat to the "proper" relationship between men and women. When women earned wages they redefined gender. Mills no longer hired married women or single mothers. Female virtue, specifically virginity, was considered the foundation of patriarchal authority. Patriarchy did not function in the factory if it was not in effect in the family. Fatherly male authority in the factory was meaningless if the factory provided young women the means to be independent of that authority. If women worked only when they were virgins, the factory maintained its patriarchal standing as father. Women worked while awaiting marriage rather than as independent females unincorporated into the family system.

The owners improved working conditions and kept salaries relatively high. Mill workers enjoyed such amenities as cafeterias surrounded by landscaped patios serving subsidized meals, factory-sponsored recreational facilities, subsidized grocery stores, medical care, chapels, housing, and schools. Workers were paid well enough to accumulate sufficient resources to acquire homes.

The bosses' strategies sometimes had mixed results. Ana (Nena) Palacios de Montoya worked as a domestic in Medellín when she met Jairo, who would become her husband. He was a driver for the local textile factory and used his contacts to obtain a position in the factory for her. Nena loved working in the mill. She and her husband bought land and built a house using yearly bonuses, loans from the mill, and the help of friends. Slowly, she constructed her dream home, adding on as the family put together enough money. Fantastically, she managed to marry and have a child without being discovered and fired from her job. The bosses obtained two good workers, their employees earned a good life, but at the same time, Nena and Jairo had clearly maintained their independence.

In Chile, as the copper mines expanded after World War I, the companies required a stable, resident, skilled labor force. For decades, however, the companies found it hard to attract a reliable body of workers. Chilean miners, like Medellín textile workers, were known for being uncooperative and mobile. At the El Teniente mine in 1922, an exasperated foreman fired close to one hundred employees for "disobedience, laziness, fighting, insolence . . . leaving the job, carelessness, sleeping on the job, gambling, thieving, and incompetence." The large corporations had to assure themselves a steady work force, and it was clear that merely offering high wages was not sufficient to attract and maintain it. Workers were used to going back and forth from the countryside to the mines, the railroads, the ports, or the cities. Miners stayed for only a short period and then returned to the rural areas. Nor was repression enough to create a passive body of workers. Led by foreign corporations, the copper industry adopted paternalistic practices, making life more livable by adding bonuses for attendance, establishing social and cultural organizations, and offering inducements to form nuclear families. The companies set up schools and clubs to inculcate respectability in the workers.

About one-third of the miners came from the south and central regions of Chile, another third from the neighboring region to the mines, and about 20 percent from the cities. The pattern for much of the era was for workers to go back and forth from their homes to the mines. Conditions were much too difficult for many to endure very long. When demand for labor grew, the companies dispatched unethical recruiters *(enganchadores)* to the rural areas to trick peons to work in the mines. These recruiters got the peons drunk and had them sign contracts (they could not read) and then loaded them onto a train to the mines. The threat of police kept the peons in line. The recruiters advanced them funds on their wages, which of course had to be repaid by working in the mines. This pattern was repeated many times. Despite huge efforts at recruiting, turnover was a constant problem.

Women moved back and forth as well. They worked as domestics and as petty traders. They owned bars and brothels or worked in them. Just like the men, many hoped to save some money and move on. They came alone and often entered into arrangements with men. The foreign companies believed that this transient and unruly population of women in the camps added to the instability and lack of discipline among the miners.

The companies set out to reform the miners' everyday habits. Management provided sports, schools, movies, libraries, and clubs. The clubs were to substitute for labor unions. The companies sought to regulate the sex lives of the workers and the women in the camps. Employers wanted "conventional families," legally recognized by the government and the Church. Married men, they calculated, would stay on the job. Alcohol, prostitutes, and gambling were responsible for the lack of discipline. The companies went so far as to force men and women found alone together to marry. Otherwise, they would have had to leave their jobs. The company fired single women who became pregnant or had abortions. Company sponsored programs taught housekeeping skills to wives. Especially important were the pointers in making ends meet. The companies feared that poverty would tear apart nuclear families. During the 1930s, some companies added a monthly bonus and an extra allowance for those workers with families. In order to obtain these augmentations to their wages, workers had to formalize their relationships. Children were legitimized and couples entered into civil unions.

These policies succeeded in creating a stable work force during the 1930s and 1940s, but did not eliminate the difficult working conditions. Therefore the miners never evolved into passivity. Union activity continued. Nor did the policies end women's involvement in economic activities. They sold food and beverages from their homes, took in laundry, and brought in boarders. There were even some female bootleggers (smugglers of illegal alcoholic drinks). Despite all the efforts of the companies, some married women managed to obtain a degree of economic independence through their involvement in the informal sector.

The Chilean state became involved in the socialization of workers during the 1930s in order to incorporate the middle and lower classes into the new conception of the nation. The government sought to build a citizenry of disciplined and responsible people. This, of course, coincided exactly with the goals of the foreign copper companies. There were new responsibilities for the lower classes: they were to be "disciplined, educated, and responsible [in order to] fulfill the demands of citizenship for the national community." Workers, nonetheless, wanted to rule their own lives. They resented attempts to control them by both the company and the unions. Miners continued to get drunk, play cards, and fornicate.

With the encouragement of the Chilean state, the copper mines created a masculinized culture of work. The difficulty and danger of the labor was to be overcome by the sense of dignity. Pride was to overwhelm the dehumanization that accompanied modern mining. What neither the companies nor the state anticipated was that along with pride went disdain for authority.

A Miner's Day at El Teniente

At four or five o'clock in the morning, a miner went for breakfast at a cantina or the house of a family. By six he was on his way to the train that would take him up to the mine. The train was dark without windows, completely enclosed to prevent accidents. The miner then reported to the foreign supervisor, who recorded his time of entry. A giant elevator then transported the miner and some six hundred of his fellow workers to the different levels of the mine to join up with their teams of fifteen people to work in the tunnels. There were three shifts. The lead miners entered the tunnel first, laying down the pipes and tubes that would bring in the compressed air and water for the drills. The miners drilled as the machine sprayed water on the wall to prevent dust from filling the cavern. Despite this precaution, the tunnels nevertheless filled with dust. Miners could see barely five or six feet ahead. Miners drilled holes and inserted dynamite in them and blew up the walls. Placement of the dynamite was delicate, skilled work. Other team members then lay the rails for the cars, which would first haul timbers for constructing the supports for the shafts and then the ore. Another group loaded the ore into the cars. These cars were then pushed to chutes, which brought them to the concentrating plants. All of these tasks required enormous strength. Miners learned their various skills on the job. When they exhibited proficiency, they moved on to better positions. Some became foremen. The concentrating mills also required much skill. This work was even more dangerous because of the toxic fumes. Because there was never sufficient protective equipment, silicosis, a respiratory disease, was inevitable. Workers would be lucky to survive a dozen years.

Mining was brutal work in terrible conditions. The climate in this part of Chile was frigid. Foremen, under relentless pressure from the companies to increase productivity, pushed the workers hard. After a few days, new miners often skipped work to recover from their aches and pains. Some workers refused to take the more dangerous assignments. Miners were in short supply and had the advantage of being able to find another job if fired.

Copper mines paid the best of any occupation in Chile. By the mid-1940s, as we see in Table 13.1, miners earned 50 percent higher wages than any other employment. El Teniente paid bonuses based on productivity. Foremen earned still higher wages and enjoyed better housing.

Table 13.1

Comparative Wages in Chile

Occupation	Average daily wage in Chilean pesos		
	1937	1941	1945
Nitrate miner	19.80	26.48	59.47
Coal miner	14.18	24.84	55.50
Copper miner	20.88	38.82	83.68
Textile worker	11.61	21.77	
Leather worker	13.70		
Shoe worker	10.32	23.05	

Source: Thomas Klubock, *Contested Communities: Class, Gender, and Politics in Chile's El Teniente Copper Mine, 1904–1951* (Durham: Duke University Press, 1998), 135–36.

Living conditions in the El Teniente mining camp were generally abhorrent. Lodgings for families had no electricity, light, or ventilation. "... [T]he barracks for single workers [were] so awful as to be irrational." Miners with their families lived in two-room apartments in barracks buildings. Often, two families shared one apartment. One family had nine children and parents: "... [W]e women had the bedroom because there were six girls and three boys, so in the big bedroom there were only women, in the other were my father with the boys, and in the other the kitchen." The company would not allow electric heaters or irons. Families used small wood- and kerosene-burning stoves, but both were expensive. There were common taps for water and toilets.

Perhaps, the worst disadvantage of the camps was the high cost of living, especially food. The cost of living in El Teniente increased 184 percent in the decade between 1936 and 1946. Nutrition suffered. Monopoly prices were at the heart of the problem. High costs badly eroded the real value of the nation's highest wages.

Urbanization and Social Change

The transformations in society were no more apparent than in the growing cities of Latin America. These changes were particularly evident in the conditions of the middle class and attitudes toward women.

The Cities

Latin American cities were overcrowded, unsanitary, overrun by epidemic diseases, and teeming with uneducated migrants from the countryside and abroad. At the beginning of the twentieth century, upper classes in Rio de Janeiro and Buenos Aires and other cities determined to dramatically transform their metropolises' physical and social space while at the same time inculcating moral values in the masses. Urban redevelopment, electrified public transportation, and massive population growth transformed the cities economically, spatially, and culturally.

The divide between the wealthy and the lower classes, however, widened and grew more obvious. Rio de Janeiro, for example, whose population was half Afro-Brazilian and where immigrants flooded in by the thousands, was really two cities. The poor, on whom the authorities cast suspicious eyes, and a tiny minority of "decent" upper and middle class folk who made up less than 20 percent of the population. The upper classes sought to impose their will on the lower classes through cleaning up downtown spaces with new health and housing codes, regulating recreation, and strictly enforcing laws against public nuisances such as prostitution.

Massive urban renewal took place in Rio de Janeiro from 1902 to 1910. Vast tracts of the working-class areas were cleared and their inhabitants moved to the outskirts. As migrants continued their flow into the city, urban services remained woefully inadequate. Terrible epidemics tormented the city. By 1920, the streets

How Historians Understand | The Voice of the Lower Classes

THE MOST DIFFICULT TASK historians confront is the construction of the past of the rural and urban lower classes. Mostly illiterate, they did not often record their own histories. The upper classes, whose fear of the masses we have discussed extensively in these pages, were in charge of governments, universities, and media and excluded the stories of those who were not of their own status in national histories. The less well-born, among them the poor, country people, urban workers, non-elite women, appeared in official history books only as no-account, lazy subjects of justifiable oppression, exotic objects of sympathy, criminals, or irrational protestors. As in the cases of the well-known Mexican historian Lucas Alamán and the liberal historians of nineteenth-century Argentina and Chile, upper class fear and disdain of the lower classes was clearly evident.

Foreign visitors, the most famous of whom was Fanny Calderón de la Barca, the wife of the Minister of Spain to Mexico, who recorded her observations of nineteenth-century Mexico, were perhaps the best sources for glimpses into the lives of everyday people. They tended, however, to see Latin Americans through the narrow focus of wealthy, white Europeans or North Americans, with their racism and condescension undisguised. Their best-selling books provided pictures of half-naked gauchos and tropical villagers, noble at their best, savage at their worst.

Pressured by the events of periodic, violent upheavals during revolutions in Mexico (1910), Bolivia (1952), Cuba (1959), and Nicaragua (1979) and the challenges of Marxism, populism, and feminism, twentieth-century historians of Latin America delved into the histories of lower class people. The first efforts used traditional methods, exploring national institutions, such as labor unions, which had records to consult.

Traditional sources seemed to provide neither description nor insight. Newspapers of the day, unless in opposition to the government—and these were rare—hardly paid attention to the poor. Few treated the lower classes with any degree of fairness. Strikes, for example, were seen as the result of the manipulations of outside agitators. Not many reporters explored the lives of the people driven to these radical actions.

In the 1960s, dismayed by the massacre of three hundred civilian protestors in Mexico City by government secret police forces, and in the 1970s, horrified by the emergence of vicious, repressive military regimes in Argentina, Chile, and Brazil, historians pushed harder to write the stories of everyday people. Local records provided the sources for this history.

The best sources for the history of common people lie in judicial, police, notary, and municipal archives, located in villages, towns, and cities. In addition, most recently, historians have discovered illuminating materials in the records of large companies. There are also some records from modern large estates. Foreign mining companies in Brazil and Chile, in particular, have proven rich depositories. Most of the archives contain "official" documents, of course, which reflect views of events that are hardly impartial.

Historians, despite the difficult conditions in local archives, such as poor lighting and ventilation, the threat of dangerous parasites from dust, and unco-operative bureaucrats, have discovered invaluable materials. Judicial archives, for example, contain the records of suits concerning marriage, criminal trials, tax protests, litigation between heirs, and land disputes. Notarial records reveal family economic holdings, wills, business transactions, and contracts. Police documents tell us what crimes were committed and by whom. Municipal records detail taxes, rules, and regulations, the activities and tactics of local officials, and the reactions of the citizenry to official actions.

Although police and court records are not always representative samples of the general population, by using them historians can uncover the extent of such activity as drunkenness, wife beating, prostitution, and banditry. They can also estimate the extent of government interference in everyday life in its efforts to discipline the lower classes.

The picture produced by these records is, of course, never complete, but they have created history where none had existed previously.

Questions for Discussion
Why do you think that historians in recent decades have focused on the lower classes? Why do you think that historians ignored the masses for so long?

of downtown were littered with abandoned girls, beggars, and prostitutes, and ravaged by disease.

Living conditions changed in Lima as well. There was an exodus from the old central districts to outlying areas (suburbs). Consumer credit allowed for the possibility of buying one's own home and created new spending patterns. Lima, however, became segregated with poor and wealthy neighborhoods clearly defined.

Perhaps the most startling example of super-urbanization during this era was Mexico City. Country people have thronged into the city in increasing numbers from 1940 right up to the present day. The capital grew from 1.5 million inhabitants in 1940 to 8.5 million in 1970. Four million had left the countryside to come to seek their fortunes in the metropolis. The number of automobiles grew exponentially, choking the city in carbon monoxide fumes. Skyscrapers sprouted in the core of the city and along the beautiful, tree-lined, statue-ornamented Paseo de la Reforma, while migrants rushed into burgeoning barrios such as Netzahualcóyotl. The government erected architectural splendors like the National Autonomous University and the Museum of Anthropology. Much of the nation's new industry was established in Mexico City—one-fourth of the country's factories were located there by 1970.

Generally, life was better in the city. In 1960, *capitalino* (resident of Mexico City) family income was 185 percent more than those in rural areas. There were more opportunities for everyone. The worst problem facing newcomers was housing (although the rising cost of living and eroding real wages were serious problems as well).

Life on the Edge: The Middle Class

The middle class expanded because government bureaucracies grew larger, foreign businesses multiplied, opportunities trickled down in growing economies, and education opened up to other than just the wealthy classes. What mattered to the members of the middle class, as it had to the gente decente in the nineteenth century, was maintaining their respectability and their distance from the lower classes. Because their economic situation was chronically precarious, middle class people, barely more financially well off than the working class, concerned themselves foremost with keeping up the appearance of their status (see Table 13.2).

Although there were minimum requirements for employment as a white-collar worker, such as rudimentary mathematics, spelling, neat penmanship, and perhaps some bookkeeping, it was crucial to have contacts—usually through family ties, but also through school chums, geography, or perhaps ethnicity. Even good references did not assure one of a position. In Peru, employers often had a prolonged (perhaps three months) probation period during which employees competed against each other for the one permanent position. Paternalism ruled the work place, and loyalty was at its core. There were no contracts or formal

Table 13.2

A Typical Middle-Class Budget in Peruvian Soles

	Soles
Rent	100
Food	240
Soap, toothpaste	20
Transportation	36
Water, electricity, garbage	14
One servant	50
Kerosene	12
Movies, once a week	20
School fees for oldest child	80
Total	572 on income of 600 (a meager sum at the time)

Source: *Ya!* No. 16 (July, 1949), p. 18–19, cited in D.S. Parker, *The Idea of the Middle Class: White Collar Workers and Peruvian Society, 1900–1950* (University Park: Penn State University Press, 1998), 212.

guidelines for salaries or expectations with the likelihood of arbitrary treatment. Paternalism did on occasion have its advantages, though, for employers might assist their employees during crises.

White-collar workers strove first and foremost to live respectable lives. In Lima, they often resided in rooms rented to them by upper class owners of large mansions in the core of the city, often in what were formerly servants' quarters. The landlords, who had fled the slums to live in the outskirts of the city, feared working-class tenants and so favored middle class renters, to whom they often lent furniture and dishes. The apartments were nonetheless crowded and not necessarily well maintained.

White-collar workers were less likely than poorer Peruvians to die of epidemic diseases such as typhoid, cholera, bubonic plague, or yellow fever. But they did succumb to tuberculosis, which accounted for one-third of all white-collar mortality and resulted from working in badly ventilated spaces or residing in damp overcrowded apartments. It is likely that they were malnourished as well. Lima, as so many other Latin American cities, was unhealthy.

White-collar workers perpetually lived on the edge. They had no emergency cushion, spending their paychecks as they got them (see Table 13.2). Pawnshops were the only source of ready credit. It was not likely that white-collar workers could save money to buy their own homes, for there were no banks to keep their savings, or to provide mortgages. White-collar workers tried to emulate the rich. They were "self-consciously concerned with prestige, honor, and distinction," which led many of those who worked in commerce in Lima to join shooting clubs or to play billiards or to wear English cashmere in the 1920s. Women followed European fashions. Because living spaces were so small and unpleasant, many people frequented cafes and streets. Walking the streets of Lima was a way to show off their respectability. Crucial to the middle class psyche was the notion that they were different from the working class. They were willing to commute for hours so they could reside in respectable areas of the city. The middle class looked for entertainment other than films, radio, and sports and began to travel.

Women made up only 1 percent of the white-collar work force in 1908 in Peru and did not enter this sector in numbers until the 1910s, with positions in the post office, telegraph, and telephone companies. In the 1920s, they moved into retail, then banking, insurance, and commerce. Five percent of all working women were white-collar by 1931. The image of the white collar, however, remained that of a young bachelor or a later version of a man with a family whose wife did not work. Respectability demanded the wife stay at home, even if, as a result, the family lived modestly on one salary. It is probable that, despite the myth, women did work outside the home.

In Peru and elsewhere in Latin America, the number of white-collar workers expanded from 1930 to 1950. Businesses grew larger and more complex. Public bureaucracies swelled. As in Chile's mines, traditional paternalism gave way to hierarchies and impersonal relations. Women entered the white-collar ranks, usually at the lowest-paid levels. After the 1930s in Lima, mestizos comprised the largest number of white collars. And white-collar workers' children eventually gained access to university education.

La Chica Moderna

Urbanization and industrial work instilled a new attitude in women, forming what the era called the modern woman. (They were known in Mexico and elsewhere as *las chicas modernas,* or modern girls.) Although at the beginning of the twentieth century women office and factory workers were a small minority of the female workforce, they caused much public discussion. Most working women, as they had in the previous century, toiled as domestics. The 1920s, however, brought the notorious flapper—racy, flirtatious, and assertive. The image of the independent, sensuous female shook the male establishment, for to them female virtue was the very center of patriarchy. In Brazil, modernity, when applied to men, indicated economic progress and healthy, rational sexual and family relations, but, when applied to women, it meant a dissolute lifestyle and loose morals.

The upper classes, government officials, and Catholic conservatives worried about the low rate of marriage among the poor, the high rate of infant mortality, and the increasing numbers of women and children in the industrial work force. Catholics sought to reemphasize traditional values. Women were crucial because not only did they reproduce, but they also educated their children. Therefore, society had to re-educate women, so they could inculcate their offspring with the proper values and attitudes. The regime of Getúlio Vargas (1930–1945) adopted policies that were intended to adjust the traditional role of women to meet new conditions while maintaining patriarchy.

The irony was, of course, that the reason middle class women were entering the white-collar work force was because it had become harder and harder to make ends meet on one salary. More middle class women took advantage of educational opportunities and went into the professions. To the middle class, women's employment did not elicit the same disapproval it had in the past.

The fashions of the 1920s were disconcerting for the upper class males who dominated Brazil (and probably a significant percentage of middle and working-class males and some females). Women wore lighter more comfortable dresses. Later in the decade, dresses and skirts came up to the knee and were worn with silk stockings and high heels. Women were revealing themselves physically as never before. Less cumbersome bras and panties replaced corsets. Short haircuts and makeup were the style. Bare arms and legs were exposed on the beach. Women smoked cigarettes in public. Films and magazines showed off the glamorous life. To stuffy upper class males, women's virtue was under attack. Dances changed, music was scandalous: The tango, foxtrot, Charleston, and shimmy were all the rage.

The Brazilian state, like the Chilean state, sought in this era to defend patriarchy from these challenges. Its targets were women and the poor, the crucial threats to their status. The first goal was to strengthen traditional marriage. To accomplish this, the government adopted protective legislation, which limited women's access to the work place and instituted social service agencies to monitor the urban poor. Industrialists even went so far as to set up model villages to control the domestic lives of their workers.

The Brazilian ruling class was willing to make minimal concessions. Early in the century, Brazilian legislation altered the wife's status to "companion, partner, and assistant in familial responsibilities," but firmly maintained the husband as head of household. Women still did not have the power to control their own property. In 1940, the government's Penal Code eliminated the distinctions between male and female adultery. There was also an attempt to end the legal tolerance of crimes of passion. Thus, women had, like the middle class, struggled enormously and succeeded in bettering conditions, but their situation was precarious. As the middle class had not achieved equal status with the wealthy and powerful, neither had women obtained equality to men.

Popular and High Culture

The transformations caused by the movement of people from the countryside to the cities and from the rest of the world to Latin America deeply affected both popular (songs, dance, folk crafts) and high culture (painting, sculpture, orchestral music). The arts were closely tied to the constructions of national identities. Improved communications and transportation not only brought people together domestically, but facilitated the introduction of foreign influences. Latin Americans struggled to find their own ways in the grounds between their own traditions (oftentimes violently rejected) and those of Europe and North America, much admired by upper classes. We observe in Latin American dancing, music, and painting, in particular, the changes wrought by industrialization, migration, and urbanization.

The tango in Argentina was a fitting symbol that represented this profound transition. Before World War I, the tango was performed primarily in the suburbs of Buenos Aires, where rural tradition was still strong. It was connected with rural music and song, such as the *payada* and the *milonga.* Songs protested against conditions in the teeming tenements and the industrialization of urban work. Rural people, newly transplanted, despised city ways as exemplified by the *cajetilla,* or dandy.

The tango melded various aspects of Argentine society. It combined the music of the rural milonga, the Spanish *contradanza,* and influences of African Buenos Aires. It was modern and urban because couples danced closely entwined. Traditional dances were performed in groups. The tango was a protest against conventional mores. As it transformed from the rural to urban, the dance left its *machista,* street-fighting, "bad" women milieu and replaced it with individual emotion. Radio and film made the tango part of popular culture. The upper and middle classes, disdainful of the dance at first, later embraced it as a symbol of Argentina.

The samba, too, was an object of upper class scorn in the nineteenth century. The Brazilian government outlawed it for a time. Nonetheless, during the 1920s samba became the symbol of Brazil's mixed heritage of African and European culture. Arising from the poor Afro-Brazilian neighborhoods of Rio, samba clubs took over Carnival (the festival before Lent) in the 1920s. Their leaders were able to shed the bad reputations of their predecessor organizations and convince parents in the poor neighborhoods to allow their daughters to participate. Thus, not only was samba—the dance of the poorest Brazilians—the symbol of the nation, but it also illustrated how women, active and public participants in Carnival, were no longer restricted to private spaces.

In painting and literature, the conflicts inherent in urbanization, modernity, and finding national identities emerged in various movements at the turn of the twentieth century, such as *modernismo* and *indigenismo*. In literature, Nicaraguan poet Rubén Darío formulated a movement known as modernismo that sought a way to express the Latin American experience. Art followed, seeking a uniquely Latin American presentation of the region's culture. Latin American artists, most trained in Europe, set aside the perspective of the Continent and looked at their homeland up close. Saturnino Herrán (1887–1918), a Mexican artist, for example, who—unlike many of his contemporaries—never studied in Europe, depicted Indians and mestizos living and working in their local environs in such paintings as *El Trabajo (Work)* (1908) and *La ofrenda (The Offering)* (1913). He was one of the first twentieth-century Mexican artists to look to the pre-Columbian past for subject matter. Ecuadorian Camilo Egas (1899–1962) painted huge horizontal panels depicting the life of Indians over the centuries since the conquest, for example, the *Fiesta Indígena (Indian Festival)* (1922).

At the heart of the Mexican search for national identity and art's place within it was Geraldo Murillo, widely known as Dr. Atl (1875–1964). He was a crucial link between European movements (such as impressionism), Mexican popular culture, the famous Mexican muralists, and the revolutionary government. Dr. Atl brought *arte popular* into the forefront in 1921 when he organized an exhibition of popular art and wrote an accompanying text, *Las artes populares en Mexico*. A talented painter in his own right, Dr. Atl's works, such as *El Volcán Paricutín en erupción* (1943), for instance, showed eclecticism in his approaches. He was an important sponsor of the muralist movement in the 1920s. Pedro Figari (1861–1938), a second-generation Uruguayan, son of an Italian immigrant, depicted life on the vast plains of the Pampas and creole and black dance. He, like Herrán and Egas, painted the lower classes in the countryside, "never before represented with such boldness and candor. . . ."

POPULAR AND HIGH CULTURE 403

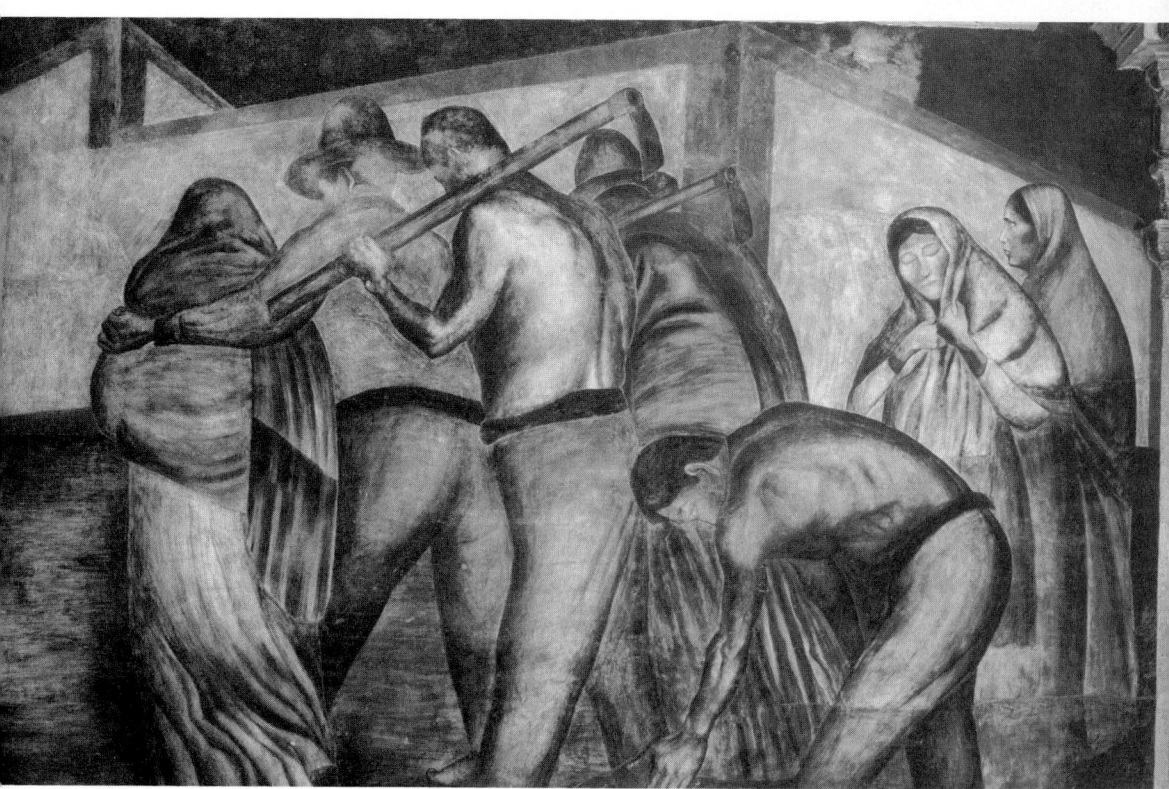

José Clemente Orozco's *La clase Obrera (The Working Class)*.

Perhaps the most well-known and the most important artistic movement that grappled with the intertwined dilemmas of modernization and national identity—most crucially the place of indigenous peoples within the Revolution—were the Mexican muralists. The most famous painters were Diego Rivera (1887–1957), David Alfaro Siqueiros (1896–1974), and José Clemente Orozco (1883–1949), but the group also included Alva de la Canal, Charlot, Fernando Leal, Xavier Guerrero, Roberto Montenegro, and Dr. Atl. "The artists faced two major challenges: that of introducing a new public monumental art requiring special technical skills, and that of creating an effective visual language for propaganda purposes." José Vasconcelos, the minister of education during the administration of President Álvaro Obregón (1920–1924), set out quite pointedly to incorporate and indoctrinate the masses through public art. Vasconcelos sought to educate the mostly illiterate Mexican population—to make them Mexicans.

Siqueiros's manifesto of 1923 set out the artists' goals: "the creators of beauty . . ." must ensure that "their work presents a clear aspect of ideological propaganda." The muralists introduced workers and country people into their art on a grand scale and rewrote Mexican history in their enormous paintings on walls. The stairwell murals in the National Palace in the Zócalo

Diego Rivera's *The Uprising (Soldiers and Workers)*.

(central plaza) of Mexico City depict Mexico's history from the conquest through the Cárdenas (1934–1940) era. Art was to the muralists inherently political. In a nation in flux during the 1920s, art seemed a way to help construct a sense of nationhood in a country blown apart in the previous decade.

The 1930s brought an intensification of the concern of artists for the lower classes. In Mexico and Peru, indigenismo (nativism) took center stage as these nations struggled, as they had for centuries, over the place of the Indian population in their societies. The Mexican muralists were the primary purveyors of the new indigenous image, romanticizing the pre-Columbian civilizations (and at the same time denigrating Spanish colonial culture). Indigenismo both in art and literature and as a political problem was a complex phenomenon. On one hand, intellectuals sought to extol the great heritages of the Indian civilizations. On the other hand, to modernizing upper classes, the Indians were backward and those more thoughtful of them sought to place the Indians in industrializing society. Pride in the accomplishments of native peoples dovetailed nicely with intensifying nationalism, which was a crucial aspect of populism, the political answer to the social question during the 1930s and 1940s. Nonetheless, to the

LATIN AMERICAN LIVES

Frida Kahlo

FRIDA KAHLO (1907–1954) was a tortured artist famous for her striking self-portraits and for her stormy marriage to muralist Diego Rivera. Long after her death at forty-seven, she became celebrated for her incorporation of distinctively female concerns, such as reproduction, children, and family, into her paintings. Critics consider her avowedly feminist in her treatment of her own body. She, like Elvia Carrillo Puerto (see Chapter 12), was a prominent example of Mexico's "new" woman who defied convention. Kahlo has reached cult status among feminists for her merging of personal emotions and politics.

Her life was determined by four factors: a terrible automobile accident that left her with a fractured spine and pelvis and constant pain throughout most of her life; her tumultuous marriage to Rivera; her inability to bear children; and her prodigious talent (though unrecognized, for the most part, while she was alive).

When she was fifteen, a bus she was riding collided with a trolley. The crash inflicted terrible injuries, which resulted in 35 hospitalizations and operations. The remainder of her life was spent in constant physical torment. Kahlo and Rivera married in 1929. They divorced in 1939 and remarried in 1940. They were international stars, consorting with world-famous artists and leftist politicians and thinkers. Rivera's notorious philandering marred their dream-like lives, though Frida, herself, had affairs as well.

Personally and professionally, Kahlo was in the forefront of the movement to incorporate popular culture into art. She was flamboyant in her dress, wearing the traditional garb of the women of Tehuantepec, the isthmus in southern Mexico, and styling her hair in indigenous coiffures with bows, combs, and flowers. She bedecked herself in jewelry. She was an avid collector of popular, folk, and pre-Columbian art. Her artistic work was rooted in pre-Columbian and colonial sources. Some commentators regard her as the Mexican artist who best combined popular art with the "modernist avant-garde." The merger of her concerns as a woman and her feeling for country people manifest themselves in her painting *My Nurse* (1937), in which she suckles on the breasts of a dark-skinned Indian woman.

In her most famous paintings, we can observe her obsessions with her pain, her love, and her barrenness. In her work *Raices* (*Roots*, 1943) she portrays herself with vines growing out of her chest as she lies in barren land. Despite her inability to have children of her own, she insists on herself as part of and a contributor to the "natural environment." In *El abrazo de amor del universo, la tierra* [Mexico], *Diego, yo y el señor Xolotl* (*The Love Embrace of the Universe, the Earth [Mexico], Diego, Me and Señor Xolotl*) (1949), she holds a baby with Diego's face in her arms, combining both her obsession with

(continued on next page)

> **FRIDA KAHLO** *(continued from previous page)*
> motherhood and her love of her husband. *Las Dos Fridas* (*The Two Fridas*, 1939. See Plate 13.) resulted from her divorce from Rivera. The two women depict her traditional and urbane sides, only the former loved by Diego.
>   In the male-dominated world of Mexican art, Frida Kahlo was unappreciated until the 1980s, when her striking depictions of motherhood and her body fit into the new feminist art history. Some historians, however, have criticized the treatment of her as a victim, obsessed with her physical and emotional pain. Overlooked, they maintain, is "her active role in the formulation of the language of art, which questioned neo-colonial values." Interpreted as "'the other,' the feminine and the unconscious," she is marginalized in a similar way in which Latin America finds itself made exotic. Kahlo, however, does not interpret Mexican women (or herself) as victims, but rather as "an assertive presence with the power of life and death."
>
> **Questions for Discussion**
> Discuss how you think that art reflects its time. Why is art such an effective instrument of social protest?

upper and middle classes, the Indians of the present were impediments to modernity.

By the 1930s, the great triumvirate of Mexican muralists, Orozco, Siqueiros, and Rivera, were painting in the United States because of the conservative environment of the regime headed by President Plutarco Elías Calles (1924–1928, and 1928–1934 as the power behind the scenes). They came back under Lázaro Cárdenas, however, and, mirroring the radical era of the Revolution, returned to the themes of utopian Indian societies before the Europeans arrived.

Brazil confronted its national and cultural identity not only in terms of Indians, but African peoples as well. Traveling the path of the Mexican muralists, Tarsila do Amaral (1886–1973) returned from her European training in the early 1920s to paint the everyday existence of poor Brazilians, who comprised the nation's reality. Another Brazilian painter, Candido Portinari (1903–1962) also depicted the "poor and the dispossessed, haggard and weak, with the staring eyes and distended stomachs of the malnourished."

In the 1920s, centered in São Paulo, modernist artists in Brazil ended Brazil's denial of its past and set about incorporating it into a national culture. They rejected regionalism and sought to make Brazil Brazilian. Mario de Andrade, the novelist, became a leader of the search for what constituted Brazilianness. Gilberto Freyre, the sociologist, sought Brazilianness in its traditions and regions. Brazil could only be whole, he argued, by allowing regional differences to flourish within the nation. Both rejected foreign models, none of which had stood up to Brazilian requirements.

Conclusion

At the core of Latin American struggles during the first half of the twentieth century were, first and foremost, economic and physical survival. Most people were poor, getting by on a day-to-day basis. Although there were great gains in education and healthcare—more people were literate and they lived longer—Latin Americans' standards of living lagged far behind those of Western Europe and the United States.

Latin Americans also grappled with the widespread effects of industrialization and urbanization. Everyday people, particularly in the countryside, fought to retain their cherished traditions and control over their daily lives. The onslaught of the factories, railroads, highways, telephone, radio, electricity, and centralized government, however, was too strong. Nonetheless, the urban and rural working classes and small landowners were remarkably independent and resilient. They selectively adopted new ways and adapted to new conditions. Their resistance to the dictates of the upper classes and military, however, caused the latter to seek drastic solutions to the decades-old social question. Two decades of violence and trauma ensued.

Learning More About Latin Americans

Baily, Samuel L., and Franco Ramella, eds. *One Family, Two Worlds: An Italian Family's Correspondence across the Atlantic, 1901–1922* (New Brunswick, NJ: Rutgers University Press, 1988). The story of Italian immigrants in Buenos Aires.

Barnitz, Jacqueline. *Twentieth-Century Art of Latin America* (Austin, TX: University of Texas Press, 2001). An interpretive history of the region's brilliant art.

De Jesus, Carolina Maria. *I'm Going to Have a Little House: The Second Diary of Carolina, Maria de Jesus.* Trans. Melvin Arrington, Jr., and Robert M. Levine. (Lincoln, NE: University of Nebraska Press, 1997). The sad story of a favela dweller.

De Jesus, Carolina Maria. *The Unedited Diaries of Carolina Maria de Jesus.* Ed. Robert M. Levine and Jose Carlos Sebe Bom Meihy. Trans. Nancy P.S. Naro and Cristina Mehrtens (New Brunswick, NJ: Rutgers University Press, 1999). The story of a favela dweller.

Farnsworth-Alvear, Ann. *Dulcinea in the Factory: Myths, Morals, Men, and Women in Colombia's Industrial Experiment, 1905–1960* (Durham, NC: Duke University Press, 2000). Women factory workers.

Fowler-Salamini, Heather, and Mary Kay Vaughn, eds. *Women of the Mexican Countryside, 1850–1990* (Tucson, AZ: University of Arizona Press, 1994).

French, John D., and Daniel James, eds. *The Gendered Worlds of Latin American Women Workers* (Durham, NC: Duke University Press, 1997). Essays on working-class women.

James, Daniel. *Doña María's Story* (Durham, NC: Duke University Press, 2000). A woman in the meatpacking plants of Argentina.

Klubock, Thomas. *Contested Communities: Class, Gender, and Politics in Chile's El Teniente Copper Mine, 1904–1951* (Durham, NC: Duke University Press, 1998). Life in the mining camps.

Moya, José C. *Cousins and Strangers: Spanish Immigrants in Buenos Aires, 1850–1930* (Berkeley, CA: University of California Press, 1998). Traces the immigrant experience from Europe to Buenos Aires.

Parker, D.S. *The Idea of the Middle Class: White Collar Workers and Peruvian Society, 1900–1950* (University Park, PA: Penn State University Press, 1998). A rare view into middle class work and society.

Parodi, Jorge. *To Be a Worker in Peru: Identity and Politics* (Chapel Hill, NC: University of North Carolina Press, 2000). Trans. James Alstrum and Catherine Conaghan. The hard life of the Peruvian working class.

14

REVOLUTION, REACTION, DEMOCRACY, AND THE NEW GLOBAL ECONOMY,
1959 TO THE PRESENT

THE PROMISE OF the post-war world for equitable politics and societies and prosperous economies was unfulfilled in Latin America. The region's leaders still grappled with the Social Question, seeking to satisfy the demands of the expanding middle and urban industrial working classes. In the early 1950s, as we saw in Chapter 12, Latin Americans turned to old dictators, such as Carlos Ibáñez in Chile and Getúlio Vargas in Brazil, or looked to new strongmen as in Colombia and Venezuela. There seemed to be no answers, only failed formulas, tired politicians, and angry, impatient military officers. The major innovation of the era was the vast expansion of the electorate. Women at last won full suffrage, although the vote by no means assured them an equal voice in political affairs. Governments eliminated literacy qualifications for political participation. The Cold War rivalry between communists in the Soviet Union and China on one side and capitalists in the United States and Western Europe on the other provided international context for the internal struggles.

The victory of the 26th of July Movement in Cuba in 1959 and the subsequent adoption of communism by the Revolution struck fear into the upper class–military alliance in Latin America. During the next 20 years, the Latin American Left surged and experienced an unprecedented degree of success. Chileans elected Socialist Dr. Salvador Allende (1970–1973) to the presidency, and the *Sandinista* Revolution in Nicaragua (1979–1990) held power for a full decade. Major leftist insurgencies took place in Colombia, El Salvador, Guatemala, and Peru. Salvadoran and Peruvian rebels came within a hairbreadth of winning their wars. But at the same time, politics polarized into brutal violence. Leftist guerrillas staged robberies and kidnappings, attacked police, and bombed buildings, and, in response, Latin American militaries embarked on a vicious reign of terror from the mid-1960s through the mid-1980s. Neither Left nor Right governments delivered sustained economic growth or social peace. Militaries ruled the major nations of the region through the 1970s and 1980s, seeking, at least in the beginning, to formulate new societies without popular organizations and political parties. Eventually, if reluctantly, the armed forces, at times humiliated by defeat or scandal, withdrew from direct control over governments in the 1980s, pushed out to a large extent by the citizens of the nations they ruled. Democracy returned to every country in the region (except Cuba) by the 1990s.

At the outset of the post-1959 era, Latin American regimes continued to adhere to the Import Substitution Industrialization (ISI) model of economic development. Ironically, as we saw in Chapter 12, as the Right triumphed, it had presided over increasing government involvement in the economy. (In the Soviet communist model the state operated the economy.) By the 1980s, however, ISI had failed. Starting in Chile under military rule after 1973, Latin America gradually embraced free market economics. With the fall of communism in the Soviet Union and Eastern Europe, there was no longer a Left alternative to capitalism. By the 1990s, it was clear that both the most extreme Left and Right regimes had ended in unmitigated disaster for most middle- and lower-class Latin Americans.

The Revolutions: Cuba, Nicaragua, El Salvador, Guatemala, Peru, and Colombia

The Cuban Revolution shattered the fragile political equilibrium of the late 1950s. The victory of Fidel Castro and his 26th of July Movement in Cuba introduced a whole new set of factors into Latin American domestic political equations. The "fall" of Cuba to communism mobilized the United States to intense involvement in the region. Fidel Castro's call for revolution throughout the region intensified the fears of the upper class–military alliance. Revolutionary

1959	1964	1970	1973	1979	1990
Cuban Revolution	Brazilian military overthrows João Goulart	Dr. Salvador Allende elected in Chile	Allende ousted by Chilean military	Sandinista Revolution in Nicaragua	Alberto Fujimori elected president of Peru

1961	1968	1974	1982
United States establishes the Alliance for Progress	Peruvian Revolution; Juan Velasco Alvarado	Juan Perón returns to Argentina	Malvinas/Falklands War (Argentina v. United Kingdom)

insurgencies rose all over the region in the 1960s and 1970s, some obviously inspired by Cuba and others the result of entirely domestic factors. Often encouraged by the United States, Latin American militaries increased their political and economic activity in response.

Cuba

Only 90 miles from the United States, filled with U.S. investment and tourists, dependent on the United States for a market for its sugar, ruled by the Caribbean's strongest dictator, and with one of the wealthiest, healthiest, and best-educated populations in Latin America, Cuba seemed an unlikely location for communist revolution in the late 1950s. Nonetheless, on January 1, 1959, the revolutionary 26th of July Movement, led by Fidel Castro and other opposition groups, overthrew Fulgencio Batista (1940–1944, 1952–1959).

Batista had dominated the island's politics since 1934. After seven years of comfortable, voluntary exile in Florida after the completion of his first term as president, Batista returned as dictator in 1952. He and his followers hoped that he would regenerate Cuba, but, as his fellow former strongmen Ibáñez and Vargas discovered, ruling was harder the second time around. Castro was one of his early opponents. Fidel Castro had grown up in the rough and tumble of student politics in Cuba in the late 1940s and early 1950s during an era of blatant corruption, open violence, and deep disillusionment. On July 26, 1953, Castro led a small band in an attack on the army barracks at Moncada in the southern part of the island. The rebels committed a series of tragic-comic mistakes leading to disaster. Castro barely escaped with his life and only by luck avoided execution when captured a few days later. Amnestied after two years in prison in 1955, he left for Mexico, where he plotted and raised money to mount a new invasion of Cuba. He returned in late 1956, making his way with a small group of rebels to the mountains in the southeastern part of the island. There he established a small guerrilla movement, supported by local rural people. During the next two years, Batista's regime crumbled both from within and without.

On the day the rebel army rolled into Havana, Castro declared that "This time the Revolution will truly come to power. It will not be…[as in the past]…when the masses were exuberant in the belief that they had at last come to power but thieves came to power instead. No thieves, no traitors, no interventionists! This time the revolution is for real." He faced a number of daunting obstacles. First, the 26th of July Movement would have to overcome its rivals among the groups that had overthrown Batista. There had never been more than a few thousand guerrilla soldiers, and no more than a few hundred trusted members of the 26th of July. Second, Castro at age 32 was the oldest of the revolutionaries. Neither he nor his followers had experience in administration, nor did they have an overall plan to govern. Castro thus needed reliable allies with expertise in governance. Third, Castro had to neutralize the United States, which had cut short Cuba's previous revolutions in 1898 and 1933.

Castro was surely the most popular figure in Cuba in 1959. Although the 26th of July Movement had not defeated Batista by itself, it was the most important group in the revolutionary coalition, and it had the only significant armed force in the country. Castro was initially very careful not to alienate crucial sectors of Cuban society and his early program was not particularly radical. None of the other organizations produced rival leadership.

The revolution began to take shape in 1960 when Castro took a number of measures against U.S. economic interests and signed a reciprocal trade pact with the Soviet Union, which agreed to buy Cuban sugar. Finally, in April 1961, Castro proclaimed his revolution socialist. He had concluded that he could not carry out radical changes while Cuba remained economically dependent on the United States. At the height of the Cold War, he found in the Soviet Union a counterbalance to U.S. opposition. During the next three decades, the Russians financed Castro's program for social justice in return for Cuban support for Soviet communism in the Third World. In addition, Castro discovered reliable allies with administrative expertise among the Communist Party of Cuba.

Two confrontations with the United States helped Castro solidify his regime. In April 1961, his army defeated an informal force of U.S. trained and supported Cuban exiles who invaded the island at the Bay of Pigs. Castro's victory made him an even greater hero than previously. In October 1962, the United States and the Soviet Union nearly went to war over the installation of offensive intercontinental ballistic missiles in Cuba. The U. S. Navy blockaded the island to prevent the arrival of additional weaponry. After a tense 13 days, the superpowers reached agreement where the United States promised not to invade Cuba in return for the Russian removal of missiles from the island. The United States, however, has maintained an embargo on trade with Cuba from that time to the present day.

The Cuban Revolution has had its ups and downs. Its economic program alternated between diversification and reemphasis on exports. Ultimately, the revolution never eliminated the nation's dependence on sugar exports. The Soviet Union replaced the United States as the predominant market for Cuban sugar and supplier of needed industrial products. Cuba became even more dependent on the Soviet Union than it had been on the United States. Three notable failed experiments marked the first decade of the Revolution in power. The first was an attempt to industrialize rapidly while diversifying agriculture. A resulting drastic fall in sugar production meant a decline in the ability to purchase necessary equipment for industrialization. Castro then called for a return to sugar, setting a target of a 10-million-ton harvest in 1970. This effort failed (though Cuba produced a record harvest) and badly damaged the infrastructure of the sugar industry. The second experiment was the attempt to create a new socialist Cuban populace. Castro sought to convince his compatriots to work for the general good, not for their own financial benefit. In the Revolution, there was employment for all. He mobilized the people through the Communist Party of Cuba and through local community organizations (Committees for the Defense of the Revolution, or CDRs). Moral incentives did not succeed in motivating most Cubans, however, and the regime abandoned them for nearly two decades. Lastly, Castro attempted unsuccessfully to foment revolutions all over Latin America, using the Cuban model of guerrilla warfare. Castro's second-in-command, Ernesto "Che" Guevara, lost his life in an effort to ignite revolution in Bolivia in the late 1960s.

Castro startled Cubans on July 26, 1970, when he admitted failure: "Our enemies say we are faced with difficulties, and in fact our enemies are right." His charisma and determination had not been enough. He then embarked on a program to institutionalize socialism. As politics grew more bureaucratic and structured, the regime, nonetheless, allowed more leeway in the economy in the late 1970s and early 1980s. Castro allowed the market and private entrepreneurs a place in daily life. Women took on a greater role in politics, holding 25 percent of the leadership positions by the mid-1980s. That all was not going as well as hoped, though, was evident in the mass migration of one hundred twenty-five thousand Cubans from their home between April and September of 1980. The second decade of the Revolution had ended in disappointment, as had the first.

As communism crumbled in Eastern Europe and the Soviet Union during the late 1980s, Castro, through his program of "rectification" begun in 1986, reinvigorated the Revolution's commitment to socialism. He returned to the moral incentives of the early 1960s. There would be no more private enterprise and markets. When Soviet and Eastern European aid ended in 1989, Castro dug in his heels. He would not surrender his socialist ideals.

The overall record of the Revolution is mixed. Among its most notable successes were universal literacy, excellent health care and training, equalization of wealth, and some advances in gender and racial equality. The most notable failures were the continued reliance on sugar exports and on a single market for that crop (the Soviet Union). Cuba also relied on the Soviet Union as a principal source of industrial products. Severe shortages of basic consumer commodities forced periodic rationing. Meanwhile, despite some advances in women's status, there was a conspicuous lack of women in the highest echelons of the government.

Nicaragua

Major upheavals in Central America occurred after World War II, when long-term dictators, pressured by U.S. diplomacy, retired or were overthrown by more progressive forces. The prolonged guerrilla wars and counterinsurgency in Central America began in the aftermath of the Cuban insurrection and resulted in the deaths of hundreds of thousands of people and displacement of millions more during the 1970s, 1980s, and early 1990s. By 2000, the nations of the region, their civil wars fought to stalemates, were at peace and democracies governed all.

In 1979, the Sandinista National Liberation Front (FSLN) in Nicaragua overthrew Anastasio Somoza Debayle and became the only leftist revolution after Cuba to win power through force of arms. It later became the only leftist revolution in Latin America to lose control of the government through fair elections. The Somoza family, Anastasio Somoza García (1935–1956) and his sons Luis Somoza Debayle (1956–1967) and Anastasio Somoza Debayle (1967–1979), ruled Nicaragua for 46 years through control of the National Guard, which operated as an enormous graft machine. Unlike in other Latin American countries, Nicaraguan dictators had precarious relations with the upper classes, who disapproved of the Somozas, but cooperated with them because they kept the masses under control. Moreover, the Somozas did not directly compete against the upper class's economic interests. There were enough spoils for both the small upper class and the Somozas.

Like many other Latin American insurgencies, the Sandinista National Liberation Front began in the early 1960s. It took its name from Augusto Sandino, who had led guerrillas against the U.S. occupation of Nicaragua during the late 1920s and who Somoza's henchmen had assassinated in 1934. Many of the movement's leaders were dead or in jail by 1968, but the movement rose again to fight in the 1970s. Its base widened as it attracted rural people, students, and the children of upper- and middle-class families. Like the Cuban guerrillas, the Sandinistas were never numerous, counting perhaps only about three thousand in 1978.

The Somoza regime began to disintegrate after a catastrophic earthquake in 1972 destroyed the capital city of Managua, taking twenty thousand lives. Anastasio Somoza Debayle incurred the hatred of many Nicaraguans when he misappropriated relief funds. In 1978, he lost the support of the upper classes when he ordered the assassination of long-time rival Pedro Joaquín Chamorro. Meanwhile, the FSLN united its squabbling factions and became a formidable force. Its soldiers took control of the National Palace in a daring raid in 1978, which clearly indicated Anastasio Somoza had lost his iron grip. After he resorted to brutal air bombing of civilians in a desperate effort to retain his power, Somoza fled on July 19, 1979. An estimated fifty thousand Nicaraguans died in the brief civil war.

The Sandinistas ruled for the next decade. They had not toppled the Somoza dynasty alone, but they, like the 26th of July Movement in 1959, had the largest armed force. The FSLN governed without national elections until 1984, when FSLN leader Daniel Ortega won the presidency. Unfortunately for the Sandinistas, they encountered implacable opposition to their regime by the U.S. administration of Ronald Reagan, which clandestinely and illegally backed the rival *Contras,* a conservative coalition, in a vicious civil war from 1981 to 1989 that cost another forty thousand Nicaraguans their lives. With the help of the other Central American presidents, the FSLN and the Contras finally reached a peace agreement in 1989.

The Sandinistas committed serious economic and administrative blunders mostly due to their inexperience. The civil war took an enormous toll not only in lives but also in billions of dollars in damages. The military draft, instituted to supply soldiers to combat the Contras, was very unpopular. But the single most important mistake of the Sandinista leadership was its failure to fully incorporate women. Much of the Sandinista guerrilla leadership was female, and many women heroes were wounded, raped, and tortured in war. Although the FSLN could not have won without their efforts, many of the movement's women felt disdained after 1979. The Sandinistas also angered traditional women, who did not want to see their children drafted into the army. They lost the 1990 election in large part because they had lost women's support.

Almost everyone in Nicaragua and abroad was surprised when Violeta Barrios de Chamorro, the widow of the martyred Pedro Joaquín Chamorro, won the 1990 election. Nicaraguans were exhausted from years of civil war and sought an alternative to the ineffective Sandinistas. The FSLN remained a powerful influence in the National Assembly, where it was the largest single party, and in the army. Nonetheless, Nicaraguans were so disillusioned with the Sandinistas that they elected two more Conservative presidents to succeed Chamorro in 1996 and 2002, the first instances in Nicaraguan history when one democratically elected president succeeded another. Despite the peace, Nicaragua still has not recovered from the devastation of years of civil war.

El Salvador

A leftist insurgency nearly won control of El Salvador in the 1980s. The nation's troubles dated back to the early 1930s, when the brutal dictatorship of General Maximiliano Hernández Martínez ordered the slaughter of thirty thousand rural Salvadorans. The upper classes, fearing another uprising, backed Hernández Martínez (1930–1944) until his overthrow in 1944. Thereafter, an alliance between wealthy coffee planters and the military governed through electoral fraud and repression. El Salvador had its first open election in 1972, but the government nullified it when it was clear that José Duarte, the opposition candidate, had received the most votes. Twelve years passed before the next legitimate election, and this time Duarte (1984–1989), who had been the real victor in 1972, won and took office in 1984.

Despite the democratic outcome of the election, a vicious civil war tore the country apart for the next five years. Guerrilla groups appeared in El Salvador in the late 1960s, with five different organizations active in the field during the 1970s. They drew their support from El Salvador's vast, exploited, migratory rural working class. In 1980, the Augustín Farabundo Martí Front for National Liberation (FMLN) brought them together. Between 1979 and 1983, the FMLN mounted its strongest challenge to the military–upper class alliance. The rebels nearly won the war, but the United States provided massive assistance to the Salvadoran army and turned the tide against them. The FMLN kept up its war after Duarte took power in 1984, reaching its peak strength in 1989, with an estimated eight thousand combatants, and briefly occupying the nation's capital of San Salvador with thirty-five hundred rebels.

Exhausted by years of civil war, Salvadorans went to the polls in 1989 and elected Alfredo Cristiani, the candidate of the National Republican Alliance (ARENA), a coalition of right-wing groups. Much as in Nicaragua, people turned to the Right to bring peace. Cristiani reached agreement with the guerrillas in 1991 and three ARENA presidents succeeded each other in 1994, 1999, and 2004.

Guatemala

The reformist regime that had overthrown long-time dictator Jorge Ubico (1930–1944) ended in 1954, when the U.S. Central Intelligence Agency sponsored a successful revolt by Colonel Carlos Castillo Armas. Castillo overturned a decade of land redistribution, labor protection, and other social improvements. His successor, Miguel Ydígoras Fuentes (1958–1963), likewise served the interests of the upper classes, but without the repression practiced by Castillo. In 1960, a guerrilla movement calling itself the Rebel Armed Forces, heartened by the Cuban example, took up arms. The military ousted Ydígoras in 1963 and then ruled behind the scenes for the next decade, waging a campaign of terror and murder in its efforts to combat the guerrillas. Two generals, Kjell Laugerud (1974–1978) and Romero Lucas García (1978–1982), won fraudulent elections and presided over intensified repression, a measure of economic gains, and an orgy of corruption. Death squads, determined to crush the rural insurgency, stalked the countryside, killing Indians, who supposedly supported the guerrillas. The scale of murder reached genocidal proportions. The war continued through coups and a string of presidents until 1996, when the government reached an accord with the rebels, ending nearly four decades of warfare that had caused two hundred thousand deaths. A semblance of democracy followed with democratically elected presidents in 2000 and 2004. As in the cases of Nicaragua and El Salvador, Guatemala lay in ruins.

Peru

From the 1960s through the 1990s, Peru experienced three distinct revolutionary movements. The first occurred when reformist military officers took control of the government in 1968 and proceeded to implement far-reaching changes. In the 1980s and early 1990s, a violent guerrilla organization terrorized the country and nearly toppled the government. Also in the 1990s, a third type of revolution took place under the auspices of a president who defeated the guerrillas, ruled as an elected dictator, and presided over an incipient economic recovery.

Ever since the 1930s, an impasse between the military–upper class alliance and Victor Raúl Haya de la Torre's American Popular Revolutionary Alliance, or APRA (see Chapter 12) had strangled Peruvian political life. By the early 1960s, there was some hope that change was possible. Unlike other strongmen of the decade, Manuel A. Odría (1948–1956) ended his regime peacefully in 1956. His successor, former president Manuel Prado (1939–1945, 1956–1962), had won a new term because he obtained APRA support by promising to legalize the party and to allow Haya de la Torre to run for president in 1962. Unfortunately, an intense three-way campaign between Haya, Fernando Belaúnde Terry of the Popular Action Party, and ex-dictator Odría ended with no one obtaining the necessary 33.3 percent of the vote required by the constitution. Haya de la Torre had received more votes than his two principal rivals, but the armed forces seized control of the government rather than allow him to assume office, even though he and his party had become much more conservative over the preceding decade. Thus, the impasse continued.

Belaúnde (1963–1968) narrowly won a replay of the election in 1963. Like many other Latin American heads of state in the twentieth century, he was elected by plurality rather than majority and was backed by a minority political party. He also did not have control of Congress and found himself caught in the middle between a wary military and an impatient Left. Not surprisingly, he was unable to govern effectively.

By 1968, the stage was set for revolution in Peru. Ironically, the old political configuration had reversed itself, for APRA had shifted its ideological stance from Left to Right, while the mid-level officer corps moved almost exactly in the opposite direction, from Right to Left. The reformist military regarded APRA as an obstacle to progress. With Haya de la Torre poised to win the presidency at long last in 1969 and Belaúnde's party hopelessly divided, the military seized power under the leadership of General Juan Velasco Alvarado. The new regime set out on what it called a "third way," advocating neither communism nor capitalism.

Velasco led a startling reform of the Peruvian economy. His hope was to establish class peace through state mediation, a strategy employed successfully by both Juan Perón in Argentina and the Institutionalized Revolutionary Party (PRI) in Mexico. From 1968 to 1975, Velasco redistributed more land than either the Bolivian or Mexican revolutions. His government granted half the nation's arable land to three hundred seventy-five thousand families, one-quarter of all rural dwellers. He also presided over an unprecedented expansion of government, doubling the state's control over the economy. As they would in Mexico and Chile, so-called technocrats took over most government functions. Like other populist regimes before him, Velasco's success rested in part on the ability to grow the economy and to improve living standards. Massive borrowing abroad financed much of his program.

In 1975, Velasco stepped down because of failing health. His successor, the far more conservative Francisco Morales Bermúdez, canceled many of Velasco's reform programs and adopted an austerity regime in order to pay the massive foreign debt incurred by the Velasco government. The military permitted new, democratic elections in 1980 and Belaúnde assumed the presidency a second time. A new constitution greatly broadened suffrage and limited the role of the armed services, but Belaúnde's new government was no more effective from 1980 to 1985 than his previous one had been 20 years earlier.

As Belaúnde struggled, a new and very dangerous threat arose in the Andes mountains—the Shining Path (*Sendero Luminoso*). Abimael Guzmán, the self-proclaimed "Fourth Sword of Marxism" (Marx, Lenin, and Mao were the others), was the mastermind of the movement, which began as a splinter of the already fragmented Peruvian Communist Party in 1970. The name derived from a quote from José Carlos Mariátegui, Peru's leading communist thinker, in which he proclaimed that "Marxism-Leninism will open a shining path to revolution." Guzmán dismissed other leftists in Latin America as traitors. The Cuban Revolution, for example, was "a petty bourgeois militaristic deviation." He also believed in violence. Sendero brutally murdered thousands of political officials, especially small landowners and those regarded as do-gooders. The awful violence intimidated many Peruvians, but also made enemies.

The Sendero organization was extremely disciplined and cohesive. Half of its leadership was female. It paid its soldiers well by Peruvian standards, using large amounts of money from taxes on narcotics traffickers. At its height, the Sendero had perhaps ten thousand guerrillas under arms and as many as one hundred thousand fellow travelers. It drew its strength from young people with poverty-stricken backgrounds, many of whom had achieved a university education only to find that neither government nor the private sector could provide them with satisfactory employment. Sendero also recruited heavily in the countryside and in the shantytowns of Lima.

By 1992, Sendero Luminoso had brought Peru to the verge of demoralization and collapse. Guerrilla victory appeared inevitable as the military seemed to fall apart and panic gripped the nation. Then on September 12, 1992, the tide turned, when the army unexpectedly captured Abimael Guzmán and much of the Sendero leadership. Without its highest echelons, the movement disintegrated. The war had cost thirty thousand lives.

Desperate for a savior as Sendero violence devastated the country, Peruvians elected little-known Alberto Fujimori president in 1990. Using the military and rural community organizations to defeat Sendero, he subsequently won reelection in 1995. With peace, the Peruvian economy grew rapidly. Fujimori governed autocratically. His third Peruvian "revolution" ended, however, when he had to flee the country in 2000 in order to avoid arrest amid major scandals. In 2001, Alejandro Toledo became the first Indian to win election as president.

The second revolution, the Shining Path, had brought the nation to its knees. Like the FMLN in El Salvador, the guerrillas had come very close to victory and the war had cost dearly in terms of human life and economic destruction.

Colombia

In Colombia, as in Peru, dysfunctional politics led to prolonged guerrilla warfare, which exacted a heavy toll on its people and economy. Colombian history had long been marred by bloody civil wars between its two major political parties, the Liberals and Conservatives. Following the overthrow of the dictator Gustavo Rojas Pinilla (1953–1957) in 1957, the two political parties formed the National Front. They agreed to alternate the presidency every four years and to distribute elected and appointed political offices equally. This arrangement endured for 16 years, finally ending the long-running violence between the two parties. But Colombia was hardly democratic during these years. The National Front permitted little dissent. Without outlets for peaceful protests, a number of guerrilla groups sprung up in the early 1960s. The M-19 group, founded in 1972, and the Revolutionary Armed Forces of Colombia (FARC) were the major guerrilla groups by the 1980s. The guerrillas often controlled various regions of the country, but they were fragmented and unwilling to unite to obtain victory. In the mid-1980s, President Belisario Betancur engineered peace between the government and the FARC and M-19. Eventually, the guerrilla groups became less interested in social justice than in narcotics trafficking and banditry. But the violence continues, often spreading to the cities. Colombia seemed to hover ever on the brink of chaos. In the only continuing insurgency in Latin America, peace seems unattainable.

The Tyrannies: Brazil, Argentina, and Chile

The threat of communist revolution, made real by events in Cuba after 1959, shook Latin American militaries. They became increasingly frustrated with democratic leadership and processes, which had allowed the Left to flourish. Their visions of themselves as political arbitrators and saviors of the nation intensified. With their allies among the radical Right upper and middle classes and the police, supported by training and resources from the United States, which viewed them as bastions of anti-communism in the Cold War, the armed services took control of many governments in the region. They conducted brutal counterinsurgency campaigns, and, in some cases, set about to totally recast their societies in order to see to it that no leftist movements could ever rise again. Violations of civil rights, torture, mass murder, and fear were their weapons. As we shall see in Chapter 15, fear pervaded daily life under military rule.

The military regimes in fact succeeded in eliminating the Left as an effective political force. From Castro's victory in 1959 to the present, only the Nicaraguan Sandinistas among all the many guerrilla movements ever took control of a national government. In Argentina, Brazil, Chile, and Uruguay, the military annihilated the Left. Leftist guerrillas conducted long, terrible civil wars in El Salvador, Guatemala, Peru, and Colombia, but the best they could achieve, in the first and last cases, was a draw. Hundreds of thousands of people, mostly noncombatants, died in these conflicts, many dragged out of their homes in terror, raped and tortured, and mercilessly killed. Rich, poor, women, men, children, bureaucrat or priest, businessman or nun—all became victims.

The United States aided and abetted Latin American armed forces and the rightist regimes that accompanied them. It was no coincidence, for example, that from January 1961 to November 1964 there were ten military coups in the region, which included, in chronological order, El Salvador, Ecuador (2), Argentina, Peru, Guatemala, Dominican Republic, Honduras, Brazil, and Bolivia, during what was the heyday of the Alliance for Progress, the U.S. program under Presidents John F. Kennedy and Lyndon B. Johnson that simultaneously sponsored economic development and counterinsurgency (see Table 14.1). The United States government envisioned military dictators as the pillars of anti-communism. The alliance between the military and the United States was instrumental in defeating guerrilla movements in Bolivia, Colombia, Guatemala, and Venezuela during the 1960s. The most notorious case was the capture and

Table 14.1

"Anti-political" Military Regimes, 1960–1990

Ecuador	1963–1966; 1972–1978
Guatemala	1963–1985
Brazil	1964–1985
Bolivia	1964–1970; 1971–1982
Argentina	1966–1973; 1976–1983
Peru	1968–1980
Panama	1968–1981
Honduras	1972–1982
Chile	1973–1990
Uruguay	1973–1984
El Salvador	1948–1984

Source: Brian Loveman, *For La Patria: Politics and the Armed Forces in Latin America* (Wilmington, DE: SR Books 1999), p. 186. "Anti-political" is Loveman's term.

execution of revolutionary Che Guevara in 1967 in Bolivia by U.S.-trained Bolivian counterinsurgency soldiers.

The dictatorships cast their politics in terms of male dominance. Soldiers considered feminists a threat to male domination and therefore the enemy. At its core, the ideology of these dictatorships sought the return to traditional gender values, with women subordinate to men and dedicated exclusively to the tasks of motherhood and home. Like society, females needed "subjugation and domination." If society was rotten, it was because all of its basic institutions, most importantly the patriarchal family, had failed. Moreover, the terror carried out by the military was intrinsically gendered. Rape was one of the most common forms of torture. These self-styled protectors of motherhood saw little irony in their practice of torturing women and dumping them, while still alive, into the ocean. Not surprisingly, women played active roles in resisting tyranny. The most famous examples were the Mothers of the Plaza de Mayo in Buenos Aires, who touted their motherhood when they marched in protest against the "disappearance" of their children.

Brazil

In many ways, Brazil's military coup of 1964 provided a model for the others that followed in one nation after another. First, the Brazilian armed forces overcame divisions between hard-liners and soft-liners, between junior and senior officers, between officers of middle- and upper-class origins, and between branches (air force, army, navy), and united for their campaign against the Left. Second, they abandoned their earlier practice of going in and out of government as conditions required and determined to run the government indefinitely. Third, the Brazilian military relied on well-trained technocrats for help in operating the government bureaucracy and state corporations, forming a combination that became known in academic circles as "bureaucratic authoritarianism." Fourth, the armed services' economic development strategy depended heavily on the suppression of wages, the attraction of foreign investment, and the accumulation of capital by the domestic upper class.

The long-term success of these strategies revolved around the middle class. In Brazil and elsewhere, the middle class often suffered economic setbacks in the wake of military takeovers. But the paralyzing fear of a Cuban-style insurgency stifled protests. In several cases, Brazil and Chile in particular, the military governments' policies brought about periods of tremendous growth during which the middle class prospered relative to the lower classes. Inevitably, of course, these upturns ended. When the middle class reached the point where fear of economic ruin loomed more heavily than the threat of communism, they began to push for democracy. By then, the militaries in most countries had proven as inept and corrupt as the civilians who had preceded them.

Brazil's fragmented politics set the stage for the overthrow of the elected government in the 1960s. As in many Latin American nations at the time, no political party earned a majority in the national legislature. Governments were often unable to act and the military grew impatient, fearing a Left takeover. Centrist Juscelino Kubitschek (1955–1960), elected president after the suicide of Getúlio Vargas, trod the precarious tightrope between Left and Right so common for the era in Latin America. Like others who preceded him, he sought to build his way to political stability and economic development. His great achievement was the construction of a new capital in the interior, Brasilia. Unfortunately for Brazil, as in Belaúnde's Peru, public works did not create stability.

Kubitschek's successor, Jânio Quadros (1961), was one of the oddest political figures of the era. Without the backing of any major political party Quadros won the 1960 election, promising to sweep away corruption. When Congress dragged its feet in adopting his reform program, Quadros announced he was quitting, just a few months after taking office. Evidently, he believed Congress would not accept his resignation and instead would vote him emergency powers. He was mistaken. João Goulart, who was vice president under both Kubitschek and Quadros (Brazilian law permitted split voting, allowing Goulart's election even though he was the running mate of Quadros's opponent) was to succeed to the presidency. The military balked. They fiercely opposed Goulart, a long time protégé of Vargas. With the serious threat of civil war looming, Goulart compromised, agreeing to turn over actual governance to a prime minister and a cabinet. The arrangement lasted for less than three years. The military, growing increasingly terrified of the Left, overthrew Goulart on April 1, 1964, and ruled for the next 21 years.

Immediately, the new regime set out to crush the Left and to establish order and discipline. General Humberto de Alencar Castello Branco (1964–1967) led the first military government. He adopted a series of Institutional Acts that severely curbed civil rights. He also framed a new economic development strategy, which emphasized industrialization financed by low wages and foreign investment. His successor, General Artur da Costa e Silva (1967–1969) further limited civil rights, closing Congress and instituting censorship, sparking opposition to the regime. By 1969, various guerrilla groups had begun operations against the dictatorship, robbing banks and kidnapping foreign diplomats, including the U.S. ambassador. These actions triggered five years of government-sponsored terror. By 1974, the military and police had eradicated all armed resistance. At the same time, both Costa e Silva and Emílio Garrastazú Médici (1969–1974) ruled over the Brazilan economic "miracle." When the boom subsided under General Ernesto Geisel (1974–1979), the military loosened its reins. By 1979, under General João Batista Figueredo (1979–1984), they prepared for transition to civilian rule.

Brazilians elected the first civilian president in more than two decades in 1985. Tancredo Neves, an old political hand, died two weeks after taking office, leaving the office to José Sarney, his vice president. Sarney faced difficult economic problems because the Brazilian military had financed its export-based, ISI, high-tariff economic program with heavy borrowing abroad. In addition to

Slice of Life — On the Street in São Paulo

NOWHERE WERE the effects of the failed politics of Left and Right more visible than on the streets of the large cities of Latin America, for nowhere were the sharp contrasts between rich and poor more evident. This was particularly important because the enormous migration of people to the great metropolises is the most crucial development of the post-World War II era.

In the years immediately after World War II, São Paulo was regarded as the "locomotive" of Brazil. Typical of its indomitable optimism, the city's motto was "São Paulo cannot stop." The city's population grew at the rate of 5.5 percent a year from 1940 to 1970. Three million people moved to São Paulo during the 1950s and 1960s. Half of the increase came from internal migration, people fleeing the terrible impoverishment of the countryside for anything better. The dream was not for everyone, however. In São Paulo, the poor live in *favelas* (ghettoes) on the city's outskirts and in run-down, stuffed tenements known as *corticos* (beehives) near the center. They are in dismaying contrast to the impressive skyscrapers, sophisticated subways, and high technology.

Street Children in São Paulo, Brazil

Wearying poverty has made life a constant struggle for survival, for there is never enough work and the children never have enough to eat. There is always too much alcohol and crime is epidemic. Anthropologist Nancy Scheper-Hughes relates the story of Biu de Ninguem. After years of living in the countryside in Northeast Brazil and a short stint in Recife, Biu migrated to São Paulo when she was in her thirties. Her common-law husband, Oscar, had determined there was a better life in the city. His brother had told him that there were high-paying jobs in the metropolis. Instead of the promised land, however, Niu, Oscar, and their children found a "filthy, crowded hovel...[in] an ugly and violent shantytown." The favela was far from the central city, with only inconvenient, dangerous buses to transport them. She and the children became quite ill and they soon returned to the countryside. Many more like her stayed.

Carolina Maria de Jesus, the author of the famous memoir of the São Paulo favelas, *Child of the Dark,* was perhaps more typical. Born in a dusty, small town

(continued on next page)

On the Street in São Paulo *(continued from previous page)*

in the backlands of Minas Gerais in 1914 (or 1915), the illegitimate child of an itinerant musician and a domestic servant in a bordello, she migrated to São Paulo as a young woman looking for a job and a better life. Unlike most migrants, she was literate, having attended school for two years and thereafter having taught herself. She worked as a domestic for several wealthy families. At 33, she became pregnant and her employers fired her. She built a shack out of scrap tin in a favela that measured 4 by 12 feet. When it rained, water poured in. She hung a sack over her window to salvage some privacy. Because the 168 dwellings in the favela had only one water spigot, women and children lined up at dawn to fill large cans. The residents bathed and washed their laundry in the neighboring river. The Caninde favela where Carolina made her home was unhealthy. Periodic flooding spread filth and disease. Carolina fed her children by foraging in garbage cans from which she salvaged and sold used paper, bottles, and cans. A good day brought in 25 to 30 cents, enough to barely provide for her family. On bad days, there was nothing. To make matters worse, daily life in the favela was dangerous. On one occasion, Carolina was stabbed five times.

The Brazilian economic miracle exacted a heavy toll on the poor of the cities, especially the children. The policies of the military regime transferred income from the poorest 40 percent of Brazilians to the richest 10 percent. Purchasing power plummeted. Government cuts in spending ended programs for children's health, welfare, and education. After the military takeover in the mid-1960s, infant mortality rates rose 40 percent. Those youths who survived infancy could expect only short, unhappy lives. Parents could no longer support their children and turned them out into the streets of the city, leading to a sharp rise in the numbers of abandoned street children. Malnutrition went along with unemployment and inflation.

Unfortunately, the transition to democracy and the restoration of the economy in the mid-1980s during the presidency of Fernando Henrique Cardoso (1995–2003) have not measurably improved the plight of the urban poor.

Questions for Discussion

Why do you suppose that the poor in the great cities of Latin America do not rebel? What happened to the strident struggle for control over everyday life in the great cities?

---

an enormous foreign debt, the military left behind a bloated bureaucracy in the government and government-run businesses.

In keeping with the tradition of electing independents without strong party affiliations as president, Brazilians chose Fernando Collor de Melo (1990–1992) when they went to the polls in 1990. The highly telegenic son of a very powerful family in the northeast state of Alagoas campaigned against corruption, much as Quadros had a generation earlier. Ironically, he proved notoriously corrupt himself, and Congress removed him from office. Vice President Itamar Franco (1992–1994) took over the presidency, the first time in Brazilian history that a peaceful transfer of power followed the ouster of an incumbent president. His finance minister, the internationally esteemed sociologist Fernando Henrique Cardoso, brought down inflation, a feat that won him the presidency in the election of 1994. As chief executive, Cardoso (1995–2003) effected important positive changes that righted the Brazilian economy.

The first Latin American nation to fall to a rightist military, Brazil appears to have endured the shortest and least severe reign of terror. It regained its political equilibrium by the mid-1990s, electing a majority president. As a result, its economic prospects were perhaps the most optimistic in the region. In 2003, former labor union leader Luís Inácio Lula de Silva, known as Lula, won election as president.

Argentina

After the fall of Juan Perón in 1955, Argentina entered an era of prolonged political paralysis and economic stagnation. Neither military nor civilian governments found common ground between the classes, nor did they find a formula for development. Military regimes divided over whether or not to include the Peronists (followers of Perón), mostly labor union members, in the political process. Alternating repression and tolerance, the military found it could not govern with or without its antagonists. The more the military attacked the Peronists, the stronger the Peronists grew.

A little less than three years after overthrowing Perón, the military returned the government to civilian rule, under President Arturo Frondizi, from a wing of the Radical Party (the party headed by Hipólito Yrigoyen years earlier). Frondizi personified the impossibilities of Argentine politics. He won the election with the clandestine support of the Peronists, but could not balance the demands of the labor unions for higher wages and lower prices with the need to stabilize the economy. The Army forced him out in 1962, when he refused to annul local elections won by the Peronists. The following year, obscure country doctor Arturo Illia (1963–1966), from a branch of the Radical Party that opposed Frondizi, won the presidency with a mere 25 percent of the vote. Amazingly, Illia lasted nearly three years before General Juan Carlos Onganía literally tossed him out into the street.

Impatient with democratic politics, hard-liner Onganía set out to reform Argentina from above without popular backing. The new dictator proclaimed his intent at national renovation "The Argentine Revolution." He outlawed political parties and expelled leftist students and faculty from the national universities. His policies spurred massive protests, led by students and automobile workers in May 1969 in the city of Córdoba. Ranking among the greatest popular uprisings in

Argentine history, the *cordobazo,* as it came to be known, underlined the political and economic impasse in which the country found itself.

The following year, several Peronist guerrilla groups began operations, one of which, the *Montoneros,* kidnapped and killed former president Pedro Aramburu (1955–1958). For the next two years, these organizations staged more kidnappings, robberies, and assassinations. The bands were comprised of young men and women in their twenties, mostly middle-class students, who had had enough of the traditional Left. Though few in number and bitterly divided among themselves, and generally ineffective despite their well-publicized escapades, the guerrillas drew a massive response from the upper classes and the military, who encouraged vicious gangs that took reprisals on the Left. One such group, "The Hand," whose membership consisted of off-duty police, kidnapped and tortured student and union leaders. Argentina descended into murder and chaos.

The army overthrew Onganía after Aramburu's death, replacing him with General Roberto M. Levingston (1970–1971), but the violence continued to escalate. General Alejandro Lanusse (1971–1973) succeeded Levingston in February of 1971 after a second uprising erupted in Córdoba. Desperate to end the upheavals, Lanusse legalized Peronism for the first time in 18 years. By this time, Perón had reached mythical status in the eyes of many Argentines. The election of 1973 brought his stand-in, Héctor Cámpora, to the presidency. Later that year, Perón returned to win a new vote, demonstrating just how desperate the military had become, allowing the hated Perón to return as its only hope to contain the Left. But Perón was caught in the middle between Left and Right, even within his own party. In failing health, the 78-year-old Perón was not up to the task of governing. He had no new solutions, only his old program of shifting income to workers. On July 1, 1974, he died.

Guerrilla warfare soon resumed and rightist police, military, and paramilitary struck back hard, killing leftists at the rate of fifty a week by early 1975 and greatly surpassing the guerrillas in their fierceness and success. Perón's third wife, María Estela Martínez "Isabelita" de Perón, succeeded him as president amidst the tumult. The army deposed her in March 1976.

The darkest chapter of Argentine history took place from 1976 to 1983, as the army sought to wipe out the Left and Peronism. Due process of law vanished. By 1978, the army had crushed the guerrillas and killed most labor union leaders down to the shop steward level. Although the brutal regime of General Jorge Videla brought a measure of peace, it proved inept at managing the economy. In desperation, the army started a war against Great Britain in April 1982. Argentine forces occupied the Malvinas (Falkland Islands) in the South Atlantic, a territory Great Britain had seized 150 years earlier. General Leopoldo Galtieri (1981–1982), the new president, had hoped to rally the nation behind the war effort. He miscalculated the British response, however. He had expected Prime Minister Margaret Thatcher to do nothing more than issue a token protest, but instead the British went to war. The military also believed the United States, an ally in the anti-communist crusade in the Western Hemisphere, would prevent the British from retaliating. Instead, the administration of Ronald Reagan, with close ties to the Thatcher government, sided with the British. For the Argentines, the Falklands/Malvinas War was disastrous, resulting in two thousand casualties. The 72-day war cost the already strapped Argentine treasury $2 billion. The great defeat greatly weakened whatever public esteem the military might have once enjoyed and forced it to give up control of the government.

Elections were held in 1983, and Raúl Alfonsín, the candidate of yet another branch of the Radical Party and an old opponent of the military terror, assumed the presidency. Picking up the pieces of the disastrous military rule was difficult. Like Frondizi and Illia before him, Alfonsín was a man in the middle. Neither the military nor the unions were willing to concede or conciliate very much. Even after the appalling revelations of mass murder and torture and the trials and convictions of many senior officers for their crimes, the army and the police remained a menacing presence in Argentine life.

Alfonsín left office in 1989 in the first peaceful transfer of power from one elected president to another in Argentina since 1928. Peronist Carlos Menem won the election with the support of the military. Menem served two terms (1989–1999) and enjoyed some success in the economy, despite rampant corruption. He privatized the nation's vast, inefficient state enterprises. Fernando de la Rua succeeded him, but soon encountered a dismaying economic crisis, which caused him to resign, with three presidents following him in fast order. A measure of calm returned in 2003, when Néstor Kirchner, a provincial governor, won election as president. But the terrible "Dirty War" from 1976 to 1983 remains an unhealed wound in the heart of Argentine politics. Thirty thousand people had "disappeared" and many were never accounted for, while many of the murderers had gone unpunished.

Chile

The tyranny that emerged in Chile was the most shocking because it had long had a reputation for democratic, nonviolent politics. After the dismal second regime of Carlos Ibáñez (1952–1958), Chileans turned to another familiar name, Jorge Alessandri (1958–1964), the son of former president Arturo Alessandri. A Conservative, the younger Alessandri barely squeaked out a victory over Socialist Salvador Allende. Once in office, he had little success in instituting badly needed economic reforms. Fearing that Allende might win the 1964 election, the upper and middle classes embraced the Christian Democratic Party candidate Eduardo Frei (1964–1970) in 1964, who easily defeated Allende. Frei's slightly left-of-center government purchased the foreign-owned copper mines and adopted extensive reforms, bettering conditions for agricultural workers, but could never satisfy more radical Chileans. Even considerable assistance from the

LATIN AMERICAN LIVES

AN ARGENTINE MILITARY OFFICER

THE YEARS FROM 1976 to 1983 were Argentina's nightmare. The military, police, and vigilantes kidnapped, tortured, and killed thousands of its citizens. Military officers threw naked, drugged civilians from airplanes over the South Atlantic Ocean. Squads of white Ford Falcons arrived at homes in the middle of the night and took away their occupants, whom no one ever saw again. Soldiers raped female prisoners. Terrorist gangs kidnapped pregnant women, taking the babies and killing the mothers. Even today, few military officers are repentant for the deeds of this era. Who were the soldiers who could have committed such acts? What was it about the institution of the military that led it to turn viciously on its own people?

In 1995, retired Naval Captain Adolfo Scilingo and a half dozen other ex-officers publicly confessed to murder. While stationed at the Navy Mechanics School as a junior officer in 1977, Scilingo had flown on two flights during which he personally threw more than thirty living people into the ocean. He reported that his superiors had told him that these were extraordinary times requiring unusual actions.

The Argentine military was at almost every point before 1976 divided into two main groups: those who would maintain the constitutional order, even if they opposed the policies of the civilian government, and those who would overthrow any civilian government. There were also splits between the generals and the lesser-ranking officers. They argued over personalities and management styles. Finally, there were disagreements between the Army, Navy, and Air Force. The military previously had taken over the government in 1930, 1943, 1955, 1962, and 1966. Although their divisions never entirely disappeared, the armed forces unified from 1976 to 1983 in what they believed was a holy mission to save their fatherland. This time they vowed to remain in control.

Captain Adolfo Scilingo, one of the Argentine military officers who admitted murdering civilians during the "Dirty War" 1976–1983).

Prior to 1976, Latin American officers trained at their individual nation's military academy. They chose their branch (cavalry, infantry, or artillery) during the first year of their four-year course. Supply officers attended the academies, but they did not develop the same bonds as the line officers. The rigorous training emphasized character and tradition. The academies turned out men who had "a very subjective and very romantic…" worldview.

New officers experienced rigid discipline. They fell under the complete authority of their commanding officer, who often took an interest in the junior officer's social life and whose approval was necessary to marry. They earned promotions periodically: sub-lieutenant to lieutenant in four years, to captain in eight. Officers attended new schools at regular intervals. Selection to the status of general staff officers through examinations assured higher ranks. Those who reached the rank of colonel after about 20 years had received a year of higher military studies, which educated them in important national concerns and they also traveled abroad, often to the United States. The Argentine military was heavily influenced by German practices prior to World War II and by U.S. doctrine thereafter.

An officer's experience throughout the twentieth century would also include eroding salaries, outmoded equipment, and an intensifying sense of loyalty to the military. The officer corps believed itself above civilian petty politics in the abstract, but was mired in them in reality. Officers saw their duty was to defend their nation, but they disdained the civilians they swore to protect.

The generation of officers that came of age during the 1970s was either from small towns in the interior or sons or grandsons of immigrants. The previous cohort of officers had included many second-generation Argentines (half of the generals in 1950). As ethnic Argentines, they were often super-patriotic. Many sons of officers followed their fathers into the military. They lived to great extent in an insular world with military friends and family, which created a mentality of the military against the world. These officers did not trust civilians. The burst of leftist terrorism in the 1970s struck hard at their psyches, traditions, and beliefs. They saw themselves under siege by international communism.

By 1976, the Argentine military was desperate. It had intervened repeatedly in politics since 1930 to no effect. The nation seemed to regard the military with respect. Peronism was a non-healing sore, but bringing back the dictator was not an option after 1974. (He was, of course, dead.) The international situation frightened them, for insurgencies were everywhere: Vietnam, Africa, and other parts of Latin America. Fidel Castro had sponsored guerrillas (unsuccessfully) in neighboring Bolivia. Reflective of their middle-class backgrounds and decades of indoctrination, the office corps struck hard against its real and imagined enemies. The results scarred Argentina forever.

Questions for Discussion

How did the Argentine military become so integral to the years of terror during the 1970s and 1980s? What factors caused the struggle between Left and Right to degenerate into brutality? How would you compare the years of the terror with some of the internecine strife during the nineteenth century, such as the civil wars between Liberals and Conservatives?

U.S. Alliance for Progress, a program designed especially to support centrist governments against the threat of leftist guerrilla movements, did not prevent a downturn in the economy. The upper- and middle-class coalition that had elected Frei in 1964 crumbled, paving the way for Allende's victory in 1970. Together, the Christian Democratic and Socialist candidates drew two-thirds of the vote. Both parties advocated reform, and, clearly, so did most Chileans.

The first elected socialist head of state in the Americas, Allende started out well, but ended in tragedy. During his first year, a strong economy based on high copper prices on world markets enabled him to shift income to the lower and middle classes. The upper class, nonetheless, remained intransigent in opposition to the new regime. In the long term, Allende's ability to govern depended on three requirements. First, the radical elements of his Left coalition had to moderate their demands so as not to frighten the military or middle class. Second, the president had to win over the middle classes, which were wary of his radical program. Finally, the military had to stay committed to civilian constitutional rule. The armed forces were divided between hard-liners, who wanted to overthrow Allende, and moderates, who upheld the tradition of Chilean democracy. Allende failed to obtain any of the three. He could not control the radical Left. Rural people occupied land belonging to members of the upper class and industrial workers took over factories. His government threatened the businesses of the middle class by adopting a range of reforms favorable to workers. Amid deteriorating economic conditions and growing violence, the hard-liners prevailed. The military rebelled on September 11, 1973, and overthrew Allende.

The commander of the army, General Augusto Pinochet, led the coup. He set about not just to rid the nation of its Socialist president, but to eliminate the Left entirely. The armed forces and allied rightist thugs imprisoned, tortured, and murdered thousands. Pinochet eliminated Congress, political parties, and labor unions. The dictator also sought to reconstruct the Chilean economy by doing away with almost all business regulations, ending state involvement in enterprises, and opening the nation to free trade.

Despite harsh repression, Chileans never forgot their democratic tradition. Finally, in 1988 a national plebiscite ended military rule. Christian Democrat Patricio Aylwin (1990–1994) won the presidential election in 1989. Chile enjoyed a measure of economic prosperity in the early 1990s. Christian Democrat Eduardo Frei Ruiz-Tagle (1994–2000), the son of the former president, won the presidency in 1993. Ricardo Lagos, a Socialist, succeeded him. Chile's successive democratically elected governments since 1989 have allowed its economy to recover to a larger extent than in Argentina. The country even experienced an economic boom in the 1990s. Nonetheless, the Chilean military remains a powerful force and quite unrepentant.

The Exception: Mexico

As we saw in Chapter 11, no further revolution took place in Mexico after the bloody decade of 1910 to 1920. Instead, a single-party political system developed that began as relatively responsive to the middle and lower classes, but which over time, despite a prolonged economic boom, became less and less in touch with its constituents and more and more corrupt. There were sporadic, serious protests against the government and a number of minor guerrilla movements, but no threat from the Left arose. The government used selective violence to keep the peace, but not to the extent of the widespread terror elsewhere. Under the auspices of the governing party, since 1946 known as the Institutionalized Revolutionary Party (PRI), Mexicans experienced such a prolonged interval of social peace and high economic growth that people called it the Mexican economic miracle. With little or no opposition at the polls, PRI presidents followed one another in orderly succession during the post-war era: Miguel Alemán (1946–1952), Adolfo Ruiz Cortines (1952–1958), Adolfo López Mateos (1958–1964), and Gustavo Díaz Ordaz (1964–1970).

From the 1940s on, the Revolution was over and in its stead the PRI chose to cooperate closely with business. But as long as the economy grew, there was enough wealth for many sectors of Mexican society to benefit. PRI policies redistributed income to the middle class and upper levels of the working class downward from the wealthiest echelons and upward from the poorest. Labor unions loyal to the party received higher wages and better working conditions. There was modest land reform, but after the mid-1960s, the government encouraged agriculture for export rather than for the domestic market, often to the detriment of small landowners and cooperatives. The regime pacified the poverty-stricken majority of Mexicans by subsidizing staples (tortillas, for example) and basic services (the Mexico City Metro) and by holding out the hope of eventual land reform to rural dwellers. Patronage and personal loyalty were paramount in the political spoils system. Power centered in the office of the president, who served for six years virtually unchecked by any other authority and then named a successor before leaving office.

By the late 1960s, however, it had become clear that the PRI was losing its touch. The party never rejected violence as a means of stifling opposition, but usually found bribery more effective. In 1968, however, amidst growing protests from students and workers and after the loss of state and local elections in various sections of the nation, PRI leaders and the army panicked when a large group met in the Plaza of the Three Cultures in Mexico City on October 2. Mexico was to host the 1968 Summer Olympic Games and the government feared embarrassment. Secret police and soldiers fired on unarmed people, killing an estimated five hundred. Many of the victims had not even participated in the rally, but were shot on their way home to the apartment complexes in the area. The massacre at Tlatelolco, as it became known, discredited the regime at home and abroad.

The discovery and exploitation of vast petroleum reserves after 1970 may have convinced the PRI leadership that, despite the party's political problems, the economy would remain strong. Instead, mismanagement, widespread corruption, and runaway foreign debt brought an end to the miracle. Most egregious were the spiraling debt and the corruption. At the height of the oil boom, foreign bankers clamored to lend enormous sums to Mexico. Borrowing was predicated on oil revenues continuing at high levels, but oil prices soon declined, leaving a mountain of loans that Mexico could not hope to repay. At the same time, corruption spun out of control as well. The presidencies of Luis Echevarría (1970–1976), José López Portillo (1976–1982), Miguel de la Madrid (1982–1988), Carlos Salinas de Gortari (1988–1994), and Ernesto Zedillo (1994–2000) were venal beyond imagination. López Portillo and Salinas each reputedly ended their terms with more than $1 billion in graft. To make matters worse, during the 1980s, the government moved away from career politicians for leadership, replacing them with to so-called technocrats (*técnicos*), well-educated bureaucrats often trained abroad. The PRI completely lost contact with the Mexican people as a result.

By the late 1980s, the PRI could no longer count on uncontested automatic victories in elections. The left-of-center opposition candidate Cuauhtémoc Cárdenas very likely won the presidential election of 1988. Computer vote tallying stopped inexplicably in the middle and, after the count resumed, Carlos Salinas de Gortari of the PRI emerged the winner with just over half the votes cast. During the late 1980s and into the 1990s, the conservative *Partido de Acción Nacional* (PAN) began to claim victories in mayoralty and gubernatorial elections. The election of 1994 marked the virtual disintegration of the PRI, when the assassination of its original candidate, Donaldo Colosio, forced the party to nominate Ernesto Zedillo. He won, but the writing was on the wall. Finally, in 2000 Vicente Fox, the PAN candidate, won a clear majority, ending the longest continuous regime in Latin American history.

The Struggle for Control of Everyday Life

Have Latin Americans given up the struggle for control over their everyday lives? For two decades, the terror overwhelmed this struggle. Globalization threatens to eliminate differences between nations and peoples. Nonetheless, many Latin Americans retain their sense of locality. And certainly, they continue to seek control over their daily lives. Local loyalties may have helped to save the nation-state from disintegration. The strong sense of local governance and tradition in the Peruvian highlands, for example, was the bulwark of opposition to the Shining Path guerrillas during the 1990s. The Shining Path, by killing village leaders and priests and by brutally intruding on local prerogatives, thoroughly alienated much of the countryside. Local organizations brought together to protect villages against the guerrillas were crucial participants in the eventual defeat of the insurgency. The deterioration of the official revolutionary political party (PRI) in Mexico, which led to its loss of power in 2000, owed in great part to its unresponsiveness to local needs and sensibilities. Power had grown over-centralized in a nation where local traditions were so strong. The victorious opposition party, the National Action Party (PAN), was to considerable extent a product of Mexico's peripheral states, particularly in the north.

Unquestionably, new factors have altered this unending struggle for control over everyday life. The vast migration from the countryside to the cities (see Chapters 13 and 15) transformed it. People no longer resided in villages, but rather in slums, barrios, or squatter settlements. The village was no longer the basis for their politics. Instead, people formed neighborhood organizations to obtain services, such as water, electricity, schools, and roads. At the work place, the new migrants confronted new adaptations. If they were fortunate, they might join a labor union. Most workers had to negotiate their own way. Those who were self-employed, as street vendors, for example, faced similar conditions. A very few joined associations that represented them, but most were on their own. The struggle for local autonomy became to a large extent irrelevant for urban dwellers. New arrivals found it difficult to maintain old traditions from their country homes. Mass media exposed dwellers to consumer culture. Consumerism and individualism undermined traditions. The decision to leave the countryside shattered the old ways. For those who remained in the countryside, much of the isolation once inherent in rural life disappeared. Few could earn their living solely in agriculture, and, as a result, even those who stayed often had to supplement their income with work elsewhere. Mexicans regularly crossed the border to the United States for planting and harvest and returned home. Bureaucratic authoritarian and dictatorial regimes determinedly undermined local prerogatives. When they set about to modernize or to renovate their societies in the 1970s and 1980s, these governments saw local governance and culture as impediments to their mission. The end of tyrannies and the comeback of democracy have given a new life to local autonomy.

The New Global Economy

As the new millennium began, then, democratic elections and relatively smooth transitions of power prevailed throughout Latin America. But these new regimes still faced the daunting economic challenges and mounting social tensions that had proven the downfall of the military dictatorships that preceded them. During the

How Historians Understand | Theories of Economic Development and History

SINCE WORLD WAR II, SUCCESSIVE theories of economic development not only have greatly influenced the policies of Latin American governments, the behavior of businesspeople, and the plight of hundreds of millions of people, but also the interpretation of historical events and trends.

During the nineteenth century, ideas advocating free trade and comparative advantage dominated. Accordingly, Latin American nations were to produce agricultural and mineral commodities for export and open their markets for imports of manufactured goods. The Great Depression of the 1930s challenged these perspectives. Economists no longer universally believed that the export of primary products was sustainable as a means to develop. In the late 1940s, the United Nations Economic Commission for Latin America (UNECLA or CEPAL), led by Raúl Prebisch, an Argentine, put forward the center-periphery paradigm, also known as structuralism. This view dominated Latin American economic thinking through the 1970s. It argued export economies tended in the long run to suffer from a decline in the terms of trade. In other words, the prices received for primary goods decreased because the demand for primary products would not rise as fast as income, while at the same time the prices of industrial products rose over time. The only way structuralists believed that Latin America could develop was to substitute domestic for imported manufactures. This encouraged Import Substitution Industrialization (see Chapters 12 and 14) as the development policy widely adopted in Latin America after World War II.

By the 1960s, however, ISI had clearly failed. Dependency analysis arose to explain Latin America's lack of development. There were two schools of *dependencia*–the neo-Marxist and the reformist. Dependency advocates believed that peripheral (underdeveloped) countries, like those in Latin America, and center nations (the United States, Western Europe, and more recently Japan) were involved in an unequal exchange that would always exploit the former and benefit the latter. Consequently, the only way to change the system was to either overthrow it, which the Marxist school advocated, or reform it. The most important translation of dependency into policy resulted in further government involvement in the economies of Latin American nations to mitigate the influence of the developed center. Ironically, in order to finance their economic interventions, governments borrowed huge sums from the industrialized nations.

In opposition to the dependency school, the diffusionist model maintained that technology, capital, trade, political institutions, and culture spread out from the advanced nations to the backward countries. Within the underdeveloped nations, there also were dual societies in which a more advanced urban sector and a backward rural sector coexisted. The diffusionists maintained that ideas and capital spread from urban to rural. Accordingly, they believed that policy should be directed so that the more advanced nations cooperate with the middle classes in less advanced nations to modernize the latter. Contrary to the diffusionists, the *dependentistas* believed that the diffusion of ideas and capital made the less developed nations dependent on the giving country and therefore widened the gaps between developed and less developed nations. This situation was duplicated in the dual domestic society.

Because no Left regime (with the exception of Cuba) endured for more than a decade in Latin America after 1945, due to the opposition of upper class–military alliances throughout the region, the intervention of the United States, and communist regimes everywhere falling into economic crises by the 1980s, Latin Americans became disillusioned with governments' strong involvement in the economy. Pressured heavily by the United States and international lending agencies such as the International Monetary Fund and the World Bank, Latin American policy makers turned to the century-old liberal paradigm, now known as neo-liberalism. The idea that market forces will eventually bring equity dominated once again.

How did these differing views affect historians? These theories overwhelmingly emphasized outside factors as causes of Latin American underdevelopment. This tended to lessen the importance of domestic circumstances. In a sense, these theories removed culpability from the upper class–military alliance, from individual leaders, political parties, traditions, and culture. They reduced the lower classes to meaningless non-participants. The emphasis on international factors tended to push aside the consideration of the regional and local, which had predominated in Latin America since pre-Columbian times, leaving out the most meaningful aspects of culture and society, and over-emphasizing economics. Finally, dependency, especially, did not incorporate change over time, perhaps the most crucial aspect of an historian's purview.

In recent times, historians have reduced their concerns with economics and turned to the occurrences of everyday life and culture. This has placed the lower classes in a more central place in their studies. There has been a shift from international to local and from great forces to people.

Questions for Discussion
Why have the various models of economic development failed in Latin America? How has the struggle for control over daily life fit into the various models of development?

half-century after World War II, the countries of the region pursued three general strategies to achieve economic development. The first was to promote and diversify exports, either by finding new primary products (oranges in Brazil or petroleum in Mexico, for example) or by using the advantage of inexpensive labor costs to manufacture goods for European or the United States markets. The second was Import Substitution Industrialization. There were two versions of ISI: one set forth by democratic governments and the other by military dictatorships. Both export enhancement and ISI required extensive government involvement, costly importation of capital goods, heavy foreign borrowing, and massive foreign investment. Widespread poverty sharply limited domestic markets, placing a brake on economic development based on ISI. The third strategy, neo-liberalism, adopted after policymakers declared ISI a failure, threw open Latin American markets and removed governments from direct participation in the economy.

Despite so-called economic miracles in Mexico from the 1950s through 1970, in Brazil in the late 1960s and early 1970s, and Chile in the 1990s, major problems hampered sustained economic growth in Latin America in the post-1959 era. The region experienced increasingly volatile cycles of booms and busts because all of the strategies for development depended on external markets, capital, and technology. Periodic downturns cost many people their jobs. Prolonged periods of steep inflation eroded the standard of living of the working and middle classes. Staggering foreign debt interest payments absorbed the preponderance of government revenues, leaving little or nothing for social welfare. The already sharp inequalities in the distribution of wealth and income widened, as the rich grew ever richer and the poor even poorer. Corruption ran rampant.

The world petroleum crises of the 1970s constituted a two-fold curse for Latin America. Not only did the rise in oil prices cause general inflation and economic downturn, but it also exacerbated the debt crisis in many countries. The members of the Organization of Petroleum Exporting Countries (OPEC) earned enormous sums from the increases in oil revenues, which they deposited in Western financial institutions. The banks faced the dilemma of where to invest this money. Latin American nations (mostly Argentina, Brazil, Mexico, and Venezuela) required vast funds to develop. Latin American nations were able to pay the interest on the debt as long as their economies grew. Badly damaged by the second oil crisis, however, Latin American countries could not pay by the early 1980s. Mexico nearly defaulted in August of 1982. Rescheduling the debt and a short-lived upturn avoided the collapse of the international banking system, but the enormous burden for Latin America was not lessened in the long term (see Table 14.2). From 1978 to 2000, Argentina increased its foreign debt tenfold. Brazil quadrupled it. Mexico increased it by 500 percent. Argentina, Brazil, and Mexico in 2000 owed more than a half billion dollars abroad.

Latin Americans continued to struggle with recurring debt crises and bouts of steep inflation through the new millennium. With the end of communism in the former Union of Soviet Socialist Republics and Eastern Europe in the early 1990s, and all the free-market reforms in China, the nations of the region had little choice but to adopt neo-liberal policies and embrace the emerging global economy. In the most striking example, Mexico joined Canada and the United States in the controversial North American Free Trade Agreement (NAFTA) in

Table 14.2

Latin American Total Disbursed External Debt, 1978–2000
(In millions of dollars)

	1978	1980	1985	1990	1995	2000
Argentina	12,496	27,162	49,326	62,233	98,547	147,000
Brazil	53,614	70,565	105,126	123,439	159,256	235,000
Mexico	33,946	50,700	97,800	101,900	165,600	163,200
Latin America	153,293	228,236	377,243	443,049	616,919	750,855

Source: ECLA, *Statistical Yearbook for Latin America and the Caribbean,* 1990, 502–503; ECLA, *Statistical Yearbook for Latin America and the Caribbean,* 2000, p. 769.

1994. Working people in Mexico, Central America, and the Caribbean find themselves competing on the international market with even cheaper labor in far-flung parts of the world. In the short run at least, this has resulted in dislocations to domestic small businesses and only minimal increases in employment.

Conclusion

Momentous changes marked the half-century after the Cuban Revolution in Latin America. Guerrilla wars and military reigns of terror caused the deaths of countless thousands and dislocated hundreds of thousands more. At times, it seemed as if the region had descended into madness. An era of democracy followed those dark days. The end of insurgencies in Guatemala and Peru in the 1990s left only one major rebellion—that in Colombia.

Though democracy rules almost every nation of Latin America, there are threatening clouds overhead. Colombia appears ever on the verge of disintegration as narcotics cartels and guerrillas control substantial portions of territory. Venezuela seems equally shaky, its people unable to reach any form of political consensus. Who can guess what will happen when Fidel Castro finally passes from the stage in Cuba? Most important, however, is the problem of how Latin America can assure the continuation of democracy when, as we will see in Chapter 15, poverty and misery pervade the region.

Learning More About Latin Americans

Gwynne, Robert N., and Cristobal Kay, eds. *Latin America Transformed: Globalization and Modernity,* 2nd ed. (New York: Arnold, 2004). Filled with statistical data and interesting analyses.

Masterson, Daniel. *Militarism and Politics in Latin America: Peru from Sánchez Cerro to Sendero Luminoso* (New York: Greenwood, 1991). Clarifies the role of the military in Peru.

Menchú, Rigoberta, Trans. Ann Wright. *I, Rigoberta Menchú: An Indian Woman in Guatemala* (New York: Verso, 1984). Heart-breaking story of rural women in Guatemala in the midst of civil war.

Miller, Francesca. *Latin American Women and Social Justice* (Hanover, NH: University Press of New England, 1991). Relates the participation of women in organized social movements.

Pérez-Stable, Marifeli. *The Cuban Revolution: Origins, Course, and Legacy*, 2nd ed. (New York: Oxford University Press, 2003). Fair-minded assessment of the revolution.

Smith, Lois, and Alfred Padula. *Sex and Revolution: Women in Socialist Cuba* (New York: Oxford University Press, 1996). Explores the disappointing treatment of women in Cuba.

Stern, Steve, ed. *Shining and Other Paths: War and Society in Peru, 1980–1995* (Durham, NC: Duke University Press, 1998). Essays on the Sendero Luminoso and its relations with people in the countryside.

15

EVERYDAY LIFE,
1959 TO THE PRESENT

THE UNPRECEDENTED REIGN of terror perpetrated by rightist military dictatorships in Argentina, Brazil, Chile, and Uruguay and the vicious civil wars between rightist militaries and rightist and leftist guerrillas in Central America, Colombia, and Peru, described in Chapter 14, created an era of deep political tensions and economic hardships. Not only were hundreds of thousands killed, wounded, and displaced, but nearly everyone else suffered uncertainty. Latin Americans risked imprisonment, torture, or death for speaking their minds in public. In countries like Argentina and Guatemala, few people were not related to or familiar with someone taken away in the middle of the night or killed by leftist guerrillas or rightist death squads. To make matters worse, military regimes often installed nonpolitical technocrats as the managers of their governments. Since neither the military nor the technocrats saw themselves as accountable to voters, their new economic programs disregarded potential repercussions on the middle and lower classes. They instituted policies that dismembered direct government involvement in business enterprises and opened national borders to free trade and foreign investment. As a result, many Latin Americans suffered extensive job losses and a large-scale erosion of their standard of living.

The reemergence of democracy, beginning in the mid-1980s, while ending the terror, did not improve economic conditions for the middle and lower classes. The new democracies continued the neo-liberal policies of the dictatorships, sharply limiting their ability and willingness to alleviate the widespread suffering. Even the best efforts of governments to improve the quality of life for the middle and lower classes could not keep up with population growth, especially in the big cities, nor did they compensate for rampant inflation. Neo-liberal policies begun by the dictatorships and continued by the new democracies, at least in the short and intermediate term, caused unemployment and undermined domestic industry, which could not compete with the flood of manufactured goods from abroad. Some countries privatized social security, which often reduced the pension benefits of middle- and working-class people.

Poverty, consequently, has remained the plight of vast numbers of Latin Americans. Everyday life, always a struggle for survival for much of the population, became far more difficult because there were never enough jobs and few occupations paid enough to support a family. Millions of men and women continued to leave the countryside to seek better opportunities in the cities, which grew far beyond the capabilities of government to provide health care, sanitation, utilities, housing, or education for the new migrants. Others migrated to the United States seeking a better life. Those who remained, the vast majority, used all of their resourcefulness and creativity to earn a living and maintain their families and culture. Men, women, and children built informal economies, taking advantage of whatever opportunities arose.

By the end of the twentieth century, all Latin Americans confronted a further challenge, this one from globalization, which transformed their economies, material culture, and communications. The impact of U.S. consumerism and popular culture, carried by the mass media all over the region, was widespread. Even in the most remote villages, one could drink Coca-Cola. Latin Americans, much like their ancestors in the sixteenth century, had to pick and choose what aspects of their tradition and what aspects of the new globalization they would retain to construct their own unique cultures. In art, as well as in politics and everyday life, Latin Americans sought to make sense of their reality. When brutal regimes suppressed their creativity, artists found new ways of expression, while at the same time they melded their views and techniques with those from abroad to construct their own Latin American art.

The Reign of Terror

The long era of dictatorships and guerrilla insurgencies tormented Latin America from the mid-1960s through the mid- or late 1980s. Citizens in all of the nations we discussed in Chapter 14 lived in fear of the police, military, guerrillas, and informal paramilitary death squads. The physical damage resulting was breathtaking. There were tens of thousands of casualties. Hundreds of thousands were dislocated from their homes. If these were not enough, civil and human rights were virtually non-existent. Regimes, such as in Chile, ruled under a state of siege, eliminating due process of law.

The human toll from war surpassed that of the incessant conflicts of the nineteenth century. Between 1975 and 1995, thirty-three thousand Colombians were casualties in the civil war. In 1997 alone, two hundred thousand people had to

LATIN AMERICAN LIVES

WOMEN REBELS

IN THE CUBAN REVOLUTION and other subsequent movements, women have mobilized in response to widespread political oppression. They have led the resistance to dictatorships in Argentina, Brazil, and Chile. They have joined the revolutionary organizations in Guatemala, El Salvador, and Nicaragua. In Bolivia, Mexico, and Peru, women have actively participated in rural and urban movements. They have fought time and again to protect their families from economic crises and political mistreatment and to end long-standing gender-based oppression. Two of these women, Vilma Espín and Doris María Tijerino, were examples of the endurance, sacrifice, and extraordinary courage and leadership women have provided to the movements for social justice.

In 1955, a young chemical engineer with degrees from the University of Oriente (in Cuba) and the Massachusetts Institute of Technology, whose father was a high-ranking executive in the Bacardi Rum company, Vilma Espín Guillois (b. 1930) joined the 26th of July Movement in Cuba, led by Fidel Castro. As a student, she had previously participated in protests against Batista, written and distributed anti-government pamphlets and joined the National Revolutionary movement. She was in Mexico briefly when Castro was in exile there, and when the 26th of July struggled in the Sierra Madre Mountains in 1956 and 1957, she was a member of its national directorate along with two other women, Haydée Santamaría and Celia Sánchez (later Fidel Castro's long-term companion). Working in the cities, she went underground, narrowly escaping arrest in May 1957. Espín coordinated the group's work in Oriente province and then took over much of the overall leadership in the province when police killed Frank País, her boss. Espín was one of the leaders of a national strike in April 1958, which failed. Espín married Fidel Castro's brother Raúl, one of the rebel commanders, after the triumph of the Revolution in 1959. She became director of the Federation of Cuban Women (FMC) in 1960, a post she held through the 1990s. She separated from Raúl in the 1980s. She served as a member of the Central Committee, the Council of State, and the Politburo, the highest leadership group of the Communist Party. The FMC came to include three million women, 80 percent of the women in Cuba. She was outspoken against the sexual double standard and other inequities that were still prevalent in Cuban society. She was one of only a small number of women to hold the top leadership posts in the government and Communist Party, which is clear indication of the mixed success achieved by the Cuban Revolution in obtaining equal rights.

Doris María Tijerino Haslam (b. 1943) was one the earliest Sandinistas. Her father worked as an engineer for the Nicaraguan National Guard, notorious

(continued on next page)

> **WOMEN REBELS** *(continued from previous page)*
>
> for its corruption and oppression. A veteran of the guerrilla insurgency from the late 1960s, Tijerino was arrested, jailed, and tortured in 1969 by the Somoza regime. She stayed in prison until 1974, when the infamous Sandinista raid on a high society Christmas party obtained the release of political prisoners. The government captured her again in 1978. Another daring raid, this time taking over the National Palace, secured her release. Tijerino was the only woman to receive the rank of full commander in the Sandinista army. She paid a terrible personal price for her involvement, however, because the Somoza government murdered two of her husbands. In postrevolutionary Nicaragua, she headed the National Women's Association, was head of the national police, and was a member of the national legislature. She kept her seat as a Senator even after the Sandinista defeat in 1989. Tijerino, like Espín, suffered from discrimination by the revolutionary government, whose men would not allow women to attain the highest ranks despite their obvious talents and wrenching sacrifices.
>
> **Questions for Discussion**
> Given the traditional role of women in Latin America, why do you think they were such important contributors to the revolutions in Cuba and Nicaragua from the 1950s through the 1990s?

abandon their homes because of intensified fighting. El Salvador suffered seventy thousand civilian deaths in its terrible civil war during the 1980s. The guerrilla war and counterinsurgency in Guatemala destroyed four hundred and forty hamlets. Hundreds of thousands fled into exile in Mexico and the United States. Forty thousand died in the civil war in Nicaragua during the 1980s. Between 1980 and 1995 in Peru, the Shining Path guerrilla movement and the government counterinsurgency led to the deaths of more than twenty thousand and produced perhaps two hundred thousand internal refugees.

The economic cost was staggering. The Shining Path, for example, caused an estimated $15 billion in damages. The real income of Peruvians dropped by one-third just in the period from 1990 to 1992. One million people lost their jobs in Lima alone. In late 1990s, because of the long civil war, three-quarters of the people of Guatemala lived in poverty, more than one-half of these in extreme poverty.

The Quality of Life

The terror brought upon Latin America by the right-wing regimes and Left insurgencies brought unspeakable misery to the region. Latin Americans, after two decades of economic growth and equalization of income after World War II, plunged once again into overwhelming poverty. One hundred fifty million people—one-third of the region's population in 2004—has an income of less than two dollars a day, the minimum needed to cover basic needs. Latin America and the Caribbean have the most unequal distribution of income in the world.

The deterioration of the well-being of Latin Americans was all the more tragic in light of the fact that after World War II a number of years of relative growth and prosperity had offered hope, reducing poverty in terms of percentage of the population and redistributing wealth to the middle and lower classes. From 1950 to 1980, per capita income rose by an average of 3 percent a year. This pushed down the percentage of the population living in poverty from an estimated 65 percent in 1950 to 25 percent in 1980. Between 1970 and 1982, the share of the income of the wealthiest 20 percent fell, and the share of the poorest rose 10 percent.

By 1980, however, after a decade of dictatorships, sustained growth ended and during the next 10 to 15 years the widespread adoption of free market, neoliberal strategies badly exacerbated conditions. From 1980 to 1985, the per capita income for Latin America as a whole dropped 13 percent. From 1982 to 1993, the number of people living in poverty in Latin America increased from 78 million to 150 million. Relatively speaking, the wealthiest nations in the region, Argentina, Uruguay, and Venezuela, experienced the sharpest increase in poverty. Argentina endured the most shocking economic descent as the percentage of poor households rose from 5 percent in 1980 to 16 percent in 1990. The gap between rich and poor widened dangerously. In Brazil, the top 10 percent of the population grabbed 51.3 percent of total income, while the share of the poorest 20 percent shrank to 2.1 percent, which represented the worst income distribution figures of any country in the World Bank's database of 65 nations.

Economic stagnation or decline, rampant unemployment, widespread underemployment, and inflation characterized the years of the terror and incipient democracy. During the 1980s, the per capita gross domestic product fell more than 20 percent in Argentina, Bolivia, Nicaragua, Peru, and Venezuela. The only countries that did not suffer net decline in gross national income from 1980 to 1992 were Chile, Colombia, and Uruguay. In Latin America, 1990 per capita income was 15 percent below the 1980 level. Per capita income in Peru fell 21 percent from 1974 to 1985. As a result, the number of poor rose to 210 million by the mid-1990s, although the percentage of people who lived below the poverty line decreased slightly.

There was a clear correlation between the establishment of right-wing regimes or the presence of a prolonged insurgency and the impoverishment of the population. The percentage of people below the poverty line in Chile, for example, went from 17 in 1970, the first year of the government of Salvador

Allende, to 45 in 1985 after a dozen years of Agustin Pinochet's dictatorship. In 1989, average wages in Chile were 8 percent less than in 1970, though by 1992 they had exceeded the 1970 level. The terror adversely affected Argentina as well, where during the 1980s, per capita income decreased by 26 percent. The percentage of people in poverty in Buenos Aires rose from 6 to 22 percent. Thirty years of war in Guatemala immersed 60 percent of the total population of ten million in poverty. Twenty-five percent of the people live in extreme poverty.

As the result of the decades of military dictatorship, civil war, and neo-liberal policies, the quality of life for many Latin Americans, as we would expect, lags behind the developed nations. The United Nations in its *Human Development Report* calculates a human development index (HDI), which puts together such statistics as life expectancy, educational attainment, and income (see Table 15.1). The HDI rank for Latin America ranges from Argentina's 34, Chile's 38, and Uruguay's 40 to Guatemala's 120. The United States ranked sixth in 2000, Ireland eighteenth, Israel twenty-second, Estonia forty-second, Thailand seventieth, and Saudi Arabia seventy-first.

Table 15.1

Quality of Life Indicators: Human Development Index (HDI) 1975–2000

Country and HDI rank 2000	HDI 1975	HDI 1980	HDI 1990	HDI 2000
Argentina #34	0.785	0.799	0.808	0.844
Chile #38	0.702	0.737	0.782	0.831
Uruguay #40	0.757	0.777	0.801	0.831
Costa Rica #43	0.745	0.769	0.787	0.820
Mexico #54	0.689	0.734	0.761	0.796
Cuba #55				0.795
Panama #57	0.712	0.731	0.747	0.787
Colombia #68	0.660	0.690	0.724	0.772
Venezuela #69	0.716	0.731	0.757	0.770
Brazil #73	0.644	0.679	0.713	0.757
Peru #82				
Paraguay #90				
Ecuador #93	0.627	0.673	0.705	0.732
Dominican Republic #94	0.617	0.646	0.677	0.727
El Salvador #104	0.586	0.586	0.644	0.706
Bolivia #114	0.514	0.548	0.597	0.653
Honduras #116	0.518	0.566	0.615	0.638
Nicaragua #118	0.565	0.576	0.592	0.635
Guatemala #120	0.506	0.543	0.579	0.631
Haiti #146		0.430	0.447	0.471

Source: United Nation Development Program, *Human Development Reports,* 1975, 1980, 1985, 1990, 1995, and 2000 cited in http://www.geohive.com/global link.php?xml=hdi2000&xsl+hdi2000.

What Does It Mean To Be Poor?

The poor in Latin America are overwhelmingly rural, female, Indian, or black and most likely live in Brazil, Mexico, and Peru. Poverty levels in the countryside are twice those in the cities. Women are more likely to be poor than men. The percentage of the indigenous population living in poverty in Bolivia in 1994 was 64.3, in Guatemala 86.6, Mexico 80.6, and Peru 79. Indigenous men and women earn between 35 and 65 percent less than whites. Afro-Brazilians are 1.9 times more likely to live in poverty than whites. Brazil has 33 percent of the region's people and 44 percent of the region's poor. Mexico and Peru account for another 11 and 9 percent of the poor, respectively. Bolivia, El Salvador, Guatemala, Haiti, Honduras, and Nicaragua together account for another 19 percent.

Malnourishment, disease, and high infant mortality are an inescapable fact of life for the poor. In 1980, over 50 million people in the region had a daily calorie intake below the standards set by the World Health Organization (WHO). Twenty million of those were seriously malnourished. In Mexico, the diets of an incredible 52 percent of the population did not meet World Health Organization standards. Urbanization and globalization increased malnourishment. In 1960, for example, Mexicans mostly ate tortillas, beans, bread, and small quantities of vegetables, eggs, and meat. Two decades later, poor city dwellers consumed more processed food (such as white bread) and soda. Consumption of milk in Mexico declined about 10 percent during the 1980s, while consumption of beans dropped even more. Mexicans ate only minimal amounts of eggs, fruits, and vegetables and 60 percent ate no meat at all, leaving them easy prey for dysentery, malnutrition, and anemia. Their diets were marked by consumption of less protein and more sugar. The complex combination of corn (tortillas), beans, and chili (hot sauce), which had provided their sustenance since the beginning of civilization, gradually was giving way to widely advertised Pan Bimbo (the equivalent of Wonder Bread) and Coca-Cola. The situation was no better in Nicaragua, where consumption of food staples fell 25 percent between 1989 and 1992 alone. Maternal malnutrition has been the primary cause of high child mortality rates, which in 1996 stood at 102 per 1000 in Bolivia and over 50 per 1000 in Guatemala, Honduras, and Nicaragua (56, 50, and 57, respectively) (see Table 15.2). In Nicaragua, the infant mortality rate in the 1990s was a stunning 138 per 1000 among the poorest sector of the population. Ironically, at the same time, overall life expectancy improved. It was 47 years in 1950 and 68 in 1990.

To be poor not only means that you would not have enough to eat and that your children would likely die before they were a year old, but that you would have limited or no access to health care, sanitation, and housing. Routine health services are not available to one out of three Latin Americans. An estimated 1.5 million people under the age of 65 die each year from causes that are avoidable. Unfortunately, neo-liberal policies have cut expenditures for health care, and, as a result, the incidence of diseases associated with poverty, such as dengue,

Table 15.2

Quality of Life Indicators circa 1996: Child Malnutrition, Mortality, Female Life Expectancy, and Access to Sanitation

Country	Child malnutrition (% of children under 5)	Under 5 Mortality (rate per 1000)	Female life expectancy at birth	Access to sanitation (% of urban population)
Guatemala	33	56	69	78
Nicaragua	24	57	70	34
Honduras	18	50	69	89
Ecuador	17	40	73	87
Bolivia	16	102	63	64
Mexico	14	36	75	81
El Salvador	11	40	72	78
Peru	11	58	71	62
Colombia	8	31	73	76
Brazil	7	42	71	55
Panama	7	25	76	
Venezuela	5	28	76	64
Paraguay	4	45	74	
Argentina	2	25	77	100
Costa Rica	2	15	79	
Chile	1	13	78	100
United States	–	8	80	

Source: World Bank, *World Development Report 1998–9* (New York: Oxford University Press, 1999), pp. 192–93, cited in Patrice M. Franko, *The Puzzle of Latin American Economic Development* (New York: Rowman and Littlefield, 1999), p. 7.

cholera, hepatitis, typhoid, and tuberculosis, have risen even in the wealthier countries of the region. Only 40 percent of Guatemalans have access to safe drinking water. In Brazil, only 55 percent of urban dwellers have access to sanitation, while in Nicaragua that figure is only 34 percent, and in Guatemala 40 percent. Less than 2 percent of Latin American sewage is treated. As a result, typhoid and cholera proliferate. The lack of health and sanitation facilities in indigenous communities allows outbreaks of influenza, measles, dengue, and respiratory infections to quickly become epidemics. For Latin America as a whole, only 63 percent of housing is deemed adequate. In 13 of the 19 nations, more than one-third of the housing is substandard. Nicaragua has the worst conditions, with only 20 percent of the housing assessed as adequate. In Bolivia, El Salvador, Nicaragua, and Peru, more than one-fifth of all housing is beyond repair. Between 20 and 30 percent of all Latin American children grow up in overcrowded lodgings (three or more in a bedroom). In Brazil, two hundred thousand children live on the streets.

The biggest hope for Latin Americans to struggle out of poverty is education, but it is seemingly unattainable beyond the first few grades. While overall educational enrollment expanded from the 1960s through the 1970s and the percentage of children ages 6 to 11 in school reached 71 in 1970 and 82 in 1980, the percentage of children ages 12 to 17 in school only went from 15 to 24. Today in Guatemala, a poor child on average will complete just one year of schooling. In Bolivia, only one-third of those who enter primary school finish. Even in Chile, a poor child will complete only six years of school. The situation worsened with the neo-liberal reduction in government expenditures as Latin American per capita public expenditures on education fell 12.5 percent during the hard times of the 1980s. Latin Americans are imprisoned in their poverty.

In another irony, while the possibilities for upward mobility are sharply limited by lack of access to education, Latin American nations have made considerable inroads in literacy. The illiteracy rate dropped from 47 percent in 1950 to 10 percent in 1995. Illiteracy among women fell from 25 percent in 1970 to 12.7 percent in 1990, although they still make up over 60 percent of the illiterate population (see Table 15.3).

Some observers saw the rapid population growth after World War II as a major cause of the increase in poverty. During the post-Word War II boom, reproductive rates rose so that by 1960 the region's population was increasing at the rate of over 3 percent per year, more than doubling between 1950 and 1980. It became clear, however, that Latin American economies could neither sustain sufficient economic

Table 15.3

Adult Literacy

Country	1970	1994
Chile	89	95
Costa Rica	88	95
Argentina	93	96
Uruguay	93	97
Panama	81	91
Venezuela	75	91
Mexico	74	89
Colombia	78	91
Brazil	66	83
Ecuador	72	90
Cuba	87	95
Peru	71	88
Paraguay	80	92
El Salvador	57	71
Bolivia	57	83
Honduras	53	72
Guatemala	44	56
Nicaragua		
Latin American Average	74	87

Source: United Nation Development Program, *Human Development Report 1997* (New York: Oxford University Press, 1997), pp. 146–48 cited in Patrice M. Franko, *The Puzzle of Latin American Economic Development* (New York: Rowman and Littlefield, 1999), p. 375.

growth to provide employment for the increased number of workers nor could governments provide services, such as health care, housing, and education, for them. Consequently, Latin American governments have implemented policies to lower the birth rate, expecting that this would alleviate poverty. Since 1980, in fact, the population growth rate in the region has declined as a result of the expanded use of contraception. The Mexican government program to encourage the use of contraceptives resulted in more than a two-fold increase in their use from 1976 to 1995 (30.2 percent in 1976 to 66.5 percent in 1995). In some areas, such as Colombia, Cuba, and Costa Rica, 70 percent of adult married women use contraception. However, the poorest Latin Americans have resisted contraception and maintained high levels of fertility. Sylvia Chant provides the example of Melia, a 27-year-old woman who lived in a one-room hut in a barrio in Puerto Vallarta, Mexico, with her husband, a construction worker, and six children ranging from 3 to 9 years in age. She was a devout Catholic who had not used nor planned to use contraception, calling her offspring "gifts from god."

Although the sharp increase in population contributed to unemployment and poverty, no other phenomenon of the post-1959 era has damaged the status and well being of the lower and middle classes more than inflation. Inflation reached staggering rates during the 1970s and 1980s (see Tables 15.4 and 15.5).

Table 15.4

Inflation in Brazil

Year	*Inflation Rate*
1950	9.2%
1960	25.4
1965	58.2
1970	16.4
1975	33.9
1980	110.0
1985	235.0
1987	416.0
1988	1038.0
1989	1783.0
1990	1477.0
1991	480.0
1992	1158.0
1993	2489.0
1994	929.0
1995	22.0
1996	11.0
1997	4.0

Source: Thomas Skidmore, *Brazil: Five Centuries of Change,* pp. 194, 225.

Table 15.5

Inflation (Average annual rate)

	1970–80	1980–85	1985	1992	1995	2000
Argentina	118.5	322.6	672.2	17.6	1.6	−0.7
Bolivia	18.8	610.9	11,749.2	10.5	12.6	3.8
Brazil	34.2	135.1	301.8	1,149.1	22.0	5.5
Chile	130.2	21.3	30.7	12.7	8.2	4.7
Colombia		22.3	24.1	25.1	19.5	8.8
Mexico	16.5	60.7	57.8	11.9	52.1	8.9
Peru	30.3	102.1	163.4	56.7	10.2	4.0
Latin America				414.4	25.8	8.7

Source: ECLA, *Statistical Yearbook for Latin America and the Caribbean,* 1990, pp. 98–99; ECLA, *Statistical Yearbook for Latin America and the Caribbean,* 2000, p. 751.

Bolivia's consumer price index, for example, rose an average of 610 percent between 1980 and 1985, with the largest increase in 1985 at over 11,000 percent. Brazil's inflation topped 1500 percent in 1989, Nicaragua's 9700 percent in 1988, and Peru's 3398 percent in 1989. Only Colombia, Guatemala, Honduras, Panama, and Paraguay escaped inflation over 30 percent per year during this era. Inflation badly eroded real wages. No one could live without difficulty during these periods of hyperinflation.

It is perhaps not surprising that in an environment where the currency might decline 2 percent in value each day, conditions created desperation. Thus, to be poor also meant that one lived amidst crime, which has risen sharply, further exacerbating the decline in the quality of everyday life. Crime in Mexico City, for example, rose by 40 percent from 1963 to 1980, by more than 40 percent more in the 1980s, and by more than 40 percent again in the first half of the 1990s. Many other cities in Mexico, such as Guadalajara and Tijuana, also suffered from surging lawlessness. Conditions deteriorated to the extent that on first-class buses between Mexican cities police subjected passengers to searches for weapons before boarding.

Informal Economy

Latin Americans have proven extraordinarily resourceful in adapting to difficult conditions. They have survived economically in great part because they have constructed an informal sector, economic activities that take place outside of regulation and law. The informal economy consists of small-scale, low-technology, family-run farms, mines, artisan shops, services, and vendors, nearly all run by Indians, blacks, mulattos, and mestizos.

Neo-liberal policies resulted in a substantial increase in the informal sector because 81 percent of the new employment they generated was in the informal or small enterprise sector. From 1980 to 1992 in Latin America as a whole, employment in small enterprises increased from 15 to 22 percent of the work force. The informal sector's share of employment went from 19 to 27 percent. With domestic service (6.4 percent), these two accounted for over half the work force. At the same time, employment in large- or medium-size businesses fell from 44 to 31 percent and public employment from 15.7 to 13.6 percent. La Paz, Bolivia, where the number of vendors in the markets jumped from fifteen thousand in 1967 to nearly double that number in 1992, provides a good example of the consequences of neo-liberalism for the informal sector.

The streets of Latin America's cities are filled with individual petty entrepreneurs, who will sell items ranging from gum and candy bars to hot food to appliances. These small businesses are usually the product of a continuum, in which migrants move to the cities, take jobs—if they can find them—as domestics and menial laborers, and then, when they are more established, begin their own enterprises, using the skills learned from parents and other family. They rely first on the unpaid labor of nuclear family, but also extended kinship networks. When necessary, they obtain additional labor from workers seasonally unemployed by the export sector, and illiterate, unskilled residents of urban slums. Some proprietors of informal sector businesses manage to rise above the poverty level. On the other hand, many are not so fortunate, for the informal economy also includes street children, small-time criminals, and prostitutes.

The informal economy not only provides a living for increasing numbers of Latin Americans, but also supplies the daily needs of much of the population. In the bustling central market of Cuzco, Peru, for example, vendors sell anything a consumer might want, such as watches, hats, medicinal herbs, clothes, and endless quantities of food, some prepared and hot. In Lima, the informal sector built most of the public markets and delivers 95 percent of Lima's public transportation. In Bolivia, half the economically active population works in small businesses. In Latin American cities, vendors set up shop anywhere that space is available. The sound of bargaining is relentless, as the market women and their customers dicker back and forth over prices. The noisy market, teeming with people and overflowing with smells of food, is still the very lifeblood of the city.

Women play exceptionally important roles in the informal economy. They dominate the markets today, much as they have since before the Europeans arrived in the sixteenth century. In Cuzco, women run the stalls, caring for children, gossiping, and helping their neighbors at the same time. Often, the women began work as domestic servants, then moved on to itinerant peddling, and lastly to the market. Necessary skills, including relentless haggling with customers to get the best prices for their merchandise, are passed on from mother to daughter or aunt to niece. Work in the market provides income, flexibility to care for children, and autonomy from males. Some women hold other jobs and work part-time in the market as well. Some vendors journey in from the countryside periodically to sell agricultural products, while others invest in a license for a permanent stall.

Women vendors in market.

Life is by no means easy for market women, though. Most of them are single mothers or widows. Competition with other sellers is relentless. They must be shrewd in their dealings with local authorities. They depend heavily on family members to help them. They must be willing to work long hours. The pressure on them is enormous. As one market woman put it: "From the time I wake up until I go to bed, it's the preoccupation a mother has to feed her children, to find food for her children, whether we sell or not, because if we don't sell, there's no food to eat."

A few examples illustrate the complex adaptations required by men and women who earn their livelihoods in the informal economy. Doña Avenina Copana de Garnica is an artisan in La Paz, Bolivia. Born in the city, she nonetheless speaks Aymara, an indigenous language, as well as Spanish. She and her husband and their six children live in small, rented quarters above their small workshop in an artisan district of the city. The upstairs has one bedroom with bunk beds. They sleep and work there. The shop has a small stove for soldering and shares space with a cooking area demarcated by a piece of cloth.

The Garnica family uses metal, cardboard, and cloth to make numerous items used in rituals and celebrations, including masks, noisemakers, whips, and costumes for miniature figures. Avelina's parents live across the street and the whole family works in the business. They learned their trades from relatives. Avelina comes from a family of costume makers. She embroiders the costumes

Slice of Life — The Barrio/Favela

THE VAST increase in the population of Latin America's great cities is the most important development in the region since the 1940s. As we have seen in Chapters 13 and 14, the enormous influx of migrants created gigantic, unmanageable urban areas. Urban shantytowns dominate these mega-cities. Known as barrios in Mexico, barriadas in Peru, and favelas (and also *mucambos*) in Brazil, they incorporate hundreds of thousands, sometimes millions, of poor people, most who have fled desperate conditions in the countryside. They are noisy monuments to the resourcefulness and resilience of impoverished human beings who, seemingly against all odds, survive, and occasionally prosper, with dignity and humor. It is one of the mysteries of twentieth-century history that they have not erupted into bitterness, resentment, and widespread violence.

The shantytowns arose in empty spaces owned by absentee landlords or by the local governments. They were always on the outskirts as the cities expanded, often on the steep sides of hills or on low regions susceptible to flooding. No one wanted these lands, for they were scarcely habitable. In some areas, residents organized and won self-government as municipalities. One such case is Netzahualcóyotl, now a city in its own right in the state of Mexico with 1.2 million residents, which began as a squatter settlement on the dried-out bed of Lake Texcoco, where the strong winds blow volcanic soil in swirls and flooding is chronic. The government sold the land during the 1920s to developers who never got their project going. Later, real estate promoters illegally sold one hundred sixty thousand plots of land to low-income people. Ciudad Netzahualcóyotl incorporated forty irregular settlements northeast of Mexico City in 1964. In the 1970s, still without services, residents protested by withholding payments. Eventually, the government furnished the services and granted legal titles. In many cities, squatters banded together to organize protests to acquire their properties legally and to obtain services. Often, the fight was hard, for frequently governments and landlords used violence against them.

The shantytowns appeared overnight as people heard by word of mouth of any empty space and assembled to occupy it. After moving in from other parts of the city or from the countryside, residents constructed their abodes with materials salvaged from others' trash, such as scrap wood, corrugated metal, cement blocks, and, sometimes, cardboard and cloth. Unrecognized by city authorities, the settlements initially had no water, electricity, or sewage, nor did they have schools or health clinics. If lucky, inhabitants could line up for hours to fill cans and bottles with water from a public spigot or the visiting water truck. Inhabitants had to pay exorbitant prices for stolen electricity.

In Rio de Janeiro, the seemingly chaotic nature of the settlements hides innovation and resourcefulness. Dwellers employ clever techniques to maximize the use of difficult space. They build their homes literally brick by brick as they accumulate enough money to add on and make their structures more permanent. Nor are the favelas locations of obsolete, retrograde remnants of rural culture. Rather, they were and are places of transition and persistence.

The shantytowns in many ways are twenty-first-century urban versions of rural villages. Just as country folk fought to maintain their local autonomy and traditions in the nineteenth and much of the twentieth centuries, the residents of shantytowns have struggled to assert their control over their everyday lives.

Questions for Discussion

How do the circumstances of twentieth- and twenty-first-century struggles for control over everyday life in urban shantytowns differ from those of villages in the countryside in the nineteenth and early twentieth centuries? How are they similar?

for the miniatures. She also cuts and pastes the decorations for the costumes. Her husband, a tinsmith, apprenticed with her aunt and makes objects out of sheet metal. The family employs seasonal workers. Avelina keeps the books and supervises the workers, often making 40-minute bus rides to their homes. The Garnicas actively promote their products through sponsorship of local fiestas, selling to tourist stores in the city, and even traveling to Peru to expand their market further.

Like Avelina Copana de Garnicas, Sofía Velázquez grew up in La Paz, Bolivia, and earns her livelihood in the city's informal economy. She began her working life helping her mother sell candles in the markets and then sold vegetables in the market on days when there was no school. Later on, she sold eggs, beer, onions, mutton, and pork. Separated from her husband, she earned enough to send her one daughter, Rocío, a teenager in the early 1990s, to private school. She continues to buy and sell pork, but she and her daughter supplement their income by working as food vendors. Rocío cooks and Sofía sells the food in front of their home. Sofía also plays an active role in community affairs. She heads the organization that controls the local market, a position that carries with it the considerable expense of sponsoring local fiestas.

Privatizing Social Security

Neo-liberal efforts to reduce the size and scope of government have led to deterioration of middle- and working-class living standards. One of the crucial new innovations was the privatization of social security programs. Chile led the way in the transformation of public pensions in the 1980s. During the 1990s, seven Latin American nations privatized all or parts of their public pension systems: Argentina, Bolivia, Colombia, El Salvador, Mexico, Peru, and Uruguay. Bolivia, Chile, and Mexico chose to privatize the whole system. Colombia and Peru have

How Historians Understand | From the Countryside to the City

THE VAST MOVEMENT OF people from rural areas to the cities that has taken place since the 1940s in Latin America has left historians with many questions. Who were/are the migrants? From where did/do they come? Why did/do they leave the countryside? Three types of analysis have arisen to explain the phenomenon: those that interpret migration as a "rational" act by those seeking to better their economic situations; those that see wider forces resulting primarily from capitalist market forces at work; and those that incorporate both individual motivations and structural causes. Generally, the latter, more eclectic approach has won the day. We realize now, the result of a long series of case studies, that although the search for economic betterment is crucial, much more enters into the decision to migrate.

Migrants are difficult to characterize. At first glance, it would appear that young single males would be the likeliest to move from rural villages. Some early observers concluded that these men had fewer attachments and had the best employment prospects. But, in fact, women have comprised the majority of migrants, especially in Mexico, Peru, Honduras, and Costa Rica. In general, however, there seems to be no pattern according to marital status or age. We cannot with certainty even maintain that the very poorest migrated. Some investigators discern that migration is selective and that only the "more dynamic members of the rural population" migrate to the cities. These were likely the best-educated and most skilled as well. Women, less educated and discriminated against, had fewer possibilities in employment, but nonetheless were the majority of migrants.

Shantytown where newly arrived migrants make their homes.

There is considerable disagreement, too, over where the migrants originated. Some investigators have found migrants overwhelmingly came directly from rural areas. Others claim a pattern of movement from village to a small town, such as a provincial capital, and then to the larger cities. Proponents of the first theory thought the migrants totally unprepared for city life. Proponents of the second offer the opposite, maintaining that the migrants were "pre-urbanized." Small cities, however, were not the same as large cities. Thus, while migration may be a step-by-step process, and this is debatable, acculturation was not so easy in any case. What seems the most likely conclusion is that migrants came from villages, small towns, small cities, and larger cities, depending on their particular circumstances. Geography and time period affected their plight.

Leaving one's home, abandoning what one knows for the unknown, was/is an act of enormous courage. But what were the reasons behind it? Were people "pushed" out by the shrinking access to and deteriorating quality of the land? Or did they leave because of the unavailability of employment due to the adoption of large-scale agriculture and widespread use of technology? The first investigators thought the relentless poverty of the countryside provided the impetus for migration. Later studies, however, found that the process was not so simple. There were both "push" and "pull" aspects to decision making. One observer called what was involved no less than a "substitute for social revolution."

One survey found that the migrants themselves mentioned economic concerns as motivations less than half the time. Migration had more to do with family (to join a spouse, to find a partner, to escape unpleasantness) or health. The same study was unable to get migrants to "describe the decision with any precision."

There was, it seems, no one reason for moving from the countryside to the cities. There was no typology for migrants. Nor was there a specific route to migration. It was too personal a process. The migrants themselves do not depict their lives as linear. Their stories are compelling nonetheless.

Questions for Discussion
If you lived in a rural area in Latin America, what would motivate you to migrate to the cities or immigrate to another country? Would you have the courage to leave your home?

parallel systems in which public and private compete for members. Argentina and Uruguay have mixed systems where members contribute to both public and private pensions. Privatization has adversely affected pensions. It appears that, although initially in the 1990s private systems produced a reasonably good return on investment, they sustained very high administrative costs (perhaps 20 percent), reducing the proceeds available for pensions. In addition, funds were reduced because there was a high rate of tax evasion.

High administrative costs and tax evasion were not the only drawbacks to privatization. Most workers were not covered. The Chilean case is instructive. The crucial weakness of its new pension policies is that they cover only about half of all workers. The unemployed and those employed in the informal sector have no pensions. Women are especially hard hit. Under the old system, they enjoyed a relatively privileged position. Now women have to work more years to qualify for pensions because child-rearing responsibilities periodically take them out of the paid work force. Moreover, working women typically earn only one-half as much as male heads of household, though single women head one-fifth of all households. This boils down to women receiving smaller pensions than men receive.

The Cities

The massive movement of people to the cities that began in the nineteenth century has continued unabated. From 1950 to 1980, 27 million Latin Americans, almost all of them poor, left the countryside for the cities. The percentage of people living in urban areas rose from 40.9 percent to 63.3 percent. In the last third of the twentieth century, the people of Latin America moved to the cities in overwhelming numbers. By 1995, the proportion of urban dwellers reached 78 percent of Latin Americans. (In the United States, they comprise 76.2 percent.) Many Latin American nations' populations are predominantly urban: Argentina's is 87.5 percent urban, Brazil's 78.7 percent, Chile's 85.9 percent, Uruguay's 90.3 percent, and Venezuela's 92.9 percent. Furthermore, the population is concentrated in a very few enormous cities. Forty percent of Chileans live in Santiago. São Paulo and Mexico City each may have as many as 20 million inhabitants. With Buenos Aires and Rio de Janeiro, these cities make up four of the ten largest cities in the world.

The statistics for Mexico City are staggering. It is spread over 950 square miles, three times the size of New York City. Mexico City contains 25 percent of Mexico's population, 42 percent of all jobs, 53 percent of all wages and salaries, 38 percent of the value of all industrial plants, 49 percent of sales of durable goods, and 55 percent of all expenditures in social welfare. Its inhabitants consume 40 percent of all food production, buy 90 percent of all electrical appliances, use 66 percent of country's energy and telephones, and purchase 58 percent of the automobiles.

The great cities are virtually unmanageable. Less than half of Brazilian urban residents have garbage collection with almost all these waste materials dumped into streams or open spaces. The only factor that mitigates this enormous environmental problem is that poor people generate less waste than more affluent people. Many lack sanitation facilities. As of 1990, only 16 percent of the households of São Paulo were connected to municipal sewage treatment plants. Consequently, human wastes contaminate the water. In Brazil, it is estimated that 70 percent of all hospitalizations are the consequence of diseases that result from the lack of sanitation. Twenty-seven percent of Latin America's urban residents—80 million people—breathe air that does not meet World Health Organization guidelines. The only factor that keeps the cities from being overwhelmed by toxic emissions from automobiles is that Latin America has relatively few autos compared to the United States.

To Be Poor in the Cities

Latin American cities are really two cities—one for the rich and the other for the poor. Lima, for example, has a modern downtown with paved streets dotted with skyscrapers. Surrounding the center are millions of people living in *barriadas,* or squatter settlements. Many of the barriadas, also known as barrios or colonias elsewhere in Spanish America or as favelas in Brazil, were rural into the 1940s and even the 1950s. Gradually, as the city grew outward and as people searched for less expensive living quarters, farmland disappeared. The residents of these settlements have migrated from the Andean highlands. Dirt roads lead through the houses built from scrap lumber, woven mats, and other materials. The stink from open sewers is noticeable. The bustle is everywhere and noise abounds. The marketplaces are busy.

Beneath the apparent squalor, the odors, and the hustle are real communities. And it is here that the twenty-first century's version of the struggle for control over everyday life occurs. In Lima's barriadas and other squatter settlements throughout Latin America, people assist each other in much the same ways as they had when planting and harvesting on collectively operated farms in the highlands. Networks of relatives and friends from their home villages make life more bearable. When Jorge and Celsa settled in Lima's Chalaca barriada, for example, Jorge's sister and brother helped them build a house on the same plot where the sister and her husband lived. An aunt also provided support. Later, Celsa's sister, her husband, and four small children moved in.

Most barriada families started with next to nothing and have painstakingly built their homes. The typical house at first had one story and was built with reed matting or wooden boards. Later, residents reconstructed with wood or perhaps brick and cement. In the city of Callao, the port for Lima, dwellers salvaged bricks and wood from the buildings destroyed by an earthquake in 1967. There were a variety of furnishings depending on the economic status of the inhabitants. Barriada dwellers cooked over small fires or kerosene stoves. Only a few dwellings had electricity, initially pirated from main lines. Since there was no refrigeration, residents bought their food at the market every day, buying only what they needed. People shared space with goats, sheep, and pigs and raised guinea pigs (a traditional South American delicacy) and rabbits in their kitchens.

The homes were functional with few possessions. A typical home might have a table and utensils hung from the walls. Sleeping areas had cots or beds with straw mattresses. Clothes were hung from poles or lines strung overhead. There were boxes or trunks for storage. Larger animals such as goats, sheep, or pigs were kept in the courtyard and ate scraps. Nothing was thrown away, for everything had its uses. Nothing was fancy anywhere.

Little by little, these settlements and similar settlements throughout Latin America acquired community governance and services. Residents built cement basins with a number of spigots and a drain area at strategic points. There people waited in long lines in early morning and in the evening to draw water. Women washed laundry and bathed their children during less busy times.

An Urban Migrant's Story

The story of Percy Hinojosa (related by Jorge Parodi) of Lima, Peru, is typical of the hundreds of thousands of Latin Americans who left their rural homes and moved to the cities in search of better lives. Percy, like many others in Peru and elsewhere, left his village at 15 because the countryside offered nothing but endless poverty. Like most migrants who arrived in Lima from the countryside, he came with at best an elementary school education. In order to find work, it was important to have relatives or friends already in the city who could provide the migrant with contacts to obtain employment in factories, but Percy did not have any personal contacts. He toiled for 12 years in various jobs until he got a steady position in a factory. He began as a domestic servant and went to school at night. He then embarked on an odyssey very typical of migrants:

> "I worked at Coca-Cola, at Cuadernos Atlas, and in the Italian bakery. Later on, I would work at Pepsi-Cola, in small shops, in furniture factories, and carpentry shops. I would work two months and a half or three and I'd be laid off. I think the companies didn't want you to have a steady job at that time."

He did everything from counting bottles to packing notebooks and sanding furniture. Percy earned enough to get by, though no more. In search of higher-paying, more secure employment, Percy entered the construction trade, but this meant long periods without work. He then got a place as an apprentice auto mechanic. He had to quit, however, when he became too vocal in trying to get a raise. Percy returned to the countryside for a year. By the time he left for Lima again, jobs were even harder to come by. Eventually, he used a contact from his earlier employment as a domestic to obtain a factory job. Like so many Latin Americans, Percy did whatever was necessary.

The Environment

The push for economic development in Latin America, as elsewhere, has come at a high cost to the environment. Air and water pollution, the deterioration of agricultural lands through overuse or misuse, and the destruction of tropical rainforest areas are among Latin America's chief environmental disasters. These conditions have exacerbated the health problems, especially among the poor that we discussed earlier.

Mexico City is one of the most disheartening examples of environmental degradation over the past half-century. The air is dangerous to breathe and the smog is so thick that residents rarely see the beautiful mountains that surround the city. Three million cars clog the thoroughfares of Mexico City, often bringing traffic to a standstill—residents sometimes refer to their freeways as the "largest parking lot in the world." Motor vehicles are the primary contributors to air pollution, emitting enormous quantities of sulfur dioxide and other contaminants into the air every day. The government has tried to clean up the air by prohibiting cars from being driven into the city one day a week and by ordering emission tests and the use of cleaner fuels. These measures have helped a bit, but not enough. Motor vehicles, however, are only part of the problem. Erosion, exposed trash and feces, untreated water seeping into the subsoil, and emissions from electric plants, refineries, petrochemical plants, incinerators, and internal combustion engines spew between 6,000 and 12,000 tons of contaminants into the air each day.

Safe drinking water is hard to find. The sewage system filters only 70 percent of the city's water. Thirty percent of municipal solid waste is not collected, and people dump it into the streets, rivers, lakes, and open fields. Lake Guadalupe, the closest lake to the Federal District, is a septic tank filled with 30 million cubic meters of residual waters a year polluted with unspeakable wastes. Consequently, agricultural products produced in the region of the lake are dangerous because they are infested with harmful microorganisms.

Outside the cities, conditions are no better. Tropical rainforests in Latin America are being depleted at an annual rate estimated between 113,000 and 205,000 square kilometers per year. This results mostly from the conversion of rainforests to open land suitable for agriculture, especially in the Amazon region of Brazil, as waves of immigrants have flowed into the area during the last third of the twentieth century. The population of the Amazon went from 3.6 million in 1970 to 7.6 million in 1980 and 18 million in 2000. The number of agricultural properties increased by 90 percent and the number of cattle herds doubled. From 1973 to the mid-1980s, farmer colonists in the western Amazon region razed 60,000 square kilometers. Fewer than half of these settlers stayed more than a year. The cutting of wood for use in homes and industry has contributed considerably to the destruction of the rainforests. Oil wastes have devastated the tropical rainforests of Ecuador. Black slime formed in pools and slush filled with toxic wastes contaminated the countryside. Seventeen million barrels of oil spills ruined the rivers. The soil is so contaminated in some areas that it is crusty when poked with a stick.

The Globalization of Culture

During the second half of the twentieth century, globalization has shaped the lives of people in Latin America and everywhere else. Borders between rural and urban, local and national, and national and international culture have broken down. Massive migration from the countryside to the cities and across international boundaries has been one factor in this profound change. The advent of modern mass communications, especially television, has perhaps played an even more decisive role, touching the lives even of people who never ventured very far from their homes. Meanwhile, newspapers, comic books, magazines, popular theatre, radio, movies, and television have deeply influenced what were formerly entirely locally focused societies. The Internet has immeasurably widened the horizons of those fortunate enough to have the resources to use it. No culture exists in isolation anymore.

Brazil provides an excellent example of how mass media had transformed culture since the 1960s. Magazine circulation increased from 104 million to 500 million between 1960 and 1985. Between 1967 and 1980, the number of record players grew by more than 800 percent. The number of commercial records went from 25 million to 66 million just during the 1970s. The expansion of television was spectacular. In 1965, there were 2.2 million televisions in Brazil. That number rose to 4.2 million in 1970 and 16 million by the 1980s. Seventy-three percent of all Brazilians had TV sets. By 1996, Brazil had become the seventh largest advertising market in the world, with advertising expenditures at $10 billion. Television accounted for more than half. The Brazilian television industry well illustrates how Latin Americans have used the mass media, not only to increase their own cultural outputs, but also to spread their culture all over the world. From 1972 to 1983, the percentage of foreign programming decreased from 60 to 30 percent. Brazil exports its truly amazing soap operas all over the world (especially to Mexico and Portugal).

Without question, the globalization of popular culture brought a steady influx of movies, music, fast food, and fashions from the United States and Western Europe to Latin America. McDonald's golden arches are a familiar icon throughout the region, and WalMart operates six hundred retail stores in Mexico, some under its own name and others that retained their original names after WalMart acquired them. The mass media have heightened demand for consumer goods in the countryside, sometimes with negative consequences for the quality of life. According to the cultural commentator Néstor García Canclini, "The penetration of consumer goods into rural areas frequently generates a crisis. New needs for industrial goods are created, forcing the rural household to rationalize production and work harder, longer hours, thus making it difficult for the peasant family to continue participating in [traditional] magico-religious practices."

Latin Americans have found myriad and creative ways to blend old and new. On Sunday afternoon in the Praça de Se in São Paulo, Brazil, one can observe *capoeira* (a form of self-defense formerly practiced by slaves, now a dance), electric guitars playing rock music, and poetic duels by *cantadores*. In Peru during the 1980s, chicha music (chicha refers to an Andean maize beer often linked with traditional rituals) enjoyed widespread popularity. A combination of elements from Andean and tropical cultures, the music illustrated the mass immigration from the countryside into the cities. Although the mixture of electric guitars with tropical and Andean rhythms appears at first instance a degradation of tradition, it may in fact be a way of preserving the memory of the past within a practical acceptance of current reality. In Latin American homes, technology and tradition exist side by side. Television sets often rest on tables, right next to altars with religious images. In Brazilian favelas, residents paint their rooms pink to remind them of their rural homes.

Latin American popular culture has found worldwide markets and enthusiasts. Growing numbers of Latinos in the United States can watch soap operas on television, attend concerts of popular Latin American musicians, and celebrate traditional holidays. In June, 2004, there were reenactments of *Inti Raymi,* the ancient Inca summer solstice festival, in cities as far away as Chicago, Seattle, New York, Brussels, Barcelona, and Budapest. The indigenous people of Otavalo in northern Ecuador have long been known as savvy marketers who sell their fine textiles to tourists visiting their picturesque community. Now a wide selection of their products is available on the Internet. Sometimes popular culture has changed its form to suit foreign tastes, while retaining cultural meaning at home. Andean music has shown a noticeable Western influence as it has become familiar to audiences around the world. In Peru and Bolivia, however, music has kept its place at the center of the annual cycle of ritual.

Transitions to the new hybrid folk art are ambiguous at times. In the late 1960s, the artisans of Ocumicho, Michoacán, in Mexico began to create ceramics depicting devil figures associated with elements of the modern world previously unknown in the village, such as police, motorbikes, and airplanes. Some observers have suggested that the devils provide a way of controlling the destructive effects of modernization, by placing them within a traditional repertory of symbols. Carlos Monsiváis, the Mexican essayist, reports an interesting twist on the intrusion of modernity into rural society that occurred when the Mexican government introduced video cameras to municipal meetings in the state of Hidalgo. The Otomí Indians, who comprised most of the population of the municipality, showed more enthusiasm about watching the videotapes of the meetings than attending gatherings in person.

International market forces and national political considerations have, without doubt, altered many local traditions. Mexican governments have encouraged handicraft production so as to provide sustenance for rural people and to thus keep them from migrating to the cities. Cultural commentator Néstor García Canclini maintains, for example, that the urban and tourist consumption of handicrafts "causes them to be increasingly decontextualized and resignified on their journey to the museum and the boutique....Their uses on the land, in the household and in rituals are replaced by exclusively aesthetic appreciation," which in turn affects how they are made and the form they take.

Art

Latin American artists have continued to develop their innovative style and techniques in the age of globalization. The stark political art of the 1930s and 1940s gave way temporarily to geometric and abstract art by the 1950s, but neither proved satisfactory to artists concerned with contemporary conditions. In Mexico, there was a reaction against the muralists, led by José Luis Cuevas, who believed the world more complicated than that depicted by Rivera and Siqueiros. Instead of depicting a world of simple contrasts between heroes and villains, these artists portrayed humans as victims of greater forces. Perhaps the most famous artist emerging from this era was Colombian Fernando Botero. He, too, dropped socialist realism. He, like Cuevas, was more comfortable going back to European painters' techniques, but Botero added exaggeration and parody in his portrayal of characteristic types in Colombian politics and society.

By the 1960s, Latin American artists again embraced social protest, but it was more diverse in its application than the socialist realists of the earlier generation. According to Jacqueline Burnitz, however, some artists working under the brutal regimes of the 1970s through the 1980s employed a "strategy of self-censorship" in which "they invented new symbols or invested previously used ones with new meaning." For example, Brazilian Antonio Henrique Amaral painted bananas in the 1970s as a parody of Brazil as a banana republic, a tinhorn dictatorship that deferred to the United States. Other artists challenged not the political state but the commercialization of art and official art institutions. This conceptual art, comprised of various media ranging from prints to performance, provided the means for ideological expression without actually confronting the terrifying regimes in power. Some artists, nevertheless, paid a high price for their veiled protests. After the Chilean coup in 1973, Guillermo Nuñez was arrested, imprisoned, tortured, let go, and then watched closely. After being jailed and tortured a second time two years later, he was forcibly exiled.

Latin American artists in the late twentieth century struggled and succeeded brilliantly in forging their own art out of the different strains of influence from their homelands and abroad. They fought to make sense out of a world of bitter poverty and profound disappointment. The explored their past and future with the same persistence, courage, and humor displayed by their ancestors for the preceding 600 years.

Conclusion

As they entered the new millennium, Latin Americans lived in a world very different from what their ancestors had known when they embarked on their journeys as independent nations nearly two centuries before. As we saw in Chapter 9, nineteenth-century governments struggled mightily to persuade their people to think of themselves as citizens of a nation rather than residents of a particular village, town, or region. Those who governed in Latin America after 1880 had a much easier time in getting people to see themselves as part of a national community. The coming of railroads, telegraphs, and telephones consolidated national territories as never before. Public education systems and mandatory military service provided ideal vehicles to inculcate patriotic values to students and raw recruits. Modernizing governments saw local governance and culture as impediments to their mission and took decisive steps to undermine both.

The development of modern mass communications in the twentieth century created national popular cultures as more and more people followed the same soap operas, read the same comic books, watched the same movies, and enjoyed the same music. Televised spectator sports also encouraged people to think of themselves as Peruvians or Mexicans or Costa Ricans as they cheered their national teams in international soccer competitions. Winning the World Cup in soccer has probably done as much as any government program to make Brazilians proud to be Brazilians and Argentines proud to be Argentines. In the age of globalization, even a nation's citizens who worked and lived abroad could partake of national patriotic observances and reaffirm their loyalties to their home countries. Each year on the night of September 15, for example, the medium of satellite TV permits Mexican citizens living in the United States to watch their president stand on the balcony of the National Palace in Mexico City and reenact Father Miguel Hidalgo's famous "Grito de Dolores," the spark that ignited the country's struggle for independence nearly two hundred years ago. The Internet and cheap long distance telephone calls enable people living abroad to keep in touch with friends, family, and local happenings back home.

Meanwhile, globalization has also generated forces that weaken national loyalties. Traditional ways of life distinctive to a particular country are rapidly giving way to international consumer culture. At the same time, strong local and regional loyalties persist alongside wider national and international allegiances. In recent years, the end of tyrannies and the comeback of democracy have allowed more local autonomy. The rise of Mexico's most active opposition party, the Partido Acción Nacional, and its ultimate success in capturing the presidency in 2000 began in part as a resurgence of regional identity, particularly in the north. Ethnic and linguistic minorities continue to reassert their languages and traditions against homogenized national and international cultures.

Whether they work for multinational corporations or continue to work in the countryside, whether they never venture much beyond the localities where their ancestors have lived for centuries or travel great distances in search of work, education, or entertainment, whether or not they have access to the Internet, and regardless of their income levels, Latin Americans of the twenty-first century still see the struggle to retain control over their daily lives as their paramount objective, and one that is perhaps as unattainable today as it has ever been in their history. For a large majority of people in the region, poverty and its related ills—malnutrition, substandard housing, and disease—seriously interfere with that quest. Even those who live comfortably for the moment can remember all-too-recent times of political uncertainty, galloping inflation, and war and terror, and fear of a return to those conditions remains strong. The natural environment that nurtured the first civilizations in the Americas and provided a host of commodities used and valued all over the world faces the dire consequences of modernization. But ever since their first ancestors migrated across the Bering Strait thousands of years ago, Latin Americans have shown great ingenuity in meeting their needs for survival and for cultural autonomy. Their energy and cultural creativity will serve them well in the years to come.

Learning More About Latin America

Scheper-Hughes, Nancy. *Death without Weeping: The Violence of Everyday Life in Brazil* (Berkeley, CA: University of California Press, 1992). The author presents a gut-wrenching picture of favela life.

Tardanico, Richard, and Rafael Menjívar Larín, eds. *Global Restructuring, Employment, and Inequality in Urban Latin America* (Miami, FL: North-South Center Press at the University of Miami, 1997). The editors include all the dismaying statistics about the present state of Latin Americans.

Timerman, Jacobo. *Prisoner without a Name, Cell without a Number* (Madison, WI: University of Wisconsin Press, 2002). Argentine Jew who was jailed during the Dirty War tells his terrifying tale.

Winn, Peter. *Weavers of the Revolution: The Yarur Workers and Chile's Road to Socialism* (New York: Oxford University Press, 1986). Winn gets inside the minds of workers to an unprecedented extent.

Glossary

Aguardiente (ah-gwar-dee-EN-tay) Sugar cane alcoholic beverage.
Arrendatarios (ah-rehn-dah-TAH-ree-ohs) Permanent workers on Colombian coffee farms.
Atole (ah-TOH-lay) Corn gruel eaten for breakfast in Mexico.
Barretón (bah-ray-TOHN) A heavy wedge with an iron tip and long, straight wood handle used to poke soil in order to insert seed.
Cacique (kah-SEE-kay) Originally, a traditional chief in Caribbean societies; later an indigenous local ruler in Spanish America; this term was also used to describe local political bosses in the nineteenth century, after Latin American independence
Calaveras (kah-lah-VAY-rahs) Skeletal figures used in celebration of the Days of the Dead in Mexico.
Candomblé (kahn-dohm-BLAY) Afro-Brazilian religion.
Cantadores (kahn-tah-DOR-ays) Singers.
Capataz (kah-pah-TAHS) Foreman on a cattle ranch.
Capitalino (kah-pee-tah-LEE-noh) Resident of Mexico City.
Capoeira (kai-poh-EH-rah) Formerly a slave dance, evolved as form of self-defense in Brazil.
Caudillo (kow-DEE-yoh) Strong leader with a local political base.
Centralist Favors strong national government.
Chica moderna (CHEE-kah mo-DEHR-nah) Modern woman.
Chicha (CHEE-chah) Maize beer drunk in the Andean region.
Cofradía (koh-frah-DEE-ah) In Spanish America, an organization of lay people devoted to a particular saint or religious observance; members maintained village churches and sponsored festivals.
Colono (coh-LOH-noh) Temporary worker on a Colombian coffee farm; medium-scale Cuban sugar planter.
Compadrazgo (kohm-pah-DRAHS-goh) Godparent relations; an individual who agrees to look after the child of another.
Concordancia (kohn-kor-DAHN-see-ah) Argentine political coalition of the 1930s with Conservatives, Radicals, and Independent Socialists.
Conservative Favors strong central government and the Roman Catholic Church.
Conventillos (kohn-vehn-TEE-yohs) Buenos Aires tenements.
Corticos (kor-TEE-kohs) Crowded slums in Rio de Janeiro.
Debt peonage Debt incurred by rural laborers on large estates in order to pay for baptisms, weddings, funerals, and to purchase supplies that debtor cannot repay.
Descamisados (des-kah-mee-SAH-dohs) Shirtless ones; working class supporters of Juan Perón in Argentina.
Enganchadores (ehn-gahn-chah-DOR-ays) Dishonest labor recruiters.
Estado Novo (eh-shta-doo-noh-voo) Dictatorship of Getúlio Vargas in Brazil (1937–1945).

Estancia (eh-STAHN-see-ah) Large estate in Argentina and Uruguay that generally raises livestock.

Estanciero (eh-stahn-see-EH-roh) Large landowner in Argentina and Uruguay; owner of an estancia.

Farinha (fah-REEN-yah) Coarse flour made from cassava.

Fazenda (fah-ZEHN-dah) Large estate in Brazil.

Fazendeiro (fah-zehn-DAY-roh) Large landowner in Brazil; owner of a fazenda.

Federalist Favors weak national government with political power vested in states or provinces.

Finca (FEEN-kah) Colombian coffee farm.

Frijoles (free-HOH-lays) Beans, a staple of Mexican diet; usually combined with corn tortillas.

Gaucho (GOW-choh) Argentine cowboy known for fierce independence.

Guano (goo-AH-noh) Bird excrement used for fertilizer, collected from islands off Peru.

Hacendado (ah-sen-DAH-doh) Large landowner in Spanish America.

Hectare 2.47 acres.

Hombres de bien (OHM-brays day bee-EHN) In colonial Spanish America, men who had honorable reputations in their communities; in the nineteenth century, decent people; professionals of some means who often managed government in nineteenth century Mexico.

Huaraches (wah-RAH-chays) Sandals.

Indigenismo (een-dee-hehn-EES-moh) Admiration for the advanced culture of pre-1500 societies in Latin America; efforts to bring native peoples into the modern economy.

Jefes políticos (HEH-fays poh-LEE-tee-kohs) District political bosses under Porfirio Díaz in Mexico.

Léperos (LEH-peh-rohs) Beggars of Mexico City.

Ley fuga (Lay FOO-gah) Shot while trying to escape; ruse used by Rurales.

Liberal Favors weak central government, opposes the Roman Catholic Church, and encourages individualism rather than collective landownership.

Liberto (lee-BEHR-toh) Slave born in Brazil after 1813 who was to remain a slave until age 21.

Matador (mah-tah-DOR) Bullfighter.

Mayordomo (mai-yor-DOH-moh) Manager of an estancia or hacienda.

Metate (may-TAH-tay) Grinding stone for corn used in making tortillas.

Molino de nixtamal (moh-LEE-noh day neex-tah-MAHL) Corn-grinding machine.

Panela (pah-NEH-lah) Brown sugar cakes.

Patron–client relations Unequal relationship between upper-class individual and lower-class individual (hacendado and peon, for example) in which the former obtains protection and patronage in return for loyalty.

Peinilla (pay-NEE-yah) Machete.

Petate (pay-TAH-tay) Sleeping pallet.

Pulque (POOL-kay) In Mexico, a fermented beverage made from the agave cactus.

Quilombos (kee-LOHM-bohs) Communities of runaway slaves in the interior of Brazil.

Rebozo (ray-BOH-soh) Narrow, long shawl for women.

Rurales (roo-RAH-lays) Rural police during era of Porfirio Díaz in Mexico.

Santería (sahn-tay-REE-ah) Afro-Caribbean religion.

Siesta (see-EHS-tah) Nap after the midday meal.

Tithe Contribution to the church of 10 percent of one's income.
Vaqueros (vah-KAY-rohs) Cowboys in Mexico.
Vecindades (vay-seen-DAH-days) Mexico City tenements.
Voudoun (VOO-doon) Afro-Caribbean or Afro-Brazilian religion.
Yerba mate (YER-bah MAH-tay) Strong tea in Paraguay and Argentina.

CREDITS

CHAPTER 8
>P. 247, The Granger Collection, New York
>P. 248, Archives Charmet/Bridgeman Art Library
>P. 255, Houghton Library, Harvard University
>P. 259, Library of Congress

CHAPTER 9
>P. 280, Dibujo de Eliseo Marenco, de la obra *La Lanza Rota*, de D. Schoo Lastra.
>P. 288, The Granger Collection, New York

CHAPTER 10
>P. 305, Photo courtesy of The Newberry Library, Edward E. Ayer Collection
>P. 317, General Library at the University of New Mexico, Donald C. Turpen Mexican Revolution of 1910 Collection, Center for Southwest Research

CHAPTER 11
>P. 338, General Library at the University of New Mexico, Donald C. Turpen Mexican Revolution of 1910 Collection, Center for Southwest Research
>P. 349, Center for Southwest Research, Zimmerman Library, The University of New Mexico

CHAPTER 12
>P. 367, Biblioteca Nacional de Chile
>P. 381, Biblioteca Nacional de Chile

CHAPTER 13
>P. 403, Schalkwijk/Art Resource, NY. Art ©Estate of Jose Clemente Orozco/SOMAAP, Mexico
>P. 404, The Jerry Bywaters Collection on Art of the Southwest, Hamon Arts Library, Southern Methodist University, Dallas, Texas (AP Photo)

CHAPTER 14
>P. 423, H. John Maier Jr./Time Life Pictures/Getty Images
>P. 428, ©Reuters/CORBIS

CHAPTER 15
>P. 451, Photo by Ellan Young
>P. 454, Photo by Ellan Young

INSERTS
>**Plate 8:** ©Reuters/CORBIS
>**Plate 9:** New York Historical Society, New York, USA/Bridgeman Art Library
>**Plate 10:** INDEX/Bridgeman Art Library

Plate 11: Time Life Pictures/Getty Images
Plate 12: Schalkwijk/Art Resource, NY. Art ©Estate of David Alfaro Siqueiros/SOMAAP, Mexico/VAGA, New York
Plate 13: Schalkwijk/Art Resource, NY
Plate 14: ©Howard Davies/CORBIS
Plate 15: INDEX/Bridgeman Art Library

INDEX

A
abolition, of slavery, 310, 346
aguardiente (rum), 362
Aguirre Cerda, Pedro, 375
Agustín I of Mexico, 264, 270. *See also* Iturbide, Agustín de
air pollution, 458-459
Alemán Valdés, Miguel, 376–377, 431
Alessandri, Arturo
　Chile under, 347, 375
　populism of, 366, 370
Alfonsín, Raúl, 427
Allende, Salvador, 409, 427, 430
Alliance for Progress, 420, 427–430
Alvarado, Salvador, 374
Alvarez, María'Elisa, 388
Amaral, Antonio Henrique, 462
Amaral, Tarsila do, 406
American Popular Revolutionary Front (APRA) of Peru, 354–355, 372, 417
anarchists, in working class, 345
Andrade, Mario de, 406
anti-Semitism, in Argentina, 368–369
anticlericalism, of Juárez, 268–269
Apaches, bounties on, 351
Aramburu, Pedro, 426
ARENA (National Republican Alliance) of El Salvador, 416
Argentina
　anti-Semitism in, 368–369
　Bourbon Reforms in, 245
　civil wars in, 277
　Concordancia of, 374–375
　debt of, 365, 436, 437*t*
　"Dirty War" in, 428–429
　export economy of
　　boom in, 332
　　concentration of commodities in, 333
　　prices in, 363
　foreign investment in, 331
　gauchos of, 305–306, 305*f*
　Great Depression in, 363
　gross domestic of, 443
　immigration to, 341, 342*t*
　industrial working class of, 337
　landowners of, political dominance of, 344–346
　manufacturing development in, 360
　middle classes of, political power of, 366
　military coup in, 420
　military of
　　cost of, 282
　　modernization of, 343
　　politics dominated by, 280
　　nineteenth century, 280*f*
　　under military regime, 420, 425–427, 444
　nationalism in, 282
　under Perón, 377–378
　political stability in, 342–343
　population growth in, 300, 335
　populism in, 366–369
　poverty in, 443, 444
　racism in, 310
　railroad of, 334
　regionalism in, 269–270
　resistance movements in, women in, 441
　small holdings of
　　discontent among, 340–341
　　life on, 314
　social security in, privatization of, 453–456
　upper classes of, political power of, 366
　urban population of, 456
　in War of the Triple Alliance, 274–275
Arias, Jacoba, 389–390
Aristocratic Republic (Peru), 347–348
Arriaga, Antonio, 230
artisans, slaves as, 308, 309
arts
　current, 462
　urbanization in, 401–407
Augustín Farabundo Martí Front for National Liberation (FMLN) of El Salvador, 416
Avila Camacho, Manuel, 376–377
Ayacucho, 251
Aylwin, Patricio, 430
Azuela, Mariano, 355

B
Bajío, revolt of, 243–245
Balmaceda, José, 346
bananas
　European demand for, 294
　export of
　　boom in, 331, 334
　　prices for, 363
bandits
　in Brazil, 353
　in Mexico, 282
banking
　central, of Argentina, 374
　modern systems of, economic development and, 292
barretón, 361
barrios, 452–453
Batista, Figueredo João, 422
Batista, Fulgencio, 377, 379, 411
Bay of Pigs, 412
beans, in diet, 320–321, 445
beef, European demand for, 294
beef industry, in Paraguay, under Francia, 290–291
Belaúnde Terry, Fernando, 417
Belém, revolt in, 285
Benavides, Oscar, 376
benefits
　for miners, 392
　for textile laborers, 391
Betancourt, Rómulo, 379
Betancur, Belisario, 419
black beans, in diet, 320
blacks. *See also* free blacks; slaves
　numbers of, 299
　Rosas supported by, 286–288
Blanco, Antonio Guzmán, 271, 343
Bolívar, Simón, 247*f*
　independence campaigns of, 245, 249–252
Bolivia
　constitution of, 250
　economy of, effect of war on, 281
　education in, 447
　export economy of
　　boom in, 332
　　concentration of commodities in, 332, 360–363
　　prices in, 363
　founding of, 250
　Great Depression in, 360–363
　gross domestic product of, 443
　housing in, 446
　independence of, from Buenos Aires, 270
　inflation in, 449
　informal economies in, 450
　military coup in, 420
　political movements in, women in, 441
　poverty in, demographics of, 445
　reforms in, 380–382
　revolution in, 378, 413
　social security in, privatization of, 453–456
　in War of the Pacific, 275
Bonaparte, Joseph, 238
Bonaparte, Napoleon, 238
boom and bust cycles, 331, 348–350, 436
Botero, Fernando, 462
Bourbon Reforms, 242–243
　impact of, 239
Boves, José Tomás, 245
Brasilia, construction of, 422
Brazil
　civil wars in, 277
　debt of, 293, 293*t*, 436, 437*t*
　demographics of, 299
　dictatorship of, 375
　diet in, 320–321
　economic modernization of, resistance to, 352
　export economy of, concentration of commodities in, 332, 360–363
　favelas of, 452–453
　foreign investment in, 331

471

472 INDEX

Brazil, *continued*
  globalization in, 460–462
  Great Depression in, 360–363
  immigration to, 341, 342*t*
  independance of, 253–260
  inflation in, 448*t*, 449
  literacy in, 337
  manufacturing development in, 360
  mass media in, 460
  military coup in, 420
  military modernization in, 343
  under military regime, 420, 421–422
  as monarchy, 264
  political dominance in, of coffee planters, 344–346
  political stability in, 342–343
  popular and high culture in, 406–407
  population growth in, 299–300, 335, 336*t*
  Portuguese exploration of, 72–75
  poverty in, 443
    demographics of, 445
  presidency of, shared, 346
  rainforest destruction in, 459
  regionalism in, 271–272
  resistance movements in, women in, 441
  rural areas of, demographics of, 298
  sanitation, 446
  slavery in
    end of, 282, 308
    on plantations, 307–312
  small farms of, life on, 314–315
  sugar industry of, economy based on, 294
  terms of trade in, 333
  upper class control of, 372, 385–386
  urban population of, 456
  under Vargas, 379
  in War of the Triple Alliance, 274–275
Buenos Aires
  cattle industry of, 293–294
  colonial, Bourbon Reforms in, 214, 245
  demographics of, 316
  economic development of, debt for, 293, 293*t*
  export economy of, 293–294
  housing in, 324
  independence of, 246
  industrial working class of, political affiliation in, 345
  living conditions in, 316
  middle class of, 337
  population growth in, 335
  population of, 300, 456
  poverty in, 444
  towns under, independence declared by, 252
bullfighting, 326
Bulnes, Manuel, 280

C

cacao beans
  European demand for, 294
  export of, boom in, 331
Cáceres, Andrés, 285, 347
Callao
  housing in, 457

  industrial working class of, 337
Calles, Plutarco Elías, 372, 406
Cámpora, Héctor, 426
Canal, Alva de la, 403
Candomblé, 312
Canudos, 352
capital, foreign
  dependence on, 295
  in economic growth, 329
  in export boom, 331
capitalism, Liberal advocacy of, 266
capoeira, 461
Caracas, independence of declared, 245
Cárdenas, Cuauhtémoc, 432
Cárdenas, Lázaro, 372
Cardoso, Fernando Henrique, 425
Carillo Puerto, Elvia, 373–374
Carillo Puerto, Felipe, 373–374
carnival season, samba in, 402
Carranza, Venustiano, 353–355
Carrera, José Rafael, 271
cassava farms, 314–315
castas, 241–242
Castello Branco, Humberto de Alencar, 422
Castillo, Ramón S., 377
Castillo Armas, Carlos, 416
Castle War of Yucatán, 281
Castro, Fidel, 379, 410–413
casualties
  of revolutions and civil wars, 440–442
  of nineteenth century wars, 281
Catholic Church
  as community, 257
  Conservative support for, 266
  credit from, economic development and, 292
  Francia and, 290
  Liberal opposition to, 266, 277–278
  modern women and, 400
  proper role of
    civil wars and, 277–279
    post-independence, 263, 266
  in villages, 315
caudillos, 263, 286–291, 287*t*
CDRs (Committees for the Defense of the Revolution) of Cuba, 413
Central America
  economic development of, debt for, 293, 293*t*
  foreign investment in, 331
  at Panama conference, 251
  as part of Mexico, 249
  regionalism in, 271
centralism
  in Buenos Aires, 270
  in Mexico, 270
  regionalism and, 269
  vs. federalism, 263, 265–267
CEPAL (United Nations Economic Commission for Latin America), 434
Chamorro, Pedro Joaquín, 414
Charlot, Jean, 350, 403
la chica moderna, 400–401, 405
chicha, 461
children, on haciendas, 307
Chile
  under Allende, 409
  democracy in, 346–347
  under dictatorship, 379

  economic development of, debt for, 293, 293*t*
  education in, 447
  export economy of
    concentration of commodities in, 332
    prices in, 363
  Great Depression in, 360–363
  gross domestic product of, 443
  independence of, 249
  industrialization of, government intervention in, 363
  manufacturing in, development of, 360
  military of
    country ruled by, 280
    modernization of, 343
    under military regime, 420, 427–430
  mines of
    labor for, 388
    working conditions in, 390–393
  mining camps of, 338–340
  nationalism in, 282
  nitrate mining in, foreign investment in, 331
  political stability in, 343
  populism in, 366, 370
  post-independence, unity of, 267, 272
  poverty in, 443–444
  resistance movements in, women in, 441
  Social Republic of, 375
  social security in, privatization of, 453–456
  urban population of, 456
  in War of the Pacific, 275
chiles, in diet, 320–321
cholera, in cities, 317
Cinco de Mayo, 348
Cisplatine War, 290
cities
  current, 456–458
  demographics of, 298
  life in, 315–317
  living conditions in *vs*. rural areas, 386
  migrations to, 317–319, 423–424
    current, 456
    in globalization, 460–461
  histories of, 454–455
  importance of, 386
  poverty in, 457–458
citizenship, in Latin American independence, 256
civil rights, under military regime, 422
civil wars, regionalism and, 267
clothing, 321–322
  of modern women, 400
Coca-Cola, 445
cockfighting, 325–326
coffee farms, Colombian, 361–362
coffee industry
  European demand in, 36294
  export boom in, 331, 332, 334
    railroads in, 334
  slaves in, 307–312
coffee plantations, 361
coffee planters, in Brazil, politics dominated by, 344–346
Collor de Melo, Fernando, 424–425

Colombia
    civil wars in, 277
    coffee farms of, 361–362
    contraception use in, 448
    under dictatorship, 379
    economic development, debt for, 293, 293t
    export economy of
        boom in, 332
        concentration of commodities, 333, 360–363
        Great Depression in, 360–363
    gross domestic product of, 443
    independence of, 249
    inflation in, 449
    regionalism in, 271
    revolution in, 409, 419
    social security in, privatization of, 453–456
colonels, in Brazil, 346
colono, 361
Colosio, Donaldo, 432
Committees for the Defense of the Revolution (CDRs) of Cuba, 413
Common Sense (Paine), 225
communications
    in economic development, 292
    in export boom, 331
communism, in revolutions, 409–410
Communist Party, reactions against, 378–379
community
    in cities, 457
    nations as, creating, 256
    among slaves, 312
Comte, Auguste, 342
Concordancia (Argentina), 372
Conselheiro, Antonio, 352
Conservatism
    in civil wars, 277–279
    in Mexico, 270
    vs. Liberalism, 265–267
        rural lower class and, 279
Constitution of 1917 (Mexico), 354
Constitution of 1812 (Spain), 240, 241, 246–248, 253
consumerism, impact of, 440
Contestado, 352–353
contraceptives, 448
Contras, U.S. support for, 414–415
cooking, urban poor and, 321, 457
Copana de Garnica, Avenina, 451–453
copper, export boom in, 331
copper mines
    in Chile, 338–340, 390–391
    wages in, 394t
cordobazo, 425–426
CORFO (Chilean National Development Corporation), 363, 375
Cofradías, in village life, 315, 390
corn, 362. *See also* maize
corruption
    economic development and, 292, 436
    in Mexico, 432
Cortes
    in Portugal, 255
    in Spain
        American delegates to, 241–242
        dissolution of, 246
        reestablishment of, 240

corticos, 324, 423
Costa e Silva, Artur da, 422
Costa Rica
    coffee farms of, 361
    contraception use in, 448
    cost of living, in mining camps, 395
    export economy of
        boom in, 332
        concentration of commodities in, 332
        Great Depression in, 363
    landownership in, 124
    urban migrations in, 454
cotton, European demand for, 294
cotton industry, in Peru, immigrants in, 342
Council of Regency, 241
credit, economic development and, 292
creoles, in independence movements, 237
crime, 449
Cristiani, Alfredo, 416
CROM (Regional Confederation of Mexican Workers), 372
crop failure, in colonial Mexico, 243
Cuba
    under Barista, 379
    contraception use in, 448
    under dictatorship, 379
    export economy of
        boom in, 332
        concentration of commodities in, 332, 360–363
        Great Depression in, 360–363
    immigration to, 341, 342t
    populism in, 370–371
    rebellion in, 377
    sugar industry in
        economy based on, 294
        foreign investment in, 331
        prices in, 363
        Soviet market for, 412
        after World War I, 360
Cuban missile crises, 412
Cuban Revolution, 409, 410–413
    women in, 441
Cuevas, José Luis, 462
culture
    globalization of, 460, 462
    urbanization in, 401–407
Cuyo, 249
Cuzco, informal economy in, 450

D
dance, in popular and high culture, 401–402
"Dance of the Millions," 360
dandy, 401
Darío, Rubén, 402
Day of the Dead, 325
De la Madrid, Miguel, 432
De la Rua, Fernando, 427
debt (national), 437t
    of Argentina, 365
    for economic development, 293, 293t
    interest payments on, 436
    of Mexico, 432
debt peonage, 302
democracy
    in Chile, 346–347
    economy and, 366

neo-liberalism in, 439–440
warfare and, 280–281
Democratic Action Party (AD) of Venezuela, 379
demographics, 299–300
dependency analysis, 434–435
descamisados, 377–378
Díaz, Porfirio, 268–269, 282
    Indians under, 351
    Mexico under, 348–351
    retirement of, 353
    stability under, 343
    succession of, 350–351
Díaz Ordaz, Gustavo, 431
dictatorships, 372–378, 409–430, 440
    economy and, 366
    of Mexico, 348–351
    of Nicaragua, 414
    post-independence, 264–265
Diego, Juan, 228
diet, 320–321
    current, 445
    of slaves, 308–311
diffusionism, 434–435
"Dirty War," 369, 427, 428–429, 428f
discipline
    of labor
        of gauchos, 306
        in mining camps, 340
    of slaves, 307
discrimination, independence movements and, 239
disease
    current, 445
    among white-collar workers, 399
Dolores, 243–244
domestic life, on haciendas, 304–307
domestic servants
    slaves as, 308, 309
    women as, 318–319
Dominican Republic
    export economy of,
        concentration of commodities in, 360–363
        Great Depression in, 360–363
    immigrants to, 342
    military coup in, 420
Dr. Atl, 402–403
drainage, in cities, 316
dried meat, in diet, 320
drinking water, 316, 446, 459
droughts, in colonial Mexico, 243

E
earthquakes
    in Managua, 414
    in Valparaíso, 347
Echevarría, Luis, 432
economic depression, 329
    Díaz dictatorship and, 351
economic development
    environment and, 458–459
    export economies and, 458–333
    and Liberalism, 266
    under military regime, 422
    obstacles to, 292–293
    from political stability, 342
    post-independence, 263
    theories of, 434–435
economic modernization, 330–335.
See also industrialization
    downside of, 332–334
    gauchos and, 306
    Indians and, 351–352

474 INDEX

economic modernization, *continued*
  railroads in, 334–335
  resistance to, 335, 352–353, 385
  rural areas and, 352–353
  village social structure and, 341
economic participation
  of lower classes, 358
  of women, 358
economies
  Cuban, under Castro, 413
  democracy and, 366
  demographic growth and, 299
  dictatorships and, 366
  government in, 359, 363, 379, 436
  informal, 449–453, 451*f*
  peacetime, 364–365
  populism and, 366, 370, 379–380
  under PRI, 431
  in rural areas, 313
  wars and, 281
  after World War I, 359–360
Ecuador
  colonial
    cabildos of, 241
    royal monopolies protested in, 243
  export economy of, concentration of commodities in, 332
  independence of, 249
  military coup in, 420
  rainforest destruction in, 459
  regionalism in, 271
education
  in colonial Brazil, expansion of, 254
  current, 446–447
  in Mexico, 377
  in Paraguay, under Francia, 290
Egas, Camilo, 402
eggs, 445
El Salvador
  export economy, concentration of commodities in, 332, 360–363
  Great Depression in, 360–363
  housing in, 446
  military coup in, 420
  military modernization in, 343
  poverty in, demographics of, 445
  revolution in, 409–410
    casualties of, 442
    women in, 441
  social security in, privatization of, 453–456
El Teniente mine, 339, 392–395
electricity, availability of, 388
enfranchisement
  in Argentina, 344–345
  under colonial rule, 241–242, 253
  of women, 382, 383*t*
enganchadores, 339, 392
entertainment, 324–326
environment, 458–459
erosion, soil, 361
Espín, Vilma, 441
Estado Novo (Brazil), 372, 375
estancias, life on, 301–312
estates. *See* haciendas
ethnicity
  in civil wars, 281
  in independence movements, 237

in nation building, 262–263
  in regionalism, 267
Europeans, immigrants, 342*t*
  Argentine encouragement of, 310
  in industry, 337
  racism and, 341
  wage labor by, 306
Eva Perón Foundation, 378
export economies
  booms in, 331–332, 334
  concentration of commodities in, 332, 363
  development of, 293–295
  diversification in, 435–436
  gauchos in, 305–306
  impact of, 333
  modernization and, 330–332
  after World War I, 365

F
factories, textile, 390–391
Falklands/Malvinas War, 426–427
family
  in barrios, 457
  as economic unit, 313
  employee stability and, 391, 392
  modernization and, 330
  among slaves, 330
  in urban migration, 454
FARC (Revolutionary Armed Forces of Colombia), 419
farinha, 314
farmers, housing of, 323–324
favelas, 423, 452–453
fazendas, life on, 301–312
Federal Wars (Venezuela), 271
federalism
  in Mexico, 270
  vs. centralism, 263, 265–267
Federation of Cuban Women (FMC), 441
feminism. *See also* women
  in industrial working class, 340, 366
  under military regimes, 421
Ferdinand VII of Spain, 238, 246
fertilizer
  European demand for, 294
  export boom in, 331
Figari, Pedro, 402
First Republic (Brazil), 346
FMC (Federation of Cuban Women), 441
FMLN (Augustín Farabundo Martì Front for National Liberation) of El Salvador, 416
folk art, hybrid, 461
Fonseca, Deodoro da, 346
foreign capital
  debt from, 437*t*
    of Argentina, 365
    for economic development, 293, 293*t*
    of Mexico, 432
  dependence on, 295
  in economic growth, 329, 348
  in export boom, 331
foreign wars, in nineteenth century, 275–276
Fox, Vicente, 432
France, export economy dependence on, 333, 363
Francia, José Gaspar Rodríguez de, 289–291
free blacks, royalist, 245

free market economics, 410, 443
free trade, Liberal advocacy of, 266
Frei, Eduardo, 427–430
Frei Ruiz Tagle, Eduardo, 430
Freire, Ramón, 280
French Intervention, 268, 279
Freyre, Gilberto, 406
Frondizi, Arturo, 425
fruit, 445
Fuentes, Carlos, 355
Fujimori, Alberto, 418–419

G
Galtieri, Leopold, 426–427
gambling, 325–326
garbage, disposal of, current, 456–457
García Márquez, Gabriel, 251
Garrastazú Médici, Emilio, 422
gauchos, 305–306, 305*f*
  Rosas supported by, 286–288
gender roles
  under military regimes, 421
  modernization and, 330
  in politics, 285–286
  reinforced by marriage, 401
  in rural areas, 313–314
  upper class influence on, 386
gente decente
  in middle class, 336
  in post independence government, 264
Germany
  capital from, in Latin American economic development, 331–332
  export economy, dependence on, 333, 363
Gerrero, Xavier, 403
ghettoes, 423
globalization, 440, 460–462
godparenthood, in villages, 390
gold, export boom in, 331
GOU (United Officers' Group) of Argentina, 377
Goulart, João, 422
government
  in economy, 359, 363, 379, 436
  form of, consensus about, 263
  in industrialization, 363
  modern women and, 400
  representative, in Spanish America, 240–241
  in villages, 312–313, 390
government loans, for economic development, 292–293, 293*t*
grain, export boom in, 331
  railroads in, 334
Gran Colombia, Republic of, 249.
  See also Colombia; Ecuador; New Granada; Venezuela
  at Panama conference, 251
Great Britain
  Buenos Aires occupied by, 246
  capital from, in Latin American economic development, 292–293, 331
  export economy dependence on, 333, 363
  in Falklands/Malvinas War, 426–427
Great Depression, 360–363
"Grito de Dolores," 244, 257
gross domestic products, 443
Grove Vallejo, Marmaduke, 370, 375

Guanajuato, 244
guano, export of, 294
Guatemala
  education in, 447
  export economy of,
    concentration of
      commodities in, 332,
      360–363
    Great Depression in, 360–363
  independence of, 271
  infant mortality in, 445
  inflation in, 449
  military coup in, 420
  military modernization in, 343
  as part of Mexico, 249
  poverty in, demographics of, 445
  revolution in, 378, 409, 416
    casualties of, 442
    cost of, 441
    women in, 441
  sanitation in, 446
Guayaquil
  in independance movement,
    249–251
  population growth in, 336
Guerrero, Vicente, 245, 248, 283,
  284–285
Guevara, Ernesto "Che," 413,
  420–421
Guzmán, Abimael, 418–419
Guzmán, Matin Luis, 355

H
Hacienda, de Bocas, work life on,
  303–304
Hacienda del Maguey, work life on,
  302–303
hacienda stores, 303
haciendas
  life on, 301–312
  villages and relations with, 312
Haiti
  export economy of,
    concentration of
      commodities in, 332
  poverty in, demographics of, 445
handcrafts, international market for,
  461–462
Haya de la Torre, Victor Ra'l, 376,
  380, 417
health care, 445–446
Hernández Martínez, Maximiliano,
  415
Herrán, Saturnino, 402
Hidalgo y Costilla, Miguel, 243–244,
  259f, 260
high culture, urbanization in,
  401–407
Hinojosa, Percy, 458
hombre de bien, in post-
  independence government, 264
homeless, in Mexico City, 324
Honduras
  export economy of,
    concentration of
      commodities in, 332,
      360–363
    Great Depression in, 360–363
  infant mortality in, 445
  inflation in, 449
  military coup in, 420
  poverty in, demographics of, 445
  urban migrations in, 454
households. *See also* family
  headed by women, 319–320

housing, 322–324
  current, 445–446, 457–458
  for white collar workers, 399
Huerta, Victoriano, 353
human development index (HDI),
  444, 444t
huts, 323–324

I
Ibáñez del Campo, Carlos, 370, 379,
  427
Illia, Arturo, 425
immigrants
  European, 342t
    Argentine encouragement of,
      310
  in industry, 337
  racism and, 341
  wage labor by, 306
Import Substitution Industrialization,
  359, 365, 410, 434, 436
imports
  reliance on, 333
  restrictions on, 365
income per capita, 443
income tax, in Argentina, 374
independence, 256f
  gauchos in, 305
  regional conflicts in, 252–253
  of Spanish colonies, 246–253
  transition to, as turning point,
    239–240
independence movements
  diversity within, 237
  Indians in, 256
Indians
  clothing of, 322
  under colonial rule
    enfranchisement and,
      241–242, 253
    in Hidalgo's rebellion, 244
  extermination campaigns
    against, 311
  in independence movements,
    256
  in military, social advancement
    of, 282
  modernization and, 351–352
  murder of, in Guatemala, 416
  numbers of, 299
  in popular and high culture, 402
  racism against, 311
  "rediscovery" of, 351–352
  Rosas supported by, 286–288
indigenismo, in art, 402, 404–406
industrialization. *See also* economic
  modernization
  under Cuban Revolution, 412
  government intervention in, 359,
    363
  import-intensive, 365
  under military regimes, 422
  World War II and, 364
infant mortality rate
  in Brazil, 424
  current, 445, 446t
  of slaves, 307
inflation
  current, 448–449, 448t, 449t
  oil prices and, 436
  in World War II, 364
informal economies, 449–453,
  451f
inheritance laws, widows and,
  319–320

Institutional Revolutionary Party
  (PRI) of Mexico, 431–432, 433
international commerce
  limitations on, economic
    development and, 292
  after World War I, 360
Internet, 460
Inti Raymi, 461
intoxicants
  in peon diet, 303
  in religious celebrations, 325
intra-regional wars, in nineteenth
  century, 274–275
Iturbide, Agustín de, 248, 248f, 258,
  283

J
Jesus, Carolina Maria de, 423–424
Jews, in Argentina, 368–369
João VI of Portugal, 253–254
Johnson, Lyndon B., 420
Juárez, Benito, 268–269, 270
Junta Patriótica, 257–258
juntas
  in Brazil, 255–256
  in Spain, 240–241
Justo, Juan B., 345, 374–375

K
Kahlo, Frida, 405–406
Kennedy, John F., 420
Kirchner, Néstor, 427
Korean War, 364
Kubitschek, Juscelino, 379, 422

L
La Paz, informal economy in, 450
labor
  in cities, 318
  for haciendas, 301–302
  for mines, 339
  for ranches, 387
  temporary
    for coffee estates, 361
    for haciendas, 301–302
labor discipline
  of gauchos, 306
  in mining camps, 340
  in textile factories, 391
labor unions
  in Brazil, 375
  in Mexico, 372
  Perón and, 377–378
Lagos, Ricardo, 430
land deterioration, 458–459
land expropriations, 329
  in Mexico, 340, 350
  in modernization, 352
  in Peru, 347
land reform
  under Cárdenas, 376
  Mexican Revolution and,
    353–355, 371–372
  in Peru, 417–418
  under PRI, 431
landownership and landholding. *See
  also* small holdings
  in Argentina, politics dominated
    by, 344–346
  in Brazil, politics dominated by,
    345–346
  concentration of, urban
    migration and, 386
  Liberal view on, 266, 277–278
  railroad disruption of, 335

landownership and landholding, *continued*
  in villages, 312–313
languages, in regionalism, 267
Lanusse, Alejandro, 426
Laugerud, Kjell, 416
Law for the Permanent Defense of Democracy (Chile), 379
lead, export boom in, 331
Leal, Fernando, 403
leftist ideologies, 372
  vs. military, 419–420, 422
legal system
  economic development and, 292
  female equality in, 401
Leguía, Augusto B., 348
  populism of, 366, 369–370
léperos, 318
Levingston, Roberto M., 426
Ley fuga, 348
Liberalism
  in civil wars, 277–279
  in Colombia, 419
  in Mexico, 268, 270
  vs. Conservatism, 265–267
    rural lower class and, 279
  women and, 366
liberto, 314
lifestyle
  in cities, 315–317, 395–398
  of lower classes, 423–424
  on haciendas, 301–312
  in villages, 312–315, 387–388
Lima
  industrial working class of, 337
  informal economy in, 450
  population growth in, 336
  poverty in, 457
  towns under, independence declared by, 252
  urbanization of, 397
  white-collar workers of, 336, 399
lime (mineral), in diet, 320–321
literacy
  in cities, 386
  current, 447, 447*t*
  expanding rates of, 337
  in Paraguay, 290
literature, in popular and high culture, 402
livestock production, railroads in, 334
living conditions
  in cities, 315–317, 395–398
  in mining camps, 395
  in small holdings, 312–315
  in villages, 312–315, 387–388
local autonomy. *See also* regionalism
  in barrios, 457
  in Liberal victory, 279
  military regimes and, 432–433
  urban migration and, 358
  villages and, 313
López Mateos, Adolfo, 431
López Portillo, José, 432
lower classes
  in economic arena, 358
  in historical sources, 396–397
  political voice of, 358
  in post-independence government, 264
    caudillos supported by, 286–288
    Francia supported by, 289–291
  political ideology of, 267
  political participation of, 283–286
  upper class fear of, 284
  racism against, 310–311
rural
  autonomy for, 285
  Liberalism *vs.* Conservatism and, 278
  upper class fear of, 310–311, 385–386, 395
  urban life of, 423–424
loyalty
  in Latin American independence, 256, 257
  in Mexican politics, 431
  in middle class employment, 398–399
  in political ideologies, 266
Lucas García, Romero, 416

M

M-19 (Colombia), 419
Machado, Gerardo
  populism of, 366, 371
  rebellion against, 377
machete, 361
Madero, Francisco I., 269, 353
maize, in diet, 320
malnourishment, 446*t*
  current, 445
Managua, earthquake in, 414
manioc, in diet, 320
Mantaro Valley, living conditions in, 389–390
mantilla, 321–322
manufactured goods, import of, 333
manufacturing, development of, 360
  Great Depression and, 363
Maranhão, civil rebellion in, 277
María, José, 353
Maria of Portugal, 253
Mariátequui, José Carlos, 352, 380, 418
market. *See also* trade
  fluctuations in, vulnerability to, 332
  national, railroads in, 334
market day, in villages, 314
marriage
  employee stability and, 391, 392
  government strengthening of, 401
  inequality in, 320
  among slaves, 312
  of urban women, 319
Mato Grosso, civil rebellion in, 277
mayordomo, 301
McDonald's, 460
meat
  in diet, 320, 445
  export boom in, 331
Medellín, textile industry of, 388, 390–391
Menem, Carlos, 427
Mesoamerica. *See also* Central America; Mexico
mestizos
  clothing of, 322
  enfranchisement and, 241–242
  in Hidalgo's rebellion, 244
  in military, social advancement of, 282
  numbers of, 299
  in popular and high culture, 402
Mexican Revolution, 353–355
  Juárez and, 269
Mexico
  bandits in, 282
  barrios of, 452–453
  civil wars in, 277, 281
  clothing in, 321–322
  colonial
    cabildos of, 241
    rebellion in, 243–245
    royal monopolies protested in, 243
  contraception use in, 448
  crime in, 449
  debt of, 293, 293*t*, 436, 437*t*
  dictatorship of, 348–351
  diet in, 320–321
  economic development of
    boom and bust cycles in, 348–350
    debt for, 293, 293*t*
  economy of, effect of war on, 281
  export economy of
    boom in, 332
    prices in, 363
  feminism in, 373
  foreign investment in, 331–332
  Great Depression in, 363
  haciendas of, social structure of, 301
  immigration to, 341, 342*t*
  independence of, 248–249
    national celebration of, 257–258
  industrial working class of, 337
  industrialization of, government intervention in, 363
  under Juárez, 268–269
  land reforms in, 376
  manufacturing in, development of, 360
  middle class control of, 371–372
  military of
    cost of, 281–282
    presidency dominated by, 280
  as monarchy, 264
  muralists of, 403–406
  nationalism in, 282
  at Panama conference, 251
  petroleum industry of, foreign investment in, 331
  political movements in, women in, 441
  political stability in, 343
  population growth in, 299–300
  poverty in, demographics of, 445
  under PRI, 431–432
    foreign investment in, 331
  railroads of, 334
  regionalism in, 270
  small holdings of, discontent among, 340–341
  social security in, privatization of, 453–456
  terms of trade in, 333
  urban migrations in, 454
  villages of, living conditions in, 387–388
Mexico City
  Carrillo Puerto in, 373
  colonial, conservative government of, 244
  crime in, 449
  demographics of, 315–316

diet in, 321
environmental degradation of, 459
housing in, 324
independence day in, 257–258
living conditions in, 316, 397–398
lower classes of
political participation by, 283
and U.S. occupation, 283–285
population of, 300, 456
towns under, independence declared by, 252
urbanization of, 397–398
women in, employment of, 318–319
middle class
in Allende government, 430
creation of, 329
diversity in, 336–337
expansion of, 398–400
Leguía supported by, 369–370
Mexico controlled by, 371–372
in military regime, in Brazil, 421
political accommodation of, 344
political power of, 366
political voice of, 337
in Radical Party of Argentina, 344–345
social mobility of, in military, 343–344
upper class allied with, 366–369
vs. working class, 399
Middle Period, 239–240
migrations, to cities, 317–319, 423–424, 440
current, 456
in globalization, 460–461
histories of, 454–455
importance of, 386
military. *See also* warfare
of Argentina
in "Dirty War," 428–429
in Semana Trágica, 368
of Bolivia, MNR and, 382
Brazil under, in First Republic, 346
of Chile, in Allende government, 430
cost of, 281–282
Liberal view on, 277–278
modernization of, 343–344
of Peru, APRA and, 380
in politics, 354–355
in post-independence government, 264
domination of, 280–281
political ideology of, 266–267
recruitment for, and political participation, 283
upper class alliance with, 343, 354–355, 417, 435
vs. leftist ideologies, 419–420
military regimes, 410, 419–421
of Argentina, 425–427
of Brazil, 421–422
of Chile, 427–430
local autonomy and, 432–433
poverty from, 443–444
milk, 445
milonga, 401
Minas Gerais

civil rebellion in, 277
presidency under, 346
minerals. *See also specific minerals*
export boom in, 331
railroads in, 334
mines. *See also specific types*
effect of war on, 281
wages for, 394*t*
mining camps, in Chile, 338–340
Mitre, Bartolomé, 270, 280
MNR (National Revolutionary Movement) of Bolivia, 372
modernismo, in art, 402
modernization. *See* economic modernization
molasses, farm production of, 362
molino de nixtamal, 388
Moncada, attack on, 411
Montenegro, Roberto, 403
Montevideo
British invasion of, 246
independence of, from Buenos Aires, 252, 270
Montoneros, 426
Morales Bermúdez, Francisco, 418
Morelos, José Maria, 244–245, 257
Morones, Luis, 372
mortality rate, of slaves, 307
Mothers of the Plaza de Mayo, 421
mucambos, 452–453
mulattos
in military
royalist, 245
social advancement of, 282
numbers of, 299
Rosas supported by, 286–288
muralists, 403–406, 462
Murillo, Geraldo, 402–403

N
Napoleonic Wars, 238
nation, allegiance to, 256
Nation Action Party (PAN) of Mexico, 432, 433
national culture, through art, 406
National Front (Colombia), 419
National Party of the Revolution (PNR) of Mexico, 372
National Republican Alliance (ARENA) of El Salvador, 416
National Revolutionary Movement (MNR) of Bolivia, 372, 378, 380–382
National University (UNAM) of Mexico, 377
National Women's Association (Nicaragua), 442
nationalism, indigenismo in, 404
neo-liberalism, 434–435, 436
democracies under, 439–440
informal economies and, 449–450
poverty under, 443
Netzahualcóyotl, 452
Neves, Tancredo, 422
New Granada
colonial, royal monopolies protested in, 243
independence of, 250
Nicaragua
export economy of, commodities in, 332, 363
Great Depression in, 363
gross domestic product of, 443
housing in, 446

infant mortality in, 445
inflation in, 449
poverty in, demographics of, 445
revolution in, 409, 413–415
casualties of, 442
women in, 441
sanitation in, 446
Ninguem, Biu de, 423
nitrate fields
foreign investment in, 331
War of the Pacific over, 275
nomadic peoples, extermination campaigns against, 311
North American Free Trade Agreement (NAFTA), 436–437
Núñez, Guillermo, 462

O
Oaxaca, inter-village conflict of, 313
Obregón, ilvaro, 354, 372
occupations, in cities, 318
Odría, Manuel, 380, 417
O'Higgins, Bernardo, 288
oil spills, in Ecuador, 459
Onganía, Juan Carlos, 425
Organization of Petroleum Exporting Countries (OPEC), 436
Orozco, José Clemente, 350, 403
Ortega, Daniel, 414
Ortiz, Roberto M., 375, 377
Ortiz de Domínguez, María Josefa, 260

P
Páez, José Antonio, 271
painting, in popular and high culture, 402–406
País, Frank, 441
Palacio Nacional de Belles Artes, 387
Palacios de Montoya, Ana, 391–392
Pan Bimbo, 445
Panama
export economy of, commodities in, 332
Great Depression in, 363
inflation in, 449
Spanish American conference in, 250–251
Panama Canal, immigrants and, 342
panelas, 362
Paraguay
under Francia, 289–291
Great Depression in, 363
independence of, from Buenos Aires, 252, 270, 289
inflation in, 449
in War of the Triple Alliance, 274–275, 281
Parián Riot, 283, 284–285
Parliamentary Republic (Chile), 346–347, 370
Partido Socialista (Socialist Party) of Argentina, 345
La Patria Nueva, 369
patriarchy, in factories, 391
Patriotas Marianas, 260
Patriotic Military Union (Venezuela), 379
patron-client relationships
in Argentina, under Radical Party, 345
in Brazil, under landowners, 346
caudillos in, 286
in Mexico, under PRI, 431
in Peru, 369–370
in populism, 366

payada, 401
Paz Estenssoro, Victor, 382
Pedro I of Brazil, 255–256, 255f, 264, 271, 283
Pedro II of Brazil, 256, 264, 271
peinilla, 361
Peixoto, Floriano, 346
peons, on haciendas, 302, 303
Pérez Jiménez, Marcos, 379
periodization, 239–240
Pernambuco, revolt in, 254
Perón, Eva Duarte de, 377–378
Perón, Juan
  Argentina under, 377–378, 426
  working class support of, 358
Perón, María Estela Martínez, 426
Peronists, 425–427
Peru
  Aristocratic Republic of, 347–348
  barriadas of, 452–453
  cotton industry of, immigrants in, 342
  demographics of, 299
  economic development of, debt for, 293, 293t
  economy of, effect of war on, 281
  export economy of, 294
    concentration of commodities in, 333
  Great Depression in, 363
  gross domestic product of, 443
  guano industry of, 294
  housing in, 446
  independence of, 249–252
  Indians of, "rediscovery" of, 352
  inflation in, 449
  manufacturing in, development of, 360
  middle classes of, political power of, 366
  military coup in, 420
  military of, modernization of, 343
  at Panama conference, 251
  political movements in, women in, 441
  populism in, 369–370, 375–376, 380
  poverty in, demographics of, 445
  racism in, 310
  revolution in, 409–410, 416–419
  Shining Path in, 418–419, 433
    casualties of, 442
    cost from, 442
  social security in, privatization of, 453–456
  upper classes of, political power of, 366
  urban migrations in, 454
  villages of, living conditions in, 387–388, 389–390
  in War of the Pacific, 275, 281
petroleum crises, 436
petroleum industry
  export prices in, 363
  foreign investment in, 331
  in Mexico, exploitation of, 432
Piérola, Nicolás de, 347
Pinochet, Augusto, 430
Plan de Iguala, 248–249
Plan of Ayutla Revolt, 279
plantations, life on, 307–312
Platt Amendment, 371
Plaza of the Three Cultures, 431–432

PNR (National Party of the Revolution) of Mexico, 372
political consolidation wars, in nineteenth century, 274
political participation
  of lower classes, 358
  popular, 283–286
  of small farmers, 362
  of women, 358
political stability
  economic growth from, 342
  modernization and, 329
Pombaline Reforms, impact of, 239
popular culture
  urbanization in, 401–407
  worlds markets for, 461
Popular Front (Chile), 375
population
  of cities, 300, 456
  increases in, 335–336
  of slaves, in Brazil, 298
population growth, 299, 300t, 447–448
populism
  domination of, 358, 367–372
  economic success and, 366, 370, 379–380, 417–418
  nationalism in, 404
  women and, 366
Portinari, Candido, 406
Portugal
  monarchy of, moved to Brazil, 253–254
  revolt in, 255
Posada, José Guadalupe, 349–350
positivism, 342
Potosí, silver mines of, effect of war on, 281
poverty
  current, 440, 442–449
  demographics of, 445–449
Prado, Manuel, 380, 417
Prebisch, Raúl, 434
Prieto, Joaquín, 280
printing presses, in Brazil, 254
public art, 403
public celebrations
  in creating community, 257
  in everyday life, 299
public works, under Leguía, 369
Puebla, demographics of, 299
Puerto Rico, cabildos of, 241
pulque
  in diet, 303, 321
  in religious celebrations, 325

Q
Quadros, Jânio, 422
quality of life, 442–456, 444t
quilombos, 308
Quito
  independence of, 249, 250
  towns under, independence declared by, 252

R
racism
  European immigration and, 341
  against lower classes, 310–311
Radical Party (Unión Cívica Radical)
  of Argentina, 366–369
  middle class in, 344–345
railroads
  construction of, 329, 348

in export economies, 331, 334–335
  foreign investment in, 331
  resistance to, 335
rainforest destruction, 458–459
ranches, social structure on, 301
rape, in military regimes, 421
rations
  for cowboys, 304
  for hacienda peons, 302
Reagan, Ronald, 415
rebellion, participation in, causes of, 354–355
rebozo, 322
Recife, revolt in, 283, 285
Regional Confederation of Mexican Workers (CROM), 372
regionalism
  in Brazil, under coffee planters, 345–346
  in Mexican Revolution, 353
  in political alliances, 358–359
  post-independence, 267–272
    economic recovery from, 291
  transportation systems and, 334
religion. See also Catholic Church
  entertainment and, 324
  among slaves, 312
  in villages, 315
Republic of Gran Colombia, 249
republics, post-independence, 264–265
Revolutionary Armed Forces of Colombia (FARC), 419
Rio de Janeiro
  demographics of, 316
  diet in, 321
  favelas of, 452
  housing in, 324
  literacy in, 337
  living conditions in, 316
  population of, 300, 456
  Portuguese monarchy moved to, 253–254
  slaves of, as domestic servants, 309
  uprising in, and abdication of Pedro I, 283
  urbanization in, 395–397
  women in, employment of, 318–319
Río de la Plata. See also Argentina
  cowboys of, 306
  estancias of, life on, 301, 304
Rio Grande do Sul
  civil rebellion in, 277
  presidency under, 346
riots, as political participation, 283
Risquez, Diego, 251
Riva Palacio, Vicente, 322–323
Rivadavia, Bernardino, 270
Rivera, Diego, 350, 403, 405–406
Roca, Julio A., 344
Rojas Pinillo, Gustavo, 379, 419
Rosas, Juan Manuel de, 270, 280, 286–288, 288f, 305
rubber, export boom in, 334
Ruiz Cortines, Adolfo, 377, 431
rum, farm production of, 362
runaway slave communities, 308
rural areas
  demographics of, 298
  discontent in
    in Argentina, 340–341

Index

in Mexico, 340–341, 350
economies of, 313
housing in, 323–324
landless peoples of, 329, 335, 340
Leguía supported by, 369–370
living conditions in, *vs.* cities, 386
in Mexican revolution, 354
migrations from, 317–319, 440
importance of, 386
modernization and, 352–353
scarcity of work in, 387
traditions preserved in, 433
work life in, 301–304
Rurales, 348

S

Sáenz, Manuela, 251, 259–260
Sáenz Peña Law of 1912, 344–345
Salinas Gortari, Carlos, 432
Salvador da Bahia de Todos os Santos, civil rebellion in, 277
samba, 402
San Luis Potosí, independence day in, 258
San Martín, José de, 249
Sánchez, Celia, 441
Sánchez Cerro, Luis M., 370, 375–376
Sánchez Navarro estate, work life on, 303
Sandinista National Liberation Front (FSLN), 409, 414–415
women in, 441–442
Sandino, Augusto, 414
sanitation
in cities, 316–317
current, 445–446, 446*t*, 456–457, 459
Santa Anna, Antonio López de, 268, 270
Santa Cruz, Andrés, 288
Santamaría, Haydée, 441
Santander, Francisco de Paula, 271
Santería, 312
Santiago, population of, 456
São Paulo
life in, 423–424
literacy in, 337
population of, 456
presidency under, 346
São Sebastião do Rio de Janeiro. *See* Rio de Janeiro
Sarney, José, 422–424
Scilingo, Adolfo, 428, 428*f*
seaports, refurbishment of, 329
Semana Trágica (Tragic Week), 345, 368–369
Sendero Luminoso (Shining Path), 418–419, 433
casualties of, 442
cost from, 442
serape, 322
sewing machines, 388
sharecropping
on coffee farms, 361
by gauchos, 306
shepherds, work life of, 304
Shining Path (Sendero Luminoso), 418–419, 433
casualties of, 442
cost from, 442
silicosis, 394
Silva, Lula de Luís Inácio, 425
silver, export boom in, 331

silver mines, decline in production of, 243
Siqueiros, David Alfaro, 403
slavery, abolition of, 310, 346
slaves
in Brazil
on cassava farms, 314–315
in military, 282
population of, 298
employment of, 318–319
independence movements and, 239, 259
lives of, 307–312
numbers of, 299
resistance by, 308
runaway communities of, 308
self-employed, 309
urban, 309
small holdings
life in, 312–315
in Peru, 389–390
smallpox, in cities, 317
smuggling, economic development and, 292
soap operas, Brazilian, 460
social mobility, military and, 282, 343–344
Social Question, 330, 365–366, 385–386
social security, privatization of, 453–456
social structure
on haciendas, 301
in Mexico City, 318
populism and, 366
in villages, 312
modernization and, 341
socialism, institutionalization of, in Cuba, 413
Socialist Party (Partido Socialista) of Argentina, 345
Socialist Republic (Chile), 372
socialists, in working class, 345
socialization, of urban workers, 388–393
soil erosion, 361
Somoza Debayle, Anastasio, 414
Somoza Debayle, Luis, 414
Somoza García, Anastasio, 414
South America. *See also specific countries and regions*
Soviet Union, Cuban reliance on, 412–413
Spain
in Napoleonic Wars, 238
representative government in, 240–241
Spanish America
administration of, cost of, rebellion against, 238
representative government in, 240–241
Spencer, Herbert, 342
squashes, in diet, 320–321
state monopolies, economic development and, 292
steamships, in export boom, 331
stimulants. *See also* intoxicants
street children, 424
structuralism, 433
subsistence, in rural areas, 313
Sucre, Antonio José de, 251, 288
suffrage, 383*t*
under colonial rule, 241–242, 253

for women, 382
sugar
European demand for, 294
export of, boom in, 331
sugar industry
in Caribbean, after World War I, 360
foreign investment in, 331
sugar plantations, slaves on, 307–312

T

tango, 401–402
tapioca, 314
taxes
in colonial Brazil, for bureaucracy, 254
economic development and, 292
on income, in Argentina, 374
in Paraguay, 290
in villages, 313
Teatro Colón, 387
Teatro Nacional, 387
technocrats
in Brazil, 421
in Mexico, 432
technology
in economic growth, 329
in military modernization, 343
television, 460–461
temporary labor
for coffee estates, 361
for haciendas, 301–302
tenant farming, on haciendas, 301–302
tenements, 324
terms of trade, 333, 434
Texas, U.S. annexation of, 275–276
Texas War, 277*f*, 282
textile industry, of Medellín, 390–391
textiles, Mexican, trade restrictions eased on, 243
Thatcher, Margaret, 426–427
"The Hand," 426
Tijerino, Doris María, 441–442
Timerman, Jacobo, 369
tin, export boom in, 331
Tlatelolco, massacre at, 431–432
tobacco, European demand for, 294
Toledo, Alejandro, 419
tortilla
in diet, 320–321
grinding machine for, 388
towns, in independence movements, 252
trade
colonial, Cortes and, 242
inter-Latin American, 364
international
limitations on, economic development and, 292
after World War I, 360
in World War II, 364
trade boom, 329. *See also* boom and bust cycles
Tragic Week (Semana Trágica), 345, 368–369
transportation
in economic development, 292
regionalism and, 334
26th of July Movement, 409, 410–412, 441

U

Ubico, Jorge, 378

UNAM (National University) of Mexico, 377
unions. *See* labor unions
United Nations Economic Commission for Latin America (UNECLA or CEPAL), 434
United Officers' Group (GOU) of Argentina, 377
United States
  capital from, in Latin American economic development, 331
  communism opposed by, Cuba and, 410–413
  export economy dependence on, 333, 363, 364
  in Falklands/Malvinas War, 426–427
  Guatemala revolution sponsored by, 416
  military regimes aided by, 420–421
  Salvadoran Army assisted by, 416
  Sandinistas opposed by, 414–415
universities. *See* education
upper class
  under Díaz dictatorship, 351
  lower class feared by, 310–311, 385–386
  middle class allied with, 366–369
  military allied with, 343, 354–355, 417, 435
  modern women and, 400
  modernity resisted by, 385
  political power of, 366, 395
  racism in, 310–311
  under Somoza dictatorship, 414
urban life, 315–317, 395–398
  cooking in, 321
  local autonomy and, 433
  in São Paulo, 423–424
urbanization, 395–398
  modern women and, 400–401
Uriburu, José F., 374
Uruguay
  Great Depression in, 363
  gross domestic product of, 443
  immigration to, 341, 342t
  imports to, reliance on, 333
  industrialization of, government intervention in, 363
  manufacturing in, development of, 360
  under military regime, 420
  poverty in, 443
  social security in, privatization of, 453–456
  urban population of, 456
  in War of the Triple Alliance, 274–275
U.S.-Mexican War, 275–276, 277f

V
Valparaíso, earthquake in, 347
Vanegas Arroyo broadsheets, 349–350
Vargas, Getúlio, 372, 375, 379, 400
vecindades, 324
vegetables, in diet, 445

Velasco Alvarado, Juan, 417–418
Velázquez, Sofia, 452
Venezuela
  coffee industry of, 294
  colonial, Bourbon Reforms in, 245
  cowboys of, 306
  dictatorship of, 379
  export economy of, 294
    boom in, 332
    concentration of commodities in, 332, 363
  Great Depression in, 363
  gross domestic product of, 443
  independence of, 241, 249, 250
  political stability in, 343
  poverty in, 443
  urban population of, 456
Victoria, Guadalupe, 270, 284
Videla, Jorge, 426
Villa, Pancho, 353–355
villages
  life in, 312–315, 387–390
  social structure in, 341
Villaroel, Guaberto, 382
virginity, employee stability and, 391
voudoun, 312

W
wage economy, in rural areas, 313
wages, 394t
WalMart, 460
War of the Pacific, 274–275, 276f, 281, 285, 347
War of the Reform, 268, 279, 281
War of the Triple Alliance, 274–275, 281
warfare. *See also* military
  cost of, 281–282
  democracy and, 280–281
  in nineteenth century, 272–279, 273t–274t
    economic recovery from, 291
    impact of, 279–282
water
  in diet, 321
  drinking, 316, 446, 459
water pollution, 458–459
wealth and class. *See also* lower classes; middle class; upper class; working class
  in civil wars, 281
  contrasts in, 299
  Francia and, 289–290
  in independence movements, 237
  in nation-building, 262–263
  in Semana Trágica, 368
white-collar workers
  employment as, 398–399
  new class of, 336
whitening campaigns, 310
whites
  numbers of, 299
  in post-independence government, 264
widows, in cities, 319–320
women. *See also* gender roles
  in cities, employment of, 318–319

  civil rights for, in Argentina, 366–369
  clothing of, 321–322
  in Cuban politics, 413
  in economic arena, 358
  on haciendas, domestic life of, 304–307
  in independence movements, 259–260
  in industrial working class, 337–340
  in informal economy, 450–453, 451f
  migration of, to cities, 454
  under military regimes, 421
  in mining camps, 339–340, 391–392
  modern, 366, 400–401, 405
  in political arena, 337–340, 358
    in Cuba, 371
  in revolutions, 441
  rural lives of, 313–314
  in Sandinistas, 415
  in Sendero Luminoso, 418
  social security for, 456
  suffrage for, 382, 383t
  in textile industry, 391
  in white-collar workforce, 399
wool, export boom in, 331
work
  in everyday life, 299
  on haciendas, 301–312
working class
  of Chile, political accommodation of, 347
  creation of, 329–330
  diversity in, 337
  Perón supported by, 378
  political accommodation of, 344
  political voice of, 337
  vs. middle class, 399
  women in, 337–340
working conditions, in mines, 339, 394
World War I, aftermath of, 359–360
World War II, 364

Y
Yanamarca Valley, living conditions in, 389–390
Ydígoras Fuentes, Miguel, 416
Yrigoyen, Hipólito
  election of, 345
  populism of, 366–369
Yucatán
  Carrillo Puerto in, 373
  caste war in, 281
  Maya Indians of, rebellion by, 311

Z
Zapata, Emiliano, 353–355, 374
Zapatistas, 353
Zayas, Alfredo, 370–371
Zedillo, Ernesto, 432
zinc, export boom in, 331
Zócalo, 316